Europe
Since
World
War

II

The Big Change

NORMAN
LUXENBURG

Southern Illinois University Press
Carbondale and Edwardsville

Feffer & Simons, Inc.
London and Amsterdam

Library of Congress Cataloging in Publication Data

Luxenburg, Norman, 1927–
Europe since World War II.

Bibliography: p.
1. Europe—Politics—1945–   2. Europe—
Economic conditions—1945–   I. Title.
D1058.L88 1973   320.9′4′055   72–75334
ISBN 0–8093–0583–6

Contents

	Maps and Illustrations	vii
	Tables	ix
	Preface	xi
1	Introduction	1
2	Democracy, Fascism, and Communism in the Interwar Period	14
3	The Breakdown of Collective Security and the Outbreak of World War II	31
4	World War II	44
5	The New Europe to the Origin of the Cold War	76
6	The Cold War	92
7	Recovery of Europe: The Postwar Decade	129
8	Post-Stalin Europe: The Fifties	167
9	The Big Change: Contemporary Europe	192
10	The Continuing Challenge	235
	Selected Bibliography	247
	Index	251

Maps

Europe in 1914   2
Europe in 1939   42
Europe at the height of Hitler's power, 1942   68
German territorial losses since 1914   74
Soviet expansion in World War II   100
Warsaw Pact and Atlantic Pact (NATO) nations, 1972   127
Europe in 1972   190

Illustrations

Generalissimo Francisco Franco   33
Alcide de Gasperi, Premier of Italy   86
Tito of Yugoslavia   118
Air view of Berlin   151
Île de la Cité, Paris   155
Macedonia, Yugoslavia   164
Konrad Adenauer, Chancellor of West Germany   180
Ludwig Erhard, architect of Germany's economic recovery   181
Harold Wilson, Labourite Prime Minister of England   186
Edward Heath, Prime Minister of England   187
Willi Brandt   188
Dusseldorf, Germany   195
La Croisette, Cannes, France   199
Club Paradis, a Black Sea resort in Rumania   207
Typical plaza, Gelanova, Spain   208
Leonid I. Brezhnev, General Secretary of the
    Soviet Communist Party   232
Andrei A. Gromyko, Soviet Foreign Minister   233
The new Europe—the Thyssen Building, Dusseldorf   237
The old Europe—a street in the older section of Zurich   238

Tables

1. Population of European and other major nations, 1800–1910   4
2. Population of the continents, 1800–1950   5
3. Population of German, French, Austrian, and Russian cities, 1850–1910   7
4. Railroad mileage, 1850–1913   8
5. Steel production, 1885–1913   9
6. Line-up of the powers on the eve of war, 1939   44
7. Output per worker in selected industries, 1935–1937   132
8. Productivity of coal mines, 1913–1948   132
9. Raw steel production, 1937–1949   135
10. Industrial and electrical production, 1937–1949   135
11. French industrial production, 1937–1949   140
12. German industrial production, 1949–1956   147
13. German crop production, 1934–1957   147
14. Persons per dwelling in Germany   148
15. French national expenditures, 1948–1952   156
16. Soviet steel and coal production, 1939–1955   162
17. Wheat yield, 1949–1950   162
18. Crude steel production, 1913–1970   196
19. Electric energy production, 1930–1970   197
20. Population, 1910–1970   197
21. Wheat production, 1928–1968   198
22. Private automobiles in European countries, 1928–1969   198
23. Number of telephones in selected countries, 1910–1969   200
24. Number of radio sets in selected countries, 1938–1965   201
25. Number of television receivers in selected countries, 1956–1969   201
26. Housing units built in Germany   202
27. Housing units in England and Wales, 1901–1966   203

28. Construction activity   204
29. Percentage of European dwellings with baths   204
30. Housing space in selected Soviet cities, 1926–1960   205
31. Number of tourists in several major tourist countries,
    1938–1969   206
32. West Europeans visiting East Europe   209
33. Number of students in higher education, 1910–1968   211
34. Number of physicians per 10,000 population,
    1900–1968   212
35. Infant mortality, 1900–1968   212
36. Birthrate in selected countries, 1911–1969   213
37. Divorce rate, 1910–1938   214
38. Number of divorces, 1935–1970   214
39. Projected and actual population for 1970   215
40. Projected population to A.D. 2000   216
41. Average annual deaths from pulmonary tuberculosis,
    1901–1967   217
42. Deaths due to tuberculosis, 1900–1969   217
43. Notifications of infectious diseases in the U.K.   218
44. Number of unemployed in selected European coun-
    tries, 1929–1970   218
45. Percentage of workers in agriculture, 1930–1967   221
46. Number of tractors in selected countries, 1939–1969   222
47. Crop yields in Austria   222
48. Wheat output in European countries   223
49. Producer price of wheat in Germany and Italy   224
50. Average wage per hour in manufacturing in Germany
    and Italy   224
51. Annual consumption of starch foods in Scandinavia   225
52. Net food supply per capita, 1948–1969   226
53. Working time required to purchase common foods,
    1967   227
54. Cost of family weekly food basket, 1967   228
55. Meat consumption per capita per year   229
56. Take-home pay of average industrial worker with
    wife and two dependents, 1969   230
57. Purchase price of common items, 1969   231

Preface

IT is the intention here to review in a readily comprehensible manner European developments in the period since 1939 and to depict graphically the tremendous political, sociological, economic, industrial, and psychological changes which have been taking place in Europe since World War II.

The data and the interpretation should make this useful both as a supplementary textbook for most courses in modern history and as a quick reference for persons desiring statistical information concerning Europe's economic, industrial, material, and social development in the twentieth century.

It is also hoped that this book will make interesting reading to many persons who have no desire to read a more involved account of the inter and intranational politics of recent European history. At the same time it is hoped that the well-informed reader will have his attention focused on certain salient features of European development.

NORMAN LUXENBURG

Iowa City, Iowa
April 1972

1

Introduction

TO the present generation as it looks back some seventy years to the beginning of the twentieth century, the Europe of that time seems like a remote world of relative placid tranquility and slowly changing ways, particularly when compared with the hectic, rapidly changing world of the present. Indeed, ever since the advent of the industrial revolution, if not earlier, each generation has looked back to the relative changelessness of the recent past. No less an observer than Karl Marx, regarding with awe the great changes taking place as a result of technological and industrial advance, wrote in 1867 that more had been produced and created by man in the preceding century than in all recorded history put together. Marx's observation could have been echoed by each succeeding generation, for the tremendous advances which Marx had seen were small indeed compared with those taking place in the next forty years. The intelligent observers of the generations coming to maturity and reaching middle age in the decade prior to World War I could not fail to be impressed by the changes and advances which had taken place in their time.

In the half century or so between the Crimean War and World War I, slavery had been abolished in the United States; Japan had emerged from isolation and had become a great and powerful modern state; Russia had liberated the serfs, pacified the Caucasus, extended its domain to central Asia, and helped open Siberia to settlement by con-

ICELAND

ATLANTIC OCEAN

NORWAY

SWEDEN

UNITED KINGDOM

NORTH SEA

IRELAND

DENMARK

BALTIC SEA

RUSSIAN EMPIRE

EMPIRE

NETHERLANDS

BELGIUM

LUXEMBOURG

GERMAN EMPIRE

FRANCE

SWITZ.

AUSTRO-HUNGARIAN EMPIRE

ITALY

RUMANIA

BLACK SEA

MONTE-NEGRO

SERBIA

PORTUGAL

SPAIN

CORSICA

BULGARIA

SARDINIA

ALBANIA

GREECE

TURKEY

MEDITERRANEAN SEA

SICILY

CRETE

CYPRUS

0   200   400   MILES

EUROPE IN 1914

struction of the Trans-Siberian railroad; and Canada and the United States had bound the Atlantic to the Pacific with bands of iron.

Whereas at the time of the Crimean War only England of the major European nations could have been said to have a representative democracy—and even there the franchise was greatly limited—by the decade prior to World War I each of the major nations had a functioning parliament which was elected by the people. While true representative democracy was severely hampered and limited, especially in Russia, the educated European observer of the early twentieth century regarded true representative government as the wave of the future.

In every major European nation, rural villages were turning into huge industrial cities; telephones, cables, and the new cheaper press were coming in to make the public almost instantaneously aware of world happenings. Most of Africa and huge areas of Asia, long neglected by the major powers, were now being taken over as several of the European nations vied with each other for colonial possessions. Newer, faster, and cheaper ship and rail transport caused a fantastic increase in trade, and nations formerly self-sufficient began to be drawn more and more into the world, rather than the national, market.

By the turn of the century electric power, recently a novelty, was beginning to find a multitude of applications. Medical and scientific advances were beginning to bring many once-dreaded diseases under control. Epidemics which only a generation before had been a terror in vast areas of Europe, were now pretty much a thing of the past. Numerous commodities, once luxuries, were becoming available to even the average tradesman in the industrialized nations. Many foods formerly raised only for the local market could now be shipped and marketed in areas far from their origin.

In every major nation illiteracy was being reduced by leaps and bounds, and free primary education was becoming available in virtually all the major nations. Even in Russia, the advances made against illiteracy in the twenty-five years prior to World War I are striking.

It would be appropriate here to more closely examine some of these changes in pre-1914 Europe. In the decade prior to 1914, there were some twenty sovereign states in Europe and numerous other independent nations throughout the world. Six of these, England, France, Germany,

1. POPULATION OF EUROPEAN AND OTHER MAJOR
NATIONS, 1800–1910
(In millions)

Nation	1800	1880	1910
Austria	14.0	33.6	56.0
United Kingdom	16.1	35.1	45.0
France	27.3	37.7	39.6
Germany	24.6	45.2	64.9
Japan	30.0 (est.)	37.0	46.7
Russia	37.0	88.0	140.0
United States	5.3	50.2	92.0

Source: W. S. Woytinsky and E. S. Woytinsky, *World Population and Production: Trends and Outlook* (New York: Twentieth Century, 1953), p. 44.

Russia, the United States, and Japan, were great military powers, and two others, Austria-Hungary and Italy, were important powers. Of very great significance among the important developments which had been taking place in these nations and which were beginning to have a profound influence on the balance of power were the demographic changes. While at the beginning of the nineteenth century, France with its almost thirty million inhabitants was far more populous than any of its major rivals with the close exception of Russia, by the beginning of the twentieth century, France had fallen behind every major power in population. Table 1 not only indicates the comparative stagnation in French population growth, but the tremendous upsurge in that of the other major nations.

The Europe of 1900 had a population estimated at 401 million people, of whom more than 325 million lived in the six major powers. The other fifteen European states together had fewer than 75 million. All of Africa in 1900 had a population estimated at 120 million; all of South America had 38 million. Of the populous Asian states, only Japan was both unfettered and united and thus able to exert a strong influence abroad. Thus, even from the standpoint

2. POPULATION OF THE CONTINENTS, 1800–1950
(In millions)

Continent	1800	1850	1900	1950
Europe	187	266	401	560
Africa	90	95	120	198
South America	9	20	38	111
Asia	602	749	937	1302
North America	6	26	81	166

Source: Woytinsky and Woytinsky, p. 34.

of numbers, Europe in 1900 was far more impressive than it had been a half century before, or than it was to be a half century later.

The growth in population of Europe during the preceding fifty years had been truly striking; it is even more impressive when it is borne in mind that emigration from Europe during the nineteenth century had exceeded sixty million, with more than half of that number coming to the United States. Thus, the number of persons of European stock in the world had increased from about 20 percent in 1800 to 35 percent in 1900.

As the twentieth century began, however, a downward trend in the birthrate in all the major European powers was already evident. For a short period, nevertheless, populations were going to continue to rise at a rapid rate in most of these nations.

While the overall population growth of the European nations had been enormous indeed, that of the cities was even more spectacular. In 1800, not one of the major European nations had had a majority of its people in the cities. By 1850, England alone had become urbanized; by 1900–1914, all but Russia had a predominantly urban population, and even there the number of city dwellers was rising rapidly. Thus, in less than fifty years, the average West European had not only ceased to farm for a living but was actually living in the cities. Quite obviously the entire manner of life was changing; different problems were going to arise.

To genuinely understand what had been taking place, it might be advisable to stop here to examine this growth of the cities. London alone in 1900, with its population of more than 6.5 million people, had more than three-fourths the population that all of England, including London itself, had had in 1800.

Berlin alone, with its 3 million people in 1910, had far more people than it and the next thirty German cities together had had back in 1850. And in the period 1900–1914, this trend to the cities was continuing. In all of Germany at the time of the Crimean War, only Berlin, Hamburg, and Munich had more than 100,000 inhabitants. Essen had only 9,000. A little more than fifty years later, Hamburg had grown from 132,000 to 931,000; Munich from 110,000 to 596,000; Frankfurt from 65,000 to 415,000; and Berlin from 450,000 to over 3 million.

French and English cities grew rapidly in the half century following the Crimean War, yet their growth was not as spectacular as that of the German cities. In 1850 Paris, with almost a million persons, was the only city in France with more than two hundred thousand inhabitants. By 1910 the population of Paris was passing three million, Marseilles 491,000, and Lyons 524,000.

Although urbanization in the Russian empire had not reached the levels it had in the Western powers, the growth of cities was enormous. Indeed, it was this very growth of the Russian cities that changed Russian history and, consequently, world history. For it was from the great concentrations of urban workers that the revolutionary parties, particularly the Bolsheviks, drew their strength. By 1910, among the numerous large cities in Russia, Kazan, Lodz, Saratov, Riga, Yekaterinoslav, and Kharkhov all had more than 200,000 inhabitants.

3. POPULATION OF GERMAN, FRENCH, AUSTRIAN, AND
RUSSIAN CITIES, 1850–1910
(In thousands)

City	1850	1880	1910
Germany			
Berlin	419	1,122	3,730
Hamburg	132	290	931
Cologne	97	145	517
Munich	110	230	596
Leipzig	63	149	590
Essen	9	57	295
Dresden	97	221	548
Frankfurt	65	137	415
France			
Paris	1,053	2,714	2,936
Lyons	177	377	524
Marseilles	195	360	551
Austrian Empire			
Vienna	444	726	2,031
Budapest	178	371	880
Russian Empire			
Moscow	365	612	1,502
St. Petersburg	485	1,133	2,019 (1912)
Kiev	61	247	505 (1911)
Odessa	90	194	498

Source: Woytinsky and Woytinsky, pp. 120–21; World Almanac (New York, 1915), pp. 706–7.

Improved transportation had helped make the growth and provisioning of the new cities possible. In 1850, England with about six thousand miles of track was the only nation with anything approaching a rail network. Ten miles an hour at that time was a satisfactory speed for a locomotive. By 1900, trains could do a hundred miles an hour, though even express runs were usually kept to about fifty miles per hour.

4. RAILROAD MILEAGE, 1850–1913
(In thousands of miles)

Country	1850	1860	1880	1900	1910	1913
Great Britain	6.6	10.4	18.0	21.9	23.4	24.5
Russia	.4	1.0	15.0	31.7	41.2	46.4
Germany	3.7	7.2	21.0	31.9	38.0	39.9
France	1.9	5.9	14.7	22.9	24.2	....
Italy	.2	1.1	5.4	9.8	10.6	12.8

Source: W. S. Woytinsky, *World Commerce and Governments: Trends and Outlook* (New York: Twentieth Century, 1955), p. 342; W. S. Woytinsky, *Die Welt in Zahlen,* 7 vols. (Berlin: Rudolf Mosse, 1927), 5:34–45.

During the period 1890–1911, France had increased her railroads by 33.9 percent, England by 16.4 percent and Germany by 42 percent.

The airplane too was a novelty. Yet between 1909 and 1913, the speed of planes increased from less than fifty miles an hour to over a hundred and sixty, and their range from one hundred and seventy miles to more than six hundred.

By the last decade of the century, electric streetcar lines were coming into operation to transport the huge urban populations, and London and Paris had their underground systems. The railways and municipal railways had been built for the primary purpose of transporting goods and passengers. Yet the very development of the railroads fostered a greater expansion of the burgeoning steel and iron industry.

Since it has often been customary to use iron and steel production figures as a gauge of the industrialization of a nation, these production figures of the twenty-five years prior to World War I should be of great interest.

Between 1885 and 1910, Russian steel production increased more than 1750 percent; German more than 1100 percent. World output of steel had increased from 0.7 million tons in 1870, to 4.4 million tons in 1880, to 12.4 mil-

5. STEEL PRODUCTION, 1885–1913
(In 1,000,000 tons)

Country	1885	1910	1913	% Increase 1885–1913
United States	1.7	26.5	31.8	1871
Germany	1.2	13.7	18.9	1575
Great Britain	1.9	6.5	7.8	411
France	.5	3.4	4.7	940
Russia	.2	3.5	4.8	2400

Source: Woytinsky and Woytinsky, p. 1118.

lion tons in 1890. By 1913, as shown in table 5, Germany alone was producing 19 million tons, about double the entire world production of only twenty-five years earlier. And the United States with a production of 32 million tons was far ahead of Germany.

This heavy industry demanded power, and coal production soared in an attempt to meet the demands of mushrooming industry, expanding cities, steam locomotives, and the fleets of commercial vessels which were handling the vastly increased international trade.

The fast means of transportation broke down the old self-sufficiency. France depended for one-third of its coal on imports. England imported four-fifths of its wheat, many minerals, all of its cotton, and so on.

In all the industrial nations of western Europe, agriculture had ceased to occupy first place in the national economy. Even in primarily agricultural Russia, industry was not only developing but doing so even more rapidly than in the countries of the West. Trade among the major nations was expanding enormously. Thus, by any measure in the prewar decade, the production and trade figures of all the leading powers could show substantial gains.

By 1914, every European country outside of Russia and the Balkans had relatively well-developed codes of factory and labor legislation, and even in Russia attempts had been made in that direction. Largely as a result of the activities of democratised municipal governments many European cities by 1914 had been endowed with a tremendous number of new and improved services, from public utilities such as water, gas, electricity, and transportation, to public parks, libraries, schools, museums, hospitals, recreation centers, and all the other amenities of modern urban life.

Educated man, harnessing power to his needs, was beginning to regard war as a barbaric anachronism. Peace conferences had been called. Attempts had been made to outlaw war, and the peace palace had been built at the Hague. Yet the major continental powers all had conscription, and if the gods of war would will it, millions of men were ready to answer the call to arms. They were ready to fight for the nation, for the fatherland in danger. No one among the continental generation about to be thrown into war thought in terms of "making the world safe for democracy." This type of idealism was to come from the new world. The soldiers going to the trenches in 1914 were fighting for the nation.

World War I, or the European civil war, dealt a smashing blow to the steady and clear progress toward improvement and liberalization which Europe had been making in the prewar decade. Each of the major nations suffered millions of casualties. The immediate costs of the war were staggering, and all the nations, except for shattered Russia, then in revolution, emerged with huge war-incurred debts.

In addition, there were the legitimate demands on the governments by the millions of war-created dependents. Added to this was the physical damage of the war which had been extensive in large areas of France, Belgium, and East Central Europe. Germany had lost important areas, disrupting even further normal economic patterns. Central Europe was in chaos as the Austro-Hungarian Empire disintegrated.

The tremendous loss of wealth by Europe, and the loss of so many of the best and most energetic people, helped prevent a resumption of normal trade which was particularly important to the well-being of both Britain and Germany. Under these conditions, the decade of the twenties was mostly a period of retrenchment while the European countries recovered from the wounds inflicted by the nightmarish great war. Just when it seemed that Europe was on the road to recovery, the Great Depression of the early thirties struck. Millions of people were out of work, with drastic consequences for the attitudes and institutions of central Europe.

Gradually, throughout the latter thirties, Europe was recovering. Living conditions, housing, health standards, and educational opportunities were all better by 1939 than they had been prior to World War I. The twentieth century could not be denied forever.

Meanwhile, the vast Russian Empire, where the Bolshevists had seized power in the closing stages of World War I, had been ravished by a ferocious civil war which continued throughout 1919. Attempts to carry the revolution into East Central Europe had failed, and the Bolshevik leaders were faced with the task of restoring the Russian economy. This proved virtually impossible to do under classic Marxist doctrines, and Lenin and the Bolshevik leaders were forced to make concessions to man's nature. "Two steps forward and one step backward," as Lenin put it. Private enterprise of a type was allowed under the New Economic Policy or NEP.

Under this NEP, which offered a profit incentive, the

Russian economy revived. It was, however, a bit too late
to save the lives of millions of persons who starved during
the famine on the lower Volga area in 1922–23. However,
by the later 1920s, Russian production had passed prewar
totals and the scars of war were mostly healed.

At this point, Joseph Stalin, who had won the power
struggle in the intraparty maneuvering following Lenin's
death, began what was to be the real Russian revolution.
Russia was to be industrialized at a speeded-up tempo regardless of the human cost. This was to be done by the
five-year plans and the planned economy. The peasants,
constituting the overwhelming majority of the Russian
population, were to be forced into giant collective farms to
work for the collective rather than themselves. This break
with the past, this compulsory changing of the life and work
habits of the majority of the Russian population, constituted
the real Russian revolution.

In every respect the costs were high. Millions died in the
resulting famines. A very strict and stringent rationing was
introduced in the Russian cities. The already large secret
police establishment was expanded into a huge empire as
millions of Soviet citizens were deported to work camps because of real or suspected hostility to the government. Of
the increased industrial production, only a small, extremely
minimal part was turned toward the manufacturing of
consumer commodities. Most was put into making those
tools and equipment which would cause a still further rise
in heavy industrial output. The net result was that there
was a sharp increase in heavy industrial output in the
Soviet Union accompanied by a sharp increase in the police
terror and a sharp decline in the already low standard of
living.

By strong and ruthless action, however, Stalin did succeed in strengthening his position throughout the thirties;
during the same period, agricultural production gradually
increased toward its previous totals. Stalin's severe and
ruthless measures prevented the development in Russia of

any organized opposition to his regime. In Central Europe, however, the severe shocks to the political and social order which had been occasioned by the World War and the great economic depression of the early thirties helped bring dangerous new forces into play.

2

Democracy, Fascism, and Communism in the Interwar Period

THE territorial provisions of the peace treaty when combined with the economic provisions, or lack of far-sighted provisions, created great problems in the postwar period which helped lead after a twenty-year armistice to a resumption of the European civil war, or World War II.

Another important legacy of World War I had been the rise of the dictatorships and the "isms." In the prewar period, and even during the war, most educated thinkers on the Continent as well as elsewhere regarded some type of a liberal democracy as the preferred form of government, a form which must inevitably triumph, replacing relics of obscurantist monarchism as the monarchies had once replaced feudalism. It seemed almost impossible that there could be a real intellectual challenge to democracy. Representative democracy had functioned best, or seemed to these people to have been functioning best, in England and the United States. The success of this parliamentary government in England had been, and is still today, often attributed to British governmental genius or some other ill-defined quality. In reality, however, there had been for all practical purposes only two systems of parliamentary government which had been used up to that time: the British system, which almost inevitably led to a two-party system, and that of France, or the two-election system which almost inevitably led to a multiplicity of parties. All the major Continental nations used, with certain variations, the latter system. Briefly, it functions in the following manner: With a multiplicity of parties it is almost impossible for any one party to have a working majority in parliament. The ruling coalitions are not usually solid and any demagogic or flamboyant statesman can make the most outlandish statements or promises, knowing full well that even if he is called to a position of responsibility, his ministry would scarcely have time in office to fulfill its promises even if the promises would be possible of ultimate realization. The government can fall; but the bureaucracy and the members of parliament remain. In England, on the other hand, the fall of the ministry would call for a general election, and all the members of parliament would run both the expense of elections and the risk of being defeated. This, of course, helps to enforce both party discipline and responsibility in government. Furthermore, there was in Europe, for the most part, no long tradition of parliamentary government, and parliamentary institutions had not grown organically on the Continent but had been more or less suddenly granted. Under these circumstances, democratic institutions in the interwar period had not been functioning as well as hoped for. As many Continental nations experienced problems and disillusionment in the interwar period, more and more persons became dissatisfied with the seeming incompetence and slow working of democratic government. More and more persons became attracted by the idea of a strong government solving their problem. There were two loud calls to the angry and discontented; one from the Communists, the other from the adherents of a strong nationalist dictatorship, generally called Fascists. In the interwar period, not one nation went Communist, but a number went Fascist, unofficially if not officially. By 1940 there was nothing visibly inscribed in the heavens that said democracy would triumph; indeed, democracy appeared to be facing disaster. The first major triumph of fascism occurred in Italy and was directly traceable to conditions caused by World War I.

At that time of that war Italy was, to use modern terminology, in many respects an underdeveloped nation with almost no natural resources. Her railroads were poor; her heavy industrial and steel production was less than a fourth or fifth that of either France or Russia; she had almost no iron, coal, or petroleum resources. In addition, she had an extremely high rate of illiteracy; figures for army recruits in 1905 show an illiteracy rate of 31 percent, a decrease of only 7 percent from the 38 percent in 1895. Only Russia of the major states had had a similar degree of illiteracy, and even there the Tsarist regime had reduced its illiteracy rate among army recruits from 62.4 percent in 1895, to 34.8 percent in 1910, to 25 percent in 1914. The Italians, pushed into war by the angry young men like the rabid nationalist poets d'Annunzio and Marinetti, who "knew too much of peace but too little of war," had expected a rather easy victory and huge gains and glory. Instead, their gains had not been large and there had been little glory in a war which had seen enormous numbers of casualties and such a smashing Italian defeat at Caporetto. There was great discontent with the government, notorious even for Italy with its political corruption and manipulations.

By 1920, prices in Italy were running about six times the prewar level, and the value of the lira was shrinking from a prewar 19.3 cents to only four cents by 1921. The workers' attempts to keep pace with the rising cost of living had led to numerous costly strikes—running at more than two thousand a year by 1921—which further adversely affected the accumulation of wealth in the country and the ability of the government to meet its financial obligations.

For the millions of Italian war veterans and the hundreds of thousands of war wounded, there was no mustering out pay and no provisions for rewards for their years of service. For a large number of these men, jobs were difficult to find and those that were available paid poorly. Under these conditions it is not surprising that ministries rose and fell rapidly, and the various parlimentary leaders such as Nitti, Giollitti, Bonomi, and Facta did not remain in power long enough to achieve any real program. Many people looked to the Socialists whose numbers grew rapidly; the socialistic confederation of labor achieved a membership of two million, quadrupling its size. However, this presaged more strikes and disorders.

In addition, the Italian Communist party, though small in numbers, was active far out of proportion to the size of its membership, promoting strikes and riots with zeal. An ever-growing number of Italians were, however, getting tired of disorder, tired of corruption, and tired of mismanagement. They wanted a strong man. The strong man was to come with nationalist support. The nationalists had not been large in number, but they were determined, and a number of events helped their growth. Italian Premier Orlando had answered Wilson's appeal to the Italians by appealing to Italian nationalism. Demagogic speeches and demagogic articles had unleashed strong nationalist passions, and further aroused the Italian nationalists. Dissatisfied with the peace treaty and determined to achieve their goals, a rather small group of these nationalists, wearing the later-famous blackshirts, gathered under the command of the poet Gabrielle d'Annunzio. In defiance not only of the Allies but of the Italian government, d'Annunzio and his followers seized Fiume. Such was the status of the Italian government at this time that it dared not act against them for over a year. It is true that there had been precedents in the work of Garibaldi for such a freebooting expedition. However, d'Annunzio's men wanted more than just a "unification of Italy" as did Garibaldi. The numerically small group of nationalists was aided at this time by the government's disregard for the veterans, and by some Socialist abuse of the veterans. Many of the latter began to band together and join nationalist societies. Benito Mussolini, who formerly had been a Socialist, was busily organizing his followers in Milan into fighting units called *fascio di combattimento.* There had been numerous other *Fasci* in Italy even before Mussolini. However, following a congress held in Milan in March of 1919, the other *Fasci* merged with his own. Nevertheless, there was no ground swell of support to Mussolini and the number of his following remained quite small. By the end of 1919, there were probably ten to twenty thousand Fascists in all of Italy. It was Socialist success and further strikes and disorders that gave the Fascists their opportunity. Mussolini began to receive financial support from a number of industrialists and others alarmed at the disorders. Both the *Fasci* and the Socialists began to organize parades and demonstrations while the fighting units of the Fascists began to battle with the Socialists in the major cities of northern Italy. In the violence of the next two years, there were probably far over a thousand persons who lost their lives, and there were even some outright assassinations. Both the army and the police stood by during these battles, the army generally not favoring the Socialists. The fact that the Italian government itself stood by helplessly on the sidelines was a clear indication to all that it was unable to really rule the country. The Socialists had to some degree resorted to violence, for they had been on the decline even prior to the violent Fascist reaction; however, the Fascists were to claim credit for having pushed them back.

By the time of the election of 1921, the Fascists, now united with the nationalists and organized as a political party, won thirty-five seats in the Italian parliament. Fascist promises and demagoguery were attracting more and more followers, while at the same time Fascist organizers were transforming the fighting units or *squadristi* into a paramilitary force, which adopted the black-shirted uniforms of d'Annunzio's followers at Fiume. While the government stood by, Fascist Blackshirts began to take over cities in northern Italy. The Socialists tried to fight back but their power was broken. Only a direct order to the army, many of whose officers sided with the Fascists, could have been able

to have suppressed the Blackshirts at this point. An irresolute government, which since early 1922 was headed by Luigi Facta, its fifth prime minister since the war, a government which had no majority and no firm policies, was certainly not the government to dare give such an order to the army. In October, Mussolini and his followers decided the fruit was ripe for the plucking and prepared for the march on Rome. Some 50,000 Fascists marched on the capital and brought about the fall of the government. The king asked Mussolini, whose personal "march on Rome" was made by railroad, to form a new government.

Despite some scattered violence and even political murder before the Fascist dictatorship was firmly established, Mussolini's regime did bring internal peace and order. It was aided almost from the beginning by an increase in productivity which many outsiders, as well as Italians, attributed to the new stability brought by the firm hand at the helm. The Fascist government adopted more or less a hands-off policy in respect to business during its first years in office, though Mussolini and his highest associates in no way believed in *laissez faire*. The efficiency of the Fascist government in making the train run on time, in keeping order in the streets, in virtually eliminating strikes, in balancing the budget and stabilizing the lira, in increasing production and productivity, were all to have an appeal in a number of countries whose economies and traditional patterns had undergone a tremendous upheaval. The pluses of fascism were more immediately visible than its minuses. Fascism in Italy was not the creation of big business, though the latter did accept it as a preferable alternative to communism. An electoral law of 1928 declared the Fascist party the only legal party in Italy. Fascism as such was an Italian nationalist movement with no logically thought-out long-range objectives of economy or government. Though certain threads of continuity run through Fascist history, Mussolini was to change his stance on many issues.

Mussolini's "march on Rome" served as an example for Marshal Pilsudski's march on Warsaw and the establishment there of an authoritarian government. Mussolini's paramilitary street forces served to some extent as models for Hitler's SA. His type of absolutism helped bring about a drift toward absolutism in both Hungary and Austria.

Indeed, of all the states in East Central Europe, democratic government was on a rather secure basis only in Czechoslovakia. One extremely important factor helping the Czechs retain democratic institutions was the intelligent, and continued leadership they had throughout the interwar period. However, the best of will and the greatest respect would not have been enough to have assured democratic government had it not been for the relatively sound economic position of Czechoslovakia. The Czechs had an economy well balanced between agriculture and industry, a good part of the industries of the old Austrian Empire having been concentrated in Bohemia. The comparatively high per capita income of Czechoslovakia in the interwar period was a powerful factor in contributing to a stable democracy.

In Russia the Reds, as a result of their victory in the civil war, were firmly in control, and there was little chance for the establishment of any parliamentary democracy there. East of the Rhine, therefore, the main struggle between the "isms" on the one hand and democracy on the other took place in Germany.

The initial efforts of the German Communists or Spartacists to establish a Red republic in Germany during the postwar chaos had been shattered, and a democratic representative democracy was established in Germany. Germany, however, had not been a united nation for a long time and true parliamentary democracy had not had a long period of development there. Any German government, in order to gain the support of the majority of the German people, would have had to solve the numerous pressing economic problems facing the nation in the interwar period. Since the German internal political and economic problems were influenced by outside demands which in turn were influenced by internal German developments, these matters will be discussed together.

The new Social Democratic government of Friedrich Ebert took over a country which had lost a tenth of its prewar population and territory. Its total national wealth in 1919 was estimated at about two-thirds of that of 1914. In addition Germany had suffered battle deaths of almost two million men and 800,000 deaths, according to later Nazi claims, through malnutrition as a result of the Allied blockade continued after the fighting stopped. Other enormous problems were created as a result of the tremendous loss of rolling stock by the terms of the armistice, the need to reroute the normal channels of internal trade because of the territorial losses, and the need to integrate an economy which had lost areas which had previously been sources of supply. The money formerly acquired from foreign investment which had helped cover deficits was no more. The merchant marine was virtually gone. The colonies with the money invested there, though not very important in themselves, were gone. There were millions of war injured and more than three million other persons, widows and dependents of war dead, with justified claims on the national treasury. In addition to these problems, the problem of the actual war expenditures, which had been temporarily met by drastically increasing the amount of currency in circulation and by internal borrowing, now had to be faced.

In the postwar period, the Social Democrat majority party in Germany was honestly trying to come to grips with these problems and trying to figure out some way of bringing economic and political order out of the situation. The position of moderate government leaders was made extremely difficult by the fact that long-range plans could not be made until Germany was presented with the final reparations bill. When finally presented in 1921, this bill was for the staggering sum of 56 billion dollars or almost the equivalent of the entire estimated German national wealth. (After sharp exchanges the bill was later cut to 32 billion.)

Since the Germans obviously could not pay this amount in gold, and since the other nations would not accept German labor in other countries for payment, the only possibility of payment would have been a tremendous revival of world trade in which the Germans, by selling enough industrial products abroad above and beyond the amounts needed to balance essential imports, would accumulate sufficient capital to pay off the Allies. Even this would of course have required an extraordinary amount of luck, self-discipline, and a long period of time. The forty-two years for payment alotted by the Allies could have sufficed given the above prerequisite; however, in a country with democratic institutions there is bound to be agitation against any government which seems to be selling out the nation's interests. It is extremely difficult to ask a people to take on a forty-two-year obligation. In the Germany of the early and late 1920s it was easy for demagogues to utilize this situation for their advantage. A campaign was begun to discredit Germany's civilian leaders. They had brought these woes on Germany; Germany had not been defeated in battle but had been "stabbed in the back" by the revolution. It was the civilian leaders of Germany who had signed the peace and admitted a German war guilt which few Germans felt. Soon some of these extremists were carrying their campaigns into the streets in a manner reminiscent of the Fascists in Italy. Lumped together, these groups of rightist extremists were called the Free Corps and in many respects were the substance from which the Nazi party later evolved. As first formed in the days after the armistice, the Free Corps had been a welcome support for the government. They had been useful in fighting the Bolshevist advance in the Baltic area and had helped keep Polish freebooters out of disputed territory. Returning to Germany, they had gone underground to avoid the vigilance of the Allies. They found a ready haven in Munich and Bavaria which in the postwar years was a hotbed for all types of extremist activity. How this group drifted into murder and terrorism and bullying is rather difficult to trace. Their first victim was Matthias Erzberger, the man who had signed the armistice. This assassination came just at the time that the crisis was developing over the reparations payments, with the Allies threatening to occupy the Ruhr if the Germans did not agree to their demands. When the Weimar coalition accepted the Allied demands, the nationalists vented their anger on Walter Rathenau, minister of foreign affairs, who was assassinated in mid-1922.

By this time the value of the mark had been declining in an alarming manner, forcing the German government to ask the Allies for a moratorium on reparations so they could bolster the mark. The French, differing with the British, refused the Germans' request for a moratorium on reparations. When, by December of 1922 and January of 1923, Germany had defaulted in her reparations payment, the French moved into the Ruhr to take over the mines and plants. The Germans answered with passive resistance, a general strike, and sabotage of equipment which brought on punitive French reaction. The effect on the German economy of the Ruhr occupation was disastrous. The mark, already probably weakened beyond redemption, now lost all value and before the end of the year its worth could only be figured out by an astronomer – something like several trillion marks to the dollar. The old currency had reached rock bottom. In the end the Germans were forced to capitulate and agree to renew reparations payments if a new formula could be worked out. For France the Ruhr occupation had been a Pyrrhic victory indeed. She had lost the sympathy of the British and the Americans, and this explains to some degree the later British hesitancy to back up the French. In addition, the occupation had proved costly for the French and their already enormous national debt had increased still further.

For Germany the costs were incalculable. But it was not merely the dollar and cents or mark loss which hurt Germany most. It was the loss of savings, policies, and pensions by millions of honest, law-abiding persons. Indeed almost the entire petty bourgeoisie had suffered. Virtually overnight they had become destitute through no fault of their own. The solid middle class which should be the backbone of a democracy had suffered a grievous blow. Many of these persons were to prove in the future susceptible to the pipes of extremists and demagogues who seemed to promise them so much. Others, though not impressed by the "ism", had lost whatever desire they might have had to rally to the defense of democracy. With this background of happenings and with the success of the Italian Fascists as a guidepost, German extremists increased their agitation in 1922–23.

By this time the name of Adolph Hitler, an Austrian-born ex–army corporal, was becoming known in Bavaria. He had taken over the leadership of a very small ultranationlist party called the German Workers Party. In Bavaria many of the rightist extremists stood for separatism and an independent Bavaria; Hitler however stood for a greater Germany. Hitler constantly kept harping on the same themes and his oratory did have an appeal. His party, which since 1920 was called the Nazi or National Socialist German Workers' Party, did not really present so much a positive program as a number of slogans which could appeal to those wanting easy answers. It appealed mainly to the young, though in many respects the party would have appeared to appeal most to the lower middle classes. During the years 1920–23 the nucleus of the organizations and ideas which were later to dominate Germany and most of Europe took shape. The *Sturmabteilung*, or SA, composed of ex-*Frei Korps* members and often just thugs, was organized at first for protection of meetings and later to beat up and intimidate opponents. With their brown shirts, they were in many respects reminiscent of Mussolini's Blackshirts. The party soon had its own newspaper, the *Voelkischer*

Beobachter [Racial Observer], which later became the official mouthpiece of Nazi Germany. An addition of importance to the party was that of Hermann Goering, a world-war fighter pilot ace who had ended the war as commander of the famous Richthofen squadron, and now took over the leadership of the SA.

The tumultuous events of 1923 helped Hitler gain followers and led to his next move. As a result of the French occupation of the Ruhr and the resultant economic paralysis, the political situation in Germany, particularly in Bavaria, had become strained. Bavaria was acting almost as an independent nation, and in Saxony and other regions the Reds, encouraged by Moscow to take advantage of the economic collapse, were attempting to set up an independent Red state. As relations between Bavaria and the central government worsened, Hitler thought that the time to act had come. He had established good relationships with the former army commander General Ludendorff and probably figured that with this added prestige he could seize Munich and then move on to Berlin, like Mussolini on Rome. On November 9 Hitler and Ludendorff and about a thousand Nazi supporters marched on downtown Munich. However, the local army commander had been expressly ordered by the Reichswehr commander to put down the revolt and was ready for Hitler. This time the military reacted differently than it had during the Kapp Putsch. The troops fired on the marchers; some sixteen Nazis were killed, and Hitler himself, captured shortly thereafter, was brought to trial and sentenced to prison.

Under almost any ordinary circumstances, in almost any well-ordered state, this would have spelled the end of an agitator's hopes. It is hardly possible that anyone could have then predicted that less than ten years Hitler's splinter extremist organization would take over Germany. However, at the trials which took place, Hitler had for the first time an important rostrum from which he could propound his cause. The trial was well reported throughout Germany

and even abroad, and Hitler's association with Ludendorff
helped raise him in the public's mind. For the first time
Hitler became known all over Germany. A lenient court gave
him a five-year sentence, of which only a little over a year
was actually spent in rather comfortable confinement in the
Landshut prison. During this period of captivity Hitler
dictated to his assistant Rudolf Hess his *Mein Kampf* which
later became the Nazi bible. The failure of his Putsch had
taught Hitler a lesson: a "march on Berlin" in the manner
of Mussolini's march on Rome could not succeed as long as
the army would oppose it. The Nazis would have to build up
their power base by working through legal channels first.

Meanwhile economic and political order had returned to
Germany. Reparations payments had been scaled down and
large-scale American and British credits helped German
recovery. As long as this fresh capital flowed in, Germany
could meet her scaled-down obligations and gradually reestablish her economic prosperity. As long as Germany
prospered—despite the constant harangues from right and
left—democracy was not seriously threatened in Germany.
During most of the remaining period of the twenties, the
Weimar Republic's leading statesman Stresemann, now
foreign minister instead of chancellor, tried to lead Germany back into the European community of nations. In
1925 Stresemann met with the English and French ministers, Chamberlain and Briand, at Locarno in Switzerland
and out of their conferences arose the Locarno treaties by
which it was hoped peace would be secured to Europe. As a
further result of the Locarno treaty Germany entered the
League of Nations.

In 1928 the moderate prosperity of the Republic was
shown in the election returns which virtually eliminated
the Nazis and gave the Social Democrats such a large vote
that one of their members became chancellor. In 1929 new
reparations were adopted whereby all foreign controls in
Germany were abolished. The following year, as a result of
negotiations, the Allies evacuated the Rhineland. Although

the Nazis and other extremist groups raged violently against either agreement, there seemed to be little threat to the existence of the Republic. The combustible material, the Nazi and extremist groups, was there, but there seemed no issue that could ignite them into a force strong enough to bring down the Republic. There was little warning of the impending economic storm that within a period of less than three years would put an end to the Weimar Republic. However, the stability of the Weimar government was based on a modest prosperity; when that prosperity began to wither as a result of the American depression of late 1929, the position of the Weimar government became more and more unstable. The raucus voices of the extremists calling for a national regeneration, a pure race, a repudiation of the war-guilt clauses, an end to reparation payments, revision of the Versailles treaty, and a strong, forward nationalist party began to attract an ever-widening following. As the ranks of the unemployed swelled and the future appeared dismal, many of the disillusioned turned to the Nazis. For those who needed easy answers to the complex problems of the day there was the facile explanation of blaming the Jews and the "stab in the back" for Germany's woes. For youth, facing a bleak future in a discredited and debt-ridden nation, there were the inspiring slogans of a united, powerful, virile state under one leader, and a call to clean out decadent democracy. The extremists grew; the Communists increased in numbers, and the Nazis mushroomed. And now, when Germany needed its solid bourgeoisie more than ever, the effects of the runaway inflation of 1923 made themselves felt. That class which should have been ready to defend democracy had suffered too much too recently. This does not mean that the Nazis just walked into power with the acclamation of the German people. Despite their enormous gains the Nazis were not able to get a majority of the vote. However, they were the largest single political party in Germany. Their ruthless paramilitary forces beat up opponents and smashed opposition presses;

and although Hitler repeatedly said he would take power
only by legal means there was always the threat of a Nazi
take-over, a take-over which no one but the army had the
strength to stop. Nazi demands for an end to the Versailles
restrictions and for a strong army had won large support
in military circles, and it was not certain whether the
army as such would interfere with an attempted Nazi take-
over.

By 1932 the number of unemployed in Germany had
risen to six million. The attempts to organize a customs
union with Austria had again been vetoed by the Allies. The
government deficit was rising as more and more government money was needed to meet the crisis. Under these
conditions the strength of the Nazi party grew rapidly. Prior
to 1920 the Nazis held only twelve seats in the parliament;
in the fall 1930 elections they won 107 seats, and in the
elections of mid-1932, a total of 230 seats.

Yet, despite the tremendous growth, the Nazis by mid-
1932 were actually beginning to lose a bit of their support.
New elections were called and the Nazis polled two million
fewer votes than formerly. Even then Hitler and his Nazis
were vastly underestimated. At the beginning of 1933 the
aged President Hindenburg was persuaded by his closest
advisers to take the Nazis into the government, giving the
post of chancellor to Hitler and a few other posts to his supporters. Hitler almost immediately dissolved parliament
and called for new elections. During the period before the
elections opposition papers were suppressed and opposition
candidates denied access to the radio, while Nazi Brown-
shirt strongarm units intimidated others. The huge Reichstag fire occurred shortly before the elections were held.
The Nazis immediately seized on this as an excuse to strike
at the Communists, whom they accused of having caused
the fire. By a special presidential decree many constitutional
guarantees were suspended while the Nazis tried to fan
the fears of an impending Communist coup. Even then, the
Nazis polled less than a majority, receiving some 17 mil-

lion out of a total of 39 million votes cast. However, with
the support of the deputies representing the four million
Nationalists, Hitler was able to induce the new Reichstag
to pass the "enabling act" giving him sweeping powers. For
all practical purposes the Reichstag had voted itself out of
existence and the Weimar Republic had expired. Just how
portentous this event was, was not really appreciated at the
time. Among those who seriously underestimated the Nazi
menace were the German Communists. They had been
anxious to bring down the democratic government of the
center, believing that even in the event of a Nazi take-over,
Hitler and his rabble would be repudiated by the people
who would then rally to the Communist banner. Largely for
this reason they refused to cooperate with the anti-Nazi
forces. Scarcely ever were people to be more sadly disillusioned. Perhaps a repudiation of the Nazis was a possibility had the economic situation worsened. However, this
did not happen. The economic situation in Germany did
improve. At the same time the Nazis viciously cracked
down on former and potential opponents to their rule. While
many Germans were appalled at the Nazi measures, there
were many who approved extreme measures and still others
who did not care what the government did as long as it
brought on employment and as long as conditions improved.

With the success of the Nazis in Germany, the cause of
democracy on the Continent east of the Rhine was pretty
well doomed. With the exception of Czechoslovakia, even
those nations which kept the trappings of parliamentary
democracy came more and more to discard democratic
freedoms. Since the impatient youth of these countries was
no longer satisfied with the slow workings of democracies,
the extremist organizations gained a greater following.
Communism was pretty much discredited, and the Russian
famine of the early thirties had done much to dampen
ardor in that direction. A greater appeal in the East Central

nations was that of the Fascists, and each of these countries soon had its equivalent of the blackshirts and brownshirts.

Thus, by 1939 Fascism was on the offensive and gaining ground. Throughout non-Fascist Europe and elsewhere, democracy was on the defensive, and communism was largely discredited.

3

The Breakdown of Collective Security and the Outbreak of World War II

WORLD WAR I had dealt Europe a shattering blow. Out of the vast popular demand that future war be prevented had come the League of Nations, the basic idea of which was "collective security." It was hoped that collective action could bring about peace and security; for alliance systems had not brought security but had helped lead to war.

The principle of collective security had been embodied in certain articles of the League covenant which stated that each member undertook to respect the integrity and independence of all the others and would join in preserving them against aggression. Under Article 16 all members promised to join in common action against any other nation which made war in violation of the covenant. This then was collective security, the hope for future peace.

In September 1931 collective security was put to the test when Japanese forces attacked Chinese positions in Manchuria and proceeded to take over that region. The League and collective security were of no aid to the Chinese. However, Japan and Manchuria seemed far away. There were still high hopes that the League might be successful in a future quarrel or quarrels closer to the European home.

In 1935 Italian forces invaded Ethiopia and proceeded to conquer that nation while Benito Mussolini proclaimed its annexation to the new Italian Empire. The Ethiopian emperor, Haili Selassie, appealed to the League of Nations, warning that if there could be no security for his country at that time, there could be no security for other nations in the future. The League did not act to defend Ethiopia; "collective security" had proved to be a hollow phrase.

Meanwhile, in the same year, the mineral-rich Saarland was reunited to Germany as a result of a plebiscite held there under League supervision the preceding year. Within two weeks of the return of the Saar, Hitler proclaimed military conscription in Germany, thus unilaterally abrogating vital provisions of the Versailles Treaty. There were some protests against this move but no action was taken. Germany speeded up armament expenditures enormously while the English and French, plagued with budget deficits and not wishing to become involved in an arms race, did relatively little toward military preparation. For the Germans, Adolph Hitler was rapidly becoming the hero who had brought back German territory, raised employment, ended many of the onerous clauses of the Versailles Treaty, and who was moving the country forward. Shortly thereafter, Hitler chose a crisis moment in international affairs, when sanctions were being considered against Italy over Ethiopia and when that signatory of the Locarno agreements guaranteeing Germany's western border was at odds with Britain and France, to send troops into the Rhineland and to announce that Germany was repudiating both the Versailles Treaty and the Locarno pact. The council of the League of Nations voted that Germany was guilty of violation of the Locarno Treaty. Although Germany was not ready for war and German officers had orders to withdraw from the Rhineland if the French moved, none acted to stop Hitler. The French would not move without British support, and the British did not give their support, partially because France had not joined them in imposing sanctions on Mussolini. Thus the last opportunity to stop Hitler without bloodshed had passed. The Germans immediately set about militarizing the Rhineland and rushing completion of a fortified line, the so-called Siegfried Line, along their western frontiers. Again the League had not been able to act effectively.

Generalissimo Francisco Franco

Meanwhile, in Spain General Francisco Franco had led his troops against the Madrid government, and in the Spanish Civil War which ensued, Hitler and Mussolini cooperated in sending aid to the Franco forces. By the fall of 1936, Hitler and Mussolini had signed an agreement creating the so-called Rome-Berlin Axis; a month later Hitler signed with Japan an anti-Comintern (Communist International) Pact, to which Mussolini adhered shortly thereafter. Thus the three large "have not" powers had formed a Rome-Berlin-Tokyo axis. The results of this Italo-German cooperation were felt almost immediately in Austria.

Austria had been in chronic economic difficulties as a result of the dismemberment of the empire in 1918. She had been hard hit by the depression. Her people were German-speaking; Hitler himself was an Austrian. It was only natural that many Austrians should regard a union with the larger German economic unit as a way out of their financial difficulties. Indeed, as early as 1931, an attempt had been made for an Austro-German customs union; this had been vetoed by the Western Allies. While many Austrians were appalled by some of the excesses of Nazism, many others were excited and stimulated by Nazi successes, and as early as 1934 local Austrian Nazis had made an attempt to seize power. It was probably only Mussolini's prompt mobilization of Italian troops along the Brenner which had prevented a German annexation of Austria at that time. After the German-Italian Axis accords there was no power ready to stand in Hitler's way over Austria.

Thus, in early 1938, when France was faced with another ministerial crisis, Hitler put pressure on Austria's Chancellor Schuschnigg to admit Nazis to key positions in the Austrian cabinet. Shortly thereafter Schuschnigg, faced with German forces massing on the borders and an ultimatum for his resignation from Arthur Seyss-Inquart, the Austrian Nazi Minister of the Interior, gave up his position in order to "save bloodshed." At the invitation of Seyss-Inquart, German troops, already poised for an invasion,

entered Austria, and Hitler proclaimed the "Anschluss"–
the annexation of Austria, the East Mark.

The Anschluss dramatically changed the whole Continental power picture. Germany now had a common frontier
with her ally Italy. From a nation of 67 million, she had
become a nation of 74 millions. The bloodless German success in Austria enormously boosted Hitler's prestige both at
home and abroad. It brought Germany to the frontiers of
Hungary and Yugoslavia, and both of these countries were
to be subjected to greater German pressures than before.
Czechoslovakia, the anchor of the Little Entente of Rumania, Yugoslavia, and Czechoslovakia, was now pretty much
surrounded by Germany and placed in a much more precarious position militarily than she had been before. With Germany on their borders, the nations of the Little Entente permitted Hungary and Bulgaria to rearm, receiving in return
a pledge of nonaggression. Obviously, this raised the prestige of the local Nazis, particularly in Hungary.

The success of Germany in Austria also raised the political stock and prestige of the Nazis and German nationalists
among the 3.5 million Sudeten Germans living in Czechoslovakia. The local Nazi leader, Konrad Henlein, became
more and more aggressive in his demands on the Czech
state. Meanwhile, anti-Czech articles began to appear in
the controlled German press, and there were rumors of
German troop concentrations along the Czech border. At the
same time, Germany was rushing its construction of the
Siegfried Line, designed, it was believed, to halt the French
should the latter honor her commitments to defend Czechoslovakia in case of a German attack. In the summer of 1938,
war clouds began darkening the European skies as Hitler
ordered maneuvers of about one and a half million men;
some French reserves were also called up and Soviet Russia
promised to support the Czechs. In September 1938, Hitler
declared in an address to the Nazi Parliament that Germany
could not sit idly by while the oppressed Sudeten Germans
were defenseless; it appeared that Germany was poised for

an attack. Such an attack would have brought on a general
European war. Neville Chamberlain, the British Prime Minister, wishing at almost all costs to avoid a war, flew to
Munich to consult again with Hitler at the latter's mountain
chalet of Berchtesgaden. Here Hitler insisted that he was
asking nothing more than self-determination. The Sudetan
inhabitants were German and wished to be part of the German state. Up to this time, Hitler had neither demanded
nor annexed any non-Germany territory. It seemed scarcely
worth a world war to prevent the unification of 3.5 million
Germans to the state to which they obviously wished to belong. Chamberlain's advisers told him that neither the British nor the French could deal with air attacks by the new
German air force, the Luftwaffe. Hitler further announced
that once his demands against Czechoslovakia were met,
he had no further territorial demands to make in Europe.
French and British popular opinion was not united. Under
these circumstances, British Prime Minister Chamberlain
and French Premier Daladier agreed to go to Munich where
they signed the Munich agreements that have since become
synonymous with appeasement. In these agreements the
Western Allies agreed not to oppose the German annexation of the Sudetenland.

Upon his return to London, Chamberlain told cheering
crowds that he had brought peace with honor, peace in our
times, and that it was preposterous that Britishers should
be donning gasmasks and digging trenches over a quarrel
in a distant land. There were other Englishmen like Winston Churchill who warned against the course being followed, but they were not heeded. It was not known that
some of the leading German generals, alarmed at the real
state of German readiness and appalled by what they considered Hitler's reckless gamble with the future of the nation, were prepared to countermand any order to move on
Czechoslovakia; and that had the Allies resisted at that
point, Hitler's position was far from formidable. At any rate,
the German annexation of the Sudetenland in October 1938

brought new woes to the Czech state. Poland now renewed her claims to the Teschen area, and the weakened Czechs were forced to cede that territory. By November they had been forced to cede still another area with about one million inhabitants to Hungary.

The losses of such territories could not help but have an effect on the stability of the remaining part of the Czech-Slovak state, where many Slovaks had long felt that the Czechs, on the whole more highly educated, were running the government from a Bohemian rather than a Slovak point of view. As Slovak demands grew, the weakened Prague government was forced to decentralize the state, making it more of a federation. As pressures mounted, Hitler summoned the Czech leaders to Berlin where, after an all-night session in which they were subjected to the threats of seeing their land devastated – the loss of the Sudetenland with its strong frontier fortifications had placed the Czech state in a militarily untenable position – they agreed to place the "fate of the Czech people . . . in the hands of the Fueh-rer." On March 15, 1939, German troops moved in and occupied Prague and set up a German "protectorate" over Moravia and Bohemia, while Slovakia became a vassal state of Germany. At the same time Mussolini was deciding that the time was favorable to strengthen Italy's position in the Adriatic and to enlarge his empire. In April 1939, Mussolini, failing to get King Zog of Albania to agree to some of his demands, ordered Italian troops to move into that country. Albania was quickly occupied and King Victor Emmanuel was proclaimed king of Italy and Albania.

In the three years from the spring of 1936 to 1939, the European and world political situation had changed drastically. It was quite obvious that the aggressors could be stopped only if they were confronted by strong military force; yet there was no certainty that any of the big powers had the will to use force to halt the dictators. In those scant three years, Ethiopia had been occupied; Japan had invaded China, occupying large territories; Italy and Germany had sent great aid to Franco's forces; Germany had abrogated both the Locarno and the Versailles Treaties, remilitarized the Rhineland, occupied Bohemia and Moravia, and had brought Slovakia and Hungary within her orbit. Italy had annexed Albania and was demanding other territories as well. The situation was far different from what it had been less than four years earlier when a weakly armed Germany had indicated she would not abide by the Versailles Treaty.

Until the German occupation of Bohemia, Hitler could justify his actions by claiming self-determination. However, in occupying what was left of Czechoslovakia, he had violated the pledge he had given at the time of the Munich crisis, the pledge that he had no more territorial demands to make in Europe. In March 1939, Hitler was no longer speaking only about self-determination but about *Lebensraum* [living space]. Until March 1939, there had been some justification for all of Hitler's demands. Now it seemed that these demands could be enlarged to include eastern Europe, and perhaps Alsace, former colonies, and who could tell what else?

Belatedly, the British and French democracies realized that they could not afford any more Munichs, that they would have to make a stand. Chamberlain had earlier stated that he would fight if any one nation attempted to dominate the world by "fear of its force." The British and French governments, therefore, jointly announced at the end of March 1939, that they would at once support Poland in the event that that nation was compelled to resist any action which clearly threatened Polish independence. The British were particularly anxious to make their position unequivocally clear, for they had often been accused of failure to do just that in 1914.

During this period, the German press began reporting Polish atrocities against persons of German origin in western Poland, and denounced the Polish terror against the German minority. By the end of April, Hitler abrogated both the German-Polish nonaggression pact of 1934 and the Anglo-German naval agreement of 1935. Almost immediately, he demanded that the free city of Danzig be returned to Germany and that Germany be given a "corridor" across the Polish Corridor; in other words, a highway and a railway line in which the Poles would have no sovereignty.

In May 1939, Italy and Germany signed a military alliance in order to put more pressure on those who were not ready to appease them. The British and French, realizing the geographical difficulties involved in trying to help Poland or any other nation in eastern Europe in the event of a German attack, began to sound out the Soviet Union for an alliance. Stalin was not sure what to believe. In the Czech crisis, the Western Allies had backed down at the last moment. Perhaps the evil capitalists would like very much to see a German-Russian war in which these two states exhausted each other. In addition, the Western Allies did not appear too ready to make concessions to Russia for an alliance. Stalin wanted a guarantee to the Baltic states. The Western Allies were a bit fearful that this would be merely a pretext for the Soviets to swallow up those states.

Meanwhile, Hitler did not stand still. Shortly after the occupation of Prague, the Germans moved into the city and territory of Memel which had been administered by Lithuania for the League of Nations. The population of Memel was mainly German; however, the brazen manner in which it had been occupied by the Nazis, coming on the heels of the occupation of Bohemia and accompanied by German demands on Poland for Danzig and the Corridor, and coupled also with Mussolini's seizure of Albania and demands for the return to Italy of Nice, Corsica, Savoy, Tunis, etc., was enough to send tremors through the chancelleries of Europe.

In April America's President Roosevelt had sent to the two Axis dictators a message in which he asked their assurances that they would not attack for a period of ten years a list of states which he enumerated. Hitler, in one of his most eloquent speeches in the German Reichstag, scornfully answered this message. Under the calm measures of analysis to which this speech could be subjected in the West, Hitler's speech could be shown to be avoiding the issue. However, to the German populace for whom all the counterarguments were not readily and clearly available, Hitler seemed right. Why was FDR asking him to guarantee Syria and Palestine, and other states? Roosevelt should ask the French and the British rather than the Germans about those places.

Britain, meanwhile, despite strong pacifist and liberal objections, reluctantly began to gird for war, and peacetime military conscription was introduced there. However, Britain was woefully unprepared. During the five preceding years, she had spent only a fraction of the sum on armaments that the Germans had. The British began pushing diplomatic measures. Mutual assistance treaties with Poland and Turkey were concluded, and the king and queen of England went on a goodwill tour of the United States and Canada in the late summer of 1939. In July 1939, as the Polish question heated up, a British mission was dispatched to Russia.

The British, having no idea the Soviets were then carrying on other negotiations, made no attempt to rush their own discussions with the USSR, and their mission was even sent by ship rather than by air. One reason the British did not hasten was that they were faced with a somewhat difficult task in their negotiations with the Soviets, and they confidently believed that Stalin would have to fight for Poland regardless of how he felt. The Poles had made it abundantly clear that they were very reluctant to admit Soviet troops to Poland—a reluctance which later events proved well founded—and negotiating a treaty acceptable both to the Poles and Stalin was not easy.

To the British and French, and to almost all outside observers, it was unthinkable that the Soviets and Nazis could come to an agreement. Hitler had railed against bolshevism for almost twenty years, and none could have been more violent than the Soviets in their denunciation of the Nazi beast. Thus it was to the amazement and shocked disbelief of the diplomatic world that the news was broken on August 23, 1939, a few days after the arrival of the Allied negotiating mission, that the Germans and Russians had signed a nonaggression pact. A diplomatic revolution had occurred.

Actually there had been signs which had been ignored. It had on occasion been hinted in some quarters that perhaps Hitler could come to some sort of understanding with the Soviets as the Germans had done at Rapallo. There were a number of German statesmen who regarded an understanding with Russia as both important and essential. Some astute observers might already have noticed that Hitler had recently been omitting certain customary and gratuitous references to Marxism as the world's curse. In May 1939, there had been a number of cautious "feelers" and conferences between German and Russian representatives. Count von Schulenberg, the German ambassador in Moscow, was known to be a strong advocate of Russian-German friendship. Yet it was only after the signing of the German-Soviet pact that the significance of the above facts was recognized in the West.

The pact itself was of tremendous importance. With this pact, Hitler could confidently face the West. The new Siegfried line, along Germany's western frontiers, the strength of which was overestimated, could keep the French and British at bay while he finished with the Poles; and in the event of a somewhat protracted war he could count on Russian supplies to avoid the worst stringencies of the blockade. The "pact of steel" earlier signed with the Italians, had been designed to impress the outside world, for Mussolini had plainly informed Hitler that Italy would remain neutral in the war because of her lack of preparedness. In the week of peace that remained following the Soviet pact, Hitler's efforts to get the Allies to back down appeared to be bearing

EUROPE IN 1939

fruit. Hitler had been further assured by his Foreign Minister Ribbentrop that the British would not fight. On the first of September 1939, after a staged border incident to convince the German public that the Poles were the aggressors, German forces swarmed across the Polish frontier while dive bombers pounded Polish bases. Two days later, when the Germans did not respond to a British ultimatum to Germany to withdraw, the British and then the French declared war on Germany. Another holocaust had begun. All the measures taken at the end of World War I, all the provisions made to safeguard the peace had failed.

This time it was a far more sober Europe that received the news of the war. In 1914 Berlin had had parades and had taken on a carnival atmosphere. Paris and the other capitals were happy that the hour of reckoning had come. In 1939, Berlin was very somber indeed, and it was with a very heavy heart that a disillusioned Chamberlain told his distressed countrymen that as a consequence of the failure of the Germans to reply to the Allied demand that Germany cease operations against Poland, England was again at war with Germany.

4

World War II

The First Years

ALTHOUGH it had been known that the Germans were arming feverishly and building an air force at a rate much faster than either Britain or France, and though the Western nations had dreaded becoming involved in a war with Germany, German strength was vastly underestimated.

In 1939 there were many who expected a long two-front war to develop, with Germany gradually reduced to submission by the Allied blockade and by the superior overseas resources of the British and French. Indeed, the Allied strategy seemed bent on holding the line in the West while

6. LINE-UP OF THE POWERS ON THE EVE OF WAR, 1939

Country	Population (In millions)	Steel production (In millions of tons)
France	41	8
Germany	80	22
Great Britain	48	13
Poland	34	2
USSR	172	19
Italy	44	2
United States	131	48
Japan	72	7

Source: United Nations, *Statistical Yearbook for 1948*, table 104. Woytinsky and Woytinsky, p. 1118.

the British built up an army and additional troops came in from the overseas dominions. The French and British had finally learned the lessons of World War I – that a well-entrenched defense in depth was far better than a reckless offense, and that given the massive firepower of modern armies, the advantage is with the defense. However, the lessons of World War I were not applicable to World War II. The airplane and the tank had revolutionized warfare as the Germans now proved in the Polish campaign. The results of the early stages of the war were, therefore, vastly different from those expected by almost all neutral observers. The Germans counted on columns of tanks racing around prepared positions to cut rear communications and dive bombers blasting defenses and supply bases from the air, so that Polish armies would be cut up, cut off, and pounded into submission. Poland was no insignificant nation. She had in 1939 some 35 million people and a sizable, well-trained army of a million and a half men; moreover, Poles had given a good account of themselves in the post–World War I fighting against the Russians and were confident of their ability to stop the Germans. The Poles had counted on their lack of roads to stop mechanized columns and on their excellent cavalry to wreak havoc among the infantry.

However, the German annexation of Czechoslovakia had greatly weakened the Polish defensive position. Had the Poles immediately retreated to the Vistula, which would have meant surrendering a giant part of their country, there would have been a much better chance for resistance. However, the aggressor chooses the time and place where he will attack, and within a very short time after their sudden assault, the Germans had bombed the Polish air force out of existence, which meant that henceforth the Germans knew the exact dispositions of the Polish forces while the Poles had no idea from which directions the attacking Germans were coming. Armored columns drove through and around the Poles, causing confusion and chaos. Bombers pounded the Polish cities and rail centers, and the weather remained fine with no rains coming to turn the Polish roads into muddy quagmires which might have bogged down the German armor. After seventeen days of fighting, the Poles were smashed and reeling. However, units were retreating to the east hoping to make a stand deeper in Poland. There the Germans would have to fight in worse terrain under worsening weather conditions, with more extended communication lines, while the Poles hoped to be supplied through Rumania. All the time, Britain would be strengthening her forces on Germany's western front. While it is doubtful that the Poles could have held out here, the sudden invasion of Poland by the Russians on September 17 made further resistance virtually impossible. The Polish government fled to exile through Rumania, although Warsaw held out until September 27. The Soviets and the Germans two days thereafter concluded a treaty of friendship and established a demarcation line between them. Actually, the Russians had annexed mostly that territory to the east of the Curzon line, territory which they had lost as a result of the war with Poland in 1920. This territory of about 14 million persons, largely inhabited by White Russians and Ukranians, was then annexed to the Ukranian S.S.R., and Nikita Khrushchev, then party secretary for the Ukraine, set about the task of incorporating the "liberated" territory into the USSR. Hitler had spoken about establishing a thousand-year Reich, and the Nazis gave every evidence of intending to establish a permanent "new order" in the territory they had conquered. Those territories which had been German prior to 1918 were immediately incorporated into the Reich along with other choice areas including the cities of Lodz and Warsaw with their environs. Over the rest of Poland, with the capital at Cracow, a protectorate on the order of the Bohemian protectorate was established under the rule of Hans Franck. Thus, from a nation of 35 million persons, a Polish protectorate of 13 million under direct Gestapo rule remained. Fourteen million more former Polish subjects had been incorporated into the USSR. In those areas directly incorporated into Germany, the Nazis began to try to attract German settlers. *Lebensraum* was to be obtained by removing non-Germans from this area into the protectorate. Although the world had had some advance warning of what Nazism might be like, and although previous Nazi gains had been accompanied by extreme brutality against Jews and persons who had expressed themselves at some time or another against the Nazis, there soon began to unfold in Poland a Nazi terror of a kind scarcely anticipated. To the German people, to whom the Poles had for some time been depicted as uncultured brutes molesting peaceful German villagers, nothing was said about the deportations, roundups, and the intention to gradually eradicate the Polish intelligentsia. Also, although the treatment of the Jews had been extremely bad from the beginning, few persons, possibly not even most Nazis, really had any inkling of what was going to develop in the succeeding years. For the German people, Hitler was the leader, *Der Fuehrer*, who had settled the score with those uncultured neighbors who had despoiled Germany and persecuted German minorities. For them it was the Poles who had attacked and reaped the just whirlwind. Now that the score had been settled, here was Hitler offering the most generous peace terms to the Western allies. It was only English hatred of Germany, so the Germans were told, a hatred caused in large measure by the "international Jewish conspiracy" that was keeping England in this war. After all, Poland, for whose defense the English had gone to war, had been smashed. For what other reasons would the English continue a costly war?

The Western Allies felt differently. They had learned that Hitler could find explanations for all actions, and now that war had come they were determined to carry it on. However, they were convinced that the best method was simply to hold the line in France till Germany would be worn down. For that reason, they had allowed whatever offensive opportunities they might have had while Germany was occupied in Poland to pass. During the fall and winter months, the Communist parties which had formerly been so active in their denunciation of Hitler were denouncing this imperialistic, capitalist war and criticizing Britain and France for continuing it. Rumors spread in France and articles began to appear in the presses of many nations about this being a business war, a phony war. Some reporters now referred to this war as the *Sitzkrieg* as opposed to the German *Blitzkrieg* of "lightning war." Reports were rampant about how German and French manufacturers were still dealing and trading across neutral Belgium and Holland.

However, the western front was comparatively quiet only because the best weather for offensive operations had passed by the time Germany could shift troops from Poland. The lessons of the Polish campaign had not been learned in the West. Besides, the French had spent fortunes in fortifying their frontier zone with Germany. This system of fortifications, the so-called Maginot Line, named after the former minister of war who helped design it, was considered virtually impregnable. For the Germans to break through at any point, it was confidently stated, would cost a minimum of two million casualties. For the Allies to try an offensive through the heavily fortified German Siegfried line would be folly, so why risk anything?

But while the war on the western front entered a "lull" period, the war at sea had begun with a series of spectacular German successes, with a German submarine even penetrating the British naval harbor at Scapa Flow and sinking a British battleship. In addition, hundreds of thousands of tons of merchant shipping were lost to the German U-Boats. For again, as in World War I, the Germans could not compete with the British in surface warships and had taken to the submarine. However, the energetic Winston Churchill had been recalled to command at the British Admiralty, where he had been in World War I, and with newer submarine detection instruments, British losses to the undersea raiders were greatly diminished.

However, the democracies seemed to have another enemy in the Soviet Union, which was supplying Hitler with the sinews of war and at the same time was making preparations to strengthen her own position. She had already annexed eastern Poland. Now taking advantage of the preoccupation of the other powers in the West, she demanded and received naval and military bases from the three Baltic republics. She then demanded that the Finns cede certain territories in the Karelian Isthmus and the area around the Gulf of Finland which would aid Soviet defenses for Leningrad; in return the Soviets would give the Finns territory to the north. This the Finns refused to do. On November 28, 1939, the Soviets renounced their nonaggression treaty with Finland. Shortly thereafter, with Russian Foreign Minister Molotov accusing the Finns of having attacked the USSR and asserting that Russia must defend herself against aggression, the Soviets launched an invasion of their small neighbor. Simultaneously, their planes attacked Helsinki. To the amazement of much of the world, the Russians ran into considerable difficulty. The weather during that winter was exceptionally cold; the Finns under General Mannerheim fought tenaciously and well, and the terrain was such as to impede mechanized columns. The Finns appealed to the League of Nations which was still sitting in Geneva. That body, thereupon, asked the Russians to cease hostilities against the Finns. To this request, the Russians blandly announced that they were not conducting hostilities against Finland but had just concluded a treaty of friendship and aid with the legitimate Finnish government and were merely helping them crush criminal elements. (Upon crossing the frontier the Russians had brought with them a group of expatriate Finnish Communists and recognized them as the Finnish government.) The rest of the world did not share that opinion, and there was a strong clamor in many countries to do something for Finland; however, there was little that could be done as long as Germany, not yet ready to destroy her alliance with the Soviet Union, stood in the way.

The Russians continued to bring up more and better units, and the Finns were gradually worn down. Thus, by the beginning of March, the latter were anxious to enter into peace negotiations. As a result of this peace, the Finns lost, among other things, their second largest city, Vipuri, and the Karelian Isthmus. It was quite obvious that only armed resistance could preserve independence and territorial integrity .

During the fall and early spring, as England converted her industry and strengthened her forces, the feeling of confidence there developed even further. Chamberlain, speaking on April 4, 1940, stated "now after seven months of war I feel ten times as confident of victory as I did at the beginning . . . One thing is certain," he added, "Hitler has missed the bus." By this he meant that Hitler had not struck while England was still unprepared. But Hitler had intended to go for other bus rides.

The Scandinavian countries were of considerable strategic importance. Denmark had been a great supplier of eggs and other agricultural products to England. Swedish industry and particularly her ores were of great importance to Germany. If Germany could seize both Denmark and Norway, she could insure herself of access to Swedish raw materials and manufactures and improve her food supply, for a Sweden surrounded by Germany would have little choice. With Norway in their hands, the Germans could have admirable air and naval bases for harassing British shipping while securing their own flanks. Scandinavia had enjoyed virtually a century of peace. An attack from the Germans was completely unexpected. To further throw the Allies off guard, the Germans made troop concentrations and feints in the West, and there was talk in Germany of the necessity of striking a decisive blow in the West soon. On April 9, German troops moved into Denmark and quietly swept into Copenhagen where the Danish king, realizing that resistance was futile, ordered that there be no opposition. The invasion of Norway, however, required an overseas landing operation, which, in the face of British naval supremacy, could be difficult if opposition were encountered in the opening stages. However, the German invasion had been well worked out and coordinated with native Norwegian Nazi sympathizers. Within a few hours, virtually all important strategic bases in the country were in German hands, though King Haakon and his chief government aides escaped to England. The Allies did land a force near Trondheim, hoping that with naval support and the aid of the Norwegians they could defeat the Germans. However, their position became untenable and they later reembarked. In Norway itself, the Germans established a puppet government under a native Norwegian Nazi, a Major Vikdun Quisling. The name Quisling shortly thereafter became synonymous with traitor.

There could be no doubt that the Nazis had scored a major success in their Scandinavian ventures. In Germany the populace was told, and still occasionally reads, that the invasion of Norway was necessary to forestall the British whose plans to seize that country as a base of operations against Germany had been all drawn up. Under these conditions, the prestige of Hitler and the Nazis soared still more with the Germans. The war had caused little real hardship as yet. Hitler kept offering peace—it was the jealous English who kept the war going. The Nazis insisted the Germans were a super race and now they were proving it. German arms were invincible. For Hitler himself, the string of unbroken successes had increased his confidence. At every step there had been advisers to tell him he was wrong and should hesitate. Before the Austrian invasion it had been General von Fritsch; Hitler had him removed, and events proved Hitler right. Before the Czech invasion, it had been General Beck; Hitler had him removed, and again Hitler had been right. Before the Polish and Scandinavian campaign, still others had urged caution, and Hitler was right. Who could argue with such success?

The Nazi successes in Scandinavia caused an uproar in

London and Paris. In both capitals it was felt that a change
in the management of the war was necessary. In London
a broken and disillusioned Chamberlain, amid cries of "resign" from his own party adherents, turned the government
over to Winston Churchill. In France, Premier Daladier had
scarcely made way for Paul Reynaud when the Nazi blitzkrieg broke with full fury.

The Invasion of Belgium and the Nazi Attack in the West

Hitler on more than one occasion had promised to respect the neutrality of Belgium and Holland. On Sunday
morning, May 10, 1940, German forces occupied Luxem-
burg and swarmed into Holland and Belgium. It was the
Schlieffen plan again, only this time with the stops pulled
out and Holland included. The Allies should not have been
caught napping. They had seen this plan in operation in
World War I. They knew that the Maginot Line defenses
only went up to the Belgian border. Prior to German rearmament the French had had joint staff discussions with the
Belgians regarding defenses in case of a German push
through their country. However, once Germany had begun
rearming and such talks became pertinent, the Belgians had
hoped to avoid provoking Germany and had abandoned joint
military planning with the French. Now they and Holland
were to reap the whirlwind. The Dutch had planned to open
the dikes and flood the country. The Germans came in with
rubber boats. Mechanized units and other forces came so
fast that Dutch plans to dynamite bridges and block roads
could not be implemented. The central heart of Rotterdam
was reduced to a rubble heap after a short aerial bombard-
ment. Within three days the Dutch government fled the
country, and within five days Holland surrendered.

With the fall of Holland, the pressure on Belgium became
overwhelming, in spite of the fact that the French and British had rushed large forces, including a large part of their
armor, to support the Belgians. The German armored col-

umns breaking through near Sedan kept going to the Channel, cutting off Allied forces in Belgium while planes, smashing communications, drove refugees down the roads, and fifth columnists caused confusions among the defending forces. Belgian fortresses such as Eban Emaul, previously deemed impregnable, were taken, and rumors were being spread about some Nazi "secret weapons." In France itself the enthusiasm and unity of World War I were lacking. The Communists and others had sown dissension among the French, and French resistance, though spirited in some areas, was not as strong as it could have been. Within less than three weeks, Belgium surrendered; the Allied forces which had gone up to save her found themselves split as a result of this Belgian action and were forced back toward the Channel over a period of six days. At Dunkirk some 330,000 British and French troops were miraculously evacuated by an armada of all types of vessels which had been scrounged up by the British. However, the latter had had to abandon all their artillery and heavy equipment and could be of no use in the continuing battle for France. With these Allied forces out of the way, the German pressure on the remaining French forces was too great. The French surrendered Paris rather than have it subjected to aerial destruction and moved the capital to Tours. The French cabinet was split on whether to continue resistance from the colonies if necessary, or to surrender. In France, the will to resist at all cost was lacking.

Meanwhile, with the Low Countries already occupied by the Germans and France reeling, Mussolini decided this was the time to act. He felt that since the war was already decided, and if Italy were to get any war booty, she must enter the conflict now. On June 10, therefore, Mussolini announced to the cheering fickle crowds that Italy was going to war against the "plutocratic reactionary democracies." In the words of the Italian Marshal Badoglio, he "wanted to show that Italians could jump from planes," and be heroes. And in the words of President Roosevelt, "the hand

that held the dagger has struck it into the back of his neighbor." But the Italian forces, though large, did not have much
influence on the actual fighting.

The Italian invasion was halted by the French; however
the German advance continued. Premier Reynaud was
forced from office and replaced by the aged Marshal Henri
Pétain, the victor of Verdun. Pétain's request for an armistice, a request which Hitler waited three days before receiving, led to the acceptance of German terms on June 22,
1940, and the armistice was signed in the same railroad
coach in the forest of Compiegne where the Germans had
been forced to surrender in 1918. By these terms the Pétain
government, consisting of many Rightists, was to rule in
southern France, while the Germans were to occupy more
than half of the country including the entire Atlantic coast.
The French forces in metropolitan France itself were to be
demobilized and all French military equipment there turned
over to the Germans. France, which only some six weeks
before was thought by many to have the finest army in
Europe, lay prostrate.

Save for the two neutrals, Switzerland and Sweden, surrounded by Axis territory, all of continental central and
northern Europe to the Russian border was now in Nazi
hands. Of the three southern peninsulas of Europe, the Nazis
appeared to have two, the Iberian and Italian, on their side,
and the Balkan lay outside the main area. The vast industrial complexes of Belgium and northern France could
henceforth be integrated into German industry. The very
speed of the conquests had kept total German casualties to
a ridiculously low figure. Some German troops were even
released to help in the harvests. The Germans were on top
of the world. They thought they had won the war. Even
many of those German officers who had doubted Hitler and
had inwardly thought him an adventurer now supported
him. Again he offered peace. He had no quarrel with the
British. Why were they fighting? For what were they waiting? The Americans? "The Americans," said Hitler, "could

not fly over; the Americans could not swim over; the Americans could not come over." The English had better come to terms. On July 19, 1940, he said:

In this hour I feel it to be my duty before my own conscience to appeal once more to reason and common sense in Great Britain as much as elsewhere. I consider myself in a position to make this appeal since I am not the vanquished seeking favors but the victor speaking in the name of reason. I can see no reason why this war must go on. I am grieved to think of the sacrifices which it will claim. I should like to avert them also for my own people. I know that millions of German men, young and old, are burning with desire at last to settle accounts with the enemy who for the second time had declared war upon us for no reason whatever. But I also know that at home there are many women and mothers. . . . (Max Domaros, *Hitler Reden* [Wuerzburg, 1963], 2:1558)

It is not to be wondered that most Germans genuinely believed in Hitler's sincerity in trying to obtain peace. But the English felt that they could not abandon the struggle and live in a Europe or a world dominated by Hitler. Churchill, in summoning the English to resist, sounded an entirely different note from that which had prevailed in France. He vowed that England would fight alone, that the English would fight on the beaches, in the cities, that they would never surrender.

There were many who thought the British position untenable, that the Germans, with air supremacy and heavy guns mounted on the Channel coast, could drive the British naval forces out of the narrow twenty-mile water zone between Calais and England and then proceed to land in England and overrun her. Moreover, in the Middle East, the Italians had launched an invasion of Egypt from Libya. There were some, including the influential American senator Key Pittman, who even advocated that the British should evacuate everything of importance from the homeland and bring the navy to Canada where, in conjunction with the American fleet, a further Nazi advance could be stopped.

However, the British position was not as bad as it appeared at first glance. War production had been rising, and Canada, Australia, and the other dominions were pouring in aid. The Channel was still a formidable barrier and the British still had unquestioned control of the sea. As long as the Royal Air Force was able to fly and as long as the Germans did not have complete control of the skies over England and the Channel, a cross-channel invasion would be an extremely hazardous undertaking. The next phase of the war, therefore, was the extended air battle over England in which Hermann Goering's *Luftwaffe*, or air force, attempted to destroy the Royal Air Force. For several months, the German bombers and fighters ranged across the Channel, inflicting very heavy damage and severe destruction. However, the German losses were high, and the RAF was not losing control of the skies. British antiaircraft defenses were constantly being improved. German pilots shot down over England were lost to the German war effort, whereas many of the British airmen who were downed were able to fight again. Thus, in this so-called Battle of Britain, the Germans ran into a determined foe in the RAF, a foe with planes of high quality, probably even better than those of the Germans. In just one week, the Nazis lost almost five hundred planes. Aid from America was beginning to flow into England too. Hitler stood at a crossroad. It was possible to try a cross-channel invasion without having uncontested air superiority. However, before such enormous risks Hitler hesitated. What might happen if he should get bogged down in an English campaign and if the Russians would hold up supplies or, even worse, attack? He himself had invoked the law of the jungle, and the Soviets in their attack on Finland had shown themselves bound by no moral scruples. Perhaps he could get the Russians to join him against the British if enough prospective booty were held out to them in the Near and Middle East. For the purpose of obtaining further Russian cooperation, Molotov was invited to Berlin in November 1940. Few outside observers, and probably not even the Soviets themselves, realized just how momentous these talks were destined to be. The talks were influenced by a number of moves the Soviets had recently made; for while Germany had been occupied in the West, Russia, alarmed at the speed of the Nazi advance, moved rapidly to add to her own territories and to strengthen her position. The Soviet Union, already in possession of key bases in the Baltic lands and responding to the "requests of the Baltic people for incorporation into the USSR," had graciously accepted them in June 1940, and Red forces occupied those countries completely. This was followed by a Soviet ultimatum to Rumania for the cession of Bessarabia and part of Bukovina to the Soviet Union. There was no one from whom the Rumanians could hope to obtain support, and they were forced to grant the Russian demands. The loss of Bessarabia was a grievous blow, but what would happen if further demands were made? Rumania had already lost almost four million of her seventeen million people to Russia; now Hungary, which was drawing more and more into the Axis orbit, was demanding the return of Transylvania. The Balkan Entente had proved a myth. The League of Nations was dead. France was prostrate; Britain seemed on the ropes; the United States was a world away. To whom could Rumania turn? On September 6, 1940, General Antonescu, the leader of the newly-established authoritarian regime in Rumania, announced that Rumania had freely entered the sphere of the Axis powers, and in October German troops entered Rumania. The Soviets were uneasy; Hungary and Bulgaria, both of which had been awarded Rumanian territory as a result of the Vienna Award of August 30, 1940, were also in the Axis camp. Now Rumania. There were obvious differences between Germany and the USSR over spheres of influence in the Balkans.

The Russian-German Split

It was again this background, therefore, that Molotov arrived in Berlin for talks in November 1940. He was especially interested in Rumania, Bulgaria, and Finland, all countries in which German influence was becoming very marked and in which the Soviets wanted the dominant voice. Regardless of how the Germans attempted to explain the presence of German troops in Rumania, the Russians felt uneasy. The Germans tried to press Molotov for an agreement; von Ribbentrop, the German Foreign Minister, insisting that for all practical purposes, the British were already defeated. The attitude of Molotov and the Russian insistence on a predominant role in the Balkans and Finland infuriated Hitler. The talks thus ended in failure, and orders were given in Germany to continue drawing up plans to attack Russia, an operation known under the code name of *Barbarossa*. One important factor which hastened Hitler's decision was the knowledge that the United States was more and more abandoning its position of neutrality and aiding the British. In 1935 the United States Congress had adopted a resolution by which it abandoned its previous concepts of neutral rights which had brought the United States into the war in 1812 and 1917. This resolution was supplemented by a neutrality act in 1937 which was intended, in the event of a foreign war, to prevent Americans from traveling on foreign ships or for United States ships to carry arms. The United States by the fall of 1940 had moved a long way from this position in spite of the neutrality act which was still in force. In September of 1940, in return for bases in Newfoundland and the West Indies, the United States transferred to the British over fifty overaged destroyers, an enormous asset in the antisubmarine war. Meanwhile, the United States itself was vastly speeding up its defense preparedness program. Later that month, for the first time in its history, the United States approved a peacetime military conscription law. The United States had 130 million people and the largest industrial plant in the world; it also had a fleet which vied with that of the British for the number one spot in the world, and it had enormous natural resources. If the United States were to become, in the words of Roosevelt, the "arsenal of democracy," time would not fight for the Axis. These were all considerations which Hitler had to ponder as he decided to attack Russia, an undertaking planned for the spring of 1941.

The attack on Russia did not come in the spring, for Mussolini, disappointed with the meager gains Italy had so far attained and seeking military glory, ordered an attack on Greece in October 1940. To the consternation of the Italians, the Greeks not only resisted stoutly, but soon were pursuing the retreating Italians into Albania itself. While the Italian expedition against the Greeks had come to grief, their campaign against the British in Egypt was faring even worse. Here the British had hurled the Italians back and were pursuing them into Libya, to which Hitler had dispatched the Afrika Korps under General Rommel. The Italian invasion of Greece opened up a possibility for the British to land troops and planes there. This represented a potential danger to any German force operating in Russia. Hitler then decided to invade Greece and secure his southern flank, even if it meant a delay in the beginning of the Russian campaign. German troops in large numbers began to enter Rumania, and both Yugoslavia and Bulgaria were induced to adhere to the tripartite pact, the former on March 25, 1941, the latter on March 1, 1941. The Russians were clearly very anxious and uneasy about German intentions in the Balkans, and although they went to great lengths to keep their part of the bargain with Hitler, the Soviets were preparing feverishly for a forthcoming war and doing their best to counter German influence in the Balkans. Thus, when a military coup in Yugoslavia unexpectedly replaced the pro-Axis government with one sympathetic to the Allies, the Soviets immediately signed a treaty of friendship with this new regime. The signs were already clear that Soviet-German friendship was not too firm. However, if the Soviets hoped they could stop Hitler's hand by such an act they were wrong. Nazi troops were already in Bulgaria and Rumania, and Hungary too had been brought into the Axis camp. On April 6 the Nazis struck with overwhelming strength against both Yugoslavia and Greece. Within twelve days, the Yugoslavs surrendered unconditionally. Yugoslavia was partitioned for daring to defy the Nazis, and an independent Croatian state was set up under a government sympathetic to the Nazis; the Hungarians moved in and occupied territories in the north which they had lost at Trianon, while Italy annexed an area of Slovenia, with its capital at Ljubljana (Laibach) and a good share of the Dalmatian coast. Meanwhile, the Greeks and a British expeditionary force which had been rushed from North Africa to aid them, were being overwhelmed by the Germans. By April 27, after three weeks of war, the Nazis were in Athens, and those British and Greek forces which succeeded in evacuating were finding sanctuary on Crete some sixty miles to the south. There they were surprised by the first successful airborne invasion in history, and the Germans took over the island after fierce fighting. The German victory at Crete was quite dramatic and certainly did improve the Axis position in the Mediterranean; however, it was a Pyrrhic victory and even further delayed the timetable for the German invasion of Russia.

Meanwhile, on March 11, 1941, the American Congress had passed the Lend-Lease Act by which tremendous amounts of American aid soon were on their way to the British. Shortly thereafter, by agreement with the Danish representatives in Washington, the United States began to occupy Greenland, and American vessels began to patrol the North Atlantic. While German troops were beginning to be transferred from the Balkans to the southern Russian frontier, a task which took a number of weeks since sufficient motor and train transportation was lacking, and since there was a necessity of keeping the Russians off guard, the United States froze the assets of citizens of the Axis powers and ordered the Axis consulates in the United States closed.

On June 22, 1941, operation *Barbarossa* began with German planes ranging far and wide behind the Russian front blasting air bases. Rumania was an eager ally of the Germans, hoping to reacquire Bessarabia and lands on the other side of the Dniestr. After several days the Finns also joined in, hoping to reacquire the lands they had lost in the winter war. Before long, the Hungarians too were brought in, partially by promises of territorial aggrandizement and partially by a staged incident in which Soviet aircraft allegedly bombed Hungarian territory. But the Germans had neglected several extremely important steps. In their secrecy, they had not informed the Japanese, and the latter had special intentions of their own. A short time earlier, the Japanese ambassador, on his return from Berlin, had visited Moscow, and there had signed a nonaggression treaty with a worried Stalin. Japan thus felt free to pursue her aims in the South Pacific while the Russians felt that their eastern frontier was much safer in the event of involvement with Germany. Also, the extra six weeks that the Balkan campaign had set back the German timetable on the invasion of Russia meant that bad weather would start scarcely four months after the invasion began, and that the Russian winter itself might begin only five months thereafter. The span of time necessary for a successful operation was thus strictly limited. However, Hitler's confidence in his own decisions had now reached a tremendous high. He had been right too frequently. Certainly, they were invading a vast territory with a population several times that of Germany. But look at what German arms had achieved! Russia was rotten to the core. Some of the generals were aghast. To unleash a two-front war while the British in the west, supplied now by their American allies, were still strong and getting stronger, was a tremendous gamble. However, they had been wrong before with their words of caution. "All I ask of you," said Hitler to a group of commanders, "is a strong push and the whole rotten house will cave in by itself."

The world awoke on June 22 to the shocked realization that Germany and the USSR were at war. Certainly, there had been warning signs. Churchill had sent warnings to

Stalin. Several columnists had hinted there was trouble.
However, to the diplomatic corps and to the news media
throughout the world this move was totally unexpected. This
time, however, German strength was overestimated, in contrast to the past when it had been underestimated. Certainly, Russia was large, but distances scarcely mattered.
Certainly, Russia had many men. But the spirit was low
and numbers meant nothing before the Nazi juggernaut.
There were many who even thought the Russians would be
defeated within two months. And indeed, the opening weeks
of war gave every indication of this. The Russians were
smashed back and suffered defeats and casualties such as
no major army had ever endured. For the Russian army
had suffered grievously as a result of Stalin's purges. No
major European army in history had ever had a purge of
its top leadership on the scale of that which had taken place
in the Red Army in the three years prior to the war. Until
recently, it was customary to think of the Soviet defeats in
the opening stages of this war as attributable primarily to
the surprise of the German offensive and to the advantage
of German mechanized equipment. Actually, the Russians
had a great numerical superiority in mechanized equipment; and although the hour and place of the German attack were a surprise, and although many Russian frontier
units were caught completely off guard, many persons, including a number of Soviet writers like General Gorbatov,
now attribute the cause for the defeats to the Soviet losses
of trained officers caused by the prewar purges.

The Germans aimed three major blows at the Russians:
one at Moscow some six hundred miles within Russia; another at Leningrad some five hundred miles inside the
country; and the third at the Ukraine, toward Kiev and beyond. From the start, Russian resistance was spotty, with
extremely stubborn resistance by some units, and lack of
will to fight by others. Within two days, Vilna had fallen;
within eight days, Lvov; within two weeks, Riga. Six hundred and fifty thousand Russian prisoners were taken in the

encirclement at Bialystok, about the same number in the battle of Vyaszma, and again as many in the battle for Kiev, which the Germans took on September 19. In many places in the Ukraine and in White Russia, the Germans were even greeted by the populace as liberators; for, as indicated previously, the population in these areas had suffered severely under the Stalinization of the preceding years. There were many Russians who did not care to fight for Stalin and the type of communism they had experienced.

However, Hitler was revealing that he had no intention of confining this operation to a battle to bring down communism, although in turning on Russia he had called for a crusade against bolshevism. This was being turned into a battle against the Slavs, for living room in the east for the Germans, for huge estates to reward the Nazi paladins. The Nazis, drunk with previous success, felt no necessity to honor the normal rules of warfare. Prisoners of war by the hundreds of thousands were driven to the rear with whips and herded in the fields like cattle. Food was often not made available to the prisoners, thousands of whom died of malnutrition and starvation. Even in the occupied territories, little provision was made for the population. Special units of troops belonging to the secret police followed the armies into the occupied area and shot Jews, Gypsies, and others deemed undesirable by the Nazi authorities. Warning voices were raised among some of the old-line commanders and political advisers. Russia was a huge country; the war was not over. The transferral of German planes to the eastern front had opened up German targets for the powerful RAF which was bombing Germany with increasing fury. For the Germans to gain a victory over the USSR, it would be wise to try to win over the Ukrainians and some of the other "subject" nationalities of the Soviet Union and to recruit disaffected Russians to fight against Stalin. Hitler, however, had been right too often, and his confidence knew no limits. "All I ask of you," he told a group of leaders, "is that the troops be National

Socialistically indoctrinated. Anybody can do the little bit of operation leadership." This was to be a German victory! Inferior Slavs were not to be allowed to share in it, and there was no better place to establish the "new order" than here. The Russian forces would be smashed far worse than the French.

However, Russia was much larger than France. Some large Russian units were encircled and destroyed, but others were able to retreat to avoid encirclement. They could fall back 100, 200, 400, 500 miles, and still Moscow and many important centers would remain in Russian hands. This was something that no previous opponent of the Nazis had been able to do. Meanwhile, some prisoners who had surrendered voluntarily or otherwise to the Nazis, escaped. Word began to drift back to other Soviet areas of what a Nazi victory was like. Persons who formerly had no desire to fight for Stalin and the Communist regime began to take another view. And Stalin himself in appealing to the Russian people to resist seemed to promise a new era. He called on the Russian troops to be inspired by the deeds and examples not of Lenin, not of Marx, but of Suvorov, Kutuzov, Dmitri Donskoy, and old Tsarist and Russian national heroes. He called for the people to fight for Russia and not for communism. To the Church and religious leaders, he held out a hope for a change and relaxed all pressure against the Church. Meanwhile, the advancing Germans were encountering many problems in the terrain and in a stiffening resistance. In the center and north, they had had to pause to regroup. To the south, the huge dust clouds engulfed the motors and many vehicles had to be repaired. The Germans were moving farther from their bases, the Russians closer to theirs. Hitler allowed himself to be captivated by the figures of two and a half million prisoners taken and some fourteen thousand airplanes destroyed. But the Russian forces were still actively in the field. Time was running short for the Germans. Some German commanders wanted to put everything into a drive toward Moscow, the Russian rail, waterway, and communication center, as well as capital, hoping thereby to smash the defending army and by capturing Moscow to deal a tremendous psychological blow to the Soviets as well. Here Hitler hesitated, reluctant to commit most of his forces to one major push. By the time the central front received the armor for its push, the fall weather had turned the roads and fields to mud, and forward advance was very difficult. Everywhere there were clear signs that Russian resistance was stiffening. Hitler had announced to the German people that the power of the Russian bear had been smashed, never again to rise; but in reality, the war was being decided against Germany in those few months. The six-week delay in the start of the campaign had proved costlier to the Germans than had been realized.

In November the cold had hardened the ground before Moscow. At this time more armor was made available to the German forces on the central front, and orders were given to take Moscow at any price. The Germans moved against tough resistance up to the suburbs of Moscow. But then, in the early December days, the Russian winter began —earlier and more severe than expected. Under these winter conditions, field radios and phones ceased to function; motors had to be warmed up for two hours before they would function; spirits sagged. The commanders, with communication systems not functioning, even lost contact with their units and had no clear conceptions of the front situation. In front of Moscow, the German war ended and the Russian war began. By December 6, the German attack was over. The myth of German invincibility was over.

New Russian troops, fresh from Siberia, appeared before Moscow, and the Russians began their first real counteroffensive of the war. On December 7, the Japanese struck. They struck not against the weakened Russian forces in Siberia but at the United States, the Dutch Indies, Malay, and all through the area of the South China seas. At this point, Hitler, furious with the United States because of the giant American aid which was being sent to Britain and Russia, and happy to have another ally, declared war on the United States.

The Entry of the United States and the Allied Victory

Just what American strategy would have been had it not been for this rash declaration of Hitler's is difficult to tell. The United States had been adopting a more and more hostile attitude toward the Nazis throughout 1941; by December of that year, the Americans were even convoying military supplies to England. However, there was strong opposition in the United States to taking the last step and actually going to war. Now that Japan had attacked the United States, the most likely American strategy would have been to devote the main effort toward fighting the Japanese. However, with the German declaration of war on the United States, the United States decided upon the policy of pursuing a holding action in the Far East against the industrially less-developed Japanese, while concentrating the main military efforts against Germany. The great weight of the United States was about to be thrown into the balance against Germany, and though 1942 was to see some great Axis drives which came close to success, the entry of the United States, possessing the industrial capacity of virtually the rest of the world combined, presaged the total defeat of the Axis powers.

The German forces in December 1941 had not been prepared either psychologically or logistically for a winter campaign in Russia. As the temperatures plunged to forty below zero, there was some panic in German headquarters, and many military leaders wanted a general retreat from Russia. Hitler, however, insisted that the front be held regardless of cost, and his will prevailed. Though German losses through both weather and military action were rather severe, the German army came through the first winter ready to renew the offensive when the weather permitted. In North Africa, the Afrika Korps had been reinforced, and the summer of 1942 was to see a great German offensive toward Egypt as well as a German offensive in Russia.

However, this time the German offensive in Russia was far more limited and modest in scope. No longer could the Germans make an effort to knock out the whole country in one campaign. This time the efforts were directed toward seizing the oil fields of the Caucasus and reaching the Volga, thus cutting important Russian river traffic. With the oil of the Caucasus and the grain, minerals, and industry of the Ukraine and the Donets Basin in their hands, the Germans would then be in a good position to withstand a long war, while the Russians would be so weakened that they would eventually collapse. At the same time, the siege of Leningrad was to be continued in the north. This siege, the greatest in history, had resulted in great privation and suffering, and perhaps as many as one million persons died of starvation and malnutrition before the siege was finally raised. Again in 1942, the Germans scored smashing initial successes, though not as great as in 1941; they drove all the way to the Volga at Stalingrad, the former Tsaritsyn, one thousand miles within Russia. Here their advance ground virtually to a stop and they were only able to advance slowly, fighting street by street within the city. Meanwhile, another Russian winter was approaching. The German Sixth Army in Stalingrad was in an exposed position. Warnings by commanders that the troops must be pulled back before the onset of winter fell on deaf ears. Hitler by now was convinced that he knew better than the generals. He had shown it repeatedly. Stalingrad was ordered held at all costs. No ground was to be surrendered. Soon the Russians in a giant counteroffensive encircled the city; however, no breakout attempt was ordered. As the winter proceeded, it proved impossible for the Germans to supply their forces within the city by air, and gradually the Russians reduced the German pocket. By the end of January 1943, some ninety thousand men, the hungry, battered

ICELAND

ATLANTIC OCEAN

NORWAY

SWEDEN

FINLAND

UNITED

KINGDOM

IRELAND

NORTH SEA

DENMARK

BALTIC SEA

SOVIET UNION

NETHERLANDS

BELGIUM

GERMANY

POLAND

LUXEMBOURG

SLOVAKIA

FRANCE

SWITZ.

AUSTRIA

HUNGARY

CROATIA

RUMANIA

PORTUGAL

SPAIN

CORSICA

I T A L Y

SERBIA

BULGARIA

BLACK SEA

SARDINIA

ALBANIA

TURKEY

MEDITERRANEAN SEA

SICILY

GREECE

CRETE

CYPRUS

▒ HITLER'S NAZI EMPIRE
╱╱╱ TERRITORY UNDER DIRECT AXIS
CONTROL OR ALLIED WITH AXIS

0   200   400   MILES

C.C. Weiss
S.I.U. Cartographic Laboratory

EUROPE AT THE HEIGHT OF
HITLER'S POWER, 1942

remnants of the three-hundred-thousand-man German Sixth Army at Stalingrad surrendered. At the same time, the Germans were losing an army of equal size in North Africa where an Anglo-American force, starting its offensive in November 1942, had succeeded in taking all of French North Africa, while Marshal Montgomery's forces drove the Afrika Korps through Libya. The Afrika Korps, trapped in Tunisia without sea support, was forced to surrender in May 1943. The loss of over a half million of their best troops with all their equipment was a loss the Germans could scarcely afford. Barring some unforeseen circumstances or new miracle weapons, Germany was doomed to defeat.

Hitler, however, had other hopes. Back in the time of Frederick the Great, a coalition of three large powers had virtually brought Prussia to her knees; however, a change of rulers in Russia led to that nation's withdrawal from the conflict, allowing Prussia to recover. The alliance of the West with a Bolshevist Russia, the advocate of world revolution, was an unnatural one. If he could only hold out long enough, the Allies would soon be bickering among each other, and Germany could still win. Or, even if the alliance held, what about the will to carry on the fight? Of great significance for all, unfortunately, was a conversation Hitler had had several years before the war with David Lloyd-George, the British World War I Prime Minister. In these talks, Lloyd-George had made the fateful statement that Germany had capitulated at five minutes to twelve. These talks reinforced Hitler's conviction that had the Germans only continued the war, war-weariness would have forced the Allied countries to withdraw from the conflict. Hitler was determined that this time Germans would keep fighting to midnight. The result was a very dark midnight indeed, not only for the German people, but more especially for those millions of unfortunate human beings who were now to experience the "new order" in all its fury.

The Soviets had always been suspicious of the West. To

avoid the appearance of contemplating any "deals" behind
the Russians' back, and to press home on the German people
the fact that this time the Germans were completely defeated, Churchill and Roosevelt, meeting at Casablanca in
1942, announced that the war would be waged until there
would be "unconditional surrender" on the part of the Axis.
This was very good terminology; however, it is generally
conceded that it increased the German will to resist even
as the war took a greater turn for the worse for them. For
after one more attempt to take the offensive in Russia in
1943, in the giant Kursk tank battle on the central Russian
front, the Nazi forces were forced from one retreat to another. At the same time, the rapidly expanding Allied
bomber fleets were bringing death and destruction to scores
of German cities.

By the summer of 1943 Allied forces had invaded Sicily,
and Mussolini had been deposed by the Fascist Grand Council, which then secretly sought ways to take Italy out of the
war. The new Italian government under Marshal Badoglio
concluded a surrender agreement with the Allies, the formal
announcement of which was to be delayed until the Allied
landing on the Italian mainland. The Badoglio government
was hoping it could concentrate enough Italian troops
around key Italian cities like Rome to hold them against the
Germans until the Allies arrived, and then join the Allies
as cobelligerants. This proved to be wishful thinking. The
Germans quickly disarmed the Italian troops, seized Rome
and virtually all the important centers in Italy, and the
Allies were forced to wage a long, arduous campaign for
the Italian peninsula. Mussolini himself was snatched by
the Germans, in a daring raid, from the mountain retreat
where he had been interned. He was then brought to northern Italy where he formed another government which ruled
northern Italy for the Germans until virtually the end of the
war.

As the Nazi commitment in Russia grew, and as the Allied air supremacy became greater and greater, resistance

to the Nazi occupiers increased in a number of the occupied countries. In France, in Yugoslavia, and in Greece, the resistance forces were quite large and caused the Germans many problems. In most of the underground movements, the Communists soon began to play a leading and sometimes dominant role due to their better organization, discipline, and experience in underground work. Gradually, they began to try to convert these movements for national liberation into new Communist-controlled governments. In the Soviet Union itself, what had originally been minor partisan activity behind the German lines began to increase as the tide of battle turned against the Germans. By the end of 1943, partisan activity was a major problem for the Germans. By this time too, the Western Allies, anxious to avoid a split in the alliance, were meeting with the Russians to lay plans for the postwar make-up of Europe. Their conclusions and agreements will be discussed later.

On the military front, the Allies proceeded from victory to victory. The U-boat menace, so serious in 1942, had been brought under control by 1943, and the subsequent development of new sonar equipment vastly reduced that danger. Allied raids by a thousand and more bombers were turning major German industrial centers into rubble, although Germany, by major efforts, actually was able to increase her production somewhat.

On June 6, 1944, the Western Allies began an invasion of Normandy, an invasion which within less than three months had pretty much cleared France of the Nazis. The successful Allied invasion convinced even many of the die-hard German generals that a prolongation of the war would result in senseless slaughter and in further ruin for Germany. On July 20, 1944, a German officer conspiracy to murder Hitler and take over the German government came close to success. With the failure of this plot, the Nazis launched a ruthless crackdown on all participants and suspects. A number of very prominent military and political leaders, including the former army chief of staff Ludwig

Beck and Erwin Rommel, former commander of the Afrika Korps, were either executed or committed suicide. The war was thus destined to go on to the bitter end, to five minutes past twelve. Now that the Germans were on the run, Germany's former allies, one by one, as in World War I, tried to make a separate peace; first had come Italy, then Rumania, Bulgaria, Finland, and Hungary. In Hungary, a countercoup conducted by the local Nazi party in conjunction with Nazi paratroopers, resulted in that country's remaining in the war until completely overrun by the Red Army. Bulgaria and Finland were forced by the terms of peace to become cobelligerants against Germany. The German reaction to the Rumanian withdrawal, the bombing of Bucharest, led to that country's joining the war against Germany. The defection of Rumania opened up the entire Balkan Peninsula to the Russians, and the Germans were soon hastening to evacuate Yugoslavia and Greece. In Paris, at the approach of the Allied forces in August 1944, the local resistance forces rose up against the Germans. The Allies had not desired to occupy the city that quickly, but now felt compelled to divert troops to rescue the French resistance fighters. In Warsaw, upon the arrival of the Soviet forces in the eastern suburbs located on the other side of the Vistuala River, the Warsaw underground rose. For reasons indicating a desire on the part of the Soviets to see the non-Communist, strongly nationalist Polish underground crushed, the Soviets halted their advance. They also refused to make their bases and airfields available for Allied planes wishing to drop supplies to the beleaguered Poles in the capital. (It should be borne in mind that Allied planes had been refueling on Russian bases after carrying out bombing raids against targets in eastern Germany.) Thus, for over two months, while the Poles were subjected to murderous Nazi pressure, the Russians remained relatively inactive on the Warsaw front. In December 1944, with the fronts temporarily stabilized, the Nazis in one last, desperate gamble to reverse the tide, began a major push in the Ardennes against the Western Allies, using troops pulled even from the Russian front. However, German strength was no longer what it had been. There were even serious shortages of fuel, and the weather lifted, permitting Allied planes to blast German supply columns. This Ardennes offensive, the so-called Battle of the Bulge, was Germany's last gasp. By March 1945 Allied units were deep in Germany, and the Russians were poised for the last drive on Berlin. By the beginning of May Hitler was dead, having committed suicide as the Russians were storming their way through his capital; American units had gone all the way to Saxony and taken Leipzig, while other American forces were entering Czechoslovakia. The Nazis capitulated unconditionally to the Allies on May 8, 1945, and the war in Europe was over.

Although the Second World War had been concluded in Europe, the Americans and the British were still at war with Japan, a war which was to last another three months. However, even before the conclusion of World War II, a third world conflict had begun, a conflict between the Communist and non-Communist world. In Europe, with the possible exception of Czechoslovakia, the borders and shape of that conflict had been drawn by the end of World War II, though there were many who did not realize it. For in no European area through which Soviet troops had passed, with the eventual exception of part of Austria, did the Soviets withdraw without first establishing a Communist government subservient to Stalin. Before discussing the new Europe which was already taking form, it would be appropriate to discuss briefly the order which had been taking place in Europe during the last three or four years of the war.

Shortly after the beginning of the invasion of Russia, the Nazis began introducing whole series of operations which, though darkly foreshadowed in some of the speeches and writings of Nazi extremists, had been thought for the most part to be mere theory, scarcely the type of thing that

▬▬▬▬▬ GERMAN EMPIRE, 1914.

1. SCHLESWIG CEDED TO DENMARK, 1919.
2. 'POLISH CORRIDOR' CEDED TO POLAND, 1919.
3. PORTION OF UPPER SILESIA CEDED TO POLAND, 1919.
4. PORTION OF UPPER SILESIA CEDED TO CZECHOSLOVAKIA, 1919.
5. ALSACE–LORRAINE CEDED TO FRANCE, 1919.
6. EUPEN AND MALMÉDY CEDED TO BELGIUM, 1919.
7. MEMEL CEDED TO THE U.S.S.R., 1945.
8. NORTHERN PORTION OF EAST PRUSSIA SEIZED BY THE U.S.S.R., 1945.
9. SOUTHERN PORTION OF EAST PRUSSIA CEDED TO POLAND, 1945.
10. CEDED TO POLAND, 1945.

GERMAN TERRITORIAL LOSSES
SINCE 1914

would be carried out. The Nazis had long spoken superrace, the Aryan race, and of the necessity of w out undesirables. The civilized world had watched aghast at the mistreatment of Jews in Germany and in the territories annexed by Germany prior to the war. Hitler had clearly indicated that the Slavs were an inferior race, and in the eastern territories conquered by Germany they were to be in a subservient position. There had been accounts of brutal treatment in German concentration camps before the war; however, the reality of what had transpired in only a few short years surpassed all but the most fantastic surmises as to how these camps would develop. For starting about 1942, the German concentration camps were transformed into death centers for millions of Jews and Gypsies, and numerous other persons who either did not meet with Nazi approval or had run afoul of the Nazis. The new territories were to be governed and settled by the superrace. However, this superrace was not simply to be the German race. The seed of this race was to be an elite German. For this purpose, special SS units were created. Considering how thoroughly these makeshift plans were carried out in the few years the Nazis had at their disposal, there is a considerable possibility that a Nazi victory would have resulted in a good part of the population of the world being controlled and a good part of Europe eventually populated by the offsprings of these persons.

In World War I, many atrocity stories had been told and exaggerated about the Germans. By the time of World War II, however, people were more sophisticated. When Allied troops broke into Germany and began discovering the concentration camps, the Associated Press refused to print the first dispatches, believing that this was sheer exaggeration. However, the Nazi reality in World War II had surpassed the horror propaganda. In the spring of 1945 the nightmare of war was over; an exhausted, hungry, and partially devastated Europe faced an uncertain future.

5

The New Europe to the Origin of the Cold War

BRITAIN and France, which had both entered the war voluntarily to stop Nazi Germany, annexed no territory. Britain neither claimed nor received any indemnities from any of the belligerents for damages received as a result of the war. The United Kingdom, in addition to having suffered heavy manpower and property losses, was saddled with enormous debts incurred during the six years of fighting. She had been forced to liquidate still further her valuable dollar-producing interests abroad and emerged from the war in a much weaker condition than was generally realized at the time. Nevertheless, her basic institutions were intact and the popular belief in democracy had been reinforced. Furthermore, the Labour government, voted into power shortly after the conclusion of the European war, began introducing a wide program of social legislation, including socialized medicine, which was intended to give "cradle to grave" security to the English people. However, the expense of these programs coupled with the continuing drain on the treasury as a result of foreign commitments caused a financial crisis for the English government which, with ups and downs, has continued to the present. For if the First World War had dried up many markets, World War II had shattered still more. The Continent was prostrate and virtually all of Eastern Europe, tributary to a hostile Soviet Union, was largely off limits to Western trade. Even areas like Holland and Norway which had escaped the ravages of the First World War had been hard hit in the second.

During the war, virtually every nation defeated by the Axis had had a government in exile headed by its prewar leaders. These, rather than the Axis-imposed puppet governments, had been recognized by the Allies and most neutral countries as the legitimate governments of their respective countries. Each of these exile governments had armed forces of various sizes fighting along with the Allies during the war. Thus, when King Haakon's government returned to Norway, there was little difficulty in reestablishing the prewar system of government. The Quislings and their supporters, representative of only a small fraction of the Norwegian population, were by the war's end thoroughly discredited, and the Communists had always been few in Norway.

The situation in Holland, where the populace had had a long democratic tradition on which to look back, was similar. The returning Queen Wilhelmina was very popular, and she was readily reinstated in office. In Belgium, there was little difficulty in reestablishing democratic institutions; however, there was a strong opposition to the retention of King Leopold, whom many Belgians regarded as a traitor for having surrendered the army in 1940 instead of fighting on and continuing the battle from overseas the way other governments, as that of Norway, had done.

France was faced with a more difficult problem. As the war progressed, the resistance movement in France grew stronger and stronger. There was a rather sizable number of active collaborators with the Nazis, some of these simple opportunists but others actively favoring the Nazi-type state. In the unoccupied zone of France under the Vichy government of Marshal Pétain, the populace had been cautioned to remain neutral in action and speech. Pétain was determined to spare France as much misery as possible and was ready to collaborate to a great extent in order to prevent further suffering to the nation. Fearing that anti-Nazi and anti-German elements of the population might indulge in activities which would provoke a German response, Pétain had introduced restrictive measures of a type commonly associated with dictatorships. "Work, Family, Nation" replaced "Liberty, Equality, Fraternity" as the slogan of the Vichy regime, and the right to openly discuss or write about political affairs was especially prohibited. At first most Frenchmen, bewildered by the crushing defeat, had reluctantly accepted the new situation. However, some had not. General Charles de Gaulle had fled to Britain immediately after the Allied defeat in Flanders and there announced that France had lost a battle but not a war, and he had summoned the French to continue the struggle with the aid of powerful allies. Under his leadership, a government in exile, a "Free French" government, was set up. There were sizable French forces in England. Well over a hundred thousand Frenchmen had been rescued from Dunkirk along with the British, and these formed a base for the de Gaulle government. In addition, the French had considerable forces overseas and a powerful fleet. For a while there had been hope that these forces outside Nazi control would gravitate to the Allies and work with de Gaulle. However, the French forces in the colonies regarded the Vichy government as the legitimate government of France and remained neutral. The British, fearful that the Axis might try to seize these French ships in violation of the terms of the armistice, and knowing that absolute mastery of the seas was essential for their very survival, determined to prevent this French fleet from falling into Nazi hands. Thus, large British naval forces suddenly appeared off Oran and other French North African bases, demanding that the French ships either join them or follow them to a British naval harbor where they would be held for the duration of the war. The French refused the ultimatum, and the British thereupon put a good share of this French fleet out of commission. This action caused a great deal of anti-British hostility; however, most Frenchmen later grudgingly realized the necessity for such a measure.

The French underground, which in the meanwhile had been growing slowly, aided somewhat by agents slipped in from England, received a powerful boost when the Germans invaded the Soviet Union. The Communists, who had previously denounced the war as a capitalist war, and for whom the war had suddenly become a holy cause for the liberation of mankind, now carried on anti-Nazi activities. The Communists, by their zeal, organization, and ruthlessness, added greatly to the underground movement. Also, as Nazi air power in the west diminished because of the necessity of transferring air units to the Russian front, the growing British and American air forces could fly over France at will, dropping agents and even supplies. The tremendous step-up in Allied air raids on Germany itself in 1942 and 1943 became known in France, and the knowledge that victory was possible brought even more recruits into the resistance movements. The brutal methods used by the Gestapo to crush the underground aroused still more fanatical hatred, and throughout 1943–44 the resistance movements grew greatly.

In late November 1942, when the Allies along with free French forces of General de Gaulle invaded French North Africa all the way from Casablanca to Algiers, they had hoped that appeals from both General de Gaulle and the more orthodox French hero General Giraud would cause the French forces in North Africa, numbering more than a hundred thousand, to rally to the Allied cause. This was not the case, and at both Oran and Casablanca there was stiff fighting. The Allies finally came to an agreement with the Vichy official, Admiral Darlan, who by coincidence happened to be in Algiers at this time. He ordered the French forces in North Africa to cease firing and announced that he would collaborate with the Allies. The Germans, now thoroughly suspicious that the unoccupied section of France might go over to the Allies, moved in and occupied the rest of the country. They had hoped to seize the rest of the still formidable French fleet then at Toulon. The French naval officers and seamen, shaken by the turn of events, hostile to the Germans, but still not supporting General de Gaulle, scuttled the fleet to prevent it from falling into German hands. As long as the Vichy government had had overseas forces and a strong fleet at its disposal, it was more able to counter German pressures. Now, it had little leverage indeed, and became more and more collaborationist. Outside of France itself, General de Gaulle was finally recognized as the undisputed leader of the free French forces. Within the country itself, many of the growing underground forces were coming under Communist leadership. However, there were large numbers in the resistance who took their orders and instructions from London. Following the Allied invasions of Normandy, and particularly the invasion of southern France on August 15, 1944, the French underground flared up everywhere, blowing up rail lines, hindering German communications, attacking small units, and even seizing whole departments. On August 19, 1944, as mentioned previously, there was a large uprising of some fifty thousand members of the underground in the capital. A French division of the Allied forces under General LeClerc was dispatched to their rescue, and shortly thereafter, General de Gaulle arrived in Paris to establish the new French government.

There were strong groups of Communists in the French resistance who would have wanted to try to set up a Communist government at that time. All through liberated France itself, groups of resistance leaders and suddenly superpatriots, were pouncing on those people who had collaborated with the Nazis during the occupation, meting out vigilante justice. By taking advantage of these semi-hysterical "trials," the better-organized group in the underground, the Communists, could perhaps have eliminated those elements most opposed to their taking control, had it not been for other important factors. These were the presence of de Gaulle on the scene with regular forces, and the fact that there was still a war to be fought. Even after the Allied occupation of Paris, a group of die-hard French Nazis had made a desperate attempt to kill off the new leaders. Partially for these reasons, the French Communists agreed to go along with de Gaulle, and the foundations began to be established for the Fourth French Republic.

In a physical sense France emerged from World War II perhaps even more shattered than from World War I. There had been tremendous damage done to transport. The number of locomotives was down from eleven thousand to three thousand. Harbor installations, bridges, railroad tracks, and other facilities had been destroyed. Many fields had been fought over and ruined. To make matters worse, a bad drought in 1945 created a very serious food situation. A sizable part of French exports before the war had consisted of products for the luxury trade. There was little market for these items in the immediate postwar period. In the period between the wars, France had spent too much capital on armaments and rebuilding and not enough on improving her industrial plants. The machinery in French plants, already in need of modernization in 1939, had become even more rundown and outmoded during the six years of war, and there had been heavy damages to these industrial installations by bombings. Raw materials were urgently needed as well.

Though French property losses had been great, there had not been the manpower losses of World War I. However, this time France had suffered a tremendous moral and psychological shock. First, the smashing defeat had hurt French national pride tremendously. Second, the years of occupation had rent the country and had seemed to tug at the very fabric of society. One could scarcely trust one's neighbor. Suspicion had been everywhere. In the fury of vengeance now wreaked upon collaborators, many persons suffered; a large number of these would have been pardoned a few years later when more sober judgments prevailed. There were great problems in regard to patriotism and loyalty to the government, because the French had had rapid changes of government. Allegiance to a government and to a nation in a free society must not be a complicated affair. During the war it had seemed patriotic to cheat, to deal in the black market, to harm the government; for anything that harmed the government hindered the German war effort. Once started, these practices were difficult to halt. In addition, the Communists had increased their following because of their role in the resistance. With the cry of "collaborator" or "Fascist" they had been able to cow into silence numerous persons who would normally have opposed them. It was easy for the Communists to dogmatically and demagogically demand huge wage increases for the miners and industrial workers who had suffered privations during the war, increases which the impoverished state of the nation's finances could not support. By such demands and by their organizational ability, the Communists were able to gain control over many of these unions— unions which they were later to call on strike, ostensibly for economic reasons, but actually for political ones. It was difficult indeed for the newly installed government to appeal for more loyalty and self-sacrifice from the war-weary populace. Only a totalitarian regime could have demanded greater sacrifices.

To the south of France, Spain and Portugal had avoided participation in the war. During the war while the Axis was winning, Franco had shown some enthusiasm for entering the hostilities in order to get Gibraltar. However, he had not really been eager and had set his entry price in the way of supplies and needs so high—some say deliberately so in order to keep the Axis from pressing him to get involved— that Spain remained outside the conflict. However, many nations have played the game both ways and turned from one side to another as soon as they felt the time appropriate to get their share of the spoil. Even the Soviet Union hung on to its nonaggression pact with Japan until the moment was propitious to strike.

In the anti-Fascist sentiment which prevailed in Europe following the defeat of the Axis, Spain was somewhat the outcast nation of Europe. Many had thought that the defeat of Hitler and Mussolini would automatically mean the end of Franco. At Potsdam the Big Three made it clear that they were against the membership of the present Spanish government in the United Nations, and in March 1946 the representatives of Britain, France, and the United States declared that they hoped that the "leading patriotic and liberal-minded Spaniards may soon find means to bring about a peaceful withdrawal of Franco and the abolition of the Falange . . ." In December 1946 Spain was debarred from the United Nations "until a new and acceptable government is formed in Spain."

Thus, at the end of the war Spain found herself not only a political outcast but in worse condition than before it because so many things she needed to purchase were not available. The country had been devastated during the Spanish Civil War, and the world had been at war and unable to supply her during the period which she needed to recover. Her sizable gold reserves which might have been used for vital purchases had been carried off to the USSR during the civil war. The land on which some 60 percent of the people lived was desperately in need of fertilizers. Formerly, Spain had purchased nitrates from Germany, but the war had stopped this, and now the virtual boycott by the United States and other nations made the economic situation more difficult for Franco's impoverished country.

However, the frightful devastation of the civil war, still fresh in memory, plus the relentless crackdown on persons of anti-Franco sentiment, assured the stability of the regime. Franco was able to trade freely with certain Latin American nations, especially Peron's Argentina, which was enjoying a postwar boom due to the great demand for her meat and grain products.

It has often been alleged that the United States supports dictators and that it was American support of Franco which made it possible for him to ride out the postwar period. Nothing could be further from the truth; indeed, the United States adopted a hostile attitude toward Franco during the immediate postwar period and actually broke off diplomatic relations with Spain. These relations were not renewed until December 1950. Despite the anathema of the other major European nations, Spain slowly continued her recovery from the civil war. Despite her authoritarian government, she was no threat to her neighbors. Neither Portugal, nor France, nor Morocco feared any Spanish inroads or subversion, and any further continuation of the nonrecognition and boycott of Spain would simply have meant further hardships for the Spanish people. There was no doubt in 1949 that Franco and his supporters were in firm control in Spain, and it is from that period that the Spanish economy began to show significant and continued advances.

Thus, England, France, Spain, Portugal, and the Low Countries entered the postwar period with substantially the same general governmental structures that they had had in the prewar period. The same was true of Scandinavia.

Italy for some time, however, presented a confused picture. A poor country even before the war, Italy had suffered enormous physical damage as a result of the fighting on her soil. Allied troops had fought against stubborn resistance from Sicily through the tip of the toe all the way up the peninsula. Italian ports, shipyards, and installations had been severely bombed. Italy's overseas possessions into which she had poured so much money were lost. Her merchant marine was shattered. Although most of Italy's fighting had taken place against the Western Allies, the Russians were demanding reparations from Italy for the damages incurred as a result of Italian participation in Hitler's Russian campaign.

For the sake of convenience, the Allied governments during the last year and a half of the war had recognized the provisional Italian government, headed at first by Marshal Badoglio. However, upon the conclusion of the war a permanent government and a new constitution had to be established for this shattered nation, this nation in which democracy and a respect for government had never rested on a firm foundation, and in which for almost twenty-five years there had been no truly representative government. During the latter stages of the war, moreover, anti-Fascist partisans, often Communist-dominated, had been operating in the north. While non-Communist members of the resistance organizations had had their attention focused primarily on the Fascist enemies, the Communists had been preparing for the postwar settlement and had accumulated large supplies of money and weapons. It is certainly plausible to believe that had it not been for the presence of Allied troops in Italy, the reins of government would have been seized by the better-organized Communists. The situation there was favorable for extremist solutions since in the immediate postwar period inflation was rampant, there was widespread famine, and many deserters and bandits, able to arm themselves from the weapons lost or abandoned by the contending forces, infested the country. The Communists agreed, however, to cooperate with a coalition government, and in December 1945 the premiership of Italy passed to Alcide de Gasperi who formed a coalition government which included Communists.

Meanwhile, there was a strong clamor for the abolition of the monarchy. King Victor Emmanuel, whose role throughout the Fascist period had left much to be desired, abdicated in favor of his son Humberto, hoping thereby to insure the continuance of the monarchy. This step did not achieve its goal. In the referendum held in May 1946, the Italians by a margin of 12.7 million to 10.7 million voted against retention of the monarchy.

The Communist party withdrew from the coalition in 1947, hoping that in collaboration with the Left Socialists they could bring down the government. The first elections

Alcide de Gasperi, Premier of Italy

held under the new constitution of 1948, which replaced the old constitution of 1848, were very critical for the future of Italy. They resulted in a smashing triumph and a clear majority for the Christian Democrats of de Gasperi. Nevertheless, the Communists did elect 132 deputies, who, in union with about 50 deputies from the Left Socialists, comprised a sizable opposition to the some 307 supporters of de Gasperi.

By this time, most problems of Italian foreign affairs had been dealt with. The 1946 Paris Peace Conference had obligated Italy to pay the USSR some 100 million dollars in reparations; however, Italy had received more aid than that from the United States. The peace treaty of 1947 had given Istria and Fiume to Yugoslavia; the Italian colonies had been placed under the disposition of the United Nations, and the Dodecanese Islands had been returned to Greece. After the signing of the Italian peace treaty, there still remained two difficult problems, those of Trieste and the South Tyrol. The thorny problem of Trieste was eventually settled by compromise. The predominantly Austrian territory of the South Tyrol, or Alto Adige, remained with Italy.

The internal problems faced by de Gasperi remained enormous, and the number of unemployed never fell below a million during his premiership. Yet by 1950 clear signs of a general trend for the better were visible, a trend which continued throughout the 1950s and the 1960s. The threat of a Communist takeover receded; however, the Italian Communist party remained Europe's largest Communist party outside the USSR.

North and east of Italy and war-spared Switzerland lay Austria and Germany, where in accordance with wartime agreements, four zones of occupation were established. In Czechoslovakia, the prewar leaders, Benes and Jan Masaryk, having previously agreed to the cession to the USSR of the Carpatho-Ukraine, or Ruthenia, were allowed to return to establish a coalition government. In these three nations, Germany, Austria, and Czechoslovakia, all of which had

had American troops on their territory in 1945, the future types of government were still in doubt in that year. In Greece as well, where British troops had landed, the situation in 1945 still was not clear. However, in all the rest of East Central Europe, in all those nations where Soviet troops had come during the war, there was to be no Soviet withdrawal without the establishment of a pro-Stalin government.

Thus, as a result of World War II, all those nations which were not invaded by Soviet troops preserved the prewar form of government. Those nations which had been largely occupied by Allied troops established governments of a representative parliamentary type, whereas those nations invaded by Soviet troops established governments of a Stalinist type. It was the establishment of a pro-Stalin Communist government in Poland and the suppression of other political elements there which in many respects caused the strongest major disagreements among the Allies, disagreements which led to the Cold War.

For it was the British guarantee of the integrity of Poland which had been the immediate cause for British entry into World War II, and it was to England that a number of Polish governmental leaders plus a large number of followers had fled upon the defeat of the Poles in September 1939. There they had been recognized as the legitimate government of Poland. They had organized forces among the Poles living abroad to fight for the Allies, and before the war was over there were some 250,000 Poles serving along with the British forces. Contacts with underground elements in Poland had been established by this Polish government, and soon, despite German surveillance and severe countermeasures, a rather large underground army had been built up in Poland itself. These forces and their leaders were strong Polish nationalists.

The Soviets, meanwhile, had never really reconciled themselves to the losses to Poland as a result of the Polish-Russian War of 1920–21 of territories east of the Curzon line, territories in which lived far more Ukrainians and White Russians than Poles. And it seems true as well that the majority of these inhabitants did not favor the extreme program of "Polinization" introduced by the Polish government in the interwar years. Nevertheless, the inhabitants of these areas, knowing the fate being endured by their compatriots in the Soviet Union during the periods of enforced collectivization and industrialization, had been quiescent under Polish rule, and there was certainly no group of any consequence working for a union with the USSR. The small Polish Communist party itself had been thought by Stalin to be so unreliable and so riddled with Trotskyites and Polish government agents that he had ordered it disbanded in 1938. Poor though Poland was in the interwar period, its prewar standard of living was superior to that of the USSR, though industrialization in the latter had been proceeding more rapidly than in Poland. For the Poles themselves, the greatest traditional enemy of their national independence had been Russia, and this along with the great role of the Catholic Church in Poland had helped make the Poles strongly anti-Communist. The Nazi-Soviet pact and the resultant invasion of Poland by the Russians, while Poland was reeling under the Nazi onslaught, further intensified the national dislike for both Russia and communism along with a burning hatred for the Nazis. Into Poland the Germans had come as conquerors and as rulers. After the failure of their first few initial attempts to set up a puppet Polish government which would collaborate with them, the Nazis ruled with an iron hand. Here there was no Quisling government, no veneer cooperation. The populace, insofar as possible, still regarded the London government as the legitimate government of the nation and as previously mentioned, liaison was established between the London government and the rapidly growing underground movement.

The attitude of the Poles toward the USSR was well known to the Soviet authorities. The Soviets, during their

advance into Poland in 1939, had taken many Polish prisoners and had arrested numerous other persons in the territories they occupied. Many of these prisoners were then
sent to various prison camps in Siberia and Russia. Some
fourteen to fifteen thousand former Polish officers and non-
commissioned officers had been interned in three camps in
the Katyn forest area not for from Smolensk.

Relatives in London and elsewhere had received letters
from these men occasionally until the spring of 1940; then
nothing more was heard from them. Following the German
attack on Russia, Stalin, anxious to strengthen Russian defenses in any way, came to an understanding with the Polish government in exile in London. General Sikorsky, the
head of this exile regime, flew to Moscow, and an accord
was signed whereby Polish prisoners in Russia were to be
recruited and formed into units to fight against the Germans. As the Poles began to search for officers for these
units, they began intensifying their requests for information about those men formerly held captive by the Russians
near Katyn. From the Russians they received only evasive
answers, and in November 1941 Stalin said they had escaped to the East. Meanwhile, relations between the Russians and Poles were none too cordial about a number of
other matters.

The Russians wanted the Poles, as they completed training, to be sent to the front as replacements for Russian
troops; the Poles wanted to have their own corps. Many of
the Poles now released had bitter memories of their impris-
onment in Russia and were anti-Soviet. In addition, the
Poles claimed that they were being poorly supplied with
equipment and food. After much squabbling, it was finally
agreed to evacuate those Polish units already raised and
send them by way of the Middle East to fight with the British. Here matters stood until, in the spring of 1943, the
Germans announced the startling discovery of mass graves
in the Katyn forest, graves containing the bodies of thousands of Polish officers allegedly murdered by the Russians.

The Germans invited delegates from the neutral nations and other observers to come to verify the find. The Russians claimed that these men had been murdered by the Germans themselves.

The Polish government in exile requested that the International Red Cross conduct an investigation.* The angered Soviets then broke relations with the Polish government in London and announced that they were raising their own Polish army among Poles in the USSR. They also announced the formation of a Polish committee, a committee which they were shortly to recognize as the legitimate representatives of the Polish people.

The Russian recognition of one Polish government and the Western Allies' recognition of another represented a division of great importance. The Russian moves to further the interests of the group they were supporting led to protests and disagreements with the Anglo-Americans. Old fears and mistrusts based on both ideology and nationalism began to be felt more and more strongly. Though the wartime Allies continued to cooperate for some time after this affair, it would be no exaggeration to say that the Cold War began with the disagreement over Poland.

---

* At the end of the war there were so many German atrocities discovered that one more or less did not seem to matter. Thus, many persons just assumed that the Germans had indeed been responsible for the Katyn massacre. However, the Russians did not raise the subject at the Nuernberg trials, and later investigation by a United States congressional committee published findings placing the guilt on the Soviets.

6

The Cold War

Early Soviet Western Disagreement

THE basic Communist doctrine had originally been world revolution. Lenin, Trotsky, Zinoviev, and virtually all the Bolshevist leaders had hoped and believed the Russian revolution would be merely the first stage of a world revolution and had done what they could to further Red revolutions in Central Europe. The suppression of the Communist-type governments which had sprung up in Central Europe toward the end of 1918 and the defeat of the Red Army before Warsaw forced Lenin to give up hopes for any immediate Bolshevik revolution. By the later 1920s Stalin, in his desire to "build Socialism in one country" had foregone putting major emphasis on revolution in other countries; for the time being, the Communist parties in those countries were intended to work toward the strengthening of Russia, economically and diplomatically. Again and again the various Communist parties throughout the world did all types of maneuvering to support Moscow's aims and policies.

After the rise of Nazism in the thirties there was little possibility of a Communist revolution anywhere in Europe; the danger in most countries was from a Fascist takeover. Therefore, although Moscow was basically hostile to the Western bourgeois democracies, she instructed her Communist supporters in a number of countries to join anti-Fascist coalitions. Among the liberals in many nations, therefore, the Communists were often regarded as allies in the struggle against fascism. The completely unexpected reversal of the Communist party line caused by the Hitler-Stalin pact of August 1939 brought about a sharp increase in anti-Communist sentiment in the West, not only in rightist circles, but in some leftist circles as well. The Soviet attack on Finland in 1939–40 intensified this feeling. Nevertheless, the sudden German attack on Russia brought Stalin the support of the Western democracies against Hitler. Immediately after the German attack Prime Minister Churchill himself had announced that although he had always been as anti-Communist as anyone, anybody who was fighting Hitler would get British aid. Thus the alliance of the Communist USSR and the Western democracies was born. American lend-lease aid, which had been made available to Great Britain only a short while before the German invasion of Russia, was now made available to the Soviet Union. In the Western camp during the period of this alliance, Churchill was always somewhat suspicious of Stalin's intentions and wanted concrete agreements and policies, whereas FDR apparently thought he could work out a genuine understanding with the Russians, an understanding based on broad principles. On the Soviet side, Stalin was always suspicious of Western, especially British, intentions. He complained that the British were getting more than their proper share of American lend-lease aid and that the Allies were not extending themselves to open a second front in 1942 and 1943. Again and again comments were made both in the Soviet press and by Soviet representatives intimating that the Western Allies might be acting behind the Russians' back. There were those in the West who maintained that there were strong reasons and justifications for Stalin's suspicions of Western intentions, and FDR believed that if he could allay these suspicions a new and peaceful world could be built on the basis of an Anglo-American-Russian understanding. For this reason, he again and again tried to build a bridge of understanding. However, the suspicions were deep and had manifested themselves on many occasions, even, as already indicated, during 1941 and 1942. There had been the mysterious flight of Hitler's deputy Rudolf Hess to Great Britain just prior to the attack on Russia. It was felt that Hess was trying to get some understanding with the British so that Germany would be free to operate against Russia. Stalin himself had accepted a similar Hitler overture less than two years before; it seemed entirely possible to him that the British might be so inclined in 1941. By 1943 the Russians were advancing steadily and their military output was rising. The American military-industrial machine was operating at wartime efficiency, and the United States had surpassed its allies in the size of its air, land, and naval forces. Although the British, by tremendous efforts, had a very high war production and large forces in the field, their position was not as strong as that of either the United States or the USSR in determining postwar policy.

Obviously the Allies were fighting with victory in mind, and certainly once it became obvious that victory would be won, definite policies had to be adopted for that eventuality. Any victory over Germany would of necessity bring Soviet forces into Eastern Europe. It was known that the Soviets were going to try to enlarge their sphere of influence and their actual territory there. Under these conditions the problem should have been faced as soon as possible, and the Western Allies either should have resigned themselves to Soviet annexations or by landing military forces taken steps to prevent them while there was still time. This they failed to do. They allowed the Soviets to move into Eastern Europe with no guarantees, except generally worded platitudes that free elections would be held. When it became apparent that the Soviets had no intentions of holding general free elections, the Western Allies had only three choices short of actually going to war. They could either have: (1) recognized the situation as it was and made no further concessions; (2) refused to recognize the situation and bring all possible pressures to bear on the USSR short of hostilities;

or (3) accepted the situation as it was, and made still further concessions in the hope of coming to a general understanding, unpleasant as the prospect of the imposition of Stalinist regimes in these areas would be. However, the Western Allies did not follow any of these courses. They adopted a policy which was not a policy. They continued to complain about what was happening before their eyes in Eastern Europe, indicating that they were not ready to accept it. This antagonized the Soviets. Yet, at the same time that the Allies were complaining, they put no real pressure on the Soviets to change their policy and even abandoned additional territories in Central Europe to the Soviets. An understanding of how these events came about is essential for an understanding of European and world history from the end of World War II to the present day.

As previously indicated, the Soviets had a constant fear that the Western Allies might come to some type of understanding with the Axis powers which would or could be directed against them. To allay any such Soviet suspicions that there might be some underhanded Western negotiations with the enemy powers, the United States and Great Britain on January 1, 1942, joined with the Soviet Union and the other members of the Allies (now known as the United Nations) in signing the Washington declaration that there would be no separate peace. The signing powers signified that they "subscribed to a common program of purposes and principles embodied in the Joint Declaration" of August 14, 1941, known as the Atlantic Charter, made by President Roosevelt and Prime Minister Churchill. In this declaration the two leaders had forsworn for their respective nations any territorial aggrandizement as a result of the war. In May 1942 Molotov flew to London to conclude an alliance whereby each state promised not to become party to any alliance directed against the other. Molotov then proceeded on to Washington, where he requested and obtained an increase in American lend-lease shipments to the USSR, although his further request for the immediate opening of a second front was not, and could not, be granted at that time.

In January 1943, when President Roosevelt met with Prime Minister Churchill at Casablanca, the Russians began to show some fears that the Anglo-Americans might be deciding vital issues without them. Partially to still such fears, Roosevelt then announced the decision to demand "unconditional surrender" from the Axis powers.

As the war progressed, however, it was necessary to decide certain impending and postwar issues. The Russians from the beginning had claimed the Baltic states, eastern Poland, Bessarabia, certain Finnish areas, and other territories. By March of 1943 the Western Allies had tentatively agreed to the Russian annexation, or reannexation of these territories, although this was a violation of the UN Declaration of January 1, 1942, whereby the Soviets had adhered to the Atlantic Charter. In July 1943 Benito Mussolini had been ousted from power, and Marshal Pietro Badoglio, the new head of the Italian state, almost immediately began to have secret contacts with Allied authorities for the purpose of withdrawing Italy from the war; the formal surrender of Italy was announced in September; however, prompt German action prevented any large areas of the country from falling into Allied hands. Nevertheless, the dramatic exit of Italy from the war, the growing American strength in Europe, the Allied landings in Italy, and the continued Russian advances required some definite understandings among the Allies as to what their immediate and postwar policies would be. In October 1943, therefore, the foreign ministers of the Big Three met in Moscow. Here it was decided that an independent Austria should be reestablished, that German war criminals should be brought to justice, and that a European advisory council should be set up to insure the "closest cooperation between the three governments." The powers expressed themselves in favor of the restoration of democratic government in Italy and agreed to establish an advisory council for matters relating to Italy. It was also agreed that an international organization to secure the peace should be set up. The Americans in particular set great hope in this organization. The United States Secretary of State Cordell Hull and his aids had not liked the old politics represented to them by Winston Churchill. There seems little doubt that Stalin and his aides went along with this international organization largely for the same reasons that some of the European leaders a century and a quarter before had gone along with Tsar Alexander's notion of a Holy Alliance – to humor their ally. There is no evidence to show that they either then or at any time during Stalin's lifetime put any faith or hope in the United Nations. At the Moscow conference preparations were also made for the meeting of the heads of the three states in Teheran at the end of November.

The Teheran and Yalta Conferences

On their way to meet Stalin at Teheran, the Western leaders stopped off at Cairo from November 22–26 to meet with Chiang-Kai-Shek, the leader of Nationalist China, for decisions relating to Pacific problems. Here it was decided to reestablish an independent Korea and to grant great power status to China.

At Teheran, a Western invasion of France was promised for May 1944, and the Anglo-Americans agreed not to invade the Balkans. At this time there were several Allied divisions available in the Mediterranean, and their landing in the Balkans was something Churchill had greatly desired. Churchill felt that such an invasion would expose the weaker side, "the soft underbelly," of Hitler to Allied attack and would bring all important targets of Germany's empire within range of Allied planes. He felt further that such an invasion might bring Turkey into the war on the Allied side. However, Churchill had a still more important reason for wanting this invasion; he wanted to get Allied troops into large areas of Southeast and Central Europe before the Russians arrived.

There are those who maintain that an Allied invasion of

the Balkans would merely have deflected the main Soviet blow and sent Soviet troops into western Europe before the Allies, while the Anglo-Americans became bogged down in the rugged Balkan terrain. Proponents of the Churchill strategy maintain that the Western Allies had the forces for both a cross-channel landing and a Balkan invasion. At any rate the Teheran decision not to invade the Balkans meant that in the final reckoning Soviet troops were on the scene to determine the future course of Central and South-eastern Europe, with the exception of Greece.

The Teheran Conference also set as its goal that "all peoples of the world may live free lives, untouched by tyranny, and according to their varying desires and their own consciences."

Thus far, by the beginning of 1944, the Soviets had agreed to an international organization for the maintaining of peace; they had adhered to the principles of the Atlantic Charter for no territorial aggrandizement; they had abolished the Communist International; and had now agreed that all peoples should be free of tyranny and free to live their lives "according to their own conscience." What more could anyone risk? There were some who had grave doubts. Declarations of principles were fine and good, but what would happen in practice? Churchill was worried. On May 4, 1944, seeing which way the winds were beginning to blow, he wrote Foreign Secretary Eden stating that problem: "Are we going to acquiesce to the Communization of the Balkans and perhaps Italy?" But some of the American President's advisers regarded Churchill as a relic of a past imperialist age, an age which would have to go. A rather naïve wartime propaganda in the United States had glorified the Russian war action to such an extent that, when added to the activities of the handful of genuine Communist sympathizers, a rather soporific effect had been produced on much of American thinking and planning for postwar Europe. Besides, the tremendous cross-channel invasion of June 6, 1944, and the subsequent arduous campaign to break out of

Normandy helped postpone some of the important decision-
making. Indeed it was not until September 12, 1944, that
the European Advisory Commission, which had been established in London as a result of the Moscow foreign ministers
conference of the previous October, agreed upon the postwar division of Germany into three zones of occupation. By
this time the Western Allies had swept across France, and
de Gaulle had established himself in Paris as the head of
the French government. In Italy Rome had fallen to the Allied forces. In the Balkans not only had Rumania agreed to
an armistice, but she had actually joined in the war against
the Axis, thus opening the entire Balkans to the Soviet
troops and putting all German forces in Greece and Yugoslavia in extreme danger of being cut off. In Poland Soviet
forces had reached the outskirts of Warsaw, where surprisingly strong Polish underground forces within the city had
risen against the Germans. It seemed quite obvious that the
war would soon end in an Allied victory, and Churchill,
worried about the lack of any real provisions for postwar
Europe and feeling that the Soviets must be confronted by a
British-American concert in order to get some limits to Russian expansion, sailed to the new world for consultations
with President Roosevelt. He was particularly anxious to
"forestall the Russians in certain areas of Central Europe"
and hoped that forces could be made available to give Germany a "stab in the Adriatic armpit" and to take Fiume and
possibly Vienna. He was keenly aware of the fact that the
Hungarians had expressed their intention "of resisting the
Soviet advance, but would surrender to a British force if it
could arrive in time." At Quebec it was decided by the Anglo-
Americans that as long as the battle of Italy continued there
would be no forces made available for any Balkan operations, outside of small units for commando-type operations
and two British brigades for Greece. At this conference the
American Secretary of the Treasury Morgenthau presented
his plan calling for the deindustrialization of Germany and
the consequent transformation of that nation into an agri-

1939 FRONTIER

1. POLAND, 1939.
2. PETSAMO AREA, FINLAND, 1940.
3. EASTERN LAPLAND AREA, FINLAND, 1940.
4. KARELIA AND VIIPURI DISTRICTS, FINLAND, 1940.
5. ESTONIA, 1940.
6. LATVIA, 1940.
7. LITHUANIA, 1940.
8. NORTHERN BUKOVINA, RUMANIA, 1940.
9. BESSARABIA, RUMANIA, 1940.
10. RUTHENIA PROVINCE, CZECHOSLOVAKIA, 1945.
11. NORTHERN PORTION OF EAST PRUSSIA, GERMANY, 1945.
12. MEMEL, GERMANY, 1945.

```
0    100    200    300
        MILES
```

C.C. Weiss
S.I.U. Cartographic Laboratory

SOVIET EXPANSION IN
WORLD WAR II

cultural land. Churchill agreed to consider the project; however, Roosevelt subsequently ran into strong objections to this idea in his own cabinet, and the Morgenthau plan was never put into operation; it did, however, have some effect on immediate postwar American policy in Germany. The Quebec and Hyde Park conferences of mid-September 1944, made no real arrangements or planning for postwar Europe, except for a few areas in West Germany designated for British and American occupation.

Events were moving too rapidly, however, to allow Churchill to sit back and leave the postwar European set-up to chance. With the strong endorsement of President Roosevelt, who could not attend because of the forthcoming presidential elections, Churchill arrived in Moscow on October 9, 1944, for consultations with Marshal Stalin. Meeting with Stalin on the day of his arrival, Churchill said to him, "Let us settle about our affairs in the Balkans. Don't let us get at cross purposes in small ways." He then wrote on a piece of paper which he handed to Stalin that Russian interests would be 90 percent in Rumania and 75 percent in Bulgaria. In Yugoslavia and Hungary British and Russian interests were to be 50–50 and the British were to have a 90 percent interest in Greece. Churchill notes in his memoirs that Stalin looked at the paper and agreed by making a "tick upon it." Thus was to be decided the fate of millions of people.

With almost no difficulty Churchill had been able to arrange agreements on most of East Europe, though he was later to be disappointed in the implementation of his "percentages agreement." About Poland, however, where the Soviets had been pursuing a most callous and cynical program, reaching an understanding was extremely difficult and very little was achieved in Moscow. At British insistence Stanislas Mikolajczk and other members of the London Polish government met with the representatives of the Russian-established Lublin government. It was quite obvious here that the Lublin government was merely a Russian-controlled operation, yet the Soviets were adamant about their Polish frontiers and the London Poles were not yet ready to give up completely. No accord was reached and indeed, as indicated earlier, it was with regard to the developing Polish situation that there occurred the first major disputes leading to the Cold War. It was the developing Polish situation that stood ominously in the background, despite apparent successes in other areas.

Almost simultaneously with the above conferences, representatives of the powers had been meeting at Dumbarton Oaks to draw up a charter for the United Nations, an international agency intended to secure the postwar peace and to succeed where the League of Nations had failed. Here it was decided to give France a permanent seat on the security council and to give each of the major powers a veto over UN resolutions.

As early as November 1944 de Gaulle was also pushing his plans for a third force in Europe to counteract both the Soviets and the Americans. This third-force idea of de Gaulle's, which he was to push for the next twenty-five years, at that time envisioned a British-French alliance–later a Franco-German alliance–as its cornerstone. It was not, however, accepted by Churchill.

A Big-Three meeting had been in the offing even before Churchill's visit to Moscow in October, and the continued advances of the Allies made such a meeting imperative. In early 1945 at Yalta in the Crimea, the leaders of the Big Three met again to finally lay firm agreements for postwar Europe. By this time, however, virtually all lands overrun by the Germans had been liberated. Thus the main decisions concerning Europe which were to be made at the conference were those dealing with postwar Germany and Poland. The fact that no real understanding was reached on Poland meant that relations between East and West were to be strained and mutual mistrust was not to be allayed. It meant further that the broad general understandings reached about postwar Germany were only partially to be implemented, straining even further the relations between the two major powers.

At Yalta, agreement was reached on the organization of a new international body, the United Nations. Because of American idealism the reaching of an accord on the UN was placed high on the Yalta agenda and much discussion was devoted to its workings. In retrospect one is forced to wonder how such great hopes could be placed on an organization which allowed to each major power, to every permanent member of the Security Council, a veto over any decision reached by the other members. It was this very point which Stalin, remembering the censorship by the League of Nations of the USSR for its invasion of Finland, specifically questioned; once he realized that the UN could take no action without unanimity of the great powers, he agreed to join it, after being granted several further concessions such as the allotting to the USSR of three votes in the General Assembly. Besides the issue of the United Nations, which as already indicated was important primarily to the Americans, the three really major problems to be tackled were the Far Eastern, the German, and the Polish situations.

At this time, February 1945, Japanese resistance was still very strong. The Japanese soldiers had shown every willingness to fight to the death and the American casualties in the island fighting against the Japanese had been heavy. Allied planners had to allow for heavy losses in considering the invasion of the Japanese home islands. For this reason it was deemed important to get Russia into that war to attack the Japanese forces in Manchuria and the Japanese industrial complex there. Stalin agreed to enter the war against Japan within two to three months after the termination of the war in Europe on condition that: (1) Russia receive southern Sakhalin; (2) there would be joint Soviet-Chinese operation of the Chinese Eastern and Manchurian railroads; (3) the USSR acquired the Kurile Islands; (4) the *status quo* in Outer Mongolia would be preserved and there would be a guarantee of a Russian outlet to Dairen, and the establishment of a Russian base at Port Arthur would be accepted. Stalin claimed that these annexations, which were a violation of the spirit of the Atlantic Charter, were nevertheless a justifiable redress for the Russian losses of 1904–5, and neither of the Western powers raised any objections.

At Yalta it was decided that Germany should be divided into four zones of occupation, one of these zones to be administered by the French, because of Churchill's insistence. A special status for joint occupation and rule of both Berlin and Vienna was decided upon. It was agreed that Germany should be disarmed and that German war criminals should be brought to trial. It was further decided that Germany should make reparations for damages she had caused and that these reparations should go to those countries which had borne the main burden of the war. The Soviets here put forth a reparations figure of twenty billion dollars of which half should go to the USSR. No definite agreements were reached in this connection, but it was decided to establish an Allied reparations commission and that annual deliveries in reparations should be taken from current German production. It was further decided to give to Poland German territory east of a line from Stettin southward along the river Oder to the western Neisse river, as compensation for Soviet territorial gains at Polish expense. At the time no real distinction was made between the eastern and western Neisse rivers. This change of borders would mean the transferral of some six to nine million Germans. The failure to definitely settle certain unforeseen German problems meant that the seeds of future trouble over Germany were being sown.

The main problem of the conference, however, was the Polish question. The Soviets claimed those prewar Polish territories which lay east of the Curzon line, and though the Western Allies would have liked to see Poland retain Lvov if possible, they were willing to compensate the Poles for territorial losses to Russia by granting Poland the important

German territories indicated above, territories which included such significant cities as Stettin, Danzig and Breslau,
in addition to mineral-rich territories in Silesia. On the
vexatious and vital question regarding a government for
Poland, the best that could be arranged was an agreement
that "the Provisional government which is now functioning
in Poland should therefore be reorganized on a broader
democratic basis with the inclusion of democratic leaders
from Poland itself and from Poles abroad. This Polish
Provisional Government of National Unity shall be pledged
to the holding of free and unfettered elections as soon as
possible on the basis of universal suffrage and secret ballot.
In these elections all democratic and anti-Nazi parties shall
have the right to take part and to put forward candidates"
(communique issued at end of Yalta Conference, quoted in
Churchill, *Triumph and Tragedy* [Cambridge, Mass.:
Houghton-Mifflin, 1953], p. 387). And it was on this very
issue and its interpretation that the wartime honeymoon
came to an end. The United States and Great Britain insisted that the Lublin government established by the Soviets
was not representative of the Polish people and that representatives of the London Poles be included in the Polish
government and that truly democratic elections be held.

It has often been maintained that at Yalta an ailing President Roosevelt was taken in by the Russians and in his
utopian vision of a new world made too many concessions
to the Soviets. While with the benefit of hindsight it definitely can be stated that the United States could have obtained several more advantages, such as access rights to
Berlin, about which, apparently, no one was concerned at
the time, it must be stated for the sake of accuracy that the
Allied position on Poland was set forth both forcibly and
repeatedly at the Yalta conference. To quote Churchill,
"Poland was discussed at no fewer than seven out of the
eight plenary meetings of the Yalta Conference, and the
British record contains an interchange on this topic of nearly
eighteen thousand words between Stalin, Roosevelt, and

myself. . . . Poland had indeed been the most urgent reason for the Yalta Conference, and was to prove the first of
the great causes which led to the breakdown of the Grand
Alliance. . . ." President Roosevelt stated that he "hoped to
see the creation of a Government of Poland which would be
representative and which the great majority of Poles would
support." And Churchill stated to Stalin, "I wanted the Poles
to be able to live freely and live their own lives in their own
way. . . . It was for this that we had gone to war against
Germany—that Poland should be free and sovereign. . . .
Poland must be mistress of her own house and captain of
her own soul" (*Triumph and Tragedy*, pp. 365–68).

The best the Anglo-Americans could obtain from Stalin
after such remonstrances was that "free and unfettered
elections would take place." There are those who state that
the Allies should have known that Stalin's word could not
be believed, that the United States and Britain should have
demanded and obtained more. However, this view does not
take into consideration the fact that in mid-February all of
Poland was in Soviet hands. The Western Allies were just
beginning to advance again after a hard, bitter month of
fighting. Japan was still in the war. Germany still had hundreds of divisions in the field. Stalin had kept hands off
Greece and honored the "percentages agreement" while the
British intervened in Athens to prevent a Communist take-
over in December; perhaps it might just happen that Stalin
would honor this pledge for Polish elections. Earlier Allied
action might have prevented the Sovietization of other East
European lands; however, the opportunity for direct intervention in Poland, if it had ever existed, was certainly gone
by the time of Yalta. Only the most extreme Allied pressure,
such as war or the threat of war, could have caused the
Soviets to throw over their Polish satraps. And indeed there
was nothing the matter with the Yalta agreement as such.
Had Russia honored her pledge to allow free elections in
Poland, the Allies would have received everything they said
they wanted. The great error was made when, after Yalta

and after it had become abundantly clear that the Soviets were proceeding to deal with Poland in their own fashion, the Western Allies continued to honor commitments made to Russia, commitments which allowed the Soviets to occupy territories of vital importance to the future of Europe. It was really the fact that the United States had no clear war aims beyond the defeat of the enemy and was too concerned with utopian dreams about the future function of the UN, which worked to the advantage of the Russians and the disadvantage of Britain and the United States.

Usually after great historical happenings there arises a so-called revisionist group of historians or the so-called debunkers. Such a group has been active in connection with describing the origins of the Cold War, maintaining that the Western Allies erred in the other direction during the last stages of World War II and in the postwar period, that instead of being too soft in their dealings with Stalin and the Soviets they were too harsh.

The above argument can best be examined in the light of the Polish story, since the grand alliance began to come apart over the Polish issue. For, indeed, in summing up the Polish episode one is led to the inescapable conclusion that once the tide of the war had shifted and the Soviets knew that they had successfully withstood the internal and external storm, they were already preparing for the postwar settlements and already had their eye not only on getting as much territory as possible but in getting control of Poland through a government of their own making. Step by step they proceeded in this direction, the first important step being the formation on Soviet soil of the Polish committee of 1943 and the organization of one Polish division, the Kosciuzko division.

Some of the further steps become clear from a greater examination of the Warsaw Uprising and the subsequent events in Poland. In July of 1944 the Russians were on the outskirts of Praga, the eastern suburb of Warsaw. The London government had succeeded in maintaining contacts with resistance fighters within Poland and a large underground Polish home army was in existence, an army loyal to the London government. Some forty thousand members of this force, under the command of General Bor-Komorowski, were in Warsaw itself. On July 29, three days before General Bor began his uprising, the Moscow radio broadcast an appeal from the Polish Communists to the people of Warsaw saying that the guns of liberation were now within hearing and calling on them, as in 1939, to join battle with the Germans. After announcing that the German plan to set up defense positions in the city would result in the ruin of the city, the broadcast ended by "reminding the inhabitants that all is lost that is not saved by active effort."

By July 31, 1944 Russian tanks were only ten miles away; the Germans announced that the Russians had started a "general attack" on the city. On August 1, 1944 resistance fighters began to fire on the Germans, who, caught by surprise, were soon driven from the city. The Russians in the meantime halted all offensive actions on this front.

On August 4 Churchill wired Stalin about the necessity of aiding the Warsaw insurgents. (It should here be borne in mind that the Western Allies rushed to the relief of Paris just a few weeks later, even though they had not wanted the responsibility of provisioning the city yet, and had, therefore, done nothing to encourage the Paris uprising at that time.) Stalin answered that the Germans had five divisions there and that the insurgents could not possibly take the city.

Since the Warsaw resistance fighters were desperately in need of all types of medical and military supplies and since the Russians apparently were not going to supply any, the Allies then asked the Russians for permission for their own planes to land for refueling on Russian bases after dropping supplies into the city. On August 16, more than two weeks after the beginning of the uprising, Andrei Vyshinsky, the former prosecutor of the "Show Trials" and now deputy Foreign Minister, explained to the United States ambassador that "the Soviet Government cannot of course object to English or American aircraft dropping arms in the region of Warsaw, since this is an American and British affair. But they decidely object to American or British aircraft, after dropping arms in the region of Warsaw, landing on Soviet territory, since the Soviet government does not wish to associate themselves either directly or indirectly with the adventure in Warsaw" (in Churchill, *Triumph and Tragedy*, p. 133).

Though time was of the essence, it was not until September 14, more than six weeks after the beginning of the uprising, that the Soviet air force began dropping supplies, but few of the parachutes opened and many of the containers were smashed and useless. The following day the Russians occupied the Praga suburb but went no further. It would seem that they wished to have this powerful non-Communist nationalist Polish force destroyed to the full. Yet it also seemed that they wanted to keep alive the idea that they were coming to the rescue. The result was a complete disaster for Warsaw and hundreds of thousands of its inhabitants. The underground was crushed. One of the last broadcasts from the city picked up in London stated: "This is the stark truth. We were treated worse than Hitler's satellites, worse than Italy, Rumania, Finland. May God, who is just, pass judgment on the terrible injustice suffered by the Polish nation, and may He punish accordingly all."

The major Russian advance through Poland was not resumed until January and by the first week of February 1945 the Russians had reached the Oder. At the same time the Polish committee which had been brought to Lublin under Soviet auspices began to assume more and more the duties of government. However, the great hostility of the Polish populace toward these persons whom they regarded as Russian puppets encouraged Churchill to inform Truman on April 15, 1945, "As I see it the Lublin government are feeling the strong sentiment of the Polish nation, which . . . views with increasing disfavor a Polish Provisional Government which is in the main a Soviet puppet."

However, it was soon to become plain that the Soviets were not to allow public opinion in Poland to stand in their way. On April 23, 1945, about one week after the Churchill message to Truman, as Soviet troops were getting ready for the final assault on Berlin, the foreign ministers of the Big Three had discussions over Poland for more than one hour. Molotov maintained to Eden and Stettinius, the new American Secretary of State, that the Soviets had made no difficulties about any postwar agreements with France and Belgium; therefore, the Western Allies should not object to what was transpiring in Poland. The British, however, strongly objected to what was occurring in Poland. Eden pointed out that "all three of us recognized the government in France and Belgium, whereas Poland had two governments, one recognized by ourselves and most of the world, and the other recognized by the Soviet government. The Soviet . . . making a treaty with the Warsaw government which we did not recognize was entirely different and made people think that the Soviet government was satisfied with the Polish government as it was" (in Churchill, *Triumph and Tragedy*, pp. 491–92). To these types of British representations Stalin contended that Poland, unlike Great Britain and the United States, had a common frontier with the Soviet Union and that the Soviet Union could never approve "a hostile government" in Poland. For Churchill

this was no answer. We had gone to Yalta with the hope that both the London and Lublin Polish governments would be swept away and that a new government would be formed from among Poles of goodwill, among whom the members of Bierut's government would be prominent. [Bierut was the Communist chief of the Lublin government.]

Indeed, it is from Churchill's account as told in *Triumph and Tragedy* that we have the most complete record of Allied attempts to restore a free Poland. According to Churchill, the British in trying to arrange a coalition Polish government put forth representative persons who were believed to be not "unfriendly to Russia." However, the Russians stalled week after week in giving an opinion about the people proposed. Meanwhile, with Russian aid, the Lublin government was establishing itself in Poland. By the end of April 1945 Churchill, realizing that precious time was slipping away, appealed directly to Stalin to help establish a Polish government conforming to the description of the joint declaration of Yalta "with proper regard for the rights of the individual."

The Soviets either ignored Western protestations or answered with platitudes as they continued to tighten their hold on Poland. Thus General Leopold Okulicki, the successor of General Bor-Komorowski, having received a written guarantee of personal safety, met with a Soviet representative in a Warsaw suburb. The following day a number of Polish leaders representing the major political parties in Poland joined them. Not one of the Poles returned from the meeting. Indeed it was not until May that Molotov even admitted that these men were being held in Russia. To quote Churchill further:

Nothing more was heard of the victims of the trap until the case against them opened on June 18. It was conducted in the usual Communist manner. The prisoners were accused of subversion, terrorism and espionage, and all except one admitted wholly or in part to the charges against them. Thirteen were found guilty and sentenced to terms of imprisonments ranging from four months to ten years, and three were acquitted. This was in fact the judicial liquidation of the leadership of the Polish underground which had fought so heroically against Hitler. The rank and file had already died in the ruins of Warsaw. (*Triumph and Tragedy*, p. 498)

The recital of these events leaves no doubt that the Soviets had no intention of cooperating with any government or any authority in Poland which would not be subservient to the Soviet cause. Had the Western Allies recognized this and acquiesced without any protests to a situation which they were obviously not prepared to resist militarily, there is

every possibility that the spirit of wartime cooperation between the USSR and the Western Allies would have continued somewhat longer. However, cooperation which is
based only on giving in on all points, including in the Polish
case even questions of principle, is not really cooperation.

The Iron Curtain

Meanwhile in March and April American forces began to
advance rapidly into Germany. By the 12th of April, the day
of Roosevelt's death, American forces had crossed the Elbe,
only sixty miles from Berlin. Before the month was out
American forces were deep into Czechoslovakia and Prague
lay open to them. Leipzig and large sections of Saxony and
Middle Germany were in their hands. And it is at this point,
rather than at Yalta, that the great errors in American
policy occurred. For the United States had had no long-term
plans for postwar Europe. Even as late as Yalta Roosevelt
had announced that the United States did not intend to keep
forces in Europe for more than two years after the war.

Nevertheless, Soviet allegations of Allied duplicity in
supposedly carrying out underhand peace negotiations with
the Germans, these allegations coming in conjunction with
the continuing Sovietization of Poland and Eastern Europe,
were leading to a hardening of Roosevelt's ideas and attitudes toward the USSR when his untimely death on April
12 brought about the sudden elevation of Harry S. Truman
to the office of president. Thus within the very first two
weeks of his term of office Truman was faced with the tremendous opportunity of seizing Berlin, Prague, and huge
important territories of Central Europe. However, Truman
and the Americans felt bound by earlier agreements to allow
Russian forces to take Berlin and Prague.

Churchill, having by this time encountered Soviet intransigence over Poland, was decidedly aware that a cold
war was in the offing and realized that neither persuasion
nor appeals to majority rule and other "bourgeois" concepts

would have much influence with Stalin. He now tried to get his American allies to use their position in Germany as a basis for bargaining with the Russians; his earlier attempts to get the Americans to seize the capitals of Central Europe had been unsuccessful for reasons already mentioned. However, if the Americans who had already occupied Leipzig and a good section of Middle Germany and Saxony would not withdraw, there would be a real basis for negotiations with the Soviets. If these territories were to be evacuated to the Soviets without any real concessions in return, however, Western hopes for influencing any developments in Poland or Central Europe would be lost.

Or to put it clearly, if the Americans moved back 120 miles in Central Europe, Poland and possibly all Central Europe would be lost. The Americans had already shown their good faith by allowing Soviet forces to occupy territories and cities such as Berlin and Prague which they themselves could have taken. In view of the obvious failure of the Soviets to live up to the Yalta agreements in respect to Poland and in view of the ominous developments in Eastern Europe, Churchill on May 12 again communicated to Truman his alarm about the policy the Americans were apparently pursuing in light of Soviet intransigence, and within a week he was already speaking of an iron curtain which the Soviets were ringing down across Central Europe.

By the late spring of 1945 Tito, too, had sent rather sizable Yugoslav units into the Venezia-Giulia-Trieste region. It was felt that any Yugoslav success there would lead to further annexations at the expense of Austria, Hungary, and Greece, and it was felt that Tito was acting with Moscow's encouragement. Truman's strong stand against unilateral Yugoslav action encouraged Churchill to rush troops to Trieste. At that time, and throughout the next several years, it was the prevailing opinion in the West that Stalin was pulling Tito's strings, and Stalin's somewhat belated protestations in June 1945 to the contrary were not believed. In this particular respect, subsequent develop-

ments would seem to indicate that Tito indeed was acting
on his own.

At the beginning of June 1945 Truman sent Harry Hopkins to Moscow to see Stalin about breaking the Polish
impasse; however, Stalin's concessions, which revived
Western hopes of an end to the deadlock, were more apparent than real. Nevertheless at the insistance of the Western Allies, Stanislaus Mikolajczk was persuaded to go to
Moscow and a new Polish provisional government was set
up. In the words of Churchill:

> It is difficult to see what more we could have done. For five
> months the Soviets had fought every inch of the way. They had
> gained their object by delay. During all this time the Lublin ad-
> ministration, under Bierut, sustained by the might of the Rus-
> sian armies, had given them a complete control of Poland,
> enforced by the usual deportations and liquidations. They had
> denied us all the access for our observers which they had
> promised. . . . (*Triumph and Tragedy*, p. 583)

By June, therefore, the very threatening Communist pressure on Trieste, the disregard for Allied protestations in
regard to Poland, and the complete take-overs in Bulgaria
and Rumania had caused grave misgivings in Washington
as well as London. Churchill, feeling that an immediate
meeting of the Big Three was essential if these developing
disagreements between the wartime allies were to be resolved without severely damaging relations, pressed
strongly for an immediate summit conference, hoping
thereby that decision could be reached before the Americans
pulled back to the areas allotted them at Yalta. Despite his
urgings, the conference which Stalin was in no hurry to
convene and to which Truman felt he could not come before
mid-July was therefore delayed until then. By that time,
however, it was too late to use position for bargaining
purposes. On July 1, the United States and British forces
had begun their withdrawal to their allotted zones, "followed
by masses of refugees. Soviet Russia was established in the

heart of Europe." For all practical purposes the European boundaries of the Cold War, with the possible exception of a not yet completely communized Czechoslovakia, had been drawn. Except for Austria there were to be no changes for more than a quarter of a century. Thus, when the Big Three met at Potsdam, just outside of Berlin, on July 17, 1945, it was against a background of growing differences and mutual suspicions. However, James Byrnes, the new secretary of state regarded his main duties as terminating the war by treaties and getting the United States out of Europe. At the conference provisions for ending the Pacific war were agreed upon without much trouble, although the successful American explosion of an atomic bomb in New Mexico on the opening day of the conference presaged an early conclusion to that conflict and meant that the Western powers no longer felt they needed Stalin's help in fighting Japan. It was in trying to come to an agreement on the postwar settlement for Europe, primarily Germany, that the conference ran into trouble. The real issues were not really solved but were given to committees to work out. Thus the conference decided that a council consisting of the foreign ministers of the three powers be established to work out peace treaties for Italy, Bulgaria, Rumania, Hungary, and Finland. This same council was intended to prepare a peace agreement with Germany when that nation had a government empowered to conclude peace. The conference also agreed that Germany should be disarmed and her military industry eliminated, and that all democratic political parties with rights of assembly and of public discussion should be allowed and encouraged throughout Germany. It was further decided that during the period of occupation Germany should be treated as one economic unit, and the Soviet Union was granted reparations from the western zone to the extent of 15 percent of certain German industries in return for food and raw materials, etc. Ten percent of such industrial capital equipment as was unnecessary for the new German peace economy was to be removed from the western zones to be transferred to the Soviet government as partial reparations. The Oder-Neisse border was accepted as the German-Polish frontier, and the Soviets were allowed to annex Koenigsberg. The three powers noted that the "Polish Provisional Government," in accordance with the decisions of the Crimean Conference, had agreed to the holding of free and unfettered elections as soon as possible on the basis of universal suffrage and secret ballot in which all democratic and anti-Nazi parties would have the right to take part and to put forward candidates; and that representatives of the Allied press would enjoy full freedom to report to the world upon developments in Poland before and during the elections.

The declarations of the Potsdam agreement relating to free elections and the presence of Western observers in Poland remained virtually a dead letter, and throughout summer and fall of 1945 the Polish situation continued to smoulder under the now-transparent veneer of harmonious relations between the Soviet Union and the Western Allies.

With Polish events and Yugoslav pressure on Trieste already undermining the "spirit of Potsdam", other Russian moves served to heighten Western mistrust. In March of 1945 the Russians had terminated their 1925 pact of friendship with Turkey and shortly thereafter began to demand certain border revisions with respect to the cities and areas of Kars and Ardahan. By December the Russians had reopened the question of navigation of the straits, and to put further pressures on the Turks, they were backing Bulgarian claims to Eastern Thrace. By the end of the year they were also giving secret aid to the Greek Communists.

In Rumania, Vishinsky had arrived immediately after the Yalta meeting and forced on Rumanian King Michael a revision of the government, putting Moscow supporters in key positions. Throughout 1945 the Communists weeded out potential opponents and strengthened their organization. Bulgaria, which had not declared war on the USSR during World War II, had been invaded by the Russians following Rumania's surrender and forced to join the war against Germany while a Communist-dominated coalition government was installed with the aid of Russian troops.

Even in northern Iran, which the Russians had occupied by agreement with the Allies so as to protect American lend-lease aid going to the USSR during the war, the Russians had established a puppet government, and in late 1945 and early 1946 it seemed entirely possible that they might not withdraw from Iran either.

In both Hungary and Eastern Germany the Russians were also making it increasingly difficult for non-Communist public figures. Here their task was made somewhat easier since they were in territory which had never joined them as cobelligerants in the war, and they could more easily brand any would-be opponents as Fascists.

Thus Eastern and most of Central Europe were in Soviet hands. In each of the countries in this area, the Communist government which was imposed upon the people as a result of Russian operations and the presence of the Russian military had a hierarchy of command directly answerable to Moscow. Many of these leaders had even spent either the entire war or a good part of the war in Moscow. There was no real chain of command that had been established with each other; the chain led to Moscow. In all the newly created armies and in the secret police, the two instruments of control in these states, the chief officials were responsible to the Russians there. In two cases alone, in Albania and Yugoslavia, the local Communists had fought their own revolution. Though it was only the breakdown of the German army and the entrance of the Red Army into Yugoslavia that made possible Tito's triumph, he was nevertheless at the time of the Russian advance into Yugoslavia in control of a complete governmental apparatus and had powerful forces at his command, forces which had been built by him virtually from the ground up. The chain of command in Yugoslavia stopped with Tito. Though in 1945–46 both the Yugoslav and Albanian leaders regarded Russia as the leader of the Communist movement and were ready to follow Moscow's lead in most any aggressive action for the

Tito of Yugoslavia

spreading of communism, they were still in control of their own party and of their own governmental apparatus. This was to have a very great significance for the future history of Southeast Europe. In 1945–46, however, this distinction and importance was not noted.

Since there was surface cooperation among the former wartime allies despite the many and widening rifts, coalition governments with Communist members were maintained in Western Europe throughout 1945–46. In both Italy and France until 1947, Communist members held important ministerial posts, though they did not hold the critical ministries involving police and security. In Eastern Europe a number of non-Communists also held positions in the governments, though the positions of real power were never out of Communist hands.

Nevertheless, the continuing communization of Eastern Europe throughout 1945, to which the Western Allies had not yet reconciled themselves, led to a continued hardening of policy and an ever-deepening chill in relations.

In March 1946 Churchill, in a speech at Fulton, Missouri, put into words the thoughts of a growing number of persons in the West when he stated:

From Stettin on the Baltic to Trieste on the Adriatic, an iron curtain has descended across the Continent. Behind that line . . . police governments are prevailing in nearly every case, and so far, except in Czechoslovakia, there is no true democracy. Turkey and Persia are both profoundly alarmed and disturbed by the claims which are made upon them and at the pressure being exerted by the Moscow government. An attempt is being made by the Russians in Berlin to build up a quasi-Communist party in their zone of occupied Germany . . . !! (*Ideas and Diplomacy*, ed. Norman Graebner [Oxford University Press, 1964], pp. 723–24)

Though American views coincided to a great degree with Churchill's, there were, however, still strong feelings that Churchill was only trying to get the United States to help

Britain maintain a balance of power. There were in addition many Americans who wanted a return to normalcy as
soon as possible, and for over another year there were still
some in the United States government, including a very
small number of actual Communist sympathizers, who did
not want the United States to confront the USSR in those
areas where the Soviets were applying pressure.

By 1946, however, the main disagreements in the Cold
War, certainly insofar as Europe is concerned, had shifted
from Poland to Germany. In the original stages it had been
French opposition, even more than Soviet, which had
blocked all attempts to set up a central German administration. By October of 1945 the Allies had suspended their
attempt to create such an administration and were proceeding to establish local administrations. Food which was
supposed to be forthcoming from the Eastern zones did not
appear, while reparations from the Western zones did not
meet the amounts the Soviets had anticipated. Millions of
Germans and Poles had flooded into the Allied zones and
had to be fed. The United States felt that to meet Russian
reparation demands the United States would have had to
continue to put money into Germany with one hand while
the Soviets were taking it out with the other. All of Western
Europe needed American food and in the Western zones of
Germany the food rations were reduced to between 1000
and 1500 calories a day. At the same time most of the
United Nations aid, or UNRRA, which was almost exclu-
sively American aid, had been going to aid those countries
of Eastern Europe which were under Soviet control and
which were more and more adopting a hostile attitude toward the United States. After further failure to reach agreements with the Soviets, the United States in May 1946
finally suspended reparations shipments from the American
zone and by July 11, the United States was already pro-
posing the merger of the British and American zones of
Germany into a Bizonia. By this time, moreover, the whole
Allied attitude toward Germany was changing. The Rus-

sians had announced their new plans which included not just the intention to use Germany as a source for receiving payments but envisioned the rebuilding of their section of Germany. At the same time they denounced the Western powers for violation of the Potsdam agreements and, in an attempt to appeal to the Germans, they denounced the Allies for keeping Germany in subjugation. The British and the Americans had meanwhile arrived at the conclusion that the economic recovery of Germany was essential for the economic well-being of Europe. Thus, when the Soviets now laid down a challenge for winning over the Germans, the United States responded. In Stuttgart in September 1946, Byrnes publicly declared that Germany's economic recovery was essential and pledged that if necessary the United States would stay in Germany to help rebuild the shattered economy. He declared further that the United States favored the establishment of a provisional government for all of Germany.

Thus the United States, which had come to Europe with the intention of leaving as soon as practical, had now indicated it was there to stay if necessary; the United States had become a European power. The spectre of a revived Germany in alliance with the United States has haunted the Kremlin's leaders ever since. From this point on the disagreements began to show themselves more and more openly.

In Greece Communist guerrillas, supported by Soviet-bloc states and using bases in Bulgaria, Yugoslavia, and Albania from which to operate, were threatening to destroy the precarious foundations of the newly reestablished and impoverished state. Britain had been supporting the Greek government in its struggle; however, by early 1947 war-impoverished Britain could no longer afford to continue its support. The United States, which had originally been critical of British intervention in Greece during the closing stages of the war, now sprang into the breach. President Truman in a message to Congress on March 12, 1947, ask-

ing for funds to support not only Greece but Turkey, stated
that

The very existence of the Greek state is today threatened by the
terrorist activities of several thousand armed men, led by Communists. . . . The peoples of a number of countries of the
world have recently had totalitarian regimes forced upon them
against their will. The Government of the United States has
made frequent protests against coercion and intimidation, in
violation of the Yalta agreement, in Poland, Rumania and Bulgaria. . . . I believe it must be the policy of the United States
to support free people who are resisting attempted subjugation
by armed minorities or by outside pressures. (*The Record of
American Diplomacy,* ed. Ruhl Bartlett [New York: Knopf,
1956], pp. 723–27)

This statement, the so-called Truman Doctrine, was an official affirmation of the policy of "containment," a policy
named after its advocate George Kennan who, writing at that
time in the journal *Foreign Affairs,* (April 1947, p. 575)
stated: "Since Communism preaches a perpetual struggle
against the non-Communist world, this preaching may be
rationalized into ruthless expansion unless it is met by the
force of determined resistance."

Truman had declared that "if we make it sufficiently
clear, in advance, that any armed attack affecting our national security would be met with overwhelming force, the
attack might never occur." And in the words of Dean
Acheson, "We have learned that if the free nations do not
stand together they will fall one by one." Thus the United
States was committed to stopping Communist aggression.
In June of 1947 the United States took still another step
away from its original goals, when Secretary of State
Marshall proposed that the nations of Europe whose economies had been shattered by the war draw up a list of their
needs so that the United States could help them recover
more easily. The invitation, although extended to the East
European nations as well, was regarded by the USSR as an
attempt to establish American dominance on the Continent.

Thus when Czechoslovakia, which had been trying to travel a neutral path between East and West, expressed interest in joining this program, Soviet and internal Communist pressure forced her not to.

The creation of Bizonia, the Truman Doctrine, the policy of containment, and the Marshall Plan, despite its economic character, are all regarded as major American steps in the Cold War.

Sovietization in the Satellites

These United States measures were countered by a stepped-up Sovietization throughout Soviet zones of dominance. In 1947 the leaders of those non-Communist parties, usually the peasant parties, which had been allowed to exist in Eastern Europe were arrested and in some cases executed; such was the fate of Maniu in Rumania, Petkov in Bulgaria, and Kovacs in Hungary. In February 1948 in Czechoslovakia, where the Czech cabinet had withdrawn under Soviet pressure its acceptance to participate in Marshall Plan largesse, a Communist coup backed by the Communist militia forced the end of democratic government there. For the first time since Potsdam, a major change in the boundaries of the Cold War had occurred. However, the Czech coup had been staged by Czech Communists without direct Soviet intervention. Members of the Communist party within Czechoslovakia had already been occupying certain key ministries in the Czech government and the Communists were able to carry off their coup without requiring any direct Soviet aid. The ease with which the Communists had seized a democratic government of a relatively prosperous and stable state, and one which had made every attempt to cooperate with the USSR, alarmed the nations of Western Europe and hastened plans for mutual defense. This was later to result in the North Atlantic Treaty Alliance.

In both France and Italy the Communist-controlled labor

unions initiated strikes which were really of a political and insurrectionary nature; however, in view of what was happening in Eastern Europe the governments of these countries reacted with firm measures.

Difficulties were encountered in the attempts to revive West Germany's production because of the tremendous amount of currency in circulation and the lack of goods to buy. For, upon occupation of Germany, the Allied authorities had begun issuing occupation marks which the United States redeemed under certain conditions at ten to the dollar. Plates for printing this currency had been turned over to the Russians even after the original disputes with them had arisen. The Soviets had printed an enormous amount of currency with which they paid for those goods and services which they did not requisition outright, resulting in additional cost to the United States taxpayers. The result was that Germany soon became flooded with an essentially worthless currency and incentive to work was virtually destroyed. For the purpose of restoring this incentive a new currency was issued in the Western zones of Germany; people were allowed to exchange up to four dollars worth of all their old marks for the new marks; all the remaining currency was declared invalid. The results were truly astonishing. From that moment the German economy began a forward surge which has continued for more than twenty years. The Soviets, who had been against a currency reform, countered by slowing down traffic on the Allied access routes to Berlin and finally by completely halting supplies to that city. For the more than two million inhabitants of West Berlin, the voters of which had expressed their anti-Communist sentiments, the situation was indeed grim. However, the Western Allies began bringing supplies into the city by air, and the economic consequence of the blockade began to hurt the economy of the Soviet zone of Germany; so after a year the blockade was ended.

The fact that the Soviets had actually blocked Anglo-American access to Berlin, and the fact that American military advisers and American military aid, replacing British, were being used against Communist guerrillas in Greece, showed just how far the former Allies had drifted by 1948, less than three years after the conclusion of victory. The Communist seizure of Czechoslovakia, the blockade of Berlin, which in the early stages looked as if it might result in a Communist takeover of that isolated city, and the moderately successful guerrilla war being waged in Greece brought communism its greatest expansion in Europe and seemed to presage even further gains. And yet, at the very time that the Communists had taken Czechoslovakia and were completing their consolidation in Eastern Europe, the first rift in the Communist monolith appeared. In June 1948 Marshal Tito was read out of the Cominform, the heir to the Comintern or Communist International, and was attacked with all the venom usually reserved for the most vicious capitalist enemies of the USSR.

In the West the split between Tito and Stalin could scarcely be believed and for a long time was not accepted at full face value; many thought it was some type of ruse. However, it was genuinely of extreme importance to the future development of communism. Tito had been a loyal Communist. However, unlike the other Communist leaders of East Europe who had been placed into power by Soviet bayonets, Tito had made his own revolution; though it is true that he would never have succeeded had it not been for the breakdown of the German war machine. Nevertheless, he had had a large and capable force in being at the war's end, a force which pursued the retreating Germans out of the country. An entire chain of command had been developed which led to him. The leaders of the secret police were also loyal to him. Thus, when Tito pursued policies which he felt were beneficial for both Yugoslavia and communism, without thinking whether they were necessarily beneficial for the USSR, Stalin was outraged and tried to organize an anti-Tito Stalinist faction within the Yugoslav Communist party. Once Tito's agents got wind of this (some, such as

Djilas, even having been approached themselves) and informed Tito, the latter knew he would have to resist or flee. For a person of Tito's background there was only one choice. Stalin tried by both economic and psychological pressures to bring down Tito; however, before the last step—open invasion—he shied. For an invasion might have produced an explosion behind his own lines in Eastern Europe and might even have brought in American intervention from Greece, where the Americans were aiding the Greek government. Stalin's next move was to make sure that there were no future "Titos" in the Eastern statellites and during the succeeding period, show trials were held in all the satellite states, trials in which those Communist leaders who had shown or even appeared to show nationalist or independent tendencies were eliminated. Among the most important figures thus executed was Laszlo Rajk in Hungary.

Tito, shortly after being ousted from the Stalinist system, closed the Yugoslav-Greek border to the Greek Communist guerrillas. Now that the Greek government could concentrate its forces against lines of infiltration from Bulgaria and Albania alone, the Greek revolution soon dwindled and by 1949 peace came to that impoverished country. Until that time there had been a number of prominent persons in the West who had regarded the failure of the Greek government to crush the insurgents as indication of the popular support these insurgents must have in Greece itself. It was now clear that the easy sanctuaries abroad and not any overwhelming popular support had been essential in keeping the Greek revolt alive.

By the summer of 1949 the main physical points of conflict in the European aspect of the Cold War had cooled down. The Berlin blockade was over; the Greek revolt was over. The Tito-Soviet split meant that the Trieste boundary issue could perhaps be settled in a lower key. The Truman Plan meant that Soviet pressure on the straits was relieved.

At the same time that the physical points of conflict had been temporarily brought under control, each side con-

C.C. Weiss
S.I.U. Cartographic Laboratory

**WARSAW PACT AND ATLANTIC
PACT (NATO) NATIONS, 1972**

allies in the form of lend-lease aid. This time, unlike after World War I, the United States realized that it could not expect to be paid for this aid in full, and shortly after the war negotiated a settlement of these accounts with most major lend-lease recipients except the USSR. Toward the end of the war, the United Nations Relief and Rehabilitations Commission had been established to help distribute relief in war-wrecked areas. Most of this aid, which came primarily from the United States, went to Eastern Europe. There was a strong reluctance in the United States to continue to grant aid, especially to governments which were unfriendly toward the United States, and therefore, this aid was discontinued by the end of 1946.

In the United States it was generally hoped and expected that a British and French economic recovery would lead to a general European and world recovery. There were no clear ideas nor were there clear intentions regarding an economic rehabilitation of Germany.

Britain

The British, meanwhile, had hoped that there would be a gradual tapering off of lend-lease aid at the war's conclusion and had hoped further that they could negotiate a large-scale loan to tide them over during the difficult transitional postwar months. However, the prevailing view in the United States was that there must be a return to normalcy as soon as possible, and lend-lease aid was abruptly curtailed upon the conclusion of the war. It might be added that among some of the idealists in United States governmental circles there was a certain latent antiimperialist feeling and antimonarchist sentiment which resented the British policies in Greece and probably did much to delay action on Britain's real needs. In the United States and elsewhere, it also was not readily realized just how much the British economic position had deteriorated because of the war. For in addition to the enormous war expenditures there

were now veterans' and dependents' payments to be met
and restitution to be made for the four million dwellings
destroyed or damaged.

For generations Britain had not been matching her imports with exports, but had been balancing payments and
meeting the deficits caused by import surpluses by the profits and interest on foreign investments, and to a lesser
degree, by income from her merchant shipping, insurance,
and banking operations. However, the war had forced the
British not only to liquidate their overseas assets but even
to run up foreign debts of some 15 billion dollars. In addition about half of her merchant marine was sunk in the
course of war. Had Britain had an abundance of natural resources or even a healthy agricultural base, the situation
would not have been so critical. However, under even the
most stringent of wartime agricultural measures the British
could scarcely produce half of the food they needed, and
cotton, oil, lumber, and many other ingredients of modern
industry had to be imported. Thus, for example, some 75
percent of Britain's wheat and 55 percent of her meat came
from abroad. During six years of virtually total war, British
industry, which had not been as productive or modern as
that of America to begin with, had been subjected to great
wear and strain.

Even before the war British industry had not been as
productive as that of either the United States or Germany,
as table 7. Thus, British productivity was considerably less
than that of the United States, in many fields only about
half as much. The coal industry provides another example
of trends in productivity and British export opportunities.
Coal exports, which had been a very important source of
foreign earnings in the pre-World War I period (87 million
tons in 1913), and even in the depressed market of the
interwar period (46 million tons in 1938), had fallen to
almost nothing in the post–World War II years (8 million
tons in 1945). Most alarming for the future of the British
mining industry was the rise of productivity in the mines of

7. OUTPUT PER WORKER IN SELECTED INDUSTRIES,
1935–1937

			(U.K. = 100)		
	Pig Iron	Steel	Cement	Coke	Cotton Spinning
U.S.	364	166	94	236	150
U.K.	100	100	100	100	100
Germany	141	141	92	152	120

Source: W. S. Woytinsky and E. S. Woytinsky, *World Population and Production: Trends and Outlook* (New York: Twentieth Century, 1953), p. 442.

some of its major competitors – and the consequent worsening of Britain's competitive position. From table 8 it becomes readily apparent that the war was responsible for a temporary lowering in the efficiency of the German and Polish mines and that the failure of the British to increase their productivity meant the British mining industry was no longer competitive in the world market. Yet British industry had to be competitive if the British were to be able to sell their wares abroad, pay off their debts, and rebuild some of their former investments. In the postwar period the Continental market was extremely limited, as these nations, too, sought to husband their meager financial resources. In

8. PRODUCTIVITY OF COAL MINES, 1913–1948
(In metric tons per man shift)

Country	1913	1938	1948
United States	3.8	4.9	5.9
Canada		2.4	3.0
United Kingdom	1.1	1.5	1.5
Poland	1.7	2.7 (1935)	1.8
Germany (Ruhr)	1.2	2.0	1.3

Source: Woytinsky and Woytinsky, p. 873.

the Americas British industry had to compete with the highly efficient United States industry. At the same time the British still had the enormous drain of meeting the commitments of a world power, which involved maintaining forces in Germany, Palestine, and Southeast Asia, as well as aiding Greece against Communist guerrillas. In addition the British people had just suffered six years of exhausting war, and in response to the demands of millions of Britons for all forms of security, medicare, old-age benefits, a system of social benefits or "cradle to grave" security was introduced. While few could deny that many of these benefits were both needed and desirable, they were costly and their institution at a time of mounting deficits worsened Britain's economic and political position. In addition to war-incurred obligations like veterans' and survivors' benefits, bombed housing restitution, etc., Britain was now saddled with a national debt which had risen in the following manner:

Year	Pounds (In millions)
1913	6.500
1920	7.828
1938	8.726
1946	23.637

Britain, therefore, felt compelled to turn to the United States with a request for a long-term, low-interest loan. This loan of $3.75 billion finally passed the American Congress by a close vote after a long, and at times acrimonious, debate. For a while it appeared that this loan might be enough to revive British economic health; however, the overseas commitments and the wartime deficits created enormous difficulties for the British treasury, and just when Britain, like all of Europe, needed good fortune it seemed that even the elements were conspiring against her. The European winter of late 1947 was one of the most severe in modern history. Gales and blizzards the like of which had not been seen in twentieth-century Britain stalled coal trains and barges, forcing electric generating plants and other factories to grind to a halt as their coal supplies dwindled. The storm also hit those Continental nations whose economic recovery was important for Great Britain's trade.

Thus, by the end of the winter of 1947 Britain was faced with larger deficits, and economic revival seemed in many respects further away than at war's end. It was this situation which forced the British to announce to the United States that they were no longer capable of bearing the burden they had assumed in Greece. At the same time steps were being taken for the granting of independence to India and the liquidation of other parts of the British Empire.

Under these conditions the American Secretary of State Marshall suggested that the European nations inventory their needs and that the United States would try to supply the essential needs for which they could not pay. Thus, in the summer of 1947, Britain and France extended invitations to the European nations to send representatives to Paris to draw up a program for economic cooperation and a list of needs to be presented to the United States. The Soviet bloc nations, at Moscow's insistence, did not attend, and the Western European nations meeting in Paris set up the Committee of European Cooperation. The committee, working hastily, drew up a list of needs which envisioned a payment deficit of some 29 billion dollars which would have to be met by the United States.

The suggestions met with much opposition both in Europe and the United States, and it was largely the Communist coup in Czechoslovakia which galvanized Congress into appropriating the funds for this so-called Marshall Plan, or European Recovery Program. The intention was to establish a unified European market of almost 300 million persons in which eventually all tariffs would be abolished. The stimulus to the European economy given by the Marshall Plan and the success of the plan can be measured from the statistics in table 9.

9. RAW STEEL PRODUCTION, 1937–1949
(In millions of metric tons)

Country	1937	1947	1949
Great Britain	13.2	12.9	15.8
France	7.9	5.7	9.1
Belgium-Luxemburg	6.4	4.6	6.1
West Germany	19.8 (all of Germany)	3.1	9.2

Source: United Nations, *Statistical Yearbook for 1949–1950*, table 109.

Industrial production in general had risen in Western Europe in relationship to 1937 as shown in table 10. The table illustrates also the increased electrical energy required by growing industry and consumer demands.

Yet, despite these substantial rises in British production and the recovery taking place on the Continent, especially Bizonia, which was a good augur for the revival of international trade, British goods were still not competitive. The British government was forced to restrict food imports in an austerity program and in 1949 to devalue the pound from more than $4. to only $2.80. In addition, the government pushed ahead with its nationalization program of many of Britain's basic industries and utilities.

10. INDUSTRIAL AND ELECTRICAL PRODUCTION, 1937–1949

Country	Percent of 1937 production		Electrical output (In billion KWH)		
	1946	1949	1937	1946	1949
Belgium	72	94	5.5	6.2	8.2
France	73	112	20.1	23.0	30.0
Bizonia (Germany)	34	89	49.0	21.8	35.7
Netherlands	75	127	3.5	3.6	6.3
Great Britain	90	116	24.2	42.7	50.6

Source: UN *Yearbook* 1949–50, tables 39, 122.

The result was that in many respects, living standards in Great Britain at mid-century still were lower than they had been before the war. Food consumption in 1947–48, for example, was only 93 percent of 1934–38 levels, and in 1948–49, it was only 92 percent of prewar averages.

Thus, as Britain entered the second half of the century, much had been done and was being done to improve social conditions there, and industrial output had risen above the prewar figures. However, the basic problems of increasing exports enough to pay for the standard of living most Britons deemed essential had not been met. Many food products, including even tea, were rationed. As the British noticed that even West Germany alone, shattered in war, was now producing more than all of Germany had produced before the war, dissatisfaction grew and the Labour government lost the general elections to the Conservatives headed by Winston Churchill.

France

Once the Allies had decided that Germany would be allowed to revive her industry, the recovery of Germany took place at a much faster rate than did that of France; however, it was French recovery that the British and Americans hoped would lead to the stabilization of Continental politics and economics. And on the surface it would appear that the outlook for France in the postwar period should not have been bad. Certainly, France had suffered frightful devastation; however, France was a comparatively wealthy country with a balanced economy, and since she had been granted the administration of the Saar, she had virtually all the basic ingredients she needed. Once wartime damages had been repaired, France could produce nearly all the food products she needed; she was not dependent on either extensive exports or foreign investments to make ends meet, as were the British. However, France had tremendous political problems which Britain did not have. France had been defeated. Her entire territory had been occupied. Respect for the institutions of government, low even in the prewar period, virtually evaporated during the war. Millions of Frenchmen had honestly supported the Pétain regime, believing it to be the legitimate government of France. A comparatively small number had supported General de Gaulle from the beginning. However, his following grew tremendously during the war, though to what extent he had popular support within the country itself was not really known. Under wartime occupation conditions, people could not trust each other, for the Nazis had willing and voluntary collaborators in France itself. In the period following the Nazi victory until the German attack on Russia, the French Communist party, at least officially, supported the Moscow line that this was an imperialist war and that the British should conclude it as quickly as possible. In the summer of 1941, following the German invasion of Russia, the Communist party switched its line and began actively to organize an underground resistance to the Germans. This underground had nothing to do with the Gaullist underground army, and established its own organization, the FTP (Francs-Tireurs-Partisans). Because of Communist experiences in conspiracy and underground work), the Communist role in the resistance movement soon became extremely important, so much so that there was some concern, based on the experience of other underground movements, that the Communists, being better organized and disciplined, could take over the leadership of the resistance movement and eliminate those who could be dangerous opponents to them. Some of the most influential Western advisers even felt that General de Gaulle would be repudiated by both the Left and the Right when he returned to France.

The Communists ignored Allied requests not to act until Allied forces had landed, and in September 1943, acting in close cooperation with General Giraud, heir to Admiral Darlan as commander of North Africa, they seized the island of Corsica just in advance of commando landings there. They then carried out a wave of executions of "Fascist sympathizers" which, of course, included their enemies as well as Fascists. Similar kinds of actions seen also in other underground movements were repeated on a larger scale when, after the Allies landed in France itself, there were many thousands of victims of such summary justice.

Although it was not certain that General de Gaulle's committee would be accepted by the resistance movements when it landed in France, the merger in 1943 of his committee with the North African administration headed by General Giraud had given it a more solid base of operations. A provisional consultative assembly representing various resistance movements of metropolitan France was established in Algiers, and this greatly enhanced the prestige of the general. Upon the Allied invasion of France in June 1944, this committee moved to France and became the nucleus of a provisional government.

General de Gaulle had not been welcomed in North Africa, and the Allies had found it expedient to recognize first Darlan and, after his assassination, General Giraud as the head of the Algerian administration. The merger of de Gaulle's committee with Giraud's North African administration in June 1943, after six months of bickering and political maneuvering, had given the committee a more solid base of operations and greatly enhanced its prestige. A provisional consulative assembly representing the various resistance movements in France was established in Algiers, and this added still further to the General's prestige and claim for leadership in postwar France. On June 3, 1944, three days before the Allied invasion of France, de Gaulle's committee renamed itself the Provisional Government of the French Republic and moved to metropolitan France shortly after the successful landings. By the end of October, the forces of the resistance were ordered incorporated into the regular army. Although the Communists and certain other groups did not like this idea, it apparently did meet with the approval of the majority of Frenchmen. The demise of these factional paramilitary forces meant that the future governmental set-up would be arrived at by the ballot, or possibly by political maneuvering, rather than by a Greek-type civil war.

In the political maneuvering which followed, there were strong attempts by the Communists and the Left Socialists to induce the Socialists to merge all the resistance groups into one. Had such a merger occurred it is possible that the Communists could have controlled this movement and used it as the springboard for the seizure of political power, with no need to appeal to the electorate. However, the majority of Socialists sided with the non-Communist groups to defeat this and other proposals of this type favored by the Communists. In the elections held under the provisional government in October 1945, the vote was split pretty evenly among three major groups, the Socialists, the Communists and the MRP or Christian Democrats. De Gaulle was proclaimed the head of the government and representatives of these three largest parties held ministries in his administration. Many reforms were carried out such as the nationalization of utilities, credit, insurance, and certain services, moves which gained de Gaulle the support of many Socialists even on other issues.

The installation of the de Gaulle coalition had given some hope for stability, and at first recovery was not too bad, everything considered. By 1946 production had reached almost three-fourths of prewar levels, and it was hoped that a bumper crop would improve matters greatly for 1947. However, the existence of a strong black market was hurting French recovery prospects. During the Nazi occupation it had even been considered patriotic to help oneself by selling and buying on the black market, for anything that discomfited the Germans was patriotic. Once the war was over and the tremendous shortages continued it was difficult to impose the discipline necessary to bring to an end the black marketing of goods and services needed to improve France's economic position. In addition, by December 1946 France was beginning to face expenses in attempting to reassert her prewar position in Indo-China, or Vietnam. These were to cause expenditures which the war-impoverished state could ill afford.

Just when it appeared that Western Europe and France might be working themselves out of the morass of postwar difficulties, they were struck by the terrible winter of 1947, already referred to in connection with its effects on Britain. Production was slowed, crop damage was tremendous;

11. FRENCH INDUSTRIAL PRODUCTION, 1937–1949

Year	Steel (In millions of metric tons)	Electricity (In billion kilowatt-hours)	Percentage of 1937 industrial production
1937	7.9	20.1	100
1946	4.4	23.0	73
1949	9.1	30.0	112

Source: UN *Yearbook* 1949–50, tables 39, 109, 122.

France alone lost an estimated three to four million acres of winter wheat, thus necessitating the importation of several hundreds of millions of dollars of wheat.

Nevertheless, the genuine rise in productivity, partially as a result of the Marshall Plan, enabled the nation to move forward. The figures in table 11 indicate clearly that French production was rising, and this was perhaps the key reason for the failure of the Communists and other extremist parties to gain more ground. However, the continuing drain on the economy caused by France's overseas commitments resulted in the squandering of much of this gain, and the standard of living did not improve to the extent that would otherwise have been possible.

A good part of the increased production was going into the replacement of materials and goods which had been wiped out during the war. And though the larger and more efficient industrial plants were good omens for the future, this did not immediately translate into improved standards of living.

One of the greatest handicaps to postwar European recovery was the coal shortage, since coal was still used for virtually all sources of power, for running the locomotives, for electric generating plants, and for heat. In Great Britain, worn-out machinery and the exhaustion of the richer seams, combined with a shortage of coal miners to keep production down. In France, too, the situation was not too good. Many of the prewar miners had been Poles who were repatriated. German prisoners who had been forced to work in the mines immediately following the war were also repatriated, and many of the foremen and mine officials were dismissed for alleged collaboration with the Nazis during the war. It was difficult to get Frenchmen to go into the mines, many of the better seams of which, as in England, had already been exhausted. In addition, a large number of the union leaders of the miners were Communist sympathizers and called crippling strikes in 1946–47. These strikes were politically motivated, but, nevertheless, got miner support. In Germany, too, in the years following the war, the mines suffered from a lack of workers caused by the repatriation of foreign workers and the retention of many German miners as prisoners. In addition, there was little real incentive for the German coal miners to produce in the commodities-short Germany of the postwar period. Thus, in 1948 France, Britain, Belgium, and Germany were still producing less coal than they had in the prewar period, whereas Poland, now in possession of mines in formerly German territory, was exceeding prewar production.

Germany

Of all the major European countries, none had suffered the frightful devastation and losses that Germany had. During the first five years of fighting, German losses both in manpower and property had been large enough. However, much of the material loss had been made good by expropriations in one form or another from the occupied territories. In the last year of the war, and particularly the last four and five months, Germany had had total war come home to her. Cologne, Hamburg, Essen, Berlin, and other major centers had been the target of repeated air raids, some by as many as a thousand bombers. In the closing months of the war Dresden had been virtually obliterated in an attack more costly in life than the atomic bombs on Japan. Berlin and scores of other cities which had been heavily damaged in air raids were shattered in the final *Goetterdaemmerung* of street fighting. Hitler had ordered that all supplies, warehouses, installations, etc., be destroyed, not only so that the victorious Allies could not use them but also to serve almost as a funeral pyre for the German race which had not shown itself capable of rising to the heights he had set for it. Though the commands were by no means completely carried out, German supplies were almost completely exhausted by the end of the war.

Millions of hungry, destitute refugees were pouring into the Western zones of Germany from areas in the East. Motor and train transport for civilians had come to a halt, and the roads were clogged with refugees, many pushing their few belongings in wheelbarrows. For perhaps the first time in history a modern state had just ceased to exist. There was no central government. In addition to the heavy physical losses and the realization that all the sacrifices had been in vain, came the knowledge, of which many were only dimly aware previously, that the Nazis, by their bestiality in occupied countries and especially in the concentration camps, had so darkened the German name that Germany was heartily disliked, even hated, throughout much of the world. In the strained conditions prevailing during the period of the collapse and occupation, many people had been shown in their worst colors.

Thus, as the German looked about him in 1945–46, he saw his country divided into four zones. Austria, which he had been led to believe was also a part of the fatherland, had been set up as a separate state, though also under Big Four occupation; East Prussia and the Sudetenland had not only been lost, but the millions of German residents there had had to flee, fortunate if they could carry any belongings with them. Millions of other Germans, residents of Posen, Silesia, and such cities as Stettin and Breslau had also been forced to join in the mass flood of refugees. Some ten million refugees had flooded into the Western zones of Germany. These Western zones which had had a population of less than forty million and now suddenly had to support almost fifty million persons, were themselves, however, the scenes of frightful devastation. The greater parts of Frankfurt, Essen, Cologne, Hamburg, Munich, Nuernberg, and scores of other cities had been battered into heaps of rubble and gutted buildings. Several million soldiers had been killed, other millions wounded, and still other millions were in capitivity; and of those in Soviet captivity there was no knowing when or if they would be released. Indeed, of the approximately one and a half million German prisoners in Russia, only a handful ever returned, and even many of those who did return were released only five or six years after the war. Money was virtually worthless; there were almost no products to be bought. Toothpaste, bicycles, radios, nails, soap, handkerchiefs, shoes, and clothes of any type were not available on the open market. Food, which was strictly rationed, was technically supposed to amount to between 1000 and 1500 calories a day; however, shortages did develop and often even these meager rations were not available. Added to this physical burden was the mental one. For as the atrocity stories came to light, they revealed that Germany, which had surrendered unconditionally, had not only lost her material wealth but her honor as well. In addition, the Allied authorities had promised to rid the country of Nazism, and in their attempts to do so were combing the country for former members of the Nazi party. Because of the nature of the undertaking and the difficulty of establishing good general criteria, many of the least guilty Nazis, those who had only joined the party to stay in their positions, were often penalized more heavily than persons whose offenses had been of a much more serious nature. Nevertheless, the de-Nazification campaign helped still further to paralyze the country. At the same time, the attempts to reestablish the economy and the currency on a firm basis were being undermined by the Russians, who were printing marks without any regard to the effect it would have on either morale or production.

As the German looked into the future, it seemed entirely possible that the Saar, and possibly even the Ruhr, would be permanently detached from Germany and that the Morgenthau Plan, relegating Germany to an agricultural land, would be carried out. Added to this burden was the realization that many things in which he might formerly have believed were now shown to have been rotten. The Americans even introduced a policy of nonfraternization for their soldiers in Germany. American soldiers were not to have personal contact with these perpetrators of atrocities. If at this dark moment an idealist did not have a religious faith, it was indeed hard to have anything solid on which to grasp for moral support.

Throughout 1945–46, gradually the rubble was cleared away; bombed-out families were reunited; electrical, postal, and rail service restored; and a number of plants put back into production, though at the same time some plants were being dismantled and being sent to Russia for reparations. Throughout 1946 and 1947, despite these gains in getting normal civilian life back into operation, the material situation had been getting even worse. The severe winter of 1947 also dealt a hard blow to recovery. During this period, however, there had been taking place a gradual change in the attitude of the occupying powers, and with the go-ahead to German industry presaged by Secretary of State Byrne's

Stuttgart speech, and the enormous lift given to enterprise by the introduction of a new currency in 1948, the West German economy began to revive at a remarkable rate. By the early 1950s, it had already passed the prewar levels; millions of returning prisoners had been assimilated into the economy, as had the millions of refugees, and virtually all of the displaced persons resident in Germany at war's end had either returned home or found new homes. In addition, a new democratic federal government had been established, a government which was gradually gaining acceptance. Though hostility to Germany ran deep in postwar Europe, the other West European nations were gradually getting ready to include Germany in their plans and hopes for an integrated European economy and possibly, an integrated European political and defense unit.

Of the major nations outside of the Soviet bloc, France had been the slowest to accept the revived Germany. French policy had been against the reestablishment of a single government for all of Germany, and the French hoped to attach both the Saar and the Rhineland to France. Gradually, however, French policy underwent some changes and by 1950 the French were ready to have West Germany included in a West European economic unit, though they were still not ready to have a rearmed Germany. In 1950, Robert Schuman, French foreign minister, put forth the plan which bears his name and which was intended to create a single market out of the territories of the member countries. Basically, this plan recognized the fact that none of the countries of Western Europe is self-sufficient in raw materials for its steel industry, though together they possess enough coal, ore, and scrap to produce iron and steel. France needs coke from Germany, Germany needs ores from France and Sweden, Belgium needs French iron ores, etc. This Schuman Plan, which was finally ratified by France, Germany, Italy, and the Benelux countries in 1952, was regarded as a giant step forward not only to an economic union, but also to some type of European federation – a sort of United States of Europe, a U.S.E. which would have far more inhabitants than either the USSR or the U.S.A. Many of the so-called "good Europeans," the Monets, the Schumans, and the disenchanted nationalists, especially in Germany, were ready to work hard for just such a confederation project. For many of these persons this Schuman Plan and the Iron and Coal Union which it established was regarded as a first step in that direction. Basically, the plan created a single market out of the territories of the member countries in which all producers would have free and equal access to raw materials at the same prices, except for the differences in transportation costs. Subsidies and government aid to coal and steel industries plus certain unfair competition methods were abandoned. It was hoped thereby to create a market for some 270 million persons in Western Europe. It was by such steps that Germany was being integrated into a Western European economy.

The attempt to set up a European defense community to include Germany, rather than just a European economic community, however, ran across stronger French delaying tactics, and it was not until several more years had passed that a compromise plan was finally adopted whereby German forces would participate in the defensive organization. In late 1950, as a result of the Korean War, the foreign ministers of the Western powers resolved to end the state of war with Germany and agreed that the participation of West German forces in an integrated European defense was desirable. However, the plan was rejected by the French Assembly in 1954, and it was only a compromise plan which included the German Federal Republic as an equal member of NATO that was finally accepted. Thus, it was not until 1955, when the sovereignty of the *Bundesrepublik* was finally recognized, that Germany became the fifteenth member of NATO.

During this period, the West German economy continued to boom. In 1950, there had still been more than a million and a half unemployed in the *Bundesrepublik*. In 1955 this

12. GERMAN INDUSTRIAL PRODUCTION, 1949–1956
(In millions of tons)

Year	Steel	Cement	Sulphuric acid
1949	9	9	1.1
1956	23	20	2.5

Source: UN *Yearbook* 1954, table 94; UN *Yearbook* 1957, tables
97, 108, 112.

was down to about 600,000, and by 1960 there was an acute
labor shortage. During the same period that the number of
unemployed had dropped from over a million, the number
of employed had risen from 13.8 million in 1950 to 17.2
million in 1955. Between 1948 and 1954, real wages almost
doubled. An example of production growth during those
years can be taken from table 12.

While German industrial production was rising steadily,
agricultural output had also increased. By the period 1948–
52, German farmers were already producing more than in
the prewar period, and in the succeeding four years agricultural output continued to rise as shown in table 13.

Electrical production was up from 39,100 million kilowatt-hours in 1949 to 85,100 in 1956. Everywhere the story
was the same. The recovery of the German economy, the

13. GERMAN CROP PRODUCTION, 1934–1957
(In thousands of metric tons)

Years	Wheat	Rye
1934–38	2,505	3,081
1948–52	2,656	3,042
1953–57	3,356	3,710

Source: UN *Yearbook 1957*, tables 12, 13.

tremendous rises in production, the stability of the German currency, and the tremendous amount of reconstruction and new building soon had many foreigners inquiring as to who had actually lost the war anyway. The relative passivity of the German worker organizations and the German workers during the late 1940s and 1950s—passivity relative to either France or Britain—was one very important reason for the continued boom there. However, despite the tremendous industrial advances, the Germans as a whole had a long way to come to overtake the English in providing many of the essentials which ordinarily enter into determining the standard of living.

14. PERSONS PER DWELLING IN GERMANY

Territory	1939	1946
Federal Republic	3.8	5.5
DDR	3.3	4.3
Berlin	2.8	3.4

Source: Encyclopaedia Britannica, 1961 ed., s.v. "Germany."

Thus, in the *Bundesrepublik*, almost one of four dwellings was destroyed, and in East Germany, the DDR, about one in eight. The result was that the number of persons per dwelling went up as depicted in table 14.

An official survey held in 1950 revealed that of the almost ten million dwellings in the Federal Republic (9.9 million), something like 550,000 were still emergency or temporary structures. In other words, in 1950 there were fewer dwellings in the Federal Republic than there had been in 1939, despite the fact that the population being housed there had risen by perhaps as many as twelve million persons. Since there had been virtually no new construction for a period of ten years, it also meant that a large number of houses which should have or would have been replaced in that time had not been, and that the other housing was ten years older. In the 1950s, a record number of new housing units were

being built in Germany—518,000 in 1953 and 541,000 in
1954. By 1954 a total of three million units had been built
since the war; however, there was still a tremendous housing shortage in Germany.

While West Germany was beginning to recover from the
shattering effects of the war, the Soviets were proceeding
toward the establishment of a Communist government in
Central Germany (*Mitteldeutschland*), now often called
East Germany or the DDR. This area, excluding Berlin, had
in October 1946 a population of some 17.3 million persons.
In April of that same year, the Soviet military administration had forced a fusion of the Socialist party in their zone
with the Communist party into the SED, or the Socialist
Unity (Einheit) Party. They had hoped to attract the large
Social Democratic Party in the West into this union and
then, on the model of Eastern Europe, to gradually take
over all important posts in the party, eliminating those Socialist leaders who proved unpliable, while keeping a handful of the others both for show and useful administrative
purposes. Otto Grotewohl, the Social Democratic leader in
the Eastern zone, accepted the merger; Kurt Schumacher,
the SD leader in the Western zones, did not. Land reform
was carried out in the Eastern zone; the Communists at
this stage were holding back on collectivization and hoping
by the distribution of more land to the farmers to gain some
more support for their party. By early 1948 steps were being
taken to set up the DDR, and the cadre of an army was already being formed with the organization of the *Bereitschaften*, or Alert Units, which by 1950 were being organized as
regular military units. On October 7, 1949, a few days after
the establishment of the Bonn government, the government
of the DDR was set up in the Berlin suburb of Pankow. At
the same time the Soviet Union continued to drain their
zone by taking reparation payments in a variety of ways.
According to Stalin, reparations had by 1950 amounted to
3.7 billion dollars; however, this figure did not include req-
uisitions taken prior to the Potsdam meeting.

In early 1950 Stalin, as a further measure of support for

the government of the DDR, announced a reduction in reparations by 50 percent to only another 3.1 billion. By 1952
the DDR set up a cleared three-mile-wide frontier strip between their zone and that of the the Federal Republic. Except in Berlin, it was impossible to cross from one zone to
another; thus, the Eastern citizens were to be cut off from
the contaminating influence of the now-prospering West.

In the same year, 1952, the armed forces of the DDR
were further increased and conscription into their paramilitary forces was introduced. Although there had been
many Soviet-type measures already introduced into the
Soviet zone, the pace began to increase in the early 1950s.
By mid-1952, collectivization was introduced into agriculture, and Soviet-style collective farms of a *Kolkhoz* type
were set up. The judicial system was revamped on the Soviet model, and production norms were introduced into the
factories. The unpopularity of these measures and of the
regime was demonstrated in June 1953 by the large-scale
risings in East Berlin, Halle, and other Soviet-zone cities.
Berlin was actually in the hands of demonstrators hostile
to the government for a number of hours. Then Soviet tanks
were brought in and the previous order restored. The sud-
denness and spontaneity of the demonstrations was a warning to the regime, and a clear indication that the mass propaganda apparatus alone could not win popular support. A
number of concessions were therefore made, and a slow-
down on certain unpopular measures was introduced. Nevertheless, with more than twenty Soviet divisions in the zone,
there was no possibility that the regime could be threatened
by internal forces.

Undeniably the regime did gain adherents throughout
the 1950s, yet its claim of winning more than 90 percent
of the vote in the elections is open to serious question when
it is noted that prior to 1961 about three million persons,
or about one-sixth of the population, abandoned their homes
and belongings and fled the East zone, despite the increasing difficulties of doing so. The construction of the Berlin

Wall in 1961 made such escape virtually impossible. Actually this drain of manpower in the East zone was strongly felt in the East German economy.

Throughout the 1950s and until the erection of the Berlin Wall, therefore, West Germany exerted a strong pull on the inhabitants of the East zone. It is rather easy to see that even aside from political considerations and the hostility toward the Soviets felt by many Germans, the relatively better living conditions in the Western zones and the rapidly rising prosperity of West Germany represented a threat to the stability of the East zone. The glaring differences between the two zones were also bad for the prestige of the world Communist movement.

Courtesy of the German Tourist Information Office

Air view of Berlin

The rising industrial and economic strength of Germany had another great significance. Germany's recovery and the continued instability of France had led by the early 1950s to a great change in American thinking about what would constitute a stable Europe. The United States still hoped for some type of European federation; however, in the realm of the practical political considerations which had been engendered by the Korean War, American planning for the physical and territorial defense of Europe began more and more to be centered on Germany, rather than France. In 1945 it had been hoped that French recovery would again give the French the ability to call more than five million men to the colors and would be a strong force for European stability. At that time it was still the American view that measures should be taken to prevent a resurgent Germany from ever again threatening France.

By 1950 it was a possible Soviet aggression, not a revived West Germany, which worried the United States. For many in France, the main problem still seemed to be a possible resurgent Germany; memories of the occupation were too recent, and they felt that the United States had reversed the priorities. By this time they felt that economic stability was just coming to France; now, as a result of the Korean War, the United States was urging them to spend more for armaments and to accept a rearmed Germany into the European defense community. During the late war and postwar period, France had been dependent upon the United States and Great Britain for military support; in the postwar period she had been dependent upon the United States for economic support. This necessity of being in a pliant and almost suppliant role rankled French sensibilities. For a century and a half intellectuals had played a greater role in France than in most nations, and many of these intellectuals were hostile in a number of respects to the United States, whom they blamed for a host of problems, some with much or partial justification, others perhaps out of a certain need for self-justification. Thus, American prosperity and materialism was condemned as though this had contributed to what they called a lack of culture in the United States, even though that prosperity had made possible a variety of cultural achievements and institutions which otherwise might not have come into being. In many respects it seemed that they were blaming the United States for the twentieth century and were seeking in "culture" psychological refuge for their lack of progress and prosperity.

At any rate, the French regarded the main European priority to be the creation of a united Europe with Great Britain. After the formation of a European army it was thought that German contingents could be included if necessary. In any type of united Europe they felt that English participation was essential to counterbalance Germany. For this reason the failure of Britain to join in the Steel and Coal Union was regarded as a great blow. Dependent upon the United States for financial support, the various French governments felt constrained to give lip-support to American promptings, but at home they did not really push the European army and the National Assembly stalled. Nevertheless, the growing French commitment in Indo-China and the minor rearmament for NATO again caused an inflationary spiral which the increased production resulting from success of the Monet and Marshall Plans had brought to a halt. The inflationary spiral contributed to the inability of the French governments to solve their financial problems and therefore contributed to their instability. For France could not reconcile herself to being a second-rate power, and in trying to play the role of a first-class power she was inevitably being dragged down to a third-rate one.

In France itself, the United States and its alliances were under attack not only by the Communists, but also by French nationalist forces; the former accused the United States of supporting colonialism and the latter resented the fact that the United States did not support France in the international diplomatic arena over North Africa and Indo-China. Meanwhile, the political and economic problems and the politi-

cal dissensions, which arose largely out of France's international commitments, obscured the fact that the country
was making very genuine progress. The rapidity with which
one government succeeded another, the great number of
strikes, and the war in Indo-China all tended to lower French
prestige abroad, whereas at home respect for the government dwindled as most Frenchmen did not realize the real
advances being made. Thus, just before the 1956 elections,
a public opinion poll taken in France showed that only 19
percent of French peasants, only 17 percent of agricultural
workers, only 23 percent of industrial workers, and only 19
percent of retired persons and pensioners believed themselves better off than five years ago. In all, 22 percent believed themselves worse off than five years earlier, and 25
percent believed themselves better off. The improvements
had obviously not been rapid enough to convince the average Frenchman. Yet the figures for France show that conditions were not only improving, but improving at a faster
rate. Thus, for example, where there had been about 100,000
dwelling units constructed in the period 1945–50, in 1955
alone there were more than double that amount. In 1952
there were 84,000 units; 115,000 units in 1953; 162,000
units in 1954; and 210,000 units in 1955; and in the year
of the poll, there were 260,000 units constructed.

While this rate of construction was lower than that of
Germany, it was still a remarkable achievement, particularly in comparison with the 1930–50 period. By 1956
France, whose population alone of the major and minor
European populations had shown a decline between 1900
and 1945, now had a higher birthrate than that of either
Germany or Great Britain. Steel production, which was running between six and seven million tons in 1951, came to
13.4 million tons in 1956. Electrical output, which had been
38,851 million kilowatt-hours in 1948, was 53,829 in 1956.
Thus, in 1957 agricultural production was up 25 percent
over 1949; industrial production was up 46 percent. By any
type of index the worker was sharing somewhat in this in-

Courtesy of the French Government Tourist Office

Île de la Cité, Paris

crease; however, figures also revealed that the average
Frenchman was spending something like eleven francs out
of every hundred for alcohol, while spending only seven
francs for health and five for housing. Yet the nation suffered from the malaise of unresolved political problems. The
government was running at a deficit of 570 billion francs
in 1950; 504 billion francs in 1951; 872 billion francs in
1952; 877 billion in 1953; and 780 billion in 1955. By 1952,
at the peak of inflation, prices were 40 percent over those
of 1950. The rising military budget had much to do with
this. Thus, whereas in 1948, the expense of the Civil Service had been more than twice that of the military, by 1952
the two were about even.

The general elections of 1954, returning an Assembly which selected Pierre Mendès-France as prime minister by an unprecedented two-to-one margin, gave the latter an exceptional opportunity to tackle some of France's major problems. The surrender of the French forces at Dien Bien Phu in 1954 indicated clearly that the French could not win the military war in Indo-China, and Mendès-France did succeed in extricating France from that imbroglio. However, scarcely was France extricated from the Far East when the North

15. FRENCH NATIONAL EXPENDITURES, 1948–1952
(In billions of francs)

	1948	1951	1952
Civil services	681	1297	1394
Capital expenditures	578	755	809
Military expenditures	332	857	1269

Source: Edgar S. Furniss, Jr., *France, Troubled Ally* (New York: Harper, 1960), p. 156.

African caldron in Morocco, Tunis, and finally Algeria began to boil. Mendès-France fell, but his successor, Edgar Faure, extricated France from Morocco and Tunis. However, the French Assembly drew the line at Algeria, which France regarded as an integral part of the nation itself. Soon France had half a million soldiers in Algeria, fighting the guerrilla forces which were being supplied by Egypt and to a lesser extent by Tunis, and which were using Morocco and Tunisia as staging, training, and shelter areas in their incursions into French Algeria.

The USSR

Meanwhile, great changes had been taking place in the USSR and consequently in the satellite nations of Eastern Europe. In 1941, as Nazi troops plunged deeply into Russia,

Stalin had made appeals to Russian patriotism and to old Russian virtues. The Communist international had been abolished and even the pressures against religion had been relaxed, and again there were many who believed and hoped that Russia's revolution was over, that the Thermidor had come. However, upon the victorious conclusion of the war, Stalin made it plain that there would be no let-up in the tempo. The Russian revolution was to go on. The Russian people were to be driven on to new productive goals. The Fourth Five-Year Plan for the years 1946–50 set as its goal not only the reconstruction of areas and industrial enterprises damaged by the war, but the surpassing of prewar production. Stalin announced that Soviet industrial output must be tripled by 1960 to make the Soviet Union "ready for any eventuality." By that time, said Stalin, the USSR should be producing sixty million tons of steel, and other heavy industrial output was to rise accordingly.

It would appear that by 1950 the Fourth Five-Year Plan had succeeded in greatly boosting Russian heavy industrial production, and steel output was probably approaching thirty million tons. However, the announced agricultural and consumer output goals, being of lower priority, were not reached. In order to enforce that discipline and sacrifice which Stalin deemed necessary to attain these production goals, governmental controls were kept as tight as ever, and in some respects actually tightened. The capital necessary for the expansion again was to be obtained by reinvesting virtually all surplus Russian production at the cost of immense privations for the average Soviet citizen. At the same time, huge amounts of capital and goods were also being extracted from the satellite empire.

Vast amounts of war reparations were extracted directly from Hungary, Rumania, and East Germany with no official accounting. By the formal treaties of peace, various sums were obtained from the above states and also from Finland, Austria, and Italy. The trade agreements which were signed with the nations under Soviet control usually resulted in

advantages to the Soviet Union; one of the reasons for the
later Soviet-Yugoslav split was the refusal of Marshal Tito
to go along with such trade agreements. These enforced
reparations were an enormous boost to the Soviet economy
in the postwar years; however, the main element in the push
forward was still the sacrifice of the Russian people.

While controls were being tightened on the economic
front, party discipline, political orthodoxy, and police controls were also tightened. In the late forties it was unwise
and even dangerous for a Soviet citizen to have foreign
acquaintances or contacts. Travel to and from the USSR,
except by official delegations, was kept to a minimum.

In the arts the new tone was given by Andrei Zhdanov,
secretary of the Leningrad party, who in 1946 was put in
charge of tightening ideological controls on Soviet authors,
scientists and creative artists after the wartime relaxations.
This crackdown on the arts has been called the *Zhdanovschina* as opposed to the *Yezhovschina* terror of the late
thirties. The principles of Socialist realism were to be enforced in the arts. The arts were to be put in the service of
the Socialist camp; bourgeois music and literature had no
place in the Soviet system. For the next seven years until
the death of Stalin in 1953, this was the guiding principle
for the artists behind the Iron Curtain.

Nationalities whose loyalty during the war had seemed
questionable were punished. Thus, the Crimean Tartars, the
Chechens of Daghestan in the Caucasus, Germans, especially in the Volga regions, and others were uprooted from
regions where they had lived for centuries and scattered
throughout areas of Siberia. As Professor Seton-Watson
states, if the British had adopted Soviet policy toward nationalities they would have executed or imprisoned all members of the Burmese army who fought alongside the Japanese and deported and scattered the population throughout
the Arctic. It has been estimated that about one-third of the
Baltic population was deported.

At war's end there were apparently something like five

million Soviet citizens living in Germany, either as prisoners or voluntary escapees; about three million of these were in zones not occupied by the Soviet forces. As a result of wartime agreements with the Soviets, many of these persons were forcibly repatriated to the USSR. At that time it was naïvely thought in many circles in the West that anybody who had taken advantage of the opportunity presented by the German advance to flee to Germany was a Nazi sympathizer. About one million persons, nonetheless, did manage to escape repatriation, and dispersed in the ensuing years, penniless, without means, and usually with a serious language handicap, to those nations which would accept them.

During the war, although millions of Russians had fought valiantly, millions of others had surrendered in what must have been the greatest mass surrenders of any war in history. Millions of others had obviously welcomed the Germans as liberators, while others had voluntarily joined the German forces, only to be rebuffed by the Nazis until too late to influence the course of the war. Millions of other Russians had been abroad for the first time. Though the Europe they had seen was war-ravaged, it was a Europe in which, contrary to what they had been told, the standard of living was vastly superior to that of the USSR. The government felt that a huge campaign of ideological rehabilitation was necessary. In part, this ideological rehabilitation was done through the party apparatus and party propaganda. In part, it was done through the exaltation of nationalism. It had been Russian nationalism, not communism, which had saved the state. Again in this war, nationalism had shown itself as perhaps the strongest force for which a people will fight. Communist doctrine had said that all peoples are equal. However, the Russian people were now to be more equal than others. They were singled out for special praise, while certain of the others were to be punished. In 1956 Khrushchev was to state that it was only the fact that the Ukrainians were so numerous which prevented them (the

Ukrainians) from sharing the fate of the deported Tartars. To reinforce the feeling of nationalism, school textbooks were to be rewritten to show the tremendous contribution of Russian thinkers and inventors to scientific and cultural advance. In some respects this was carried to a ludicrous extent. A current witticism which circulated in Moscow, though somewhat dangerous to repeat, was, "We invented everything, but the Americans have everything."

In a dictatorship, much of what occurs is understandable only when the dictator himself is understood. Much of what happened in Russia in the late 1940s and early 1950s is understandable only in light of an understanding of Stalin. In those last years there is much about him and internal party politics which is clouded in mystery and quite difficult to understand. It does seem certain, however, that Stalin was preparing for another tremendous purge on the order of that of the mid-thirties when he met his death.

First there had been the rather sudden death of Zhdanov and the gradual liquidation of a large part of the Leningrad party apparatus without the public knowing that this purge was taking place. It was only several years later that the names of some of the persons executed became known. For example, it was only confirmed much later that Voznesensky, former chairman of the state planning committee whose book published in 1947 had won wide praise and whose views had been condemned by the Central Committee in 1949, had been removed from his position and executed. Then had come the statements in the newspapers that the public must be vigilant, the same type of terminology which had signaled the purges of the thirties. Then had come the case of the Kremlin doctors; a number of the most important physicians in the USSR, whose services were limited to the care of the top officials of the Kremlin, were arrested and charged with all types of fantastic plots. They were accused of having injected poison into Zhdanov, of plotting to kill off the top leadership. It was also noted that most of the doctors arrested had Jewish names, and that their arrest was coupled with barbed remarks and thinly veiled anti-Semitic references in the Soviet press. Just how far this campaign might have led was anybody's guess when, in early March 1953, the world was astounded to hear of Stalin's illness and death. His death ushered in a new period in Soviet and European history. It is interesting, therefore, at this time to evaluate the progress the USSR had made since the war.

By the time of Stalin's death in 1953, the Soviet Union had not only repaired virtually all the physical damage suffered by the war, but had raised production levels in almost all fields of industry to far beyond what they had been. The USSR was by this time an atomic power; her technological institutes were turning out scientists and engineers at an increasing rate. The economies of the East European countries with their almost one hundred million people had been integrated with that of the Soviet to the advantage of the latter. Anti-Soviet Ukrainian partisan groups, active for several years after the war, had been crushed, and millions of persons whose loyalty for one reason or another had been suspected were in scattered concentration camps, mostly in Siberia. Undoubtedly, there were millions of Soviet citizens who were dissatisfied that little of the production increase for which so many sacrifices had been made had filtered down to the people. On the other hand, there were other millions of Soviet citizens who were enthusiastic about the enormous strides the country had made and for whom the production figures were justification enough for virtually any excesses of the regime. The increase in production figures is shown in table 16.

In agriculture the yields were not so impressive. However, these comparative figures were not readily available to the average Russian, and it would have been a rare individual who would publicly have pointed them out. The Russian wheat yield per acre was the lowest of any major country.

Food production was low enough to cause a semifamine in the Ukraine in 1946–47, and the food situation remained

16. SOVIET STEEL AND COAL PRODUCTION, 1939–1955

Year	Steel production (In million tons)	Coal production (In thousand tons)
1939	18	125
1946	13	114
1952	34	215
1955	45	277

Source: UN *Yearbook* 1957, tables 39, 112.

poor throughout the Stalin years. In housing, too, the situation in prewar USSR and in the 1950s showed less housing per inhabitant available in every major city than back in 1926, before the five-year plans. However, housing, clothing and a variety of diet were not important to the Red planners. Heavy industry and a host of trained technicians and scientists were what the regime wanted. In the meantime, standards of living could be sacrificed for the golden future.

When Stalin died in 1953, the Soviet Union was already the second industrial and military power in the world. She had the technicians to exploit the enormous resources of

17. WHEAT YIELD, 1949–1950
(Two-year average
in 100 kilograms per acre)

Germany	10.6
France	7.5
Canada	4.2
Yugoslavia	4.9
Hungary	5.4
United States	4.3
USSR	2.9

Source: W. S. Woytinsky and E. S. Woytinsky, *World Population and Production: Trends and Outlook* (New York: Twentieth Century, 1953), p. 546.

the country and, as already indicated, the economies of one hundred million East Europeans were integrated into that of the USSR. The imposition of Stalinist-type governments and Soviet-type collectivization had proceeded differently in the various East Central European nations.

The Eastern European Satellite Nations

During the war a national liberation committee for each East European country had been organized. The German National Liberation Committee was headed by Walter Ulbricht, the Czech by Klement Gottwald, the Polish by Jakub Berman, the Hungarian by Matyas Rakosi, the Rumanian by Anna Pauker, and the Bulgarian by George Dimitrov. Some committees served as nucleis for organizing forces among these nationals resident in the USSR; others were to serve as nuclei for governments friendly to the USSR. The Soviets then negotiated treaties with these governments. The non-Communist government of Czechoslovakia had negotiated with the Russians—they had had a long friendship with Russia—and eventually gave up Ruthenia.

In most of the Eastern nations through which the Red Army passed, the prewar regimes had not been overly popular, and people were genuinely ready to push through a number of land redistribution and other social reforms. For this reason parties wanting reforms had a good deal of support. In these countries, therefore, the Communists forced coalitions between the Socialist parties and the Communist parties in a "popular front." In all these countries the Soviet moves had been in three steps. The first was to punish the rightists and Fascists, by which many would-be foes were automatically eliminated. This was followed by the organization of coalition governments with other parties of the Left and Center. However, of the coalition parties, the Communists were usually the best organized, and had control of armed forces, the police, the justice departments, and information. Gradually, in the third phase, the other parties

Macedonia, Yugoslavia

were forced to merge with the Communist party in which a few of their leaders, such as Grotewohl in Germany, were kept along for show purposes.

By the time of the organization of the Cominform in 1948–49, all the nations in the Soviet bloc had adopted constitutions and administrations modeled on that of the USSR. After the Tito split, however, Stalin, fearful that nationalism might rear its head even among the Communist leadership of the Eastern nations, moved vigorously to prevent any such occurrence. Throughout Eastern Europe there were rather large-scale arrests and show trials of many prominent Communist leaders suspected of having nationalist, Tito-type tendencies. Among the prominent persons who fell from power in this period were Laszlo Rajk in Hungary, who was executed, and Wladislaw Gomulka in Poland, who was arrested. As Stalin had suspected the loyalties of certain nationalities during the war, at the beginning of the fifties he began to grow suspicious of the Russian Jews, or at least suspicious of many of them. The Soviet press began to carry caricatures of Jews and make barbed remarks about "homeless cosmopolitans," by which was meant the Jews.

Among the causes for this attitude were the fact that many Soviet Jews seemed to show some enthusiasm for the new state of Israel. Also, many Soviet Jews had relatives living abroad because of emigration when allowed, arrests, and wartime deportations, and flight during the war. In the Soviet Union foreign contacts of any type were suspect. The Kremlin's thinly veiled anti-Semitic campaign had its reflection in the satellites such as Czechoslovakia, where Rudolf Slansky and a number of other defendants were sentenced to death, and in Rumania, where prominent Jewish personages like Anna Pauker were forced out of positions of authority. In a number of satellites the removal of these people who had been returned to their country by Soviet bayonets helped bring the party leaders a little more support, for the new leaders were regarded somewhat as national leaders, even though they were Communists.

With the imposition of Soviet-like justice and constitutions, it was only natural that Soviet-type planning with emphasis on heavy industry and the collectivization of agriculture would be introduced into the satellites. The result of this was a raising of the worker's norm, and a shortage of agricultural and consumer products. This led to threatening discontent, which after Stalin's death was to manifest itself in several places, such as Berlin, in riots.

Thus, by the early 1950s, at the same time that Western Europe had been joining with the United States in a North Atlantic defense pact, Eastern Europe had had a series of show trials intended to crush "national" Communist leaders and to insure both the future development of the satellites along Stalinist lines and their continued cooperation with the USSR. By 1949 mainland China had been taken over by the Communists, and by the following year, British and to a lesser degree French contingents were fighting alongside the Americans and South Koreans to repel an invasion of South Korea by Communist North Korea. The USSR did not directly intervene in this Korean conflict; however, the Red Chinese did send in large numbers of troops. To most of non-Communist Europe and the United States it seemed that, with the single exception of Yugoslavia, the world was faced by a Communist monolith, with headquarters in Moscow, intent on taking over the world in one manner or another.

8

Post-Stalin Europe:
The Fifties

IN 1952, the Cold War in Europe was in full swing. Almost all of Eastern Central Europe, representing more than half of Europe's territory and virtually half its population, was under the control of the USSR. Over this vast empire one man, Joseph Stalin, was able to rule and to impress his desires and programs with the absolute power of the Eastern potentates of old. The iron curtain separating this empire from the rest of Europe had by 1952 been transformed in many places into an absolute physical barrier, with barbed wire fences, machine gun towers, and free-fire no-man's-zones just behind. In the Soviet Union and the satellites it was dangerous for persons to have foreign contacts, to be seen speaking with foreigners, or to listen to foreign radio broadcasts. The iron curtain not only was a physical barrier preventing the free flow of persons, it was also preventing the free flow of ideas. The number of Western correspondents permitted in Moscow, for example, had been cut to eight, and even these were extremely limited as to what they could see or do. By 1952 in the Far East no solution had been reached for the Korean War. In Europe itself the first stirrings of a reviving West Germany, its projected integration into the American-led North Atlantic Treaty Organization, and the setting up of American airfields within range of most important Soviet targets were further sources of aggravation of Cold-War tensions. The United States felt that the Soviets had moved into virtually all territories where there had been no Allied presence, had established their puppet regimes, disregarding the will of their peoples, and were using the resources and energies of those nations for the aggrandizement of Soviet and Communist power. The Soviets felt that the United States was trying to undermine their attempts to set up regimes friendly to themselves in bordering states and felt themselves menaced by the bases the United States was erecting within striking range of all their major centers.

In 1952 the nineteenth Russian Communist Party Congress, the first party congress since 1939, had been convened. All indications from this congress were that there was to be even more centralization in the party and a stricter control of even the lower ranks. It was suspected abroad at the time, and later confirmed by Khrushchev, that the resolutions adopted at this congress presaged a purge of the old party elite. Almost immediately after this congress, new purges began, both in the Soviet Union and in the satellites. The effects were felt even in the Communist parties abroad, such as in France, where various leaders were removed. In January 1953, as previously noted, there was the announcement in Moscow of the discovery of a fiendish plot by a number of Kremlin doctors, a plot to murder a number of leading Kremlin persons; there was a call for increased vigilance, and a mounting crescendo of warnings. What could it all mean? The similarities to the purge atmosphere of the 1930s were striking. The party leaders and army leaders could not have been oblivious to the fact that in those purges of the thirties a good share of their leadership had been liquidated.* At any rate, in 1952 the first persons

* As Bertram Wolfe has so appropriately indicated, there has never in the entire history of mankind been an army which has produced more than single isolated cases of traitors in any single generation in any general staff or officers' corps. Under these circumstances it seems amazing that believers in the Soviet system could have given credence to the idea that their system had become so much more corrupted than any other in all of history that more than 70 percent of its higher officers had been turned into traitors.

against whom the new purges were directed were the elite of the country, party officials, and officials of the non-Russian republics.

The whole campaign of vigilance and suspicion was building up when suddenly in late February it was called off. Less than two weeks later on March 4, 1953, Moscow radio broadcast the news that Stalin had suffered a stroke, and two days later his death was announced. Obviously an era had come to an end. For Stalin had impressed his will on Russia like Ivan the Terrible and Peter the Great before him.

The new leaders of the USSR moved quickly both to make sure that there would be continuity in the leadership and also to insure their own safety, which might have been in jeopardy in the purges had Stalin lived. Almost immediately Stalin's personal secretariat was abolished—this secretariat which inspired fear even in the highest men in the regime. Virtually at the same time the supreme Soviet decided not to allow the positions of head of party and head of state to be concentrated in the hands of one individual, and "collective leadership" was decided upon; Georgi Malenkov, who had seemed the likely successor to Stalin, was thus defeated in his attempt to gain control of the party apparatus and the instruments of power. The Soviet Union was to be ruled by collective leadership.

Almost simultaneously with the announcements of collective leadership and with the abolition of the Stalin private secretariat, a general amnesty was announced for many categories of prisoners. It was further announced that the Kremlin doctors had been released from detention and that the recipient of the Lenin award, whose denunciations had helped bring about their arrest, had been forced to return the medals. It was quite evident that some campaign of de-Stalinization was taking place and that the purges were over. However, in any state, and especially in a police state, whoever controls the police power rules. Thus, as long as the head of the secret police, Lavrenti Beria, retained absolute control over his own special military forces and the secret police, the other Soviet leaders could not really feel safe. In July, three months after the death of Stalin, it was announced that Beria had been arrested. His execution for antiparty and antistate activities was subsequently announced.

Meanwhile, the new regime was being faced with foreign problems of great magnitude. In mid-June the workers of East Berlin and other cities in the Soviet-established East German state had risen in resentment over many grievances, especially the imposition and increasing of Soviet-styled production norms. It was only on the second day of the disorders, after the uprising had spread and the workers had actually seized control of Berlin and several other places, that Soviet tanks were sent in to quell the risings. It was obvious to all that neither here nor in Poland had the propaganda yet produced a population friendly to the Soviets.

The fall of Beria and the dismantling of certain agencies of his apparatus meant also that the Soviet control of a number of agencies in the satellites was also to be weakened. In Russia it meant a still further releasing of political prisoners and a further relaxation of the terror. Some Soviet writers who had not dared to stray from the straitjacket of Soviet realism began to stir. A new hope was felt by many that the "thaw" of the revolution had come. *The Thaw*, the title of a work by Ilya Ehrenburg, a prominent Soviet writer and journalist, was the name given to this period of relaxation in the censorship, when for the first time in more than twenty years some Soviet writers again felt free to begin writing criticisms of shortcomings in the country and even in the system. The regime felt it could not tolerate a condition where the writers were beginning to find fault with the very system itself, and a new crackdown on the writers was instituted.

However, the new crackdowns, though serious, did not have the complete terror of Stalinist days. Though they were effective in silencing overt criticism, many writers were not completely cowed, though temporarily silenced. The succeeding fifteen to twenty years, unlike the preceding fifteen to twenty years of Socialist realism, were to see a constant pressure by a number of writers for more freedom for the creative writer. The new leadership did not pursue a steady, single-minded course either in respect to literary censorship or in respect to establishing new foreign and domestic priorities. The domestic set-up had been stamped by Stalin. Any changes meant a de-Stalinization to some degree. Yet any sudden de-Stalinization might set forces in motion which could not be controlled. In addition, many of the party leaders and the *apparatchiki* were convinced Stalinists. For this reason many of the moves of the Soviet leadership in the period from 1953 to 1956 seem contradictory, first a move away from Stalinism, then a tightening of the reins. Yet an overall glance at that period reveals a general, moderate de-Stalinization, a definite relaxation of the terror. This relaxation had its reflections in the satellite states.

This period of "thaw" and silent de-Stalinization led to a moderate relaxation of Cold-War tensions. The Korean War was brought to a conclusion; the new Soviet triumvirate met with the Western leaders in a moderately amicable mood at Geneva where a temporary solution of the Vietnam war was agreed upon. West and East were able also to agree upon a peace treaty for Austria which led in 1955 to the withdrawal of all foreign troops from that country and the reestablishment of Austrian independence. Russian leaders now even appeared in public, traveled abroad, and became human beings instead of cold portraits. Most ebullient and outstanding of this new type of leadership was Nikita Krushchev. During this period he began to stand out more and more from the collective leadership. The history of triumvirates had almost always shown that three is a crowd at the pinnacle of power, and, as the Roman triumvirates had dissolved as one man had seized power and as the Russian Communist triumvirate after Lenin's death had led to Stalin alone having power, so by 1956 Khrushchev was emerging as the most equal of the equals. He it was who in 1955 had traveled to Yugoslavia to visit with Tito to try to effect a reconciliation within the "Socialist" camp. There he had admitted the possibility of different roads to socialism. This represented a great departure from Stalinist days when Moscow was the only source of all Communist truth.

By this time as well the realities of a more complex industrial society brought on increased demands for a change in the old Stalinist bureaucratic methods of operation. There had already been some silent de-Stalinization. Obviously the renewal of relations with Tito, who had been so vilified in the Soviet and satellite press, and the change of a number of policies had led to misunderstandings and disagreement within the party itself. At the Twentieth Party Congress in 1956 in a secret speech known as the de-Stalinization speech, Khrushchev exposed the Stalinist excess and the horrors of the purges. Whether it was to set the party line straight, to gain support for himself, to set the historical record straight, or for whatever other reason is not too important; what was important was that Stalin, the infallible leader of the Communist faith, had been not only dethroned, but shown to be a neurotic, suspicious, and cruel tyrant. Almost immediately the de-Stalinization speech became known in party circles not only in Russia but in the satellites. A monarchy demands a monarch, an autocracy demands an autocrat, and a theocracy demands a high priest. Stalin, who was all of these things for the Communist world, was now dead. The Communist world could never be the same again.

As the Soviet Union had been throwing off some of the shackles of Stalinist rule, it had been loosening the shackles which controlled the satellites. In 1955 Moscow had concluded with the Eastern European nations the Warsaw military alliance pact. While a Russian marshal had been put in charge of the combined forces, there was nevertheless a slight change from the past when Moscow had simply decided everything. Now there was an attempt to legalize relations among these states. By this time as well, the trade relations between Russia and the satellites were beginning to take on more the character of legitimate trade operations rather than simply a Soviet exploitation of the satellites as had been the case during Stalin's lifetime. The fact that Tito, whose main original crime had been that he had wanted meaningful trade relations rather than a one-way exploitation, was now reinstated in the Kremlin favor meant that those persons in the satellites who had suffered for so-called Titoist tendencies must have suffered unjustly, and that those persons who had disagreed with Stalinist ideas and had suffered for that also had suffered unjustly. Blind faith and the cult of personality had been denounced. There was no longer the absolute. There now began to take place in Poland and Hungary serious questioning of past attitudes in the party. Russian control of the instruments of terror had been relaxed, and the opposition party began to be heard more frequently. In Poland, Gomulka, Spychalski, and other leaders who had been purged earlier were released and rehabilitated. Certain extreme Stalinists began to lose their positions in the state service and especially in the secret police. Some 36,000 political prisoners were released. In Hungary, as in other satellites where persons had been arrested and executed for Titoist leanings, the rehabilitation of innocent people began to take place. It was only natural that people began to ask what had been the role of their Stalinist leaders; why had they permitted and even led such repressions in the past. Criticisms of illegality and of Stalinism began to mount in the satellites. In the USSR attempts were now being made to contain the flood which had been unleashed. Stalin's good points were being emphasized. For Poland and Hungary it was too late. By the fall of 1956 it had become obvious that in Poland Gomulka was going to be elected first secretary and that his "reform" candidates were going to get the leading positions. Stalinists and others such as Marshal Rokossovski, a Pole by heritage but a marshal in the Russian army, whom Stalin had put in charge of the Polish armed forces and installed as a member of the Polish Politburo, were about to lose their posts. A reform was sweeping the Polish party. This was much more serious than anything the Kremlin leaders had intended. Russian troop movements were reported and a Russian delegation headed by Khrushchev, Molotov, and Mikoyan landed at Warsaw. For a while, apparently, the situation was quite tense. Gomulka is reported to have threatened to call on the population for help if the Russians invaded. Finally an agreement was reached whereby Gomulka was allowed to assume office; however, limits as to Polish freedoms were set. From this point on, Poland, though still a Communist state, definitely ceased to be merely a satellite in the truest sense.

The success of the Poles inflamed the situation in Hungary, where anti-Communist feeling among the population and anti-Stalinist feeling in the party were running high. By October 23–24 demonstrations had broken out in Budapest, demonstrations which had led to an unleashing of the popular fury against the secret police and the Stalinists.

Events in Hungary then moved rapidly. Soon revolt had seized the entire nation. The peasants dissolved the communes. The workers struck and joined the demonstrations. Cardinal Mindzenty, the imprisoned Catholic leader, was released by the insurrectionists. Secret police agents were being lynched by mobs and by October 30 the new government appointed by the Central Committee of the Hungarian Communist Party abolished one-party rule in Hungary and recognized the new revolutionary councils which had been formed. By the first of November, within one week of the beginning of the uprising, the government had negotiated with the Soviets the withdrawal of Russian troops from the capital. While further negotiations were taking place and while the Soviets were declaring their readiness for the withdrawal of Russian troops from Hungary, new Soviet troops were pouring into the country and taking up positions for an attack on the capital. A few days later, without warning, Russian forces using phosphorous shells and tanks pushed into Budapest and after severe fighting took over the city. A Communist government headed by Janos Kadar and made up of more pliable persons was installed by the Soviets. Leaders of the one-week government, including Premier Nagy, who had left the relative safety of the Yugoslav embassy trusting to a Soviet safe conduct promise, were arrested, and their executions were announced later.

The suppression of the Hungarian revolt was a lesson to the would-be reformers in Czechoslovakia and other satellites who had begun to stir after the heady news of reforms in Poland and Budapest. October in both places had come to an end. The warning was clear for Poland as well. Although Gomulka and the Poles had won certain liberties of action, the Soviets had made it quite plain that there were definite limits beyond which they could not go. Yet October had left its mark in East Central Europe. It had been clearly shown in Poland, in Hungary, in Germany, and elsewhere, that ten years of indoctrination had neither won the masses over to the new regimes nor to a love for the USSR. The Soviets had reasserted themselves and saved their satellites empire by means of the stick. However, now for the first time they felt constrained to use the carrot as well. Not only could the satellites no longer be simply exploited, it was necessary even to dip into Russian reserves to provide loans to help reestablish the damaged Hungarian economy. Living standards in the satellites, abysmally low, could not be ignored with impunity and could not be allowed to sink lower. Although in the main sense the Hungarians had definitely lost their revolution, they had won some real objectives and made genuine gains.

Whatever Soviet power or prestige might have suffered in late 1956 as a result of the Hungarian uprisings, however, was more than counterbalanced in 1957. Man's memory is short and soon many of even those Western leftist intellectuals who had objected vehemently to the Soviet repressions in Hungary were beginning to forgive and forget and were returning to the criticism of their more customary target, the United States. As far as power and prestige was concerned, the Soviet launching in 1957 of a small artificial earth satellite, Sputnik, more than compensated for any losses the USSR had sustained the previous year. A chill ran down the backs of many observers in the West. Many who had previously regarded the USSR as a technologically backward state suddenly began to fear that the Soviets had made the most fantastic scientific achievements. Articles began to appear in the press implying that the Soviets had an enormous scientific and technological lead over the United States. The feat of sending a small bit of metal in orbit around the earth was compared with the sending of a guided missile from Russia to hit the dome of the Empire State building in New York. The psychological impact of Sputnik was tremendous, not only in the United States where it stimulated the Congress to push money into a largely dormant rocket program, but in the Communist world. This was especially true for China, where the Soviet propaganda regarding this technological triumph apparently was believed. The real leaders of the Soviet Union realized that Sputnik had not seriously affected the balance of power. Many Chinese Communists and other Communist leaders throughout the world did not. This was to be one of the causes of the later split in the Communist world. During this period of 1957, Nikita Khrushchev had managed to outmaneuver his political rivals, especially among the old-line Stalinists, and to emerge as an even more dominant figure on the Soviet scene.

Although the suppression of the Hungarian revolution, the continued spending on heavy industry, and the pushing of the space program were all features reminiscent of Stalinism, Khrushchev's supremacy meant a relaxation of the terror apparatus. No longer did political foes have to fear for their lives when they were defeated in the party infighting. Khrushchev, impressed by growth figures in Soviet industry and by the success of Sputnik, announced plans to overtake and surpass the United States in total output by 1965 or 1970 and bring a higher standard of living to the Soviet people. Though these plans did not even approach fulfillment, the promise to bring a higher standard of living was one that had to be met partially. By the end of the 1950s Khrushchev seemed firmly ensconced in power. So, too, did the satellite leaders; Kadar in Hungary, Gomulka in Poland, Novotny in Czechoslovakia, and Ulbricht in East Germany.

Tito, whose prestige had risen greatly during the period of Khrushchev's attempted rapprochement with Yugoslavia, had been cut down to size during the period of the Hungarian suppression and its aftermath. His attempt to establish a "third road" to communism had been shown to be impractical. Yugoslavia was too small a power base from which to begin. Nevertheless within that nation itself his prestige was high and throughout the fifties as well as the sixties he remained firmly at the helm.

In the Iberian peninsula both Franco in Spain and Salazar in Portugal had no real challenge from within the country, and the 1950s saw a gradual improvement in the conditions in these countries.

In England the decade of the fifties belonged to the Conservatives, who assumed power again in 1951. However, their return did not really mean desocialization of Britain. A few industries were denationalized; however, the omelette could not be unscrambled. Under the Conservatives the postwar austerity measures came to an end and prosperity returned to Britain. As a result of the return of prosperity, marred somewhat by the Suez crisis in the mid-1950s, the Conservatives, under the skillful leadership of Harold Macmillan, entered the 1960s in a very strong position.

Internal French politics remained pretty much on the same course of governmental instability throughout the fifties. The underlying cause was the continuing drain on the nation's matériel and spirit occasioned first by the war in Indo-China and then the wars in North Africa. It had been difficult for the French to give up Indo-China, Tunis, and Morocco. It was almost unthinkable to give up Algeria, the home of the legion, and the home of more than a million *colons* who regarded themselves as French and whose forbears for generations had been living in Algeria. The regular army as well, the army that had seen its efforts in Indo-China and elsewhere come to naught, now vowed there would be no further retreats. Yet a rising tide of pressures in France led to ministerial and governmental equivocating on the Algerian issue. As home pressures mounted, it appeared that the French government would abandon Algeria. At this point the army in North Africa and the local *colon* leaders not only ceased to follow Paris orders but began to prepare for an actual invasion of metropolitan France. Units of the fleet and the overseas colonies began to rally to the leadership of these new "committees of public safety" which were being set up. Almost by chance these committees proclaimed General Charles de Gaulle as the symbol of their unity. However, de Gaulle had no desire for an illegal military *Putsch*. He insisted on being legally installed in office. With the paratroopers of the North African command poised on Corsica, the leaders of the Fourth Republic gave way and accepted de Gaulle, who then put his program and constitution before the French people for ratification. De Gaulle's new constitution provided for the establishment of a stronger executive, a president with real power elected for five years. The French people had had enough of unstable, constantly changing governments. They wanted a man. They voted for de Gaulle and his program.

The *colons* and ultras had backed de Gaulle believing that a strong nationalist like the general would not abandon Algeria. However, as the fighting continued and began to strain French resources beyond any reasonable degree, and as the situation seemed beyond French resources to bring to a successful conclusion, de Gaulle made the decision that probably only he of all Frenchmen could have made with any hope of carrying it out successfully. He agreed to allow free elections to permit the Algerians to decide their own destiny; this meant independence from France and the expulsion of the French *colons*. This decision of de Gaulle brought on another revolution of the North African army and for a while the situation was very precarious for de Gaulle; however, his will finally prevailed and the insurgent troops were disarmed without fighting. Free of the Algerian imbroglio, France in the 1960s began once again to prosper greatly and for almost a decade de Gaulle, though by no means an illegal tyrant, was able to decide French policies with probably less restraint than the dictators of many of the totalitarian states. Thus both France and the United Kingdom entered the sixties with Conservative governments in power.

In Western Germany, the phenomenal economic recovery of that amputated state enhanced the prestige of Chancellor Konrad Adenauer and the public's acceptance of the laissez-faire economic policies of his economics minister Ludwig Erhard. As the 1960s began, Adenauer's German conservative party, the Christian Democrats, were firmly in office, as they had been throughout the fifties.

In Italy there had been no strong political figure on the Conservative side who had been able to fill the void left by the retirement of Alcide de Gasperi in 1953. The result was a weakening of the Christian Democratic hold on power and the growing necessity of that party's leaders to form coalitions with other parties in order to remain in power. As the 1960s began, there were grave and serious threats to the continued existence of democratic government in Italy.

At the beginning of the sixties the Western European allies of the United States were regarded as (and felt like) junior partners of the United States. The failure of Britain and France to act successfully at Suez in 1956 and their vulnerability to the oil squeeze occasioned by the closing of that canal had seemed to presage once and for all the final decline of the European powers. Throughout the 1950s one after another they had been forced to give up their colonies

Courtesy of the German General Consulate, Chicago, Illinois

Konrad Adenauer, Chancellor of West Germany

and positions of predominance abroad. Yet at the same time that Europe had been withdrawing from its overseas commitments it had been gaining in wealth and productivity. Indeed, Western Europe had the economic wealth, the manpower, and the technology to be a superpower—if any

*Ludwig Erhard, architect of Germany's economic recovery, who
served as Economics minister and Chancellor*

of the two major states would unite in common action. Wealth means power, however, and even individually the Western European states were able by the early sixties to exert more of an influence than had been the case in the late fifties. This change became apparent only gradually. By the mid- and later sixties it was obvious.

In 1962, when the Soviets' moving of rockets into Castro's Cuba resulted in the so-called Cuban missile crisis, the United States acted without consulting its allies, though it did inform them. The Soviet withdrawal of the missiles from Cuba and the resultant relaxation of Soviet pressure over Berlin seemed to signalize to the Western Europeans that the Cold War was entering a new phase, perhaps even fading away. Like de Gaulle, some felt that the rewards of pursuing an independent policy were greater than those of remaining a junior partner in the American alliance. Germany was still to some extent an international outcast. The United States was far away. The French were Europeans. If de Gaulle could get German cooperation, particularly German money, to help develop France's atomic and military potential, a Paris-Bonn axis under de Gaulle's leadership would be able to control the Common Market nations, and France would emerge as a power with greater industrial and technological resources at its control than the Soviet Union, able to negotiate with the super powers on an equal basis indeed. This was the Gaullist dream, a dream which caused him to veto English admission to the Common Market. For in his opinion the English, who had enjoyed a special relationship with the United States, were not sufficiently European and their presence in the Common Market in the early and mid-1960s would doom his chances of controlling it. In the early 1960s the leading statesmen of Western Europe were eagerly looking forward to the realization of an age-old dream, the unification of Europe into some type of federation, a United States of Europe. It was felt that the Common Market, having proved itself economically, could be transformed into a political unit. The time was ripe. The de Gaulle vetoing of England's entry turned back the clock in this respect. The moment was lost and as a result European unity was perhaps further from realization in 1970 than it had been in 1950.

Throughout the 1960s there were various groups in Germany, the so-called Gaullists, who felt that Germany's security rested better with a European France than with an American United States which might abandon European interests in coming to a *modus vivendi* with the USSR. After the Sino-Soviet split, which came into the open in the early 1960s, de Gaulle began to speak more openly of a Europe from the Atlantic to the Urals. The danger of any Soviet move against Western Europe seemed remote, and some Europeans began to feel that being involved in an American alliance would bring them into the firing line.

Perhaps out of personal pique at wartime humiliations, perhaps out of genuine Machiavellian politics, perhaps too, out of personal irritation at the failure of the United States and Great Britain to heed his suggestions and directives, de Gaulle began to embark on a series of measures which were intended to weaken the position of the American and British currencies. France, by conservative policies holding down the standard of living, had managed to accumulate gold and dollar reserves throughout the early 1960s. Britain's economic slump plus the continued drain on the United States gold reserves occasioned partially by the Vietnamese war, partially by investments abroad, and partially by a very unfavorable tourism balance, among other things, had caused speculators to buy gold and unload pounds and dollars. At this point de Gaulle began to demand gold for the dollars he had been holding. Clearly this represented an attempt to dethrone the dollar, an attempt that came close to success. Certainly the dollar and the pound were in extreme danger, partially as a result of the French actions. All the West European currencies were related to the dollar, and many nations used dollars and dollar credits instead of gold or hard metals as backing for their currencies. Any change in the value of the dollar in relationship to the purchase price of gold would have had enormous repercussions on the financial world and the economic situation of those nations outside the Soviet bloc. However, by 1968 the financial picture was changing somewhat. The French economic position was not improving as much as had been expected, and the French hoard of gold could be kept intact and increased only by neglecting to some degree important improvements at home. In 1968 the skimping on the education budget, comparatively low factory wages, and a score of other secondary issues brought on serious street riots and major strikes in France. The economic costs of these strikes was such that France had to begin releasing her carefully hoarded supplies of gold and the mounting pressure for devaluation in the latter part of 1968 was no longer on the dollar but on the franc. Again speculation against the franc was so rampant that billions of dollars flowed out of France as a hedge against a devaluation, and pressure began to be exerted by the major Western nations for the Germans to up the value of their D-Mark, so as to prevent further pressures for devaluation of the other currencies. This pressure was resisted by the Germans with the result that the French government, after having refused to devaluate and after waiting out the storm of speculation, suddenly and dramatically devalued the franc in mid-1969. However, the entire currency situation was still clouded as 1969 drew to a close. There was not enough gold in the world to back the major currencies which were pegged to the dollar, which was valued at thirty-five dollars for one ounce of gold. If United States dollars would be accepted as backing in place of gold the situation could be stable. If, however, the United States continued to have an unfavorable balance of payments, eventually confidence in the dollar would have to weaken. If all the nations holding dollars as backing then were to demand gold, the gold hoard of the United States, already greatly depleted, could never meet all the claims against it.

The French strikes and riots of the spring of 1968 seriously damaged the prestige and assurance of General de Gaulle, although he won a strong vote of confidence from the French people in a referendum held shortly after the disorders. When he again insisted on a vote of confidence from the populace on a relatively minor issue, again as in the past threatening to resign if the vote went against him, the electorate turned him down. For they no longer seemed to be faced with de Gaulle or chaos. Elections were held smoothly and Georges Pompidou was elected to succeed de Gaulle as president, all transferrals of power being carried out smoothly. Pompidou, though a Gaullist, was not as interested in a great France as was de Gaulle. He was far more interested in a prosperous France. The result would obviously be a curtailment of prestige and military projects.

In the United Kingdom the Conservatives gave way in 1964 to the Labourites. However, English industry was not improving its competitive position in the world market. The balance of payments and balance of trade for Britain in the latter 1960s was usually unfavorable and austerity measures again had to be introduced. Despite the fact that British goods were already being priced out of world markets, a great number of strikes were helping drive British costs of production upward. Dissatisfaction expressed itself in the elections of 1970 which brought the Conservatives back to power. As the British economic position declined, more and more Britishers felt that the solution to their economic problems was to join the Common Market. Kept out by de Gaulle, they hoped that the atmosphere would be better with his departure from power. However, the situation in the early 1970s was not as propitious as it had been earlier, for new problems and obstacles had arisen. For one example, the Common Market had by this time inaugurated a complicated common agrarian policy. For Britain to accept these policies and prices would have caused a doubling in Britain of the cost of butter. There could be many rational, intelligent, and technical reasons for joining the Common Market.

Harold Wilson, Labourite Prime Minister of England

However, the British housewife could see butter rising from
less than forty cents a pound to ninety cents. And the British
housewife had a vote. Nevertheless conservative Prime
Minister Heath was determined to bring Britain into the
Market. In West Germany the main election issue of late
1969 had accidentally become whether the D-Mark should
be up-valued. Chancellor Kiesinger's personal appearance
and manner almost balanced the declining popularity of his
party. In the elections of 1969 enough Germans felt disenchanted with the Christian Democrats to allow a coalition

Edward Heath, Prime Minister of England

Willi Brandt, Mayor of Berlin and Chancellor of West Germany

headed by Willy Brandt to take office. For the first time since before Hitler a Socialist was the first minister in Germany. Yet as the decade drew to a close, as West Germany like other countries saw a vocal militant minority of radicals and Left-radical students stage protest demonstrations and confrontations with the authorities, ominous rumblings were heard from the Right. A new nationalist party was rising. The New National Germany Party reminded many onlookers of the old National Socialist party, the Nazis, though the new nationalists denied any connection. While they were not yet a major force in German politics and continued to lose ground in 1970 and 1971, they were in the wings, and a major crisis or major disorders perpetrated by the new Left could help them gain wider acceptance. Meanwhile the Italian coalitions had been becoming more and more unwieldy. By 1969 it had become extremely difficult to hold a coalition together long enough to form a government. Despite the economic advances of the fifties and the sixties, Italy still had the lowest per capita income of all the major Western democracies and had a host of social and economic ills handed down from the past. Democracy was not on firm footing in Italy as she entered the last third of the century. This was reflected in elections in 1971 which showed a startling rise in the strength of the neo-Fascists.

Thus the early 1970s saw the major European nations busy with internal political and economic problems. None of the leaders had as yet rallied a large majority of the people to his standard, and only Pompidou seemed to have the qualities which could succeed in that respect in the near future. Pompidou himself was facing a very cynical and skeptical French public, a public from which it is a tremendous feat to get half the population in favor of any policy for any length of time. For the people of these major nations, big power politics and war dangers had seemed to recede. The real dangers had been around for a long time. "Wolf" had been called too often. The tinder boxes of the Middle East, Berlin, etc., could go off at any time. Yet it

9

The Big Change:
Contemporary Europe

IN 1970 the geographical frontiers of the Western
European states were virtually the same as they had been a
century earlier. As the political map of Western Europe of
1939 had shown little difference from that of 1913, so the
political map of that area in 1970 showed even less change
from that of 1939. The great European territorial changes
between 1913 and 1970 had occurred in Central and East
Central Europe. The successor states to the Habsburg Empire, with the exception of the reemerged Poland, and East
Central Europe which had so greatly altered the map of
Europe after World War I, retained in 1970 pretty much the
same boundaries they had had in 1919. The greatest territorial changes occurring in East-Central Europe after World
War II had been the amputation of Germany's eastern territories, most of which went to Poland though some went to
Russia, and the establishment of a separate second German
state in what had formerly been Middle Germany. Thus,
Western Europe had had virtually no territorial changes in
seventy years and East Central Europe had had a series of
great changes. Yet none of the territorial changes had led to
the creation of any new great powers. Of the European
states in 1913, there were six—Austria, Italy, Germany,
France, Great Britain, and Russia—which could claim to be
great powers. In 1970 only Russia, now a superpower, could

still truly be regarded as a great power. Germany's shattering defeat in World War II had ended her great-power status. The great growth of the French economy and the rise of the French gold reserves under de Gaulle in the 1960s had allowed many in that country to hope, even after the withdrawals from Algeria and elsewhere, that France would regain her world position. However, the Paris street rebellions of 1968 and the defeat of de Gaulle during the elections of that same year ushered in what appeared to be a new period of French history, one in which that nation seemed ready to be "a Holland or a Sweden with a better climate."

For Great Britain the retreat from a position as a world power had taken place gradually over a period of twenty years. In the 1970s she could no longer count on the support of Canada, South Africa, Australia, and New Zealand, as she had been able to do in the two wars. Neither could she any longer rely on being able to recruit large numbers of Indian troops. By the 1970s Britain was returning more and more to Europe, becoming more and more Europe-oriented, and the future direction of West European politics depended more and more on how Britain's belated attempts to join the new European community progressed.

Thus France, Germany, and Great Britain, the three giants of European and world politics prior to World War I and World War II, had by 1970 given up their pretensions to world power. Italy and Austria, which might have laid claim to great-power status in 1914, could have no such pretensions a half-century later. Not only had these powers given up pretensions to great-power status, they had rather completely liquidated their overseas possessions and were not anxious to become strongly involved in other parts of the world. The single European exception to this was that one European power, Russia, which in 1970 was a greater world power than she had been in 1914. Yet the decline of the political predominance of Western and Central Europe often obscures the fact that other changes had been taking place, changes of great importance. And though people could speak of the decline of France, of Germany, and of Great Britain, the fact still remained that the generation of West Europeans coming to maturity in 1970 had greater material, educational, health, cultural, and travel opportunities than any other generation of their predecessors. To make a sweeping generality, they were the best-paid, best-fed, best-housed, best-clothed, and the best-educated generation of Europeans. Yet though the material conditions of life had improved by 1970, there were chronic problems besetting the economies and currencies of France and Britain. The existence of two Germanies, and other legacies from the past, cast clouds over the German situation.

There are those who believe that the important changes in nations are those which take place along the frontiers and in the power indices. While both of these are, of course, extremely important and often will reflect themselves on the living standards of the populations of the countries considered, a mere study of the political problems and development of the European states will not really convey the tremendous changes which have been taking place in the last two generations, changes in the manner and standards of living. Although tremendous power and political changes had occurred in Europe in the first forty years following World War I, they had not really reflected themselves on the manner of life once war damage had been removed. A trip through most European cities and the European countryside in 1939 or even in 1953 would, therefore, not have shown the great changes which had been taking place under the surface, changes only tangentially influenced by border revisions or size of armies. These changes which had been occurring with greater and greater speed were to be much more apparent before ten years had passed. For in the more than fifty years which have passed since World War I and particularly during the last fifteen years, Europe has indeed been transformed.

The great change and the greatest revolution which had

Courtesy of the German Tourist Information Office

Dusseldorf, Germany

taken place in Europe since World War I, and at a much more rapid rate since the mid-1950s, was the improvement of technology and productivity both on the farm and in industry.

Industrial Advances and Material Improvements

This improvement is reflected in the tremendous increases in the total output as indicated by tables 18–21 which illustrate some of the main indices in industrial and agricultural production.

In all these nations, therefore, both heavy industrial production and electrical power output had increased many

18. CRUDE STEEL PRODUCTION, 1913–1970
(In millions of metric tons)

Country	1913	1948	1964	1969	1970
France	4.7	7.2	19.8	22.5	23.8
Germany	18.9	5.6*	37.3	45.0	45.0
Italy	.9	2.1	9.8	16.4	17.2
Japan	.2	1.2	39.8	82.0	93.3
U.S.A.	31.8	80.4	115.5	128.2	119.3
USSR	4.9	18.6	85.0	111.0	115.9
U.K.	7.8	15.1	26.7	27.0	28.3
Spain	.2	.6	3.0	6.0	7.4

Source: League of Nations, *International Statistical Yearbook for 1926*, table 50; W. S. Woytinsky and E. S. Woytinsky, *World Population and Production* (New York: Twentieth Century, 1953), p. 1118; UN *Yearbook* 1954, table 109; UN *Yearbook* 1970, table 122; UN *Monthly Bulletin of Statistics*, March 1972, table 38.
* Henceforth, all postwar figures in tables regarding Germany refer to West Germany only.

times, whereas the population growth for the European nations listed here had been very moderate.

Though the increase in industrial output had indeed been spectacular, the rise in agricultural output was in many respects even more impressive. This can be readily seen from the figures in table 21.

This phenomenal increase in the production of numerous commodities, an increase far in excess of the population growth, created a prosperity which improved standards of living and helped to break down class barriers.

In the Europe of the pre–World War I generation, the average work week was fifty hours or even more. In the Europe of the 1960s, the work week was approximately forty hours. It is the nature of many persons to buy more than they can afford. Thus, individuals can often be encountered in any country in which real economic and wage advance has taken place who will stoutly maintain that living conditions have not improved in the last ten or fifteen year, and that a worker's salary scarcely allows a person

19. ELECTRIC ENERGY PRODUCTION, 1930–1970
(In million kilowatts)

Country	1930	1948	1964	1970
France	15	29	94	140
Germany	29	39	161	243
Italy	11	23	77	117
Japan	14	36	180	360
U.S.A.	115	337	1,084	1,638
USSR	8	66	459	740
U.K.	12	48	183	249
Spain	3	6	30	56

Source: UN *Yearbook* 1948, table 116; UN *Yearbook* 1952, table 119; UN *Yearbook* 1970, table 140; UN *Monthly Bulletin of Statistics,* March 1972, table 48.

to exist. Since charts showing the cost of living indices and the rise of wages are often boring and scarcely intelligible to some, it is perhaps more pertinent, in order to indicate the tremendous rise in living standards, to present statistics which are virtually self-explanatory and cannot be refuted.

20. POPULATION, 1910–1970
(To the nearest million)

Country	1910	1960	1970
France	40	46	51
Germany	65	55	62
Italy	35	50	54
Japan	50	93	105
U.S.A.	92	181	205
USSR	140	214	243
U.K.	45	52	56

Source: W. S. Woytinsky and E. S. Woytinsky, *World Population and Production: Trends and Outlook* (New York: Twentieth Century, 1953), p. 44; UN *Demographic Yearbook for 1968,* table 4; UN *Monthly Bulletin of Statistics,* March 1972, table 1.

21. WHEAT PRODUCTION, 1928–1968
(In thousands of metric tons)

Country	1928	1938	1962	1968
France	7,655	9,801	14,054	14,646
Germany	3,854	5,578	4,592	6,198

Source: UN *Yearbook* 1948, table 13; UN *Yearbook* 1969, table 43.

As can be readily seen from table 22, as late as 1928, there was only a comparative handful of automobiles in Europe. While the number had increased greatly by 1937, and by 1953 was far greater than it had been in 1937, it was still a rare European indeed who could afford a car in 1953. At that time cars even six years old and older commanded prices far beyond the earning power of the average person. Rapid as the increase in automobiles had been in the 1950s, the increase in the 1960s was even more rapid and has been proceeding at an increasing rate.

Thus, by 1967, the United Kingdom alone, with more than ten million autos, had more cars than all of Europe together had had only thirteen years earlier, and both France and West Germany had more cars than did the United

22. PRIVATE AUTOMOBILES IN EUROPEAN COUNTRIES, 1928–1969
(In thousands)

Country	1928	1937	1948	1953	1959	1968	1969
Austria	23	32	34	74	341	1,056	1,124
France	758	2,020	1,519	2,020	5,019	11,500	12,000
Germany	343	1,108	283	1,251	3,556	11,322	12,194
Italy	142	271	219	613	1,644	8,178	9,028
Spain	...	...	83	108	233	1,577	1,999
U.K.	934	1,833	2,020	2,797	4,981	10,949	11,365

Source: UN *Yearbook* 1948, table 120; UN *Yearbook* 1957, table 137; UN *Yearbook* 1966, table 154; UN *Yearbook* 1970, table 148.

Courtesy of the French Government Tourist Office

La Croisette, Cannes, France, shows the numerous automobiles in France

Kingdom. While it was undoubtedly true that a large number of persons had more than one car, an increase from two million to ten million cars in France, and an increase from 1.1 million to ten million in West Germany in the period from 1953–66 meant that there were now more than twenty million cars, the overwhelming majority of very recent vintage, for a population of only about 105 million. Millions of persons in 1966 could obviously afford cars who could never have done so in the pre-1953 Europe.

Though this increase was taking place at a more striking rate in the 1960s than it had in the 1950s, the rate of increase was bound to slow down in the 1970s in such countries as England, France and Germany, which were rapidly reaching the motorcar saturation point, whereas countries like Spain, Greece, Yugoslavia, and possibly even the iron curtain nations could look forward to great increases in the number of motor vehicles.

The telephone as well had been a luxury that most working-class families apparently felt they could not afford, not only in the pre–World War I but even in the pre–World War II period. In all countries the number of phones was increasing. Table 23 indicates how the telephone had become a commonplace item in the European home in the period from 1948 to 1969.

Perhaps it is necessary to dwell on these figures just a bit to realize the enormity of the change. As late as 1948, the entire Italian nation had only 659,000 telephones; eighteen years later Italy had ten times as many. Britain alone had more phones than she and all of Western Europe, including Spain, France, Italy, and Germany, had had only eighteen years before.

In 1950 there were no television stations in Europe, and even the radio was something of a luxury, although within the grasp of the average West European worker. By the 1960s it was a rare person not only in Western, but even in

23. NUMBER OF TELEPHONES IN SELECTED COUNTRIES, 1910–1969
(In thousands)

Country	1910	1920	1937	1948	1966	1968	1969
France	212	419	1,552	2,233	6,554	7,503	8,100
England	609	912	3,018	4,871	11,284	12,799	14,100
Japan	110	298	1,311	1,230	16,011	17,331	19,900
U.S.A.	6,996	12,669	19,450	38,205	98,789	109,255	115,200
Germany	968	1,767	3,623	718	9,532	11,249	12,500
Italy	63	107	424	658	6,467	7,752	8,500
USSR	.....	.....	.....	.....	7,872	10,800	12,000

Source: W. S. Woytinsky, *Die Welt in Zahlen*, 7 vols, (Berlin: Rufolf Mosse, 1927), 5:141; UN *Yearbook* 1949–50, table 137; UN *Yearbook* 1970, table 159.

24. NUMBER OF RADIO SETS IN SELECTED COUNTRIES, 1938–
1965
(In 100,000s)

Country	1938	1953	1965
Czechoslovakia	1.034 ('37)	2.7	3.7
France	4.706	8.4	15.3
West Germany	11.500	12.2	26.0
Italy	.978	4.9	10.7
Spain	.281 ('40)	1.3	4.6
United Kingdom	8.589	13.3	16.2
United States	41.000	114.0	240.0
USSR	6.980 ('40)	17.6	74.0

Source: UN *Yearbook* 1957, table 189; UN *Yearbook* 1968, table 216.

Eastern Europe who did not have a radio, and even a television set had become standard equipment in the majority
of West European homes.

In addition to radios and television sets, a host of appliances, such as refrigerators, vacuum cleaners, and washing
machines, which had become commonplace in the United
States in the 1930s, had come into a vast number of West
and even some East European homes in the later 1950s, and

25. NUMBER OF TELEVISION RECEIVERS IN SELECTED
COUNTRIES, 1956–1969
(In 100,000s)

Country	1956	1963	1967	1969
Czechoslovakia	.060	1.6	2.6	3.0
France	.442	4.4	8.3	10.1
West Germany	.704	8.54	13.8	16.0
Italy	.367	4.3	7.7	9.0
Spain	.003	.9	2.7	5.5
United Kingdom	6.570	12.8	14.5	15.8
United States	42.000	61.9	78.0	81.0
USSR	1.324	10.4	22.7	30.7

Source: UN *Yearbook* 1957, table 191; UN *Yearbook* 1968, table 217;
UN *Yearbook* 1970, table 212.

continued to be purchased at an increasing rate in the 1960s and going into the 1970s.

The new prosperity did not manifest itself just in cars, telephones, televisions, and household appliances. In housing as well, Western Europe was making giant strides forward beginning in the early 1950s, whereas Eastern Europe began to concentrate on housing about the end of the 1950s and the beginning of the 1960s. In West Germany alone in the period between 1962 and 1966 approximately 600,000 housing units were constructed each year, or about three million in a period of less than five years. More than two-thirds of these units had four or more rooms; and of this two-thirds, about half had five or more rooms. When it is borne in mind that in 1950 in the whole Federal Republic, there were only about 9.9 million dwellings of which more than half a million were emergency accommodations; and when this is compared with the more than eighteen million units there in the 1960s, the enormous scope of this housing development becomes more evident. It is interesting also to compare the figures of 550,000 or 600,000 units constructed per year in the sixties with those of Hitlerite and Stresemann Germany.

In Great Britain as well, the improvement in housing is striking. In 1966 there were more than fifteen million

26. HOUSING UNITS BUILT IN GERMANY

Overall View		Since World War II	
1929	171,800	1949–51	973,200
1933	178,000	1952–54	1,474,847
1937	340,000	1955–58	2,062,462
1959	570,478	1959–60	1,077,774
1967	572,000	1961–63	1,620,636
1969	500,000	1964–65	1,125,405

Source: *Schlag Nach* (Mannheim, 1967), p. 387; UN *Yearbook* 1968, table 143.

27. HOUSING UNITS IN ENGLAND AND WALES, 1901–1966
(In millions)

Year	Population	Housing Units
1901	32.5	6.710
1911	36.1	7.550
1921	37.9	7.979
1931	40.0	9.400
1951	43.8	12.389
1961	46.1	14.646
1966	47.1	15.449

Source: Great Britain Central Statistical Office, *Annual Abstract of Statistics*, 1968, tables 56 and 57.

dwellings in the United Kingdom as compared with 12.4 million in 1951, and only 9.4 million in 1931. These statistics should not be lightly passed over. For they show that the number of dwellings in England and Wales had increased more than 250 percent since 1901, and the population had only increased by less than 50 percent. This represents a virtual doubling of the number of units per capita. Of these seventeen million dwellings listed for the United Kingdom, less than half a million are listed as multiple dwellings and the rest are listed as one household space. Of the almost seventeen million "one household space" dwellings, less than 1.3 million have less than four rooms, and 3.5 million have four rooms. Thus, more than two-thirds of the dwellings have five or more rooms, with the largest category having six.

In France and virtually all the countries of the West, a similar housing boom was being experienced. Just how great this construction boom was can be judged from table 28.

A still clearer picture of the great increase in new construction can be obtained by converting some of these percentages into numbers. France, which constructed 423,000 new dwelling units in 1967, would have completed only

28. CONSTRUCTION ACTIVITY
(In percent of 1963 construction)

Year	France	Germany	U.K.	USSR
1938	34	35	86	17
1948	56	..	68	27
1960	82	83	92	90
1967	130	112	120	134
1969	165	123	119	148

Source: UN *Yearbook* 1968, p. 327; UN *Yearbook* 1970, table 135.

110,000 units had she been building at the prewar rate of 1938; Germany, which constructed 572,000 new units, would have completed fewer than 190,000; and the USSR would have produced fewer than 270,000 new units rather than the 2.3 million actually constructed.

While there are a number of persons who insist that today's quality of construction is not the same as in the past, and it would be an involved procedure either to refute or confirm such affirmations, there is no doubt that insofar as such modern conveniences as baths and waterclosets are concerned, the European dwellings of today are far better equipped than they were even as recently as twenty years ago.

29. PERCENTAGE OF EUROPEAN DWELLINGS
WITH BATHS

Country	1951	1962
France	10.4 ('54)	28
West Germany	51.8 ('56)	64
Italy	10.7	29
United Kingdom	62.4	79
East Germany		22

Source: UN *Yearbook* 1968, table 207; UN *Yearbook* 1962, table 176.

Undoubtedly the less crowded and more sanitary housing was one of the contributing factors to the tremendous decline in the rate of tuberculosis and other infectious diseases.

In Eastern Europe, where housing was largely neglected until the late 1950s in order to accent heavy industry, figures show a somewhat different result. Thus, between 1926 and 1940 the number of square feet of dwelling space per city inhabitant in the USSR decreased, a decrease which continued until 1956. After that time a greater attention was allotted to civilian needs with the result that a marked improvement was noticeable by 1960, an improve-

30. HOUSING SPACE IN SELECTED SOVIET CITIES, 1926–1960

City	Approximate Average Square Feet of Housing Space per Inhabitant				Approximate Population
	1926	1940	1956	1960	1960
Moscow	89	75	80	108	6,208,000
Leningrad	138	89	87	99	3,445,000
Kiev	107	87	86	109	1,174,000
Baku	74	68	69	92	1,038,000
Gorky	68	73	73	90	1,003,000
Average (for first 24 cities)	81	78	76	95	

Source: Robert T. Holt and John E. Turner, *Soviet Union: Paradox and Change* (New York: Holt, Rinehart & Winston, 1962), p. 58.

ment which continued into 1970. Though the Soviet Union had still not yet reached its minimum goal of a hundred square feet per inhabitant by 1970, the housing situation there was greatly improving.

Tourism in Europe

The new prosperity, shorter working week, better roads, more private cars, better and cheaper airplane flights, and, above all, paid vacations all combined to touch off a wave of tourism in the 1950s and 1960s far in excess of anything hitherto dreamed of. An idea of how quickly technological advance had moved in air travel can be gained from noting that the Dutch airline KLM in 1967 was handling more passengers with only forty-eight planes than she had been able to carry in 1959 with ninety-five airplanes; at the same time the planes were flying more miles and carrying more freight. By 1960, tourism easily had become the leading single item in international trade. Millions and millions of Europeans were taking vacations in other nations and in other parts of their own countries, and the ease and frequency of travel was beginning to break down the provincialism so common in the Europe of the recent past. In the pre–World War I period, international tourism had first begun on a large scale, and in the period between the two wars it had developed even further. Interrupted by World War II, tourism had revived to the extent that by 1951 it was already exceeding prewar levels. Just how low these levels were compared to those of ten and fifteen years later can be judged from table 31.

By 1970, millions of Britons, Germans, and Frenchmen, plus a host of other nationals, flew to the Spanish, Italian, and Yugoslav resorts with greater ease and in greater num-

31. NUMBER OF TOURISTS IN SEVERAL MAJOR TOURIST COUNTRIES, 1938–1969
(In millions)

Country	1938	1947	1956	1967	1969
U.K.	.300 est.	.340	1.107	4.300	5.800
France	1.000 est.	.750	4.300	12.000	12.100
Spain	. . .	. . .	2.728	16.400	21.700
Austria	. . .	.020	2.836	6.800	7.840
Italy	. . .	. . .	12.665	27.620	29.789

Source: UN *Yearbook* 1948, table 125; UN *Yearbook* 1968, table 163; UN *Yearbook* 1970, table 156.

bers than they had formerly attended resort areas a few scores of miles away in their own countries. One-month vacations for workers were common in all the major countries, and in the course of just one weekend during the holiday season, it was not at all unusual for a half million Parisians or Londoners to leave their cities for the resorts. Each year was bringing about two million American tourists to the Continent. The great growth of leisure time brought on by improved technology and the prosperity it had created, plus the ease of transportation, plus television and other mass-communications media was breaking down the insularity of small regional European nationalism. The Germans and French in 1970 knew and understood each other much better than they had in 1935 or 1910. Italians, numbering

Courtesy of the Rumanian Tourist Office

Club Paradis, a Black Sea resort in Rumania

probably two million, were working in Germany, Switzerland, and France. Yugoslavs, Greeks, Spaniards, and Por-
tuguese by the hundreds and hundreds of thousands were
employed in the more industrial nations to the north. And
in this respect as well Europeans were drawing together. By
1970, even the Iron Curtain seemed to be becoming a less
formidable and more penetrable barrier as tourists by the
hundreds of thousands flocked to the older and the newly-
established resorts in Hungary, Bulgaria, and Rumania.
Organized tours by bus, plane, and ship were also going to
the USSR, and the Czech and Polish tourist agencies were

Courtesy of the Spanish National Tourist Office

Typical plaza, Gelanova, Spain

openly advertising for tourists in West European newspapers. If old hatreds and misgivings could be allayed by
closer contacts and understandings, Europe was certainly
on the right path only twenty-five years after it had nearly
destroyed itself by misunderstandings and mutual antago-
nisms. By the mid-1960s, there were one hundred million
persons participating in the international tourist traffic, of
which three-fourths were West Europeans, and this number
was rising by between 10 and 15 percent per year.

For certain nations the flow of foreign currencies brought
by this ever-increasing flood of tourists helped make it pos-

32. WEST EUROPEANS VISITING EAST EUROPE

Country	1963	1965	1969
Bulgaria	34,000	134,000	360,000
Hungary	150,000	300,000	497,000
Czechoslovakia	300,000	520,000	607,000

Source: UN *Yearbook* 1970, table 156.

sible to meet their critical balance-of-payments problems.
By 1964 Spain and Italy were each netting about one billion
dollars a year in foreign currencies as a result of tourism,
whereas Germany lost a net of about 600 million dollars,
and the United States lost over a billion dollars as a result
of the excess spending of its citizens abroad.

As already noted, Eastern Europe too, anxious to acquire
hard currencies, was opening up its borders to tourist travel,
though restricting very much the amount of money its
citizens could spend abroad. Although the travel to Eastern
Europe was still far below the yearly rate of twenty million
tourists to Italy or Spain, the increases in tourism taking
place there were striking.

Yet this one-way flow of currencies out of certain countries
could have a negative effect in the long run. Germany was
still more than able to balance its tourist outflow in the early

1970s; however, for the United States, losing more than a billion dollars a year, the negative tourist balance could become a real problem. It had, after all, been the one-way flow of species to the East over the centuries that had drained the Roman Empire of its hard currency, creating the tremendous money problem which helped bring down the empire.

Though the greater tourist flow and the greater exchange of labor had done much to help Europeans understand each other, and though there was much greater mutual understanding in Europe in 1970 than there had been in either 1913 or 1938, there were a score of old misunderstandings and national animosities which did not die easily. It still would take only a minor incident to show that Italians and Tyrolese or Serbs and Croats did not really trust each other. The arrest of leading Croatians in 1971 and Tito's crackdown on "Croatian nationalism" showed that all animosities between Serbs and Croatians were far from ended. There were many national differences which still had to be resolved in the last third of the twentieth century, yet the thoughts and hopes of virtually all Europeans were strongly for the retention of peace regardless of any border injustices.

Population Growth and Health Improvements

The rising productivity and resulting prosperity did not manifest themselves only in increased tourism and purchases. The increased productivity and resulting prosperity meant that there was more money to deal with social, health, and educational problems. While the advances in these areas seemed painfully slow to some, they were nonetheless considerable when compared with the Europe of half a century earlier. Thus, in the field of education and in the process of eradicating illiteracy, the achievements in the twentieth century, and particularly in the last twenty-five years, are especially striking. In every European country, illiteracy as such had been virtually stamped out among the newer generation, though there are still hard-core pockets of illiteracy especially in Portugal. The growth in higher education, too, had been spectacular.

Even more impressive is the fact that this change is taking place at an increasing rate, that the increase in the last five years is as great or greater than in the previous

33. NUMBER OF STUDENTS IN HIGHER EDUCATION, 1910–1968
(In thousands)

Country	1910	1930	1950	1960	1966	1968
England, Wales	10	46	107	177 ('61)	311	347
Sweden	4	8	17	37	84	116
Austria	29	16	25	39	50	56
Hungary	10	12	27	29	52	52
Germany	63	113	123	265	407	431
France	41	74	140	272	537	622*
Italy	24	45	145	192	342	420
United States	214	972	2,297	3,583	6,390	7,513
USSR	35	737 ('35)	1,247	2,396	4,123	4,470

Source: *Annuaire Statistique de la france* (Partie Internationale, 1954); UN *Yearbook* 1948, table 155; UNESCO *Statistical Yearbook for 1969,* table 2:12; UN *Yearbook* 1970, table 203.
* The figures for some of these nations have included students in teachers' training schools. A more accurate picture for 1968 could be obtained by adding ten thousand normal school students to Sweden's total, 28 thousand to France, and 250 thousand to Italy.

decade, and that it is just as impressive in the peripheral areas of the continent as in the main nations.

The increased number of students is also reflected in the increased number of doctors and the fact that there is money available to support them.

The increase in medical knowledge, the greater number of physicians available, the improved means of diagnosis, the improved diets and housing, and the shorter hours and better conditions of work have led to a great diminishing in the cases of infectious diseases and in infant and maternal mortality. In 1900 every major European country had had

34. NUMBER OF PHYSICIANS PER 10,000 POPULATION, 1900–
1968

Country	1900	1930	1949	1967	1968
France	3.9	6.1	7.6	11.8	13.0
Germany	4.6	6.2 (approx)	. . .	15.9	17.2
Belgium	5.3	6.0	11.2 ('50)	. . .	15.9
Netherlands	4.5	6.9 (approx)	6.9 ('50)	11.8	11.9

Source: Woytinsky and Woytinsky, p. 228; UN *Yearbook* 1968, table 206; UN *Yearbook* 1969, table 198; UN *Yearbook* 1970, table 200.

an infant mortality rate of at least 150 per thousand births, and some had a rate of more than 200. By 1966 France, England, and Germany were all below twenty-five, and Spain, Italy, and Russia, all of which had had such enormously high rates earlier, were below thirty-five and were rapidly closing the gap. Holland, England, Sweden, Finland, Denmark, and Norway had even lowered their rate to below twenty. In England maternal deaths in childbirth, which in 1900 had numbered 4.7 per thousand, had declined to .9 by 1950, and to .2 by 1967. Quite obviously, the enormous number of lives saved here, which made it possible for the population to expand despite the far fewer number of pregnancies, added years to the productive labors of

35. INFANT MORTALITY, 1900–1968
(Number of deaths within first year per thousand births)

Country	1900	1938	1966	1968
Wales and England	153	52	19.6 (UK)	18.8 (UK)
France	164	66	21.7	20.4
Germany	186	60	23.6	22.8
Spain	203	109 ('35)	36.0	32.0
USSR	268	. . .	26.1	26.4
U.S.A.	. . .	51	23.7	21.8

Source: Woytinsky, *World Population and Production*, p. 167; UN *Statistical Yearbook for 1969*, table 19; League of Nations *International Statistical Yearbook*, 1939–40, table 7.

women and freed millions of women from enormous hardships. Even in the United States, with its relatively low infant mortality rate, life expectancy increased by more than
nine years in the period from 1930–32 to 1966, increasing
from 62 to 71. Perhaps the liberation from having to bear
so many children was the real emancipation of women in
Europe.

36. BIRTHRATE IN SELECTED COUNTRIES, 1911–1969
(Per thousand population)

Country	1911–13 yearly average	1937–39 yearly average	1969
USSR	46	. . .	17.2 ('68)
United States	25.1	17.3	17.7
Japan	34.9	28.7	18.3
Austria	24.9	15.9	16.5
Germany	27	19.9	15.0
Czechoslovakia	29.6	17.0	15.5
Hungary	34.3	19.7	15.0
Italy	31.7	23.3	17.6
Poland	37.8	24.7	16.3
United Kingdom	24.1	15.5	16.6
France	18.1	14.7	16.7
Sweden	23.6	14.9	13.5

Source: League of Nations *International Statistical Yearbook*, 1939–
40, table 6; League of Nations *International Statistical Yearbook*,
1926, table 2; UN *Monthly Bulletin of Statistics*, January 1971, table 2.

Interesting, too, is the overall shift in birthrates in the last
thirty-five to forty years. It becomes apparent from table 36
that by the 1960s, European birthrates were becoming more
uniform.

However, this "emancipation" had its negative aspect as
well. For the emancipation of women loosened family ties,
and the number of divorces in Europe increased greatly.
Here too the twentieth century, in its bad aspects as well as
its good, arrived in Europe about twenty-five to forty years
after it did in the United States.

37. DIVORCE RATE, 1910–1938
(Per thousand marriages of previous decade)

	1910	1930	1938
United States	100.2	163.4	201.1
England, Wales	2.2	11.5	19.1
France	46.9	60.4	87.0
Denmark	39.8	86.4	109.1

Source: Woytinsky and Woytinsky, p. 190.

An interesting phenomenon is that in the years immediately after the war, the number of divorces shot up astronomically; in England in 1947 there were 138.5 per thousand, and in France in 1946 there were 207. However, these reflected the abnormal circumstances of the war, and therefore they are not included in table 38.

Thus, the divorce figures for the post–World War decades show a gradual return to normalcy, though they are still above prewar figures.

Perhaps because of the greater economic opportunities and better housing, the marriage rate had risen slightly in Western Europe. Because of this and because of the improved infant mortality rate and better health measures, the

38. NUMBER OF DIVORCES, 1935–1970

Country	1935	1946	1950	1966	1970
Austria	728	13,351	10,534	8,643	. . . .
Hungary	5,644	. . .	11,263	20,623	23,300
France	21,004	51,946	35,143	36,500	37,000
England & Wales	3,942	17,059	30,331	38,352	59,000
Denmark	2,992	7,500	6,868	6,726	. . . .
Germany	50,259	48,422	84,740	58,730	59,000
USSR	. . . .	. . . .	. . . .	646,000	638,000

Source: United Nations *Demographic Yearbook for 1968*, table 33; UN *Demographic Yearbook 1951*, table 26; UN *Demographic Yearbook 1970*, table 23.

population throughout all of Western Europe showed a slight, steady, and healthy increase throughout the 1950s and the 1960s. The gloomy population forecasts of the various study bureaus and of the League of Nations which had been made in the 1930s and 1940s and which seemed to bear out Oswald Spengler's prophecy of the "Decline of the West," were being proved wrong by 1970, as table 39 indicates.

As already indicated, however, the League of Nations was not unique in predicting a decline in population for the

39. PROJECTED AND ACTUAL POPULATION FOR 1970
(In Millions)

Country	Projected	Actual
England & Wales	37.1	48.8
United Kingdom	46.8	55.7
Austria	6.3	7.4
France	36.9	51.3
Sweden	5.8	8.0
Poland	41.4	32.5
USSR	251.0	242.8

Source: Woytinsky and Woytinsky, p. 255; UN *Monthly Bulletin of Statistics,* March 1972, table 1.

West. Two commissions of the British Royal Commission on Population in 1949 saw three possibilities of future population development in the United Kingdom. Two of the three foresaw a decline in British population by the turn of the century, and one saw a very minor inching up if the family size increased.

In France in 1946, the Institut national de la statistique prepared ten estimates for the future population of France to 2000. Not one of them envisioned the population reaching fifty million by that time. The most optimistic forecast was a population of 48.6 million by A.D. 200. The 1970 totals of more than fifty million French and fifty-six million British certainly gave hopes for a brighter future for those nations despite their decline as powers.

Yet, though West Europeans could feel more comfortable regarding their own population problems, there was the ominous prospect of uncontrolled population explosions in the underdeveloped and poorer areas of the world. According to recent prognostications which seem quite likely to be fulfilled (of course they could be significantly changed by unforeseen factors), the future populations are as shown in table 40.

40. PROJECTED POPULATION TO A.D. 2000
(In millions)

Year	Developing areas	Highly developed areas
1960	2,103	855
1975	2,816	1,012
2000	4,979	1,288

Source: *Schlag Nach*, p. 345.

This demographic monster looming up on the horizon has led some observers to believe that the real world conflict is not between the East and the West, but largely between the technologically developed and the technologically underdeveloped countries. And, indeed, the birthrates of some of these "developing" nations are frightening when their present rate of technological development is borne in mind. On the other hand, there are the encouraging examples of Eastern Europe and Japan where the birthrate, so enormous only a generation ago, has declined so in recent years.

Next to the dramatic drop in infant mortality rates, perhaps the most apparent success in the battle against premature deaths in Europe had been the decrease in the number of people afflicted with tuberculosis.

The cold percentage rates of table 41 can be translated

41. AVERAGE ANNUAL DEATHS FROM PULMONARY
    TUBERCULOSIS, 1901–1967
    (Per 100,000 population)

Country	1901–5	1965	1967
England	134	4	3
Austria	340	15	13
France	249*	13	10
Germany	186	12	10
Hungary	394	21	21
Italy	112	11	8
Spain	148	19	13

Source: UN *Demographic Yearbook for 1968*, table 20; A. D. Webb, *New Dictionary of Statistics*, (New York: Dutton, 1911), pp. 188–89.
* Figures for France in 1901–5 and 1965 are for urban population only.

into more readily meaningful human statistics which show the decline of the actual number of deaths due to tuberculosis.

Even in Great Britain, which already had the best health rates for TB and pneumonia among the major European nations in 1953, the improvement in the 1960s is striking.

Apart from all the human misery which was spared by the avoidance of these diseases and infant deaths, the extra production and the financial savings made thereby meant

42. DEATHS DUE TO TUBERCULOSIS, 1900–1969

Country	1900	1938	1953	1969
England	60,000	25,509	8,902	1,092
France	. . . .	49,480	15,687	4,371
Italy	58,000	34,892	13,017 ('52)	4,652 ('67)
Germany	106,000	42,697	13,281 ('52)	5,988 ('67)

Source: *Annuaire Statistique de la france for 1954* (Paris, 1955); *Partie Rétrospective Internationale*, p. 25, table 1, p. 29, table 3; UN *Demographic Yearbook for 1970*, table 19.

43. NOTIFICATIONS OF INFECTIOUS DISEASES
IN THE U.K.

Year	TB	Pneumonia	Whooping cough
1957	42,411	45,399	94,206
1967	15,824	10,032	37,815
1969	14,528	9,208 ('68)	6,132

Source: Great Britain, *Annual Abstract of Statistics for 1970,*
table 56.

that funds and materials were available for other purposes
which formerly were expended during illness.

Employment, Agriculture, and Nutrition

One enormous factor in 1972 making for a better outlook
than in interwar years was the tremendous decline in unemployment. Indeed, unemployment, a major problem in
the interwar years, was scarcely a factor in the new Western
Europe, and the number of positions available in some
countries by 1970 far exceeded the number of job-seekers.

Thus in 1972 when the total urban populations were expanding and were much greater than they had been in
1929, unemployment was, with the single doubtful exception of Italy, far less than it had been in 1929. Most of what

44. NUMBER OF UNEMPLOYED IN SELECTED EUROPEAN
COUNTRIES, 1929–1970
(In thousands)

Country	1929	height of depression	1937	1958	1967	1970
Germany	1,899	5,576	912	683	444	144
Austria	192	406	321	123	65	58
Italy	301	1,006	874	1,759	689	616
U.K.	1,262	2,829	1,529	501	559	640

Source: UN *Yearbook* 1948, table 11; UN *Yearbook* 1951, table 10; UN *Yearbook*
1969, table 22, UN *Monthly Abstract,* March 1972, table 8.

unemployment there had been in 1970 was not due to scarcity of jobs available. Indeed France, Switzerland, and Germany were then absorbing the unemployed and under-employed of a host of nations. Whereas in 1960 there had only been some 276,000 foreign workers in Germany, by 1970 there were about two million. France had about three million and even Switzerland was faced by the problem of having about one million foreign workers among its labor force.

Indeed the employment picture in Germany was so good in the 1960s that immigration had passed emigration. In 1965 there were 73,851 immigrants and only 69,059 emigrants, as compared with 18,441 immigrants and 65,800 emigrants in 1955, and 7,795 immigrants and 22,986 emigrants in 1938.

Immigration not only follows the flag, but also follows the dollar or whatever is the greatest pay. In the late 1960s the take-home pay of the typical German industrial worker was the greatest in Europe (except Sweden). In 1969 the average monthly salary (in U.S. dollars) in France was $170.25; in England, $199.60; in Germany, $209.28. As German wages and real purchasing power rose in comparison with English, the trend of workers toward England declined and that toward Germany increased. Greater employment opportunities in France, Germany, and Switzerland increased this trend. By 1972, however, the American policies relative to improving the balance of payments were causing a slowing down in the rate of industrial growth in West Germany, Switzerland, and certain other countries. Fears for the stability of the American dollar cast a shadow over the outlook for continued rapid improvement.

In the fields of nutrition the new prosperity was being manifested in all of Western Europe, where the average man was eating much better than ever before. The average West European could afford much more in the way of food than in the past. A large part of this was due to both the improved methods of agriculture which were making possible better yields than ever and, to a lesser extent, the better means of transportation and marketing of farm commodities. It is impossible to overestimate the importance of this phenomenon and how it has affected the outlook of the average European. In 1970 there were already huge surpluses of butter and other commodities in Europe, and agricultural shortages and hunger were discussed in Western Europe and the United States only in an academic fashion. Except for certain comparatively small pockets of poverty in the affluent societies, hunger is something which deals primarily with those nations who have a population explosion in underdeveloped areas of the world. In 1949–50, however, many people were still wondering whether Europe itself could ever be properly fed. Even the United States in the post–World War II years, anxious to increase its food supplies to meet the European emergency, had given top immigration priority to farmers and was not interested in attracting ordinary scientists, doctors, and other professional persons. In 1950, hunger and food shortages which had haunted the USSR for more than thirty years continued to plague both the Soviets and the satellites. In this respect, the recovery and improvement of agriculture which held food prices down is every bit as amazing, if not more so, than the recovery and improvement in industrial productivity. By 1970 fewer people were producing more food on less land. It was requiring fewer and fewer persons to feed the population of Europe.

The fact that fewer people were needed on the farm to feed the population meant that more persons were available to contribute to the total output of wealth of the different countries. Just how great this shift in manpower was is revealed in table 45.

Farm machinery was making it possible for fewer workers to get more done. Taking just the tractor which had found virtually no widespread application outside the United States before 1930, and relatively little application until after World War II, we note that its use increased tremendously by the late 1960s. (See table 46)

45. PERCENTAGE OF WORKERS IN AGRI-
CULTURE, 1930–1967

Country	1930–1944	1967
Yugoslavia	74	53
Bulgaria	71	44
Rumania	72	59
Poland	59	42
Hungary	55	31
Spain	56	34
Czechoslovakia	32	16
France	33	18
Germany	18	11
Austria	31	20
Italy	49	25
Sweden	36	12
United Kingdom	8	4
United States	23	6
USSR	82	33

Source: Food and Agricultural Organization of
the United Nations (FAO), 1960, table 5; FAO,
1968, table 5.

The greater use of farm machinery to replace horses and
other farm animals meant that millions and millions of
acres formerly used to raise feed for these animals could
now be freed to raise crops for human consumption. Countries like Germany which as recently as 1938 had had 3
million horses, by 1960 had only a half million. In Russia
the number had declined from 30 million in 1910 to 11
million in 1960.

However, the use of tractors to replace manpower and
to allow more lands to be used for feeding humans rather
than for feeding horses and other draft animals, was only
part of the story of the tremendous agricultural revolution
which was taking place. Improved methods of agriculture,
increasing use of fertilizers, and better scientific knowledge
was increasing the yields per acre. And again the increase
in productivity was taking place at a more rapid rate than
earlier in the century.

46. NUMBER OF TRACTORS IN SELECTED COUNTRIES,
1939–1969
(In thousands)

Country	1939	1952–56	1967	1969
United States	1,447	4,348	4,822	4,790
France	30	268	1,107	1,230
East Germany	60*	29	139	146
West Germany		384	1,257	1,340
Hungary	7	22	68	67
Italy	39	124	509	584
Poland	1.5	45	151	186
Spain	10	22	191	220
USSR	484	788	1,739	1,908

Source: Woytinsky and Woytinsky, p. 516; UN *Statistical Yearbook for 1968*, table 27; UN *Statistical Yearbook for 1970*, table 28.
* Total of East and West Germany for 1939

Taking Austria as a rather typical example, table 47 notes great increases in productivity. Table 48 indicates how total wheat output in Europe has risen.

The increase in agricultural productivity in the first half of the twentieth century had been impressive. However, the productivity has increased at a faster rate in the last twenty

47. CROP YIELDS IN AUSTRIA
(In hundred kilograms per hectare)

Crop	1934–38 (average)	1968
Wheat	17	34
Rye	15	29
Barley	18	32
Oats	15	27
Maize	25	54
Potatoes	138	267
Sugar Beets	261	440

Source: FAO, 1969, tables 14, 15, 16, 94; FAO, 1954, part 1, tables 1, 6, 7, 8.

years. The tremendous rise in the productivity of countries
like Yugoslavia and Greece which had had such a comparative low output previously is no more remarkable than the
huge increases in the outputs of Germany and the United
Kingdom which already had had such large yields. The huge
increase in the use of artificial fertilizers helped maintain
the increase, improve yields, and prevent soil exhaustion.

48. WHEAT OUTPUT IN EUROPEAN COUNTRIES
(In thousands of metric tons)

Country	1934–38 (average)	1968
France	8,143	14,646
Austria	417	1,045
Hungary	2,220	3,360
Greece	756	1,515
Germany	4,086	6,198*

Source: UN *Statistical Yearbook for 1948,* table 13; UN
Statistical Yearbook for 1969, table 43.
* West Germany only.

France, for example, which in 1938 had used only 297,-
000 tons of phosphate fertilizers, was using 668,000 tons in
1956 and 1,587,000 tons in 1968–69. Spain, which had been
using only 60,000 tons in 1938, was using 389,000 in
1968–69. The use of nitrogen fertilizers had risen just as
dramatically; the USSR which had been using less than
500,000 tons in 1956 was using over 3 million tons by 1969.
   The results of this increased efficiency and technology
were reflected in the prices of many food commodities; thus
the price of wheat per kilo remained virtually constant
during the years 1951–66, while the level of wages in many
countries doubled. Tables 49 and 50 give figures for Italy
and Germany as examples of this phenomenon.
   The fact that much more was being produced both per
acre and per man hour expended meant that agricultural
prices did not rise proportionally. The producer price of

49. PRODUCER PRICE OF WHEAT IN GERMANY AND ITALY
(Per 100 kilograms)

Year	Germany		Italy	
	In U.S. dollars	In marks	In U.S. dollars	In thousand lira
1951	10.5	44.2	10.6	6.6
1959	10.1	42.6	10.4	6.5
1968	9.3	37.2	10.1	6.3

Source: FAO, 1969, table 169; FAO, 1960, table 126.

wheat per pound actually declined in Canada and the United States between 1950 and 1966, while shipping costs per ton of grain between those grain producing areas and Europe generally declined in that period.

Thus as salaries rose in proportion to the purchase price of food, the average worker could afford better foods, and all the Western European nations showed a marked increase in the per capita consumption of such foods as meats, dairy products, and fruits. For example, just in the years between 1954 and 1966 the annual per capita meat consumption in Austria rose from 129 to 173 pounds, in France from 188 to 277 pounds and in Spain from 39 to 73 pounds. During the same period the per capita potato and starch consump-

50. AVERAGE WAGE PER HOUR IN MANU-FACTURING IN GERMANY AND ITALY

Year	Germany (In marks)	Italy (In lira)
1953	1.59	169
1961	2.90	248
1967	4.60	426
1969	5.28	489

Source: UN *Statistical Yearbook for 1969*, table 173; UN *Statistical Yearbook for 1970*, table 175.

tion declined in Austria from 262 to 217 grams per day and in France from 262 to 218 grams per day, while in Spain this intake remained about the same. In the Scandinavian lands the amount of potatoes and flour consumed declined as shown in table 51.

Table 52 should be useful for a better idea of nutrition trends in the years 1954–69, realizing that already in 1954 people were eating better in Western Europe than they had twenty and thirty years earlier.

It can be seen that in the countries considered, the amount of meat consumed per capita has shown a steady

51. ANNUAL CONSUMPTION OF STARCH FOODS IN SCANDINAVIA
(Per capita in kilograms)

Country	Potatoes		Flour	
	1934–38	1964–65	1934–38	1964–65
Denmark	120	106	94	75
Finland	181	108	128	90
Norway	130	96	119	74
Sweden	122	96	95	69

Source: Nordic Council, *Yearbook of Nordic Statistics for 1967* (Stockholm, 1968), p. 115.

rise while the amount of cereal grains has shown a steady decline. It is obvious that a steadily increasing number of persons are able to afford meat and more expensive products and have been able to reduce their consumption of grains and other starch products.

Improved nutrition, improved housing, new antibiotics, and better hygienic and medical knowledge were all factors helping to keep down the number of days lost through illness.

The relative decline in food prices and the increased availability, partially through improved transportation distribution, of previously rare items was an enormous factor in the improvement of living standards, and even health.

52. NET FOOD SUPPLY PER CAPITA, 1948–1969
(In grams per day)

Country	Meat				Cereal			
	1948–50	1954–56	1963–665	1968–69	1948–50	1954–56	1963–665	1968–69
Austria	83	129	173	188	355	322	271	255
France	152	188	206	227*	333	305	250	225*
Federal Republic of Germany	80	138	179	200	314	260	203	191
Spain	...	39	73	115	...	320	279	242
U.K.	136	187	202	205	291	243	215	202
Yugoslavia	...	64	74	85*	...	509	534	514*
Italy	42	58	98	129	410	369	360	357
United States	224	252	276	299	210	189	178	178

Source: Food and Agricultural Organization of the United Nations, 1969, table 135.
* Figures for France and Yugoslavia listed under 1968–69 are for the preceding year, 1967.

53. WORKING TIME REQUIRED TO PURCHASE COMMON
FOODS, 1967
(In minutes per kilo)

City	Beef	Pork	White Bread	Rye Bread	Milk (liter)	Butter	Eggs (dozen)
New York	45	36	13	17	6	44	13
Moscow	222	233	56	27	31	367	167
London	83	162	13	13	12	44	28
Paris	337	314	16	43	16	217	63
Munich	252	106	31	17	11	112	37

Source: Keith Bush, "Radio Liberty Research Paper," no. 18, 1967,
pp. 18–20.

Yet, though food prices in Europe had declined very much relatively, food as such constituted a much larger share of the household budget for the average European family than it did for the American family. Table 53, based on average industrial wages in the different countries, shows the amount of working time that is necessary to purchase certain common foods.

Indeed taking what might be considered to be a typical weekly food basket for a family of four—a basket which would, however, probably be below that of the average industrial worker in the United States and above that of the average industrial worker in France or Russia—we find that the hours of work required to buy such a basket would vary as shown in table 54.

While prices in Munich, London, and Paris are obviously higher than in smaller towns and cities in the same countries, they nevertheless give some indication of the percentage of income that the average European worker has to devote to food. Yet the relatively small rise in population in Europe and the improving agricultural technology and yields should in the near future cause food products to take a lesser share of income, thus allowing more money to be spent for other commodities.

by 1970 the German worker was earning more even in actual wages than his English or French brothers, and he was working fewer hours. By 1970 industrial wages in the major European nations compared as shown in table 56.

Yet even in Germany the outlook was clouded. German competition had proved too strong for France and certain other nations and Germany had yielded to pressure to increase the value of her currency. This move had made German goods less competitive in the world markets. In 1971 and 1972 for the first time in years, German workers appeared restless and despite huge wage increases – between

56. TAKE-HOME PAY OF AVERAGE INDUSTRIAL
WORKER WITH WIFE AND TWO DEPENDENTS,
1969
(In U.S. Dollars)

Country	Per month	Per hour
United States	$460	$2.62
USSR	119	.68
United Kingdom	199	1.06
France	189	.96
West Germany	209	1.11

Source: Keith Bush, *Radio Liberty Research Bulletin*,
CRD 257/69, July 23, 1969.

1968 and 1970 the average industrial wage in Germany had risen from 4.9 to 6.1 marks per hour and was continuing to increase rapidly – there seemed no guarantee of continued labor peace in Germany, that labor peace which had contributed so greatly to the prosperity of the *Bundesrepublik*.

Table 57, by taking some common items and comparing their purchase prices, should provide an indication of the purchasing power of these and other wages listed in the preceding table.

In Germany, England, and Italy, the governments in office had only the barest of majorities; in Germany and Italy, they did not have even a majority but had been forced to join in

57. PURCHASE PRICE OF COMMON ITEMS, 1969
(In U.S. Dollars)

Item	U.S.	USSR	U.K.	France	W. Germany
1 pr. cheap nylon stockings	.59	2.22	.59	.27	.69
Men's socks, blue nylon	1.00	3.33	.60	.99	1.48
Men's black leather shoes	12.00	33.33	10.80	8.98	12.25
Men's office suit	35.00	133.33	43.20	38.70	55.00
Transistor radio	12.00	31.00	14.00	22.00	11.00
Television (59 cm B/W)	150.00	473.00	173.00	180.00	97.00
Rent, modest apartment	100.00	7.40	114.82	117.00	75.00
Electricity per KW hour	.03	.04	.02	.05	.03

Source: Bush, *Radio Liberty Bulletin*, No. 33 (1969), pp. 18–20.

coalitions to be able to form a government. In France, where George Pompidou had obtained a distinct though not too large majority at the polls, the economic losses of 1968 and early 1969 had not been recovered. Pompidou had to produce results fairly rapidly or the strong labor unions—many of them Communist-dominated—waiting in the wings were ready to call strikes which could again send the economy into a tailspin.

In Spain an aging Francisco Franco was making plans for an orderly succession to his rule. However, a totalitarian regime requires a strong hand at the helm, and it was difficult to say which way Spain would go after Franco's passing. In Portugal, the successor to Dictator Salazar was trying to lead the country into democratic parliamentary democracy, and there, too, it was not certain whether the transition would be without major upheavals. However, the first free elections held without incident in the fall of 1969 augured

*Leonid I. Bhezhnev, General Secretary of the Soviet Communist
Party*

Andrei A. Gromyko, Soviet Foreign Minister

well for this. In 1969 and 1970 the hard-line Communists in East Central Europe had gained ascendancy over elements in the party in favor of liberalizing the regimes. What had seemed a clear trend away from Stalinism in the 1960s had been reversed. The Soviet intervention in Czechoslovakia in 1968 and the crackdown on Dubcek and his elimination along with his followers from positions of authority in the Czech Communist party was a clear warning to the other satellites that Moscow was determined to control their further development. Rumania, which had seemed to be charting its own course, had been reined in, and though the Soviets had not yet interfered militarily there, the lesson for Rumania was clear.

On the whole, Soviet-dominated East Central Europe seemed stable as Europe approached the last quarter of the century. Yet the 1971 Polish workers' riots at Gdansk, Stettin, and a host of other Polish cities, which brought about the fall of Gomulka, gave evidence that this apparent stability could be shaken.

10

The Continuing Challenge

IN 1910 there were eight major powers in the world, six of which were European, and only two, the United States and Japan, which were not. In 1940 there were seven major powers, World War I having resulted in the total elimination of Austria-Hungary as a great power, although Germany had regained major power status. In 1970 there were only two superpowers, the United States and the USSR. All the major nations of Central and Western Europe — Britain, France, Germany, and Italy — had lost their positions as major world powers, either directly or indirectly as a result of World War II. Outside of Europe, China, though economically and industrially backward, had become a great power, whereas a progressing and economically and industrially advanced Japan had not yet regained major power status.

During this same period, however, Europe had advanced to new heights of productivity and well-being, despite two world and civil wars. The tremendous increase in European industrial production, in the use of chemicals, in urbanization, in automobile congestion etc., had created a host of ecological problems and there were many pessimists who looked with extreme disfavor on the industrial progress of Europe. Yet the fact remains that in 1900, electric lighting, sewage systems, public transportation, telephones, airplanes, automobiles, refrigerators, public health service, old-age benefits, unemployment insurance, compulsory and free public education, public swimming pools, indoor plumbing, and a host of other benefits were either in their infancy or virtually unknown in most of Europe. Infant mortality rates ranged from seven to nine times as much as they did in 1970. European countries in which more than two hundred out of every thousand new-born babies died within the first year of life thus had had their rates cut to thirty and twenty-five per thousand, and the rate was continuing to decline. In 1900, the average weekly hours of work ranged from fifty-five to sixty in the major nations; in 1970, they were down to about forty to forty-six hours. In standards of living, in real wages, in numbers of luxuries available to the average person, in opportunities for paid vacations, travel, decent housing, more nutritious food, more education, and better health care, every European country was further along in the 1970s than it had been in 1900 or 1938 or 1950. Yet as the German writer Goethe had observed almost two centuries ago, Western man cannot really be content. By 1970 he had accustomed himself very quickly to the new luxuries and wanted more. The man whose dreams had once been limited to having a one-week paid vacation a year was dissatisfied now when he had only two or three weeks. Indeed a three- to four-week vacation was already standard in France and Germany. Many people who had once regarded a bicycle as a luxury were no longer content with lower-priced automobiles like Volkswagens and Fiats.

This does not mean that increased luxuries, increased leisure time, social benefits, and medical care had failed to bring any contentment. The majority of West Europeans were apparently generally satisfied with the improvements taking place since the late 1940s. However, there was an increasing number, though still a pronounced minority, of students and "thinkers" of the new, as well as the older, generation who violently raged against the materialism of Western society and Western democracy. The more conventional leftist radicals looked to the USSR as their ideal. Many of the newer leftist idealists looked about and seeing injustices, poverty, and imperfections blamed "the system," but did not look to Moscow for leadership. Many of these

The new Europe—the Thyssen Building, Dusseldorf, Germany

The old Europe—a street in the older section of Zurich

persons hoped that by destroying "the system," some new perfect society could emerge from the ruins. For these extremists even the example of Soviet Russia was too moderate. They looked for more extreme measures and models to follow. Khrushchev had preached coexistence and had been unwilling to risk the gains of the USSR by pushing revolutionary movements to the point where they could lead to war. This had been one of the prime reasons for the split between him and Mao. The heroes of the extremists, therefore, were the Maos, the Che Gueveras, and the Fidel Castros. A revolution against the existing order must be carried on regardless of the dangers and costs, they maintained.

In the early 1970s, political philosophies were, therefore, more tied in with economic philosophies. And by this time there were four or five major economic-political philosophies competing for man's favor. First, and perhaps least important in contrast to the 1930s, was the Fascist philosophy. Discredited by World War II and having no strong central base of operations, Fascist philosophies did not have their former appeal to youth. However, there were a few signs of a Fascist revival in Germany, Italy, and France. Spain still had an authoritarian, Fascist-type regime, and the Greek Military Junta which seized power in the late 1960s was accused by many of having instituted that type of government. Nevertheless, fascism in the early 1970s had a relatively small appeal in the major European democracies. In the countries behind the Iron Curtain, most of those persons disenchanted with communism seemingly longed for some type of political democracy, not fascism.

The Russian type of communism and the Chinese type of communism were appealing primarily to those to the extreme left of center in the non-Communist countries who were dissatisfied with the rate of progress toward social and economic justice.

In most of non-Communist Europe the population was divided not among the competing philosophies of the ex-

treme Left and extreme Right, but among the philosophies
of the two more conventional parties, the democratic conservative and the democratic socialist parties which stood
for social progress and prosperity, but were opposed to any
great and violent change to achieve these results, feeling
that technological advance and the normal processes, having already produced such great strides in the twentieth
century, would continue to do so and could thereby trans-
form society before the century was out. Too much tamper-
ing with the existing mechanism, they felt, would not only
not really speed up advance but would cause more suffering
than benefit. While both parties stood for social progress
and prosperity, the democratic socialist parties differed from
the democratic conservatives in pushing more strongly to
equalize income and have more governmental control and
interference in business and enterprises; however, they, unlike the supporters of the Maoist and Soviet philosophies,
wanted to achieve this without abridging freedom of protest,
freedom of elections, and other basic freedoms of the representative democracies.

By 1972 neither Communist China nor Cuba had made
enough economic progress to attract supporters anxious to
improve their living standards quickly. The European nations and the United States, along with such states as
Canada, Australia, Japan, etc., were still not only the leading
industrial nations of the world, but had the highest standards
of living. The appeal of Mao and Castro was based on the
fact that they had thrown off the shackles of the past,
cleaned up their cities, and were combating famine and
illiteracy on a scale not done before. Their supporters maintained that a dozen years in Cuba and twenty years in
China were still not enough to really show what they
could do.

However, circumstances were far different in most European states from what they had been in China and even in
Cuba. Largely for that reason, Maoism and Castroism had
little appeal even in the poorer countries of Europe. The real
struggle of philosophies there was between the Soviet-type

philosophy and Western-type parliamentary philosophy. For many persons in intellectual circles in the early 1970s, freedom as understood in the past did not have the former appeal. For many of these people, economic advances were more important than what they referred to as so-called freedom of speech, freedom of elections, and so forth.

Throughout most of the rest of the world and in intellectual circles in the democratic European countries, the statistics of democratic achievements were being compared with the statistics of Communist achievements. In certain circles within the Communist world as well they were being closely observed. However, free criticism there was strictly proscribed. The Soviets had shown by their interventions in Hungary in 1956 and in Czechoslovakia in 1968 and 1969 that free criticism was not compatible with their type of communism. They had also shown that unless there were to be war or some unforeseen great weakening of Moscow's power, the Soviet bloc would remain intact. There could be no real open competition for man's mind there. The competition that would take place would be in the non-Communist world.

This then was the continuing challenge. It could be maintained to Communist sympathizers that the workers of every major non-Communist West European and Central European state had a higher standard of living than did those of the Soviet Union or the satellites. Communists would maintain that these nations had always enjoyed a higher standard of living and that the Soviets were making more progress. They could maintain that the citizens in Communist countries did not have to worry about either medical care expenses or unemployment compensation. By way of answer it could be pointed out by others that Great Britain already had full medical coverage, that most of the nations of Western Europe had certain forms of health coverage of one nature or another, and that there were already in existence in all these nations various forms of unemployment compensation.

Quite obviously the average industrial worker in the

"workers' and peasants' states" did not enjoy the material advantages of the workers in the Western nations. However, many Western intellectuals did not consider this important. When the honored representatives of the foreign intelligentsia came to the USSR, most of the mundane problems attendant with human existence were taken care of for them. Their hotel rooms were already arranged and prepaid, as were their meals.

What was often noted by these persons was the tremendous literary activity, the great number of cultural events, the great number of government-supported theaters, the interest in poetry, and so forth. And in this respect the Soviet government had done more to encourage the arts than had the Western governments. However, the fact that the government supported writers and other artists and that books were as a rule cheaper than in the West was only part of the story. The creative artist had to be wary not to exceed the limits set by the party. In Stalinist days an inadvertent slip could mean Siberia. In the 1960s some writers, like Sinyavskii and Daniel, could still be sent to Siberia; however, it was no longer the case of a chance word being held against them. Nevertheless, the sentencing of certain writers and the inability of other writers to publish works which were felt to be not in the party's interest meant that the arts were being straitjacketed. While more and more people were enjoying performances in the theaters and concert halls, the fact was that there were strong controls exercised on the arts from above.

The balance sheet in 1972 showed a lower general standard of living in housing, food, clothing, and luxuries in the Soviet Union and Eastern Europe for the most part, with the citizen insured against health, retirement, and unemployment problems; a controlled arts and cultural program supported by the government there made productions available to more persons and enabled more people to indulge their talents in the arts, yet restricted free expression in those fields as well.

In the West tourists by the tens of millions, including many from the industrial proletariat, were traveling to other nations discovering new cultures, new habits. In the USSR too, tourism was rising; yet foreign travel, especially outside of the Iron Curtain, was still beyond the dream of the average Soviet citizen.

Thus, since the Communist revolution and the end of World War I more than half a century ago, tremendous advances had been made in Eastern and Western Europe and in Northern and Southern Europe. In Eastern Europe, industrial, economic, and educational advance had taken place under communism. In North, Central, and Western Europe, these advances have taken place under representative democracies. In Spain the advances had occurred under an authoritarian government.

Dictatorships of all persuasions have had and continue to have their active propagandists who can use figures impressively. In 1972 these figures could easily show that in Europe tremendous advances have been made and are being made under freedom and democracy. It will be interesting to see whether free societies in the future will be able to continue to give their citizens more butter, clothing, and housing as well as freedom.

Selected Bibliography

Index

Selected Bibliography

Statistical Information

Excellent sources for statistics of individual nations are the statistical yearbooks they publish. For some nations, such as Great Britain and France, these go back well into the last century. For other nations such as Austria it is only comparatively recently that regular and comprehensive statistical studies are readily available. The various statistical studies of the United Nations have been improving and becoming more comprehensive during the last fifteen years or so. Some of the more valuable statistical studies used in this work are:

Annuaire statistique de la france. Several of the earlier editions such as the yearbook for 1954 have excellent comparative figures for many of the European nations.

League of Nations. *Statistical Yearbook,* for the 1920s and 1930s. These League of Nations studies, while not as comprehensive as the later United Nations data, contain a great wealth of information not otherwise readily available.

Statistisches Jahrbuch der Bundesrepublik. "Internationale Übersicht" section has good comparative data.

United Nations publications:
  Statistical Yearbook, for the years since 1948.
  Food and Agricultural Organization Yearbook, since 1948.
  UNESCO Yearbook, since 1948.
  Demographic Yearbook, since 1948.
  Monthly Bulletin of Statistics.

Woytinsky, W. S. *Die Welt in Zahlen,* 7 vols. Berlin: 1927.

———. *World Commerce and Governments: Trends and Outlook.* New York: Twentieth Century, 1955.

Woytinsky, W. S. and Woytinsky, E. S. *World Population and Production: Trends and Outlook.* New York: Twentieth Century, 1953. A good interpretation and résumé of many statistics and an excellent handy reference; however, its figures for most of the European nations are not comprehensive enough for any thorough study.

Recommended Background Reading

Ardagh, John. *The New French Revolution.* New York: Harper and Row, 1968.

Benns, Frank Lee. *Europe Since 1914 in its World Setting.* New York: Appleton-Century-Crofts, 1954.

Besson, Waldemar. *Die Aussenpolitik der Bundesrepublik.* Munich: R. Piper, 1970.

Brzezinski, Zbigniew. *The Soviet Bloc, Unity and Conflict.* New York: Praeger, 1965.

Churchill, Winston. *The Second World War,* 6 vols. New York: Houghton Mifflin, 1953.

Crankshaw, Edward. *Khrushchev: A Biography.* London, 1966.

Djilas, Milovan. *The New Class.* New York: Praeger, 1957.

Dmytryshyn, Basil. *USSR: A Concise History.* New York: Charles Scribner's Sons, 1965.

Florinsky, Michael T. *Russia: A History and an Interpretation,* 2 vols. New York: Macmillan, 1959. Background a bit too detailed for the average reader. Only goes up to the revolution.

Furniss, Edgar S. *France, Troubled Ally.* New York: Harper, 1960.

Hall, Walter P. and Davis, William S. *The Course of Europe Since Waterloo.* New York: Appleton-Century-Crofts, 1957. A good solid history, giving the political background to contemporary events.

Kaser, Michael. *Comecon Integration Problems of the Planned Economies.* Oxford: Oxford University Press, 1965.

Leonhard, Wolfgang. *The Kremlin Since Stalin.* New York: Praeger, 1962. Excellent.

Leuthy, Herbert. *France Against Herself.* Cleveland: Meridian, 1955.

Lowenthal, Richard. *World Communism: The Disintegration of a Secular Faith.* Oxford: Oxford University Press, 1966.

Lukacs, John. *History of the Cold War.* New York: Doubleday, 1961.

Mann, Golo. *History of Germany Since 1789.* New York: Praeger, 1970. Translated from the German.

Mayne, Richard. *The Recovery of Europe: From Devastation to Unity.* New York: Harper, 1970.

Rauch, Georg von. *A History of Soviet Russia,* 4th ed. rev. New York: Praeger, 1964.

Riasanovsky, Nicholas V. *A History of Russia.* Oxford: Oxford University Press, 1963.

Sampson, Anthony. *The New European.* London: Hodder and Stoughton, 1968.

Shirer, William L. *The Rise and Fall of the Third Reich.* New York: Simon and Schuster, 1960. A readable best seller by a correspondent in Germany in the opening years of the war. While it has had some justified criticism from pure historians, it can be read to good advantage by the average student interested in the period of Nazi Germany.

Treadgold, Donald W. *Twentieth Century Russia.* Chicago: Rand McNally, 1961.

Trefousse, Hans Louis. *The Cold War: A Book of Documents.* New York: Putnam, 1965.

Viansson-Ponté, Pierre. *Histoire de la République Gaulienne.* Paris: Fayard, 1970. Concerned primarily with the years 1958–62 until the definitive de Gaulle victory over the "Algérie française" movement.

Werth, Alexander. *France 1940–1955.* New York: Henry Holt, 1956. A very readable book written with some of that stylish anti-American bias which one finds among certain left-leaning Continental intellectuals.

————. *Russia at War.* New York: Dutton, 1964. A rather detailed and sympathetic treatment of World War II from the Russian side.

Williams, Philip M. *French Politicians and Elections, 1951–1969.* Cambridge University Press, 1970.

Wolfe, Bertram D. *Khrushchev and Stalin's Ghost.* New York: Praeger, 1957.

————. *Marxism: One Hundred Years in the Life of a Doctrine.* New York: Dial Press, 1965.

Index

Acheson, Dean (1893–1971), 122
Adenauer, Konrad (1876–1967):
  photograph, 180; mentioned, 179
Afrika Korps, 59, 67, 69, 72
Agriculture: improvement in output, 220–23; percent of workers in, 221; tractors in, 222; fertilizers in, 223
Albania, 37, 59, 117, 121, 126
Algerian Revolt (French officer revolt), 178–79
Algerian War (of France), 156, 179
Alsace, 38
Annunzio, Gabrielle d'. See D'Annunzio, Gabriele
Anti-Comintern Pact, 34
Anti-Semitism: Nazi and, 27; Nazi brutality in Poland, 47; Nazi shooting of Jews in Russia, 63; Nazi concentration camps, 75; in USSR 1951–53, 160–61, 165; in Soviet satellites, 165
Antonescu, Marshal Ion (1882–1946), 57
Ardennes Offensive (1944), 73
Atlantic Charter, 95–96, 104
Atom bomb, 115
Austria: annexation (Anschluss) by Germany, 25, 34–35; peace treaty, 171; crop yields, 222; mentioned, 20, 28, 34, 96, 113, 115, 129, 157, 171
Axis: formation of, 34

Badoglio, Marshal Pietro (1871–1956), 53, 70, 85, 96
Balkan Entente, 57
Baltic States: Soviets acquire bases in 1939, 49; Soviets annex, 1940, 57
Barbarossa (operation), 58, 60
Beck, General Ludwig (1880–1944), 51, 72
Belgium: German attack of 1940, 52–53; opposition to King Leopold's return, 77; postwar industrial recovery, 135; number of physicians, 212
Beneš, Eduard (1884–1948), 87
Berchtesgaden, 36
Bereitschaften, 149
Beria, Lavrenti (1899–1953), 169–70
Berlin: blockade, 124, 125, 126; wall, 151
Berman, Jacob (1901–), 163
Bessarabia: annexation by Soviets, 57
Bierut, Boleslaw (1892–1956), 110, 114
Big Three: at Teheran, 97; at Yalta, 103; at Potsdam, 115; mentioned, 83, 96, 102, 110, 114
Birthrate, 213
Bizonia, 120, 123, 135
Blackshirts, 24
Bohemia: Nazi protectorate, 37; mentioned, 20
Bor-Komorowski, General Tadeusz (1895–1966), 108, 111
Brandt, Willi (1914–): photograph, 188; mentioned, 189
Brezhnev, Leonid I. (1906–): photograph, 232
Britain: population, 4, 197, 215; urbanization, 6–7; railroad development, 8; parliamentary government in, 14–15; Locarno agreements, 26; Munich and appeasement, 36; guarantees to Poland against Hitler, 38; entry into World War II, 43; shipping losses in World War II, 48; Dunkirk evacuation, 53; Battle of, 56; destroyers from America, 58; defeat in Greece, 60; Labour victory, 1945, 76; Atlantic Charter, 95; Teheran Conference, 97–98; percentages agreement, 101; Yalta, 102–5; Polish problem, 103–14;

withdrawal from Greece, 1947, 121; economic crisis resulting from WW II, 131–33; productivity in, 132; Marshall Plan and resulting economic advance, 134–35; Conservative Victory of 1951, 136; de Gaulle opposition of, 182–83; Common Market, 183–85; Labour Victory of 1964, 185; electrical output, 197; number of automobiles, 198; telephones, 200; radios and televisions, 201; housing, 202–4; tourism, 206–7; number of students, 211; infant mortality, 212; birthrate, 213; divorce, 214; incidence of TB and pneumonia, 217–18; number of unemployed, 218; wages and standard of living, 219, 226–31; percentage of workers in agriculture, 221; number of tractors, 222

Bukovina: Soviet annexation, 57

Bulgaria: rearming permitted by Little Entente, 35; Vienna Award of August 30, 1940, 57; entrance of German troops, 59; attempt at peace settlement, 72; agreement between Churchill and Stalin, 101; attempt at peace treaty, 115; invasion by Russia, 116; Greek Communist bases supported by Soviet bloc states, 122; violation of Yalta agreement, 122; West Europeans visiting, 209; percentage of workers in agriculture, 1930–67, 221; meat consumption per capita, 229

Bulge, Battle of the, 73

Bundesrepublik: formation of, 128, 146, 151; industrial production, 1949–56, 147; crop production, 1934–57, 147; steel production, 196; electrical output, 197; population, 197, 215; wheat output, 198; number of automobiles, 198; telephones, 200; radios and televisions, 201; students, 211; physicians, 212; infant mortality, 212; birthrate, 213; divorces, 214; incidence of TB, 217; number of unemployed, 218; wages and cost of living, 219, 226–31; percentage of workers in agriculture, 221; number of tractors, 222;

wheat output, 223; meat consumption per capita, 229

Byrnes, James (1879–1972), 115, 121, 144

Cairo Conference (1943), 97

Carpatho-Ukraine, 87

Casablanca Conference (1943), 70, 96

Caucasus, 67

Chamberlain, Austen (1863–1937), 26

Chamberlain, Neville (1869–1940), 36, 38, 43, 50, 52

Chiang-Kai-Shek, Generalissimo (1886–), 97

China: split with Russia, 183

Christian Democratic Party (German), 179, 186

Churchill, Winston (1874–1965): warnings against appeasement, 36; appointed First Lord of Admiralty, 48; appointed Prime Minister, 52; summons English to resist, 55; at Casablanca Conference, 70, 96; and German attack on Russia, 93; and Teheran Conference, 97–98; Moscow meeting with Stalin in 1944, 101; Yalta, 103–6; question of postwar Polish government, 103–14; "Iron Curtain" in Fulton, Missouri speech, 119; re-elected Prime Minister, 136

Coal: and British economy, 131, 134; productivity, 132; postwar shortages, 141; Soviet output, 162

Cold War: beginning of, 91; roots of, 92, 114; development, 92–128, 167, 171, 182. See also Potsdam Conference; Yalta Conference

Collective Security, 31, 32

Comintern, 125, 157

Common Market: Britain and, 185–86; mentioned, 182, 185

Communism. See Ideologies

Communist Parties: in Italy, 17, 19, 123–24; in Germany, 27, 28, 29; in France, 123–24, 137–41 passim. See also Satellites

Concentration camps, 75

Conservative Party (Great Britain), 136, 185

Construction activity, 204

Consumer goods: automobiles, 198; telephones, 200; radios and televisions, 201
Cost of living, 228–31
Crete: German invasion of (1941), 60
Croatia: crackdown on Croatian nationalism, 1971, 210; mentioned, 60
Cuban Missile Crisis, 182
Curzon Line, 46, 88, 104
Czechoslovakia: Nazi takeover, 1939, 36–39; Communist takeover, 1948, 123, 134; Soviet invasion, 1968, 234; mentioned, 20, 35, 87, 115, 191

Daladier, Edouard (1884–1970), 36, 52
D'Annunzio, Gabriele (1863–1938), 17, 18
Danzig (Gdansk): Polish riots of 1971, 234; mentioned, 39
Darlan, Admiral François (1881–1942), 79, 137, 138
DDR (Deutsche Demokratische Republik): organization of, 128, 149; housing, 148, 204; uprisings in 1953, 150, 170; number of tractors in, 222; meat consumption in, 229
De Gasperi, Alcide (1881–1954): photograph, 86; mentioned, 85–87, 179
De Gaulle, Charles (1890–1970): rise of, 78–81; heads French government in Paris, 1944, 99; tries to create third force with Britain, 102; merges committee with General Giraud, 138; proclaimed by Algerian putschists, 178; grants free elections for Algeria, 179; vetoes English admission to Common Market, 182–83; Paris riots of 1968, 185, 193
Democracy: favorable outlook in pre-World War I period, 14; comparison of English and Continental, 14–15; loses to fascism, 15–16, 29; in Czechoslovakia, 20; reestablishment in Low Countries and Norway, 76; in France, 81; in Italy, 85; unstable in Italy in 1970s, 189; in conflict with the "isms" in the 70s, 240–43

Demography. See Birthrate; Population
Denmark: Nazi attack on, 50; food consumption in, 225
Depression, 27
De-Stalinization speech, 172–73
Divorce rate, 214
Doctors' plot (Kremlin), 160, 168, 169
Dresden: fire bombing, 142
Dubcek, Alexander (1921–), 234
Dumbarton Oaks Conference, 102
Dunkirk evacuation, 53

East Germany. See DDR
Eban Emaul fortress, 53
Ebert, Friedrich (1871–1925), 21
Eden, Anthony (1897–), 98
Education: number of students, 211. See also Illiteracy
Ehrenburg, Ilya (1891–1967), 170
Electric output. See Production
Enabling Act (Hitler's power seizure), 29
Erhard, Ludwig (1897–): photograph, 181; mentioned, 179
Erzberger, Matthias (1875–1921), 23
European Institutions: Advisory Commission, 134; Defense Community, 146; Common Market, 182, 185. See also Marshall Plan
European Recovery Program. See Marshall Plan

Facta, Luigi (1861–1930), 17, 19
Famine, Russian, 12
Fascism: rise of, in Italy, 15–19
Faure, Edgar (1908–), 156
Federal Republic of Germany. See Bundesrepublik
Finland: Soviet attack on, 49–50, 56, 93; peace with USSR, 72; cobelligerent against Germany, 72; attempt at peace treaty, 115
Fiume, 17, 19, 87
Five Year Plan: First Plan, 1928, 12; Fourth Plan, 1946, 157
Foreign workers: in Western Europe, 219
Fourth Republic (France), 81
France: population, 4, 197, 215; urbanization of, 6–7; railroad development, pre-1913, 8; steel production in, 9, 196; two-elec-

tion system, 14–15; occupation of
Ruhr, 1923, 23; German militarization of Rhineland, 32; Munich
Appeasement, 36; entry into
World War II, 43; defeat in
Flanders, 52–53; German breakthrough at Sedan and French surrender, 53–54; rise of de Gaulle
and the Free French, 78–81; Allied invasion of French North
Africa, 79; Allied invasion of
France and Paris uprising, 80;
Communists in Underground,
80–81, 137; Establishment of
Fourth Republic, 81, 138, 139;
during Nazi ascendancy, 136–
39; recovery after World War II,
136–41; recovery under Marshall
Plan, 140; German rearmament
and Cold War, 152–54; housing,
154; electric output, 197; wheat
output, 198, 223; number of automobiles, 198; number of telephones, 200; housing, 203–4;
tourism, 206; number of radio
and television sets, 210; number
of students, 211; number of physicians, 212; infant mortality,
212; birthrate, 213; divorce rate,
214; TB in, 217; wages, 219; percentage of workers in agriculture, 221; number of tractors,
222; purchasing power, 226–31
Franck, Hans, 46
Franco, Generalissimo Francisco
(1892–): photograph, 33; mentioned, 34, 38, 82, 83, 84, 177,
231
Franc-Tireurs-Partisans, 137
Free French movement, 78
Frei Korps, 22, 24
French Communists in resistance,
80–82
French Fleet: after French surrender in World War II, 78
French Underground, 79–80
Fritsch, General Werner von (1880–
1939), 51
Fulton,   Missouri   (Churchill
speech), 119

Gaulle. See De Gaulle, Charles
Gdansk. See Danzig
German Democratic Republic (East
Germany). See DDR

German Federal Republic. See Bundesrepublik
German Officer Conspiracy, 71. See
also Hitler
German rearmament (post–World
War II), 152
German-Soviet Pact of 1939, 41
Germany: population, 4, 197, 215;
urbanization, 6–7; railroad development, pre-1913, 8; steel production, 9, 196; losses in World War
I, 11, 21; Spartacists, 20; economic dislocation caused by
World War I, 21; reparations for
World War I, 21–22; Frei Korps
and rightists, 22–24; French occupation of Ruhr, 23; inflation
and ruin of middle class, 23–24;
rise of Hitler, 24–29; Locarno
Treaties and entry into League of
Nations, 26; Weimar prosperity
and the Great Depression, 27; unemployment, 28; enabling act
and Hitler's taking of power, 29;
reunification of Saar in 1935, 32;
conscription proclaimed, 1935,
32; repudiation of both Versailles
and Locarno Treaties, 32; re-
militarization of Rhineland, 33;
Anschluss, 34–35; Sudeten Crisis
of 1938, 35–36; protectorate over
Bohemia established, 37; Memel
taken, 1939, 39; Polish crisis and
demands for Danzig and Corridor, 38–39; nonaggression pact
with USSR, 41; attack on Poland,
43; England and France enter
war, 43; destruction of Polish air-
force, 45; victory in Poland and
re-partition of, 46; attack on Norway and Denmark, 50–51; attack
on the Low Countries, 52; victory
in Flanders and France, 52–54;
offer of peace to England, 54–55;
attempt to control air over England, 56; split with Soviets, 56–
58; Vienna Awards of 1940, 57;
Afrika Korps to Libya, 59; attack
on Yugoslavia and Greece, 60; attack on Russia, 60; mistreatment
of prisoners, 63; failure before
Moscow, 65; declaration of war
on the United States, 65; defeat
at Stalingrad and Tunisia, 67–
68; defection of Italy, 70; defec-

tion of Rumania and Finland, 72;
rise of Paris and Warsaw under-
grounds, 72; German capitula-
tion, 73; atrocities, 75; currency
reform, 124, 125; post–World
War II recovery, 141–47; housing, 148–49. See also Bizonia;
Bundesrepublik; DDR; Hitler;
World War II
Giraud, General Henri (1879–
1949), 79, 137, 138
Goering, Marshal Hermann (1893–
1946), 25
Gold crisis, 183, 184
Gomulka, Wladislaw (1905–), 165,
173, 174, 175
Gottwald, Klement (1896–1953),
163
Great Britain. See Britain
Greece: Italian attack on, 59; Nazi
attack on, 60; meat consumption,
229; mentioned, 99
Greek Communist revolt, 106, 116,
121–22, 125, 126, 134
Gromyko, Andrei A. (1909–): pho-
tograph, 233
Grotewohl, Otto (1894–1964), 149,
165
Gypsies: extermination by Nazis,
63, 75

Haaken VII, King of Norway
(1872–1957), 51, 77
Health: infant mortality, 212; number of physicians, 212; TB and
certain other diseases, 217–18,
241; nutrition, 229; medical coverage, 241
Heath, Edward (1916–): photograph, 187; mentioned, 186
Henlein, Konrad (1898–1945), 35
Hess, Rudolf (1894–), 26, 94
Hindenburg, Field Marshal Paul
von (1847–1934), 28
Hitler, Adolph (1889–1945): rise
of, 24–29; sends troops into
Rhineland, 32; Rome-Berlin Axis,
34; Anschluss, 34–35; Sudeten
Crisis, 35–36; occupation of Bohemia, 37; Lebensraum, 38; Danzig and Polish Corridor, 38–39;
German-Soviet Pact of 1939, 41;
peace offers to England, 47, 55;
in World War II, 49–55 passim;
61–66 passim; suicide, 73; men-

tioned, 83, 93, 94, 109, 111, 142,
189
Holland: German attack on, 52–53;
return of Wilhelmina to, 77; postwar recovery of, 135; number of
physicians in, 212
Hopkins, Harry (1890–1946), 114
Housing, 202–5
Hull, Cordell (1871–1955), 97
Hungary: Anschluss brings Nazis
to borders, 35; Czechs cede areas
to, 1938, 37; within German orbit, 38; Vienna Award of 1940,
57; join Nazis in attack on USSR,
61; attempt to withdraw from
war, 72; countercoup by local
Nazis, 72; agreement between
Churchill and Stalin, 101; attempt at peace treaty, 115; Sovi-
etizing government, 117; wheat
yield, 162, 223; West Europeans
visiting, 209; number of students, 210; birthrate, 213; divorces, 214; deaths from TB, 217;
percent of workers in agriculture,
221; number of tractors, 222;
meat consumption, 229; Soviet
intervention, 1956, 241

Ideologies: political "isms" during
interwar period, 14–15; rise of
fascism in Italy, 15–19; rise of
nazism, 24–29; communism, 92–
93; fascism in the 1970s, 239;
Maoists in the 1970s, 238–40;
Soviet-type communism in the
1970s, 241–43; Western-type democracy in the 1970s, 240–41.
See also Cold War
Illiteracy: in European countries, 3,
16
Indo-China: United States in, 183;
mentioned, 140, 153, 154, 156,
171, 177, 178
Infant mortality rate, 212
Iran, 117
Italian Communists, 85–86
Italy: railroad development, 8; illiteracy, 16; rise of fascism and
Mussolini, 16–19; Fiume, 17; attack on Ethiopia, 32; Rome-Berlin Axis, 34; attack on Albania,
37; "Pact of Steel" with Hitler,
41; entry into World War II, 53–
54; attack on Greece, 59; war in

Lybia, 59; Allied invasion of Sicily, 70, fall of Mussolini, 70; devastation following war, 84; recovery, 85–87; abolition of monarchy, 85; Trieste dispute, 87; election of de Gasperi and Christian Democrats, 87; steel production, 196; electrical output, 197; number of automobiles, 198; number of telephones, 200; number of radio and television sets, 201; housing, 204; tourism to Italy, 206; number of students, 211; birthrate, 213; TB rate, 217; number of unemployed, 218; percentage of workers in agriculture, 221; number of tractors, 222; wages and purchasing power, 224; strikes, 229

Japan: attack on Manchuria, 31, 37; anti-Comintern Pact with Germany and Italy, 34; Rome-Berlin-Tokyo axis, 34; attack on United States, 60–61; nonaggression treaty with Stalin, 61, 83; war continuing, 73; USSR enters war against, 103; steel production, 196; electrical output, 197; population, 197; number of telephones, 200; birthrate, 213
Jews, 27, 47, 63, 75, 160, 161, 165. See also Anti-Semitism

Kadar, Janos (1912–), 175, 177
Kapp, Dr. Wolfgang: Kapp Putsch, 25
Karelian Isthmus, 49, 50
Katyn Forest massacre (1943), 90–91
Kennan, George (1904–), 122
Khrushchev, Nikita (1894–1971), 46, 159, 168, 171, 172, 174, 176, 177
Kiesinger, Kurt Georg (1904–), 186
Korean War (1950–1953), 146, 152, 166, 167, 171
Kosciuzko Division, 107
Kremlin Doctors' Plot. See Doctors' plot
Kursk tank battle (1943), 70

Labour Party (British), 76, 136, 185

League of Nations, 31, 32, 33, 39, 57, 102
Lebensraum, 38, 47
Le Clerc, Marshal Philippe Marie (1902–1947), 80
Lend-Lease Act, 60, 93, 117, 130
Lenin, Vladimir (1870–1924), 11, 92
Leningrad, 67
Leopold III, King of Belgium (1901–), 77
Literacy, 3, 16
Little Entente, 35
Lloyd-George, David (1863–1945), 69
Locarno Pact, 26, 32, 38
Lublin government, 101, 105, 109, 110, 111, 114
Ludendorff, General Eric (1865–1937), 25–26
Luftwaffe, 36, 56
Luxury items. See Consumer goods

Macmillan, Harold (1894–), 177
Maginot Line, 48, 52
Malenkov, Georgi (1901–), 169
Manchuria: invasion by Japan, 1931, 31
Maniu, Iuliu (1873–1951), 123
Mannerheim, Baron Carl Gustaf (1867–1951), 49
Marshall, General George, 122, 134
Marshall Plan, 122–23, 134, 140, 153
Marx, Karl (1818–1883), 1
Masaryk, Jan (1886–1948), 87
Memel, 39
Mendès-France, Pierre (1907–), 156
Michael I, King of Rumania (1921–), 116
Mikolajczk, Stanislaw (1901–1966), 101, 114
Mindzenty, Cardinal Joseph (1892–), 174
Mining. See Coal
Molotov, Vyacheslav (1890–), 49, 56, 57, 58, 95, 110, 174
Montgomery, Field Marshal Bernard (1897–), 69
Morgenthau, Henry, Jr. (1891–1967), 99
Morgenthau Plan, 99–101, 144
Moscow Conference: 1943 (Big

Three), 96; 1944 (Churchill and Stalin), 101
Mussolini, Benito (1883–1945): rise of, 17–19; attack on Ethiopia, 32; aid to Franco in Civil War, 34; formation of Rome-Berlin Axis, 34; invasion of Albania, 37; "pact of steel" with Hitler, 1939, 41; attack on France, 1940, 53–54; attack on Greece, 1940, 59; deposition of, 70

Nagy, Imre (1895–1958), 175
NATO, 123, 128, 146, 153, 166, 167
Nazi Party: rise of, 24–29
Nazi-Soviet Pact. See German-Soviet Pact of 1939
Normandy: 1944 invasion of, 71, 98
North Atlantic Treaty Organization. See NATO
Norway: Nazi attack on, 50; food consumption, 225; mentioned, 77
Nutrition, 225, 226, 227

Oder-Neisse Line, 104, 116
Okulicki, Colonel Leopold: arrested by Soviets, 111
Oran, 78
Orlando, Vittorio (1860–1952), 17

Paris: 1944 uprising, 72; 1968 street riots, 185
Paris Peace Conference (1946–1947), 87
Pauker, Anna (1893–1960), 163, 165
Percentages Agreement (Churchill-Stalin), 101
Pilsudski, Marshal Joseph (1878–1935), 20
Poland: crisis of 1939, 38–41; Nazi protectorate, 46; establishment of Communist rule, 88–91, 105; coal mine productivity, 132; birthrate, 213; percent of workers in agriculture, 221; number of tractors, 222; meat consumption, 229; workers' riots of 1971, 234. See also Gomulka, Wladislaw; Katyn Forest massacre; Mikolajczk, Stanislaw; Okulicki, Colonel Leopold; Pilsudski, Marshal Joseph; Potsdam Conference; Sikorski,

General Wladislaw; Warsaw; Yalta Conference
Polish Corridor, 39
Polish Underground, 99
Pompidou, Georges (1911–), 185, 189, 231
Population, 4–7, 215–16
Potsdam Conference, 83, 115, 116, 121, 123, 149
Production: steel, 9, 135, 140, 196; post–World War II period, 132–36, 140, 147, 154, 162; electric, 135, 140, 197; 1960–70 period and overall view, 192–233. See also Agriculture; Coal
Purges (Russian officers, 1938–1939), 62

Quebec Conference (1944), 99
Quisling, Major Vikdun (1887–1945), 51

RAF (Royal Air Force), 56, 63
Railroad development (pre-1914), 8
Rajk, Laszlo (1909–1949), 165
Rakosi, Matyas (1892–1971), 163
Rapallo Treaty (1922), 41
Rathenau, Walter (1867–1922), 23
Reichstag fire (1933), 28
Reparations: Germany, 21–23; World War II, 115, 120, 142; post–World War II (non-German), 157
Resistance: French, 79–81
Reynaud, Paul (1878–1966), 52, 54
Rhineland: occupation by Hitler, 32–33
Ribbentrop, Joachim von (1893–1946), 43, 58
Rokossovski, Marshal Constantine (1896–1968), 173
Rommel, General Erwin (1891–1944), 59, 72
Roosevelt, Franklin D. (1882–1945): request for guarantees from dictators, 1939, 39–40; Casablanca Meeting, 70, 96; desires for harmony with Soviets, 93; Atlantic Charter, 95; Quebec meeting with Churchill, 99; Morgenthau Plan, 99, 101; Yalta, 105–6; death, 112
Ruhr occupation, 23
Rumania: cession of Bessarabia to USSR, 1940, 57; enters Axis

camp, 57; German troops enter, 1940, 57–58; enters war against Russia, 60; changes sides in war, 72, 99; imposition of Stalinist government, 116–17; percentage of workers in agriculture, 221; meat consumption, 229

Russia. *See* USSR

Russo-Finnish War (1939–1940), 49–50

SA (*Sturmabteilung*), 24, 25

Saar, 32, 138, 144

Sakhalin, 103

Salazar, Antonio (1889–1970), 177, 231

Satellites: imposition of satellite regimes, 163, 166

Schlieffen Plan, 52

Schulenburg, Count Friedrich Werner von (1875–1944), 41

Schuman, Robert (1886–1963), 145

Schuman Plan, 145–46

Schuschnigg, Kurt von (1897–), 34

Schutzstaffeln. *See* SS

Second World War. *See* World War II

SED (Socialist Unity Party, East Germany), 149

Sedan: German breakthrough in 1940, 53

Selassie, Haili (1891–), 32

Seyss-Inquart, Arthur (1892–1946), 34

Siegfried Line, 33, 35, 41, 48

Sikorski, General Wladislaw (1881–1943), 90, 91

Sino-Soviet split, 183

Slansky, Rudolf (1901–1952): execution of, 165

Slovakia, 37

Social Democratic Party (German), 21, 26, 149

Socialist Parties: Italy, 17–18, 85–87; France, 139. *See also* Labour Party; SED; Social Democratic Party

South Tyrol, 87

Soviet Union. *See* USSR

Spain: Spanish Civil War and Axis, 34; Spain and Axis in World War II, 82; Big Three hostility toward, 83; United States and, 84; gradual economic improvement in, 177; steel output in, 196; electric

output in, 197; number of automobiles in, 198; number of radio and television sets in, 201; tourism in, 206; infant mortality in, 213; TB in, 217; workers in agriculture in, 221; number of tractors in, 222. *See also* Franco, Generalissimo Francisco

Spanish Civil War, 34, 83

Spartacists, 20

Sputnik: first Soviet launching, 176

SS, 75

Stalin, Joseph (1879–1953): five year plans, 12; collectivization, 12; Polish crisis of 1939, 39–40; German-Soviet Pact, 41; nonaggression pact with Japan, 61; Nazi invasion of 1941, 62–63; appeal to the Russian people, 64; Polish Communist Party, 89; Katyn affair, 90; international communism, 92; attitude toward West in World War II, 93–94; at Teheran, 97; Moscow meeting with Churchill, 1944, 101; at Yalta, 103–4; Polish question and Warsaw uprising, 105–15 passim; at Potsdam, 115; split with Tito, 125–26; DDR, 149–50; fourth Five Year Plan, 157; new purge and Kremlin doctors' plot, 160–61, 168–69; national Communists, 165; de-Stalinization, 171–73; mentioned, 73, 161, 162, 163, 166, 170

Stalingrad, Battle of (1942–1943), 67–69

Steel production. *See* Production

Stettinius, Edward (1900–1949), 110

Straits: Russian pressure on Turkey, 116

Stresemann, Gustav (1878–1929), 26

Strikes: days lost, 229

Stuttgart: speech, 121; American rebuilding of Germany, 145

Sudeten Crisis, 35–37

Suez Crisis (1956), 180

Sweden: birthrate, 213; percent of workers in agriculture, 221; per capita food consumption, 225; strikes, 229

Switzerland, 54

Tartars: deportation by Soviets, 158
Teheran Conference, 97–98
Thaw, the, 170
Third International. *See* Comintern
Tito, Marshal Joseph Broz (1892–): photograph, 118; crackdown on Croatian nationalism; 210; mentioned, 113, 114, 117, 125, 126, 158, 165, 171, 172, 173
Tourism, 206–9
Tractors, 222
Trieste: Italo-Yugoslav dispute over, 87, 114, 116, 119, 126
Trotsky, Leon (1877–1940), 92
Truman, Harry S. (1884–), 109, 110, 112, 113, 114, 121
Truman Doctrine, 121–22, 123, 126
Tunisia: trapping of Afrika Korps, 69
Twentieth Party Congress (1956), 172

Ukraine: anti-Soviet partisans, 161; mentioned, 46, 89, 159
Ulbricht, Walter (1893–), 163
Unconditional surrender, 70, 96. *See also* Casablanca Conference
Unemployment, 218
United Nations, 83, 95, 96, 103, 107
United Nations Relief and Rehabilitation (UNRRA), 120, 130
United States: Roosevelt requests guarantees from dictators, 39–40; aid to English, 56; 1935 Congress abandons previous concepts of neutral rights, 58; 1937 neutrality act, 58; old destroyers to England, 58; occupation of Greenland, 60; patrol of North Atlantic, 60; Lend-Lease Act, 60, 93, 129–30; Japan attacks, 60–61; Germany declares war, 60–61; Roosevelt and Churchill at Casablanca want Axis "unconditional surrender," 70, 96; taking of part of Czechoslovakia, Saxony, Leipzig, 73; relations with Spain, 83, 84; Atlantic Charter, 95, 96; Big Three in Moscow, 1943, 96; Yalta, 102–7; Roosevelt dies and Truman is president, 112; American troop pullback from Saxony and Central Europe, July 1, 1945,

114; and Russian reparation demands, 120; Truman Doctrine, 121–23; Marshall Plan, 122–24, 134–35, 140; Morgenthau Plan, 144; Stuttgart Speech of Byrnes, 145; attempts to integrate Germany in European defense community, 152–53; French resentment of, 153; NATO, 166, 167; reaction to Sputnik, 176; Cuban Missile crisis, 182; steel output, 196; electric output, 197; number of telephones, 200; number of radio and television sets, 201; number of students, 211; infant mortality rate, 212; birthrate, 213; divorce rate, 214; percent of workers in agriculture, 221; number of tractors, 222; food consumption, 226; cost of living and earning power, 227–31
Urban growth, 6–7
USSR (Union of Soviet Socialist Republics): population, 4, 197, 215; prerevolutionary urbanization, 6–7; steel production, 9, 196; NEP (New Economic Policy), 11; famine, 12; collectivization, 12; first Five Year Plan, 12; Polish Crisis of 1939, 39–40; German-Soviet Pact, 1939, 41; nonaggression pact with Japan, 61; purges, 62; Nazi invasion of 1941, 62–63; Katyn affair, 90; Polish question and Warsaw uprising, 105–15; split with Tito, 125–26; fourth Five Year Plan, 1946–50, 157; new purge and Kremlin doctors' plot, 160, 161, 168–69; establishment of Stalinist regimes in satellites, 163–66; de-Stalinization, 169–71, 172–73; suppression of Hungarian revolt, 174–75; electric output, 197; number of telephones, 200; number of radio and television sets, 201; construction activity, 204; housing, 205; number of students, 211; infant mortality rate, 212; birthrate, 213; number of divorces, 214; percent of workers in agriculture, 221; number of tractors, 222; wages and cost of living, 226–31; meat consump-

tion, 229; suppression of Czechoslovakia, 234; writers in, 242

Venezia-Giulia-Trieste, 113. *See also*
   Trieste
Versailles Treaty, 27, 28, 32, 38
Vichy government, 77, 78, 80
Victor Emmanuel III, King of Italy
   (1869–1947), 85
Vienna Award (1940), 57
Vietnam. *See* Indo-China
Vishinsky, Andrei (1883–1954),
   108, 116

Wages, 224, 230
Warsaw: underground, 72, 107–11;
   uprising, 107–9, 111; mentioned,
   72
Weimar Republic, 23, 26, 27, 29
West Germany. *See Bundesrepublik*
Wilhelmina, Queen of Netherlands
   (1880–1962), 77
Wilson, Harold: photograph, 186
World War I: effects on European
   economies, 10–11; promotes rise
   of "isms", 14; effect on Italy, 16;
   effect on Germany, 20–22; gives
   birth to League of Nations, 32;
   effect on Austria, 34
World War II: outbreak of war, 43;
   British-French entry into war, 43;
   German invasion of Poland, 45–
   46; German invasion of Norway
   and Denmark, 50–51; German invasion and conquest of Holland
   and Belgium, 52–53; fall of
   France, 54; Hitler offers peace,
   55; Churchill summons English
   to resist, 55; Battle of Britain, 56;
   German domination of the Dan-
   ube, 57; Molotov-Ribbentrop
talks, 57–58; United States over-
age destroyers to Britain, 58;
Italian attack on Greece, 59; military coup in Yugoslavia, 59–60;
German attack on Greece, 59–60;
Lend Lease Act, 60; Rumania
joins Hitler, 60; Hungary joins,
61; German invasion of USSR,
1941, 61–65; Japanese attack on
Pearl Harbor, 65; United States
enters war, 65; German defeat at
Stalingrad, 67–68; German defeat in North Africa, 68; Western
allies invade Italy, 70; Western
allies invade Normandy, 71; defection of German allies, 72;
Warsaw Underground revolts,
72–73; Russians take Berlin, 73;
concentration camps, 75

Yalta Conference (1945), 102, 103,
   104, 105, 106, 110, 112, 113, 114,
   122
Yugoslavia: adheres to Tripartite
   (pro-Axis) pact, 59; anti-Axis
   coup, 59; Nazi invasion of, 60;
   resistance to Nazis, 71; Germans
   evacuate, 72; Churchill-Stalin
   agreement on, 101; Trieste dispute, 113–14, 116, 126; triumph
   of Tito, 117; Khrushchev visits
   Tito, 172; percent of workers in
   agriculture, 221

Zhdanov, Andrei (1896–1948), 158,
   160
Zhdanovschina, 158
Zinoviev, Girgori (1883–1936), 92
Zog, King of Albania (1895–1961),
   37

THE WAKE *of* FORGIVENESS

THE WAKE

— of —

FORGIVENESS

Bruce Machart

Houghton Mifflin Harcourt

BOSTON   NEW YORK

2010

For information about permission to reproduce selections from this book,
write to Permissions, Houghton Mifflin Harcourt Publishing Company,
215 Park Avenue South, New York, New York 10003.

www.hmhbooks.com

Library of Congress Cataloging-in-Publication Data
Machart, Bruce.
The wake of forgiveness / Bruce Machart.
p. cm.
ISBN 978-0-15-101443-9
1. Czechs — Texas — Fiction. 2. Spaniards — Texas — Fiction.
3. Horse breeders — Fiction. 4. Landowners — Fiction. 5. Vendetta — Fiction.
6. Lavaca County (Tex.) — Fiction. I. Title.
PS3613.A272525W35 2010
813'.6 — dc22   2009047459

Book design by Brian Moore

Printed in the United States of America

DOC 10 9 8 7 6 5 4 3 2 1

For my mother . . .

and for Marya — this and any that may follow

Some years ago, I acquired a map of Lavaca County, Texas, that was printed in 1896, and I noted that a large parcel of land had been owned at that time by one Mr. Patrick Dalton. Because Dalton is a name that goes back many generations in my family — as my godfather's name, as my own middle name, as my son's name — this seemed, since I had just begun to imagine the fictional town of this novel, a kind of serendipity. Two years later, once the novel's landscape had become all but indelible in my imagination, I discovered that there exists, way up in the northeast corner of the state and some 350 miles from the events of this story, an actual Dalton, Texas, an old timber settlement with a current population of fewer than one hundred residents. Hence the need for clarification: Though Lavaca County and many of the towns and landmarks depicted in this work are quite real, as are some historical figures who appear as minor characters, all are used fictitiously. Likewise, Jackson Gregory's novel *Judith of Blue Lake Ranch* was in fact serialized in the *Shiner Gazette* during December of 1924, but I have fictionalized it here, altering to varying degrees both its characters and storyline. The Dalton, Texas, of this novel is entirely a product of my imagination.

It is good for a man that he bear the yoke in his youth. He sitteth alone and keepeth silence, because he hath borne it upon him. He putteth his mouth in the dust; if so be there may be hope.

—LAMENTATIONS 3:27–29

The harvest is past, the summer is ended, and we are not saved.

—JEREMIAH 8:20

A Winter Harvest

FEBRUARY 1895

THE BLOOD HAD COME hard from her, so much of it that, when Vaclav Skala awoke in wet bed linens to find her curled up against him on her side, moaning and glazed with sweat, rosary beads twisted around her clenched fingers, he smiled at the thought that she'd finally broken her water. He pulled back the quilt, a wedding gift sent six years before from his mother in the old country, and kissed Klara on the forehead before climbing from bed to light the lamp. He struck a match, and there it was, streaked down his legs and matted in the coarse hair on his thighs—dark and half-dried smears of his wife's blood.

And it kept coming. He saddled his horse and rode shivering under a cloudless midnight sky to the Janek farm to fetch Edna, the midwife. By the time they made it back, Klara's eyes were open but glazed in such a way that they knew she wasn't seeing through them anymore. Her pale lips moved without giving voice to her final prayer, which entreated the child to come or her own spirit to stay, either one.

When the baby arrived, their fourth boy, blood slicked and clot flecked, he appeared to have been as much ripped from flesh as born of it. Klara was lost, and Edna tended to what had been saved, pinching the little thing's toe to get the breathing started, cleaning him with a rag dipped in warm milk and water, wrapping him in a blanket.

Vaclav Skala stood at the foot of the bed, grinding his back teeth slowly against a stringy mash of tobacco he'd chewed flavorless half an hour before. He watched Edna, a slight young woman with narrow hips and long hair as black as her eyes. She bunched pillows beneath the dead woman's shoulder blades and behind her head before resting the baby on his mother's stomach. Taking one of Klara's breasts between her thumb and finger, she puckered the nipple so the baby could get hold of it. The little thing threw his hands up about his face and worked his legs beneath the blanket, and Edna held him unremittingly to the breast until he hollowed his cheeks and found it with his mouth. "It's no hind milk in her yet," she said, "but he might get some of the yellow mother's milk. We'll be needing a wet nurse. It's several up county who might do it."

Vaclav stepped back into the doorway and looked down the dark hallway toward the room where his other three boys were sleeping. "We'll be needing a hell of a lot more than that," he said. "Let him get what's left of her if he can. He's done taken the rest."

Just before dawn, after Edna had washed the body and wrapped it in clean bedding, Vaclav carried it out and up into the loft of the barn so the boys wouldn't find her when they woke. Then he dragged the drenched mattress from the house and out through the young pear grove to the hard-caked plot of earth where he planned one day to build his stable. There, beneath the wash kettle, he kindled a fire with last year's fallen mesquite branches. The mattress was soaked through and heavier than Klara's body had been, and Vaclav found himself cursing its weight even while he recalled how Klara had stitched the ticking and stuffed it with goose feathers before their wedding night; how, when he lay pressed for the first time between her tender skin and the soft warmth of the bed she'd made for him, he'd startled his bride, so loud was his laugh.

Now, as the horizon gave way to the pink glow of another south Texas dawn and the mockingbirds came to life in the pear grove, Vaclav worked his knife along the mattress seam, undoing his wife's work, as he would find himself doing for years. With several inches

4

of the stitching cut away, he reached in and pulled out the feathers, one bloody handful after another, and fed them to the fire, which spat and sizzled before blazing into yellow flames and thick white billows of smoke.

In the near pasture, the cattle stood lowing against the fence, and had Vaclav been paying attention the way he usually did, he would have puzzled at their behavior, wondering what it was that kept them clustered against the fenceline instead of in the center of the parcel near the three square bales of hay he'd set out for them the day before. Instead, he stood staring into the fire, adding the steady fuel of feathers, looking into the flames so he wouldn't have cause to look at his hands, which were chapped and creased deeply with calluses and stained with the blood of the only woman he'd ever been fond of.

The townsfolk would assume, from this day forward, that Klara's death had turned a gentle man bitter and hard, but the truth, Vaclav knew, was that her absence only rendered him, again, the man he'd been before he'd met her, one only her proximity had ever softened. He'd known land in his life that, before a few seasons of regular rainfall, had been hard enough to crack a plow point, and he knew that if, by stubbornness or circumstance, that earth became yours to farm, you'd do well to live with the constant understanding that, in time, absent the work of swollen clouds and providence, your boots would fall loudly, giving rise to dust, when you walked your fields.

With the sun breaking clear of the horizon and the ticking gutted of its down, Vaclav whittled his knife against a brick of lye soap and added a handful of shavings to the boiling kettle water. He squinted against the sharp fumes of Klara's strong soap, and when he got the bloodstained ticking into the kettle, the water roiled and frothed red like so much sick stew.

Softly, a cool wind came up from the north and swirled the smoke around the kettle and out into the newly lit morning. Across the pasture, hidden in the far hedgerow near the creekside stand of trees, three half-starved coyotes raised their twitching snouts to catch a breeze laced of a sudden with the hot, iron-rich scent of blood. Their mouths flooded with anticipation as they hunkered their bellies low and inched forward, shifting their feet beneath them and waiting, their reticence born more of caution than patience. In the pasture, the cows went to lowing again, pressing themselves together against the fencewires.

With a twisted mesquite branch, Vaclav moved the ticking around in the boiling liquid and then threw that wood, too, on the fire. When he turned toward the house and weaved his way through the grove, he found the back door swung open, his three young boys standing just inside wearing nightclothes and wet cheeks. The oldest, Stanislav, was only five, but he held on to his brothers' shoulders the way a father would. The wind gusted enough to ripple Vaclav's shirt, and when it calmed he heard the baby crying inside. Standing in the bare yard, he took his plug of tobacco from his shirt pocket and tore off a portion with his teeth. Edna appeared behind the boys and turned them away from the door. "Their breakfast's gone cold on the table," she said. "They're asking after her."

He nodded and spit tobacco juice into the hard earth near the porch, and then, without washing his hands or taking off his boots, he stepped into the house where, for all but one wailing newborn, as in the pasture and the hedgerows, even hunger had been plowed under by fear.

Turning the Earth

MARCH 1910

HIS TWO GOOD horses he saves for racing, for the straight make-shift furlongs of the moonlit creekbed, for the chance to take more land from his godforsaken neighbor, Patrick Dalton, whose Scots-Irish surname remains on the town map and postmark but no longer on the largest deed in the county. Nowadays, that deed is in Vaclav Skala's name, for just shy of six hundred acres, nearly a third of it taken, over the past four years, by wit and force and fast horses from Dalton himself.

As likely to spit tobacco juice on a woman's shoes as to tip his hat at her, Vaclav has, since his wife's death fifteen years ago, only one source of weakness: his pair of towering roan quarter horses. For them, there are well-oiled leather bridles and carrots pulled straight from the mineral-rich earth. For them, hand-forged shoes and alfalfa and sweet feed and as many good mares to mount as he can find without insulting their bloodlines.

The horses, they're beautiful, though no longer the most beautiful in Lavaca County, and they don't work the fields. They race, they rest, they eat, they mate, and they race. They don't pull a plow. That work Vaclav leaves to his four sons, and when Guillermo Villa-señor drives his two Spanish-bred stallions and three olive-skinned daughters up the farm-to-market road from town, and when the carriage clears a thick stand of mesquite trees with arthritic branches and thorns long enough to skewer a foot in a way only careless bare-foot boys and Jesus might fully appreciate, and the girls get their

9

first glimpses of their future husbands, what they see, instead of blond-haired and handsome Czech farm boys, like they've been told by their father to expect, are weathered young men straining against the weight of the earth turning in their wake, their necks cocked sharply to one side or the other, their faces sunburned despite their hats and peeling and snaked with raised veins near the temples, their boots sliding atop the earth they're sweating to unearth. The four of them work harnessed two abreast in front of their father, who's walking in their work, one foot in each furrow, spitting stained juice between his front teeth and periodically cracking a whip to keep the boys focused and the rows straight.

The boys are moving toward the carriage—which is coming toward them, coming to change everything—but at first they don't see it, don't see the horses or the puffs of dust coming up from their hooves, don't see these fine animals, longer of leg than any the boys have known before and higher of step, their withers soaked through and shining black with sweat despite the cool morning breeze, their carriage one of wealth and women and a future the boys could not have dreamed up if they'd been left, any short night of their lives, to their beds long enough to dream much anything at all.

Here in these parts, in the black-soil heart of Lavaca County, where the Czech farmers have run off all but the last of the red-haired and ruddy settlers who came before them; where, if a man has two bits' worth of good seed and a strong back and a certain degree of stubbornness—that and a good wife who lives long enough and with enough of God's favor to grant him sons—he might harvest two hundred acres of cotton without calling on even his neighbors for help; here, where men make their own worth, they don't have much use for outsiders, and until this week there's been neither a man nor woman in the county who's often laid either an eye or a thought on a Mexican.

IN THE LAST three days, Villaseñor and his two armed escorts have been busy throwing their weight – and nearly their weight in gold – around town. On Monday, in town at the First Federal Bank and Trust, where Lad Dvorak sat at his desk working through the inventory list of the Butler farm foreclosure, Guillermo came tracking mud through the doors with his men. His hair was black and oiled back and tinged with gray in such a way that he looked to have spent the duration of his life walking into the same wet and gypsum-laden wind. His spectacles he wore down low on his nose, and he spoke with an accent that sounded to the tellers more refined somehow than their own.

One of his men stood at the door with his rifle while the other brought in the saddlebags, some eight of them in all, and then they held the door open and refused to do their business until the rest of the customers were cleared out and the doors bolted. Guillermo's daughters were taking lunch at the inn, forbidden, as usual, to accompany their father on occasions where money changed hands, of which there had been hundreds over the years, and perhaps, had they been in the bank, Lad might have been rendered as slack jawed and inarticulate by their lovely Spanish features as he was presently by the weight of their father's saddlebags.

Lad lifted the first of them to his desk, saying, "Most of it's silver, I'm betting."

"A man should know better than to make his bets blind," Villaseñor said. "I wouldn't have my good horses shod with silver."

Lad laughed and worked his fingers through the patchwork of bristled hair on his chin while Villaseñor's men stood with their rifles held casually and crosswise beneath their bellies, their thumbs hooked behind their belts. Lad figured them for nearly forty, but they wore the mustaches of boys, combed straight and too thin to hide the skin of their upper lips. Their shirts were laundered, creases pressed in the sleeves, but their boots were caked with mud and, by the smell of it, dung. They were two of the shortest men Lad had ever seen, and he snorted and jerked his head at them and said, "If it's something worth protecting in these bags, mister, I'd expect your boys here to be a shake bigger than a pair of well-fed housewives."

The men didn't flinch, and Lad knew then that they didn't speak English. Villaseñor acted, too, like he hadn't heard. He took his spectacles off, pulled a folded handkerchief from the vest pocket of his suit coat, and when he replaced the spectacles, he squinted and a tight smile creased the corners of his mouth while he spoke to his men in Spanish. They laughed, turned their backs, and went toward the door. The two tellers backed away from their windows, eyes wary. One of Villaseñor's men unlatched the door and went outside. The other propped his gun against the far wall, pulled a cigar from his shirt pocket, and waved the chewed end beneath his nose before putting it in his mouth. He unbuckled his belt and dropped a hand down into the front of his britches to make some adjustments, and when he got himself situated to his liking he pulled the belt tight under the slump of his belly and buckled up. He had an audience in the two tellers, and he gave them a wink and went back to sucking on his cigar.

When his partner came back in the door, he carried a smallish box that looked, for all its varnish and shine, like a coffin built for a rich man's tomcat. He turned the bolt on the door and put the box beside the first saddlebag on Lad's desk.

"And what of this?" Lad said.

"That's *my* wager," the old man said. "I'm betting that after we weigh these coins and you hand me a voucher, you and your boys are going to need what's in this box."

"Is that so," Lad said, winking at his tellers. "And what would that be?"

"Shoeblack. My men's boots need some attention."

Now they all had a laugh, and Lad called his men over to help weigh the gold, which they had to do in small batches because the old triple-beam scale on the premises was calibrated with only a five-pound counterweight. By the time they finished, Lad Dvorak was perspiring and salivating both. Here was a new account worth all the cotton in Lavaca County, and a fair share of the land, at that.

The men took the saddlebags to the safe, and before he wrote out the voucher Lad shook Villaseñor's hand and asked if he needed some of his balance in bills. The man raised his brows, pulled a fat fold of American currency from his coat, and removed the clip. "It doesn't seem so," he said, removing three five-dollar bills and letting them fall to the varnished bureau top.

Lad had his tellers sign as witnesses to the transaction and handed Mr. Villaseñor his voucher. "It's a pleasure," he said, "having your business. Did you need some smaller change for these?"

"The pleasure is mine," the man said. "And those bills are for you. And for your men."

"Beg pardon?"

Villaseñor lifted the lid of the box and removed two cans of shoeblack, a brush, and a felt strop. "My wager," he said, running his thumb through the stiff bristles of the brush. "The way I see it, I can leave my money here in your bank, or I can withdraw it tomorrow and do my business over in Shiner or Yoakum. I'm betting you'd rather I didn't, and I'm betting, because this is true, that when I get back in an hour from having a word with Monsignor Carew about my daughters' Nuptial Mass, you and your boys will be just about finished putting a shine to these undersized men's boots. Five dollars apiece is more than fair — don't you think? — all things considered."

Now Lad's fingers were back in his beard and his ears were flushed with blood. "I'm certain," he said, "that you would be happier with the twenty-cent shine they'll get around the corner at Wasek's barbershop, but let me be the first to congratulate you on your daughter's wedding. Who's the lucky man?"

"I don't believe I said." Villaseñor fished a cigar from his suit coat. "Not to you, I didn't. And I'd be happier, sir, if you didn't presume to tell me what would make me happy. That money there, it's yours. And so is my business, assuming these little farmwives here, who've put more men in the ground for me than yours have swindled for you, have, by hour's end, boots in which I can see myself well enough to shave."

Then he bit the tip from his cigar, ground the tobacco with his back teeth for more than a wordless minute, and sent from his lips onto the bureau top a long string of thick black spit. He lighted his cigar and the whole room went suddenly and sweetly ripe with its smoke. "There," he said, "another token of my generosity, Mr. Dvorak. If your spit's too good for my men's boots, then you can use mine."

FOR TWO DAYS thereafter, the talk about town was constant as the lowing of cattle in the pastures. While the townswomen sat together quilting or stood clustered in kitchens, polishing copper pots or latticing dough over pies filled with fruit canned the previous summer, their lips moved faster than their hands. Faster, their husbands said, than their minds.

Gathered in the icehouse, the men took long pulls on their pilsners and shook their heads, feigning indifference, but at home, even after sweating behind plows or beneath the weight of hay bales, they found themselves these days with more patience for their women's words. They'd sit at their tables long after they'd eaten, elbows on each side of their coffee cups, and they'd listen to the stories the women brought home.

The Mexican had rented the whole second floor of the Township Inn for a month. Paid in advance, he did. Then there was Sy Janek's wife, Edna, who claimed that, on her way home from delivering the Knedlik twins, she'd seen the girls, all three of them, riding black horses after dark, running the animals hard out behind Patrick Dalton's granary and into the pecan grove by the north fork of Mustang Creek. In dresses they were, with a foot in each stirrup and God only knows what, if anything, between their tender parts and the saddle leather. There was Father Carew, who'd canceled both Masses for this coming Saturday and would say, when pressed, only that this Villaseñor fellow had wedding plans, and for more than one wedding, and that to secure the church he'd brought with him a Papal Indulgence, the first Carew had ever seen, and three Sundays' worth of collections in cash. And then there was Patrick Dalton, who'd been seen taking lunch with Villaseñor and his men at the inn, and who had called Lad Dvorak to tell him that he'd run suddenly short of room at his stable, that the banker would have to come fetch the drays Dalton had boarded for him all these years in exchange for prime interest rates at the bank. These wives, the broad-hipped women who bore bad news and children both with a sad but softened look around the eyes, claimed Dalton had been seen smiling at the feedstore while he ordered two hundred pounds of molasses oats, smiling even while he shouldered them out to his wagon, two forty-pound sacks at a time.

And this is where the men of Lavaca County stopped listening.

This is where they breathed in abruptly through their noses and pushed their chairs back from the table and took their coffee out into the swirling night air, which was growing cold of a sudden and sharp with pecan and mesquite and oak from the chunkwood fires smoldering in their smokehouses. They stood out on their porches or out back of their barns, and while the low moon slid behind thin bands of clouds and they pulled tobacco from the bib pockets of their overalls and rolled cigarettes with callused thumbs, they grew more certain than ever of their wives' willful foolishness, of their forthright and feminine need to believe the world a far more mysterious and alluring place than it was. Patrick Dalton, the men knew, hadn't smiled in coming up on four damned years, not since the night when he'd for the first time lost an acreage-staked race to Vaclav Skala.

They'd been there, after all, and in their memories they'd borne witness to the race the same way their wives had borne their children—with the assurance that they'd each played a vital and thankworthy role, and with the misguided confidence that, for having done so, they would remain forever attuned to both the memory of the bearing and the born alike.

And so it was that on this March night, smoking out behind their barns, the men of Dalton, Texas, and its hinterland drew from the oft-unswept corners of their memories dozens of mismatched and contradictory notions of a night four years back, a night that, by all accounts, had seen them standing in the shuddering light of two rock-ringed finish-line fires, their undershirts starched yellow with the dried sweat of an August day's work, their backs to the creek where they'd floated their jars of corn whiskey and beer bottles to keep them cool. They'd stood drinking and smoking, comparing crop yields and woman troubles, making half-dollar bets with their neighbors while the riders readied themselves.

Some forty yards to the west, just beyond the swinging cattlegate, Vaclav Skala's youngest, Karel, sat his pop's biggest roan stallion. The boy's neck, like his brothers', was kinked from so much time harnessed to a plow, warped such that his head cocked sharply to the left and made him look a little off-kilter in the saddle. Still, there was an ease in the way he handled the animal, a casual confidence that kept his boots slid back in the stirrups so that it appeared he rode only on his toes, the reins held so delicately between fingers and thumbs, held the way a lady might hold her most precious heirloom linens after washing.

He turned the horse a few times back beyond the gate and edged him up alongside the Dalton boy on the county's newest horse, a nervous, twitching red filly his daddy had shipped in from Kentucky or Tennessee or some-damned-where. The boys kept the animals reined in just the other side of the gate while their fathers shook hands.

These were the communal truths, the recollections the landowners and townsmen shared the way they kept in common a constant worry over rainfall and boll weevils and cotton futures. What they didn't know, though they might have suspected as much, was that Vaclav had taken in those days to praying shamelessly of a Sunday that pestilence might visit the Dalton herd, and that Dalton had once that summer crept in the moonlight among the outermost

17

rows of Skala's melon crop, injecting the ripe fruit with horse laxative. These two, given a normal night, would have sooner sat bare assed on a cottonmouth nest than exchange pleasantries with each other, but here they were, something about the night and the onlookers and the improvident stakes pushing to each man's lips at least the pretense of sporting civility — *Good luck, then, neighbor* — before they went to inspect their animals.

Dalton pulled on the saddle straps and slapped his son on the leg, leaning in to offer some last bit of advice. As for Vaclav Skala, he didn't say a word to his boy. He'd said what he needed to half an hour before when he handed young Karel his crop. His mouth moved only to work the tobacco. He spat juice into the weeds and scratched at the arc of blond curls he had left behind his sun-speckled crown, pulled a nine-inch blade from the sheath on his belt and held it up to his horse's nose, letting it glint there awhile in the flickering hint of firelight while the animal got a good, strong smell of its steel.

The men of Lavaca County looked questions at one another and shook their heads, laughing together by the fire nearest the creek. *That Vaclav's a few deuces shy of a deck,* someone said.

But he's shored up straight compared to Laddie, ain't it? Where is it you're going after this, Dvorak? Bury a bishop?

And sure enough, Lad Dvorak had been there, all turned out in one of the suits he wore to work, his eyes wide enough with unease to give the lie to the rigid set of his jaw. He was holding a little .22 revolver stiffly at his side, and he looked, when he moved, like he considered his steps before taking them, each an act of pained determination, the walk of a man whose bowels had seized up on him, or who was heading to the confessional with something venial to cut loose from his conscience.

Suspect of anything that couldn't be learned from acreage or animals, the locals wondered if that's what education did to a man. Sure, he'd drawn up the papers for Dalton, making the whole wager legal as the sale of heifers or hay, but you couldn't trust a man who walked flat pastureland like he'd gone all day plugged up by his own turds. He might have held liens on half the acreage in Dalton and Shiner, but he sure looked a silly son of a bitch holding a gun.

Still, it had been left to him to fire the shot that would send the horses and their riders churning dirt through a half mile of dust and darkness, up around the thick and twisted stand of water oaks just shy of the parcel's far hedgerow, and back to the fire-lit finish line where now all the men stood waiting, pointing and laughing at Dvorak, who held his pistol so tentatively in front of him that the barrel drooped downward like the willow tip of a divining rod.

Got-damn, Lad, that ain't your dead daddy's pecker you're holding. Put a squeeze on it the way you do them purse strings of yours.

Lad squinted into the darkness and shrugged it off. There wasn't a man here who hadn't yet come to him for a loan, and if his position of power wasn't apparent in the way he held a gun, he more than made up for it with his willingness to foreclose on a loan, with the reticence of his Sunday smile, the simple withholding of which could set a man's wife to fretting in the pews, praying her husband hadn't missed a payment.

To be certain, as Patrick Dalton swung the gate out and the horses threw their heads around and lifted their tails to drop great clods to the turf, Lad would have his hand in this, too. He came out from the fenceline, watching, on account of his new shoes, where he stepped, and when he positioned himself a few yards out of the way near the pine saplings clustered alongside the creek, he waited for a nod from Dalton, one from Skala, and then he raised his arm and pointed the gun at a sky strung brightly with stars.

Since the first wagonloads of Czech settlers rolled onto the flat and fertile land of south Texas from the port of Galveston, folks had joked that if a sober man rode over these Texas plains from the coast, and if he thought, before nearing Lavaca County, that he saw in the distance even the slightest rise, even the gentlest hint of a valley, then what he was noting was nothing more or less than the very curvature of the planet. Here in Dalton, between the two forks of the creek, the land offered its first embellishment, a gentle swell that came to a two-hundred-acre plateau and then fell away to sloughs near the water's edge. And so it was on that night, despite the indecisive summer winds, that the highland discharge of such a small caliber gun brought farmwives even a half mile away to their kitchen windows and caused their sleeping children to twitch in their beds.

The horses reared and surged, and the smoke from Lad's gun flew up in a windswept whirl and circled itself like a confused spirit into the creekside trees. The boys got up fast in their stirrups, and by the time they urged their animals up to speed, hoof sod flying behind them as they tore past the cheering line of men and between the two fires and into the darkness, eleven-year-old Karel was laying it on thick with his whip.

This boy had been outriding his older brothers since he was nine, and when his old man bragged on one of his sons—which was rare and only brought on by drink and never within earshot of the boys themselves—the words he found himself slurring were always the same: *That youngest of mine, men, he could whip some fast into a common ass.*

The truth, Karel knew, though he could not have yet put it into words, was that the horse wanted the whip, wanted it the same way Karel wanted his pop's strap, the stinging and unambiguous urgency of its attention, and, for Karel, the closest he got to his father's touch.

Now he kept his crouch tight and marveled as always at the way the ride smoothed out the faster the horse ran. He would come, in later years, to find the same comfort in hard loving, in the convergence and confusion of violence and tenderness, but tonight he knew only the nervous thrill of it, the hot smelter of fear and joy found only in this kind of abandon, in riding for a stake in another man's land, in riding for the father who had refused to hold him on the day of his birth, or any day thereafter, in riding into a darkness that his adjusting vision was only now beginning to brighten, and while he alternated pops of his crop on the animal's hindquarters, he kept Billy Dalton in the corner of his eye, making sure to hold him close and on his outside flank as they approached the quarter-acre stand of oaks they were to circle before heading back to the fires and their fathers at the finish line.

The horse, Whiskey, the youngest and fastest of his father's prized pair, wanted to turn it all loose, wanted to shred acres of sod with his hooves and fill the night with the hot breath of his nostrils. Karel could feel it as he squeezed his thighs to bring the horse into the left-hand turn, the rippling ribbons of muscle beneath the animal's hide, the quivering resistance to the slightest tension on the reins. And then, just before the moss-veiled cluster of trees with their low-hanging, skeletal branches, the Dalton boy stood in the stirrups and cut back behind Karel to take the turn clockwise instead.

Whiskey threw his head to the left and broke stride, and Karel snapped the crop across the right flank and crouched into the turn, keeping the horse tight against the treeline and, because of the cant of his neck, squinting his eyes against the branches that reached out, slapping at his shoulder and face, snagging and snatching clumps of hair along the way.

The Dalton boy was out of sight, orbiting the same sizable stand of oaks in the opposite direction, and for Karel, now, there was only the sound of wind and hoof strikes, the hot pumping of breath from the horse, the memory of his old man's words when he'd handed him the crop half an hour before, the stuttering seconds before two horses would meet headlong at all but full speed.

Sooner than he expected, Karel looked up to find the Dalton horse coming on hard, Billy tucked forward and low behind the filly's windswept mane, his look one of tight-eyed determination. It was a matter of who would hold his ground and who would veer to the outside, and it was, Karel knew, one horse or the other, rather than the rider, that would likely make the decision if left to the last second.

It was Karel, too, who knew that wasn't going to happen.

When the horses were ten yards shy of colliding, Karel dug a knee into Whiskey's left flank and the horse swung out to the right, away from the trees, and then, as the Dalton boy's lips turned up at the corners and he leaned in harder, thinking he'd gained an irremediable advantage, Karel pulled his crop back sharply and, just as the horses passed, he did what his father had told him to do.

What the men of Lavaca County remember correctly is that Karel Skala broke first into the firelight, and that he blew past them at full stride before standing in the stirrups, his head cocked, as always, so far off-kilter, and slowing the horse into a wide circle out beyond the cattlegate before cantering back to where his father and brothers awaited him. Patrick Dalton went red-faced with disbelief as he stood taking it in, watching his landholdings dwindle, sucking snot up through his nose and spitting it, one last time, into the soil he'd just lost. And then waiting, waiting while Karel dismounted and handed the reins to his father, waiting while the older Skala boys gathered around their brother, slapping him hard on the shoulders and laughing. Waiting a full minute or more until the other boy, his own son, came ambling atop his filly out of the night, his right arm twisted into his lap, the shoulder hanging loose of its socket, the left side of his face puffed up and split open from cheekbone to chin.

The men standing creekside, they either pulled forth or pocketed coins, crept back to the creek for their jugs, circled around the horses, and watched while Lad Dvorak handed over both fifty-acre deeds to Skala. The Dalton boy, he was protesting, his eyes awash in tears, his face gone to a sickly blue around the wound. "The son of a bitch," he said. "I was winning."

Skala took the deeds, folded them into the back pocket of his trousers. One of the men handed him a bottle of whiskey and he bubbled it good before offering it to Dalton. "Looks like your boy caught a tree branch," he said. "They hang low around that turn, ain't it?"

Dalton refused the bottle, took his son's arm and pulled down on it and then raised it straight-elbowed until it popped back into the joint while the boy howled, crying in earnest now. "It's more than enough of that," Dalton told him, and he grabbed Billy by the hair and dragged him out into the saplings by the creek. There was some breathless whispering out there, more of the boy's complaints, and then Dalton, loud enough that everyone could hear: "It's worth fifty goddamn acres, then, is it? That's what you'll have me believe, boy? A stripe on the face?"

Dalton stomped back out into the firelight, his shoulders forward. On his face, fitful furrows. He was heading straight for Karel, who took a step or two back before standing his ground beside his father.

"Skala," Dalton said, sucking more snot. "Can I make loan of your boy's crop for a spell? My boy can't seem to keep a bead on his."

Karel looked up at his father, who was working a big wad of tobacco with his molars, nodding. Karel handed over the crop and Dalton snatched it, heading back toward the trees, snapping it against his thigh until he was once again out of sight but not nearly out of earshot: "Now, you chickenshit. You little pigtailed sister. You tell me when it feels like fifty acres' worth of hurt, and we'll see when I agree."

IT's KAREL WHO first sees the carriage, who stands straight against the weight of his brothers' progress and brings the plow point to its sudden and subterranean stop. "Shit, boy," his father says. "Is it someone told you to quit?"

The boy jerks his head up toward the road where the wheels and horses are stirring dust in their slow approach. The carriage is a two-seat covered surrey paneled in dark hardwood, varnished and gleaming and coming forward in the midmorning light. Harnessed abreast, the two sizable horses step with such a regulated cadence that their hooves hit the ground in tandem.

"Couple fine horses," Karel says.

"Talking when you should be listening," Skala says, "ain't it?" But he, too, is taking note of these animals, both of them shining oil black with broad blazes white as bleached cotton. The four boys stand transfixed, their necks cocked such that from the carriage they appear to the girls each to be puzzling some monumental and impenetrable question.

Guillermo Villaseñor brings the surrey to a stop and gives Skala a nod before setting the brake and climbing down. He smoothes the sleeves of his dark suitcoat and produces a handkerchief with which he cleans his spectacles. The three girls stay in the shaded back seat while the horses blow and tramp idly in the dirt. Karel's eyes move from horse to girl, girl to horse, awed in equal parts by each of these striking animals, the stallions with their brushed black manes and

24

long forelocks, the girls in their flowered dresses that scoop down at the neck just enough to afford a boy a view of their delicately ridged clavicles and the tanned topmost slopes of their breasts.

My *word,* Karel thinks, and his father lets loose the plow handles, hangs his whip there, and bends forward to swipe the spent tobacco from his mouth with a finger before pulling his plug from his bib pocket and biting off a new portion. He sets to chewing, then he heads out to where Villaseñor is waiting by the road in a tailored suit, his hands held out from the waist with the palms open to the fields as if to say that he's brought nothing of harm or help, either one.

The boys free themselves from the harnesses and Stanislav runs his fingers through his hair and tucks his shirt into his trousers. And then they stand there, toeing the soil with their boots, crossing and uncrossing their arms while their father walks to meet the Mexican at the edge of the cropfield.

All of the morning there's come a cool breeze just strong enough to rustle the mesquite trees up the road and ripple the boys' shirts, and now the sun works its way in and out of the clouds. Out east toward the creek, a red-tailed hawk has been circling and gliding, circling and gliding, and when it tucks its wings and drops to the earth in its swooping dive, a covey of quail bursts from the scrub grass and all of them make their escape but one. The boys, they have their backs to it, but the girls see it, and the youngest one, the one sitting closest to the field, the one with lovely full lips and wide animal eyes, opens her mouth slightly at the sight, and Karel stands straight and locks his knees against these new stirrings in his stomach, and those below. He has seen the wet tip of her tongue.

On the road, Villaseñor puts his hand out and Skala looks at it and spits into the dirt. "You needing directions?" he says.

Villaseñor smiles and pulls his hand back and narrows his eyes as if he's studying a man across from him at cards. "Not in the least," he says. "I'm precisely where I mean to be."

"Well, I mean to be plowing my fields, not standing around like an old woman on the church steps, so why don't you let me to it."

"I will, sir. I will. Thing is, I've got an enterprise in mind that could leave you with twice the fields you have presently. I've heard it in town you've more land than anyone in Dalton, perhaps more than anyone in the county, and I'm thinking you wouldn't mind having a good deal more." He pulls a cigar from the breast pocket of his coat, turns his back to the breeze, strikes a match with his thumbnail and puffs the thing lit.

"They're saying at the feedstore it's a Mexican in town passing time with Patrick Dalton, and I'm thinking if you're that Mexican then you can take your fancy buggy and your *enterprise* and your little split-tails there and turn them all *presently* around and go on back to town."

The man neither flinches nor frowns. He works at the cigar and lets the smoke roll in his open mouth and drift into the breeze. "Dalton's stabling my horses. Nothing more. And I'm Spanish, Mr. Skala. My ranch, sir, was down in Guanajuato, some three thousand hectares, beef cattle and horses, but that's finished now. Still, my family, I can assure you, is not of mixed blood, though that too will be finished, soon enough. Sometimes a man has choices in such matters and sometimes he has not."

"That's a fact," Skala says. "I'm expecting you've got a choice for me, then, am I right?"

"My girls," the old man says, "they're of age. They need husbands."

"Hell," Skala says, "it's a mess of needs go unmet around here."

"I'm willing to pay to see that this one doesn't. Two hundred acres per daughter, cash or land, if there's land enough around to be had."

Now Skala laughs and spits and turns to have a look at his boys, who are standing just this side of the furrows now and moving their eyes from the carriage to Villaseñor without moving their heads.

"Shit," he says. "What use is more land if I'm out the bodies to farm it?"

Villaseñor considers telling the man that he might buy some good workhorses instead of tethering his own flesh and blood to a plow, but instead he takes the cigar from his teeth, puts two fingers in his mouth and whistles sharply, waving his cigar at the carriage.

The girls climb down from the surrey and walk out front of the horses and stand there in a line like they're at auction and somehow prideful of it. They offer the boys closed-lipped smiles that appear soft and kindly but a far cry from shy, and they stand without moving their feet or swinging their arms and in this way they seem as at ease here in the bare daylight on another man's land as they might in their own bedrooms. The wind plays against their dresses, which flare out gently over their slight hips, and the hems fall a few inches below the knee and ripple there against their taut brown calves.

They do not avert their eyes, and neither do the boys.

Across the road, a threesome of Skala's shaggy heifers comes to pull at the brittle grass around the fenceposts, and then, taking note of the men, they push their square heads over the top wire of the fence and cross their eyes and commence to lowing.

Villaseñor raises a hand to his daughters and another out to the boys in the field. "They seem interested enough in one another," he says. "Why should we break their hearts?"

"*We* ain't doing a damn thing, not together we ain't. And I'll break a heap more than their hearts if they go taking Mexicans for wives, you mark it." Now he turns to make his way into the field, saying, "Boys, get back in front of that plow. I'm all talked out."

Villaseñor waves his cigar again at his daughters and then presses the kindled end dead against the heel of his boot while the girls climb back into the surrey. Stan runs a hand through his hair, takes another long look at the girls as they mount the carriage, and Villaseñor laughs when he catches sight of it. "Mr. Skala," he says. "I hear from Dalton you've got a pair of good-running horses."

27

Skala reaches the plow and takes his whip in hand and twirls it like a down-flung lasso in the furrows beside him. Without looking back toward the road, he says, "Well, he'd be one to know."

"Claims he does."

"I reckon he learns then, even if he learns slow."

"Perhaps, then, you'd rather wager than cut a deal. Win some land and keep your hands all the same — assuming you win, of course. Would you consider that?"

Skala coils the whip and hangs it on the plow handle. He clears his throat, turns to Karel, and looks a question at him. The clouds race overhead, and the hard wind blowing up cold from the west snaps the leather riggings against one another. Karel smiles, ducks into his harness, and tightens the straps.

Vaclav fingers the whip coiled up on the handle while the clouds throw their fast shadows onto his land, then he turns back toward the road and gives the Mexican a nod. "I just now did," he says.

IN THEIR ROOM after dark, while the three older boys lie back on their beds, bare chested in just their long drawers, hands clasped behind their heads, Karel sits on the floor working cottonseed oil into the horses' bridles. The moonlight slants its way into the room to play there against the lamp smoke hanging in the air.

"It don't matter to me which one I get," Stan says. "So long as I get one of them."

Thomàs rolls onto his side to face his brothers while he smiles and cups a hand over his crotch. "Generous of you, big brother. Then I'll have me the little one with the kissing lips. You boys see the brisket on her? Oh, Lord. I do believe she makes my sticker peck out."

Eduard sits up, his lumpy feather pillow in hand, and hurls it at Karel, who ducks out of the way and shoots his brother a look. "Poor little boy," Eddie says. "He's going to be stuck here with nothing but his own hand greased with cottonseed oil."

"Worse," Stan says. "Stuck here alone with Pop."

"It's your dream," Karel says, going back to his work, "so have it whichever a way suits you. There ain't no way I'm losing that race."

"I aim to have it a mess of ways what suit me," says Thomàs. "I aim to have it sunup, sundown, and Sundays."

• • •

That night comes the first dream Karel will ever remember carrying with him past dawn, one that will visit him often enough over the years that he will come to wonder, when he wakes, why it so troubles him still. He's standing over his father in the barn while the man hunches forward to hold Whiskey's pastern bent back between two knees and pull from the hoof a shoe that is cracking in hairlines at the nail holes. It goes unstated, but it's clear that Karel has undershod the horse and that the hind heels are now underrun and that Vaclav Skala believes his son to be about the piss-poorest farrier on the planet.

Still, the job is routine. Karel has cross-tied the animal and now there's nothing left for him but to lean against the horse and breathe in the smells of animals and hay and sweat while he watches his father's deft hands at work. Whiskey stands patient as ever in this endeavor, but when the shoe is pried loose and Vaclav drops the hoof to the dirt unshod, the horse lifts it as if he's gone half lame and throws his head about, snorting and blowing. Karel keeps his hand on the animal's neck and talks to him softly, but when Vaclav reaches down again to have a look at the hoof, the horse sidesteps and kicks, and there's a sound like what you get if you stomp a boot heel down hard on a green pecan, only louder, much louder, when the hoof strikes Vaclav Skala's forehead and drives him back into the dirt and hay.

But this is not what jerks Karel awake in bed. Instead, he keeps dreaming as he always will, watching himself run over to his father, who lies groaning and facedown with his arms thrown out to each side, the horseshoe still in one hand, the hay dust borne up by his impact hovering over him, a thousand airborne particles glinting in a kind of murky and suspect halo over the man whose fall has given rise to them.

Karel bends over the old man, whose visible eye is open but rolling too loose in its socket, and when he stands straight again, the blood rushes to the boy's head and the whole world goes red of a sudden. He stumbles, lurching to one side to catch his balance, and there's that sick sensation you get when you're out along the creek-bed and your boot comes down on a bullfrog, all that fleshy give before the abrupt and splintering and skeletal resistance.

And then his father is screaming, sitting up and cursing red-eyed and furious, holding before him an outstretched arm and a quivering hand, the horseshoe still flat, defying gravity, against the man's downturned palm despite his fingers, which are straightened and thick knuckled and now running with blood in thin streams from the back of the man's hand, a hand tufted with blond hair and run through such that the points of two shoeing nails have come up sickly between the bones and through the skin and show themselves nesting in the swollen and bloody punctures.

Upright in bed with sweat-drenched sheets adhered to his skin, Karel blinks the dream back and sits listening to his brothers' throaty breathing while his eyes try to find purchase in the darkness. The window is so black it appears to Karel the world outside has been reduced to two unlit dimensions, and because he knows himself awake now, he has no choice but to puzzle some sense out of it. He puts the night at some late hour after the moon has passed through its arc and gone on to brighten other dark horizons. After midnight, then, long after, and the horses, always still at this hour, are complaining such that he can hear them through the dense pear grove that stands between the back porch and the stable. What the devil, he thinks, and he throws back the sheets.

After pulling on his socks and trousers, Karel slips into an undershirt and slides the suspender straps over his shoulders before feeling his way down the hall with a hand on each wall and stepping into his boots by the back door. They've lost two calves in the last six months to coyotes, so Karel grabs the J. C. Higgins .22 they keep leaning and loaded against the backdoor molding. He checks his trouser pockets to make sure he's got matches, and then he steps out into the windless night that's loudly alive with tree frogs and crickets and with the panicked animals in the stables.

He pulls the lantern down off the nail that's driven into the door frame, and when he gets the wicking lit, he heads down the steps with the rifle in his right hand and the light in the other. The horses sound like they're all but gone mad, stamping and knocking themselves against the stall planks and speaking loudly out against whatever has come to torment them.

Karel moves through the grove rather than around it, hoping to conceal himself long enough to get a good bead on whatever it is he's about to shoot, but once he clears enough of the trees to get a view of the stable doors, Karel's guts flash hot with adrenaline. The slide-to door of the stable stands gapped open a foot or more, which would be normal enough, Karel knows, were there not a flickering and yellow light at work inside and a dark horse standing in the shadows between the stable and the water tank, its head sweeping back and forth as if listening at once to the other horses and to whatever it senses moving in the grove.

Karel leans his gun against a tree and blows out the lantern. He takes a knee behind the tree, one he's climbed dozens of times as a kid on account of its low berth of branches and its sweet summer fruit, and now he hunkers there with his rifle leveled at the open door and waits while his guts work against themselves in such a way that Karel wonders if a man can set himself afire with only the friction of his own fears.

He doesn't wait long there before the stabled horses grow muted and still and the entrance falls void of its glow so abruptly you'd swear there was a darkness inside capable of consuming even firelight.

Karel's eyes go useless and he thinks about how, in winter hay season, a day baling in the freezing wind can make it so even a tepid bath is too hot to sit down in all at once. Got-damn, he thinks, and he concentrates, tries to see with his ears, to find beneath the commotion of tree frogs and insects some more human and telling sound. At first he believes he's imagining it, dreaming it as acutely and convincingly as he's dreamed nails through his father's flesh, but when the slightest of a breeze pushes through the grove and the critters stop their calling from the trees to take note, there they are — footfalls, out beyond the cattletank in the yard.

Karel tries to follow them with a gun barrel he can't quite see the length of, but then his eyes begin finally to find some depth in the darkness, to see into the black rather than only the black itself, and he leaves the lantern there among the surfaced roots of the tree and makes out across the dirt with his rifle raised.

When he comes upon them, the animal sidesteps and nickers and its ears come forward. The rider startles, lets loose the reins, and sits the horse staring at him.

She's beautiful, and he damn near shoots her.

"Get on down from there," Karel says, taking his finger from the trigger.

She widens her big black eyes at him and parts her lips and sits there running her fingers between the horse's ears and down its white blaze. "And if I'd rather not?" she says, her voice smooth and cool as river-bottom stones.

She's in the same dress she'd worn in the carriage, only now its hem is riding up on account of the saddle. He drops his eyes to her legs, bare to the thigh above her riding boots, and he feels like it's nothing inside him but hot liquid swirling around his bones. He motions at her with the gun barrel and tries to drop his voice low, tries to mean it when he says it: "Then I reckon you'll be the handsomest dead woman I ever see."

Her hair falls straight and dark in front of her shoulders, a few wisps pasted to the corner of her mouth. She looks down at the gun and works visibly to keep a smile reined in while she pulls her hair back behind her ears. Then she takes hold of the pommel and swings down from the saddle. She's slight enough that she scarcely ducks her head when she stands beneath the horse's throat to rub its neck. "Do I look so dangerous?" she asks.

Karel considers the question for a moment before he realizes the gun's still leveled at her. "Either that or you're lost," he says, and he drops the barrel and holds the rifle at his side. "The hell you think you're up to in there?" he says, nodding at the stable.

She steps from under the horse and it nudges at her with its great head and sniffs and nibbles at her hair, and Karel goes cool with something akin to envy, a kind of longing he feels often in the presence of animals. There's only the trace of a northern breeze, and he takes a sideways step, hoping he might get downwind enough of her to find her scent there in the air amidst the traces of woodsmoke and turned earth and cattle.

Gathering the reins in her hands, she holds them out to Karel. "I only wanted to see them," she says. "So here. Have your fill. Fair is fair."

There's not yet so much as a hint of light on the horizon. Karel rests the butt of the gun on the ground and leans against the barrel while the horse jerks its head up against the reins and works its jaw from side to side against the bit. "I don't have to handle a horse to outrun it," Karel says, but then he notes her hand there, extended with the reins, and curses himself. If he'd reached for them, he might have touched her.

Now she raises a brow and slides the toe of her boot around in the dirt as if she's intent on drawing something of importance, something he might understand. "No," she says, "I don't suppose you do. That's an impressive pair of horses in there."

Karel glances at the stables, then back toward the house, then down at what she's drawn in the dirt. He's gone his whole life asking himself unspoken questions about his mother, and now something about the cool, unlit morning and this girl in her dress and riding boots has him wondering if his mother ever sat horseback, ever rode while he was inside her for those months when, unlike every month since, he could touch her, even if he didn't know he was doing it, when they were together in that way and both alive and maybe riding together amidst the morning light and the fields of alfalfa and the smells of coming rain and late-cut hay.

The girl walks her horse to the cattletank and waters him. She

34

acts, for all the world, as if she's paying a friendly, daylight visit to an old acquaintance.

"You better git," Karel says. "Pop catches you here it'll be hell to pay."

The girl reaches down between her knees and gathers her dress hems together in one hand, then she slides a boot into the stirrup and swings herself into the saddle. Her skin shines even in the darkness, and her lips look swollen and tender and wet when she smiles. "And what about you?" she says. "What if it's you who catches me?"

Karel lifts his rifle and flexes his fingers around its forearm and smoothes over with his boot the work she's done there in the dirt. "Just see that it isn't," he says.

The girl taps a heel to the horse's ribs and its oily eyes roll in its head as she swings him around, and then she tosses her hair to one side and looks back at Karel over her shoulder. "I will," she says. "Tomorrow night. When we race."

Karel tries to laugh, but what comes out of him is a sound more like that of the critters in the trees than that of a man who's filled up with certainties. "Is that a fact?" he says. "Your father lets his girls do his racing for him?"

"He likes to win."

"Well," says Karel, "seems only fair that you tell me your name, don't it? Before you leave me in the dust, I mean."

She turns the horse back at him and walks it up slowly so that she's looking directly down on him, her eyes so deep and full of their dark allure that Karel imagines she could pull him out of his boots and into the saddle with nothing more than a look. She curls a few strands of the horse's mane around her finger and wets her lips with her tongue, and, before she gives her horse a heel and gallops him into the early morning fields, she leans down over Karel such that her hair brushes against his face and he breathes her in and she smells of lavender and of beeswax and of sweet feed, and then her voice is in his ear and she's whispering: "Ask me Saturday, and I'll tell you it's Skala."

35

A Breeding of Nettles

DECEMBER 1924

THE YEAR'S COTTON was long in, all three hundred and fifty bales of it dried and ginned and shipped overland to Port Lavaca back in September. The money was in the bank, the Mexican pickers paid and sent on their way. Both cuts of late hay had been baled and stacked three deep in the loft — all in time for calving season — and now Karel Skala was waiting for but two withering Hereford heifers and one wide-hipped wife to drop their young into the world.

Early of the morning, with the sun striking a bright line on the horizon and the wind worrying the twisted branches of the mesquite trees behind the barn, Karel stood sipping coffee and watching his mixed herd of cattle graze beneath a low line of heavy clouds sliding in from the west. December, and still warm enough to break a sweat working in shirtsleeves. He had a habit, Karel did, on account of his crooked neck, of leaning to the right at the waist so as to set the world level in his sights. Upstairs, buried with his father's old watch beneath bank papers in his bureau, there was a photograph some fourteen years old of him and his brothers on the day of their father's funeral. They'd been standing out in the grove among the pear trees he now owned, smoking cigarettes and meaning to say something kind about their pop but saying nothing instead, looking squint-eyed into the evening sun, all four of them young and blond-haired and blue-eyed and kinked badly at the neck, compensating as best they could — he and Stan leaning to the right, Thom and

Eddie to the left. Well over a decade had gone by since they'd been together that way, standing leisurely if uncomfortably in one another's company, pretending they could ever level off a world that had put their mother in the ground and left their father standing for so many years with tobacco-stained lips, red-faced and ever ready with his whip.

But Karel didn't have time to think of such things, of his brothers and what had become of them, of their rich and lovely Spanish wives, of all the land that had fallen into their laps. There simply weren't hours enough for such thoughts, not even with the year's hottest and hardest days behind him. His Sophie had it in her mind to drive to evening Mass in Praha for the Feast, for the Jolly Club dance afterward, and there'd never been, in the five years they'd been married, any talking that woman out of a chance to spend time on her knees beneath the painted ceiling of St. Mary's, no matter how pregnant she was.

"What you aiming to do?" he'd asked her over breakfast, nodding at her belly. "Squeeze her right out in the pews?"

Sophie had whipped her apron at him and smiled. "If it's the Lord's intention, Karel, I expect I will. Besides, how is it you're so sure-fire certain it's a girl?"

"Same as always. Dreamt it was a boy."

She shook her head and went back to shaping dough for the kolaches she meant to take to the dance. "Well, Karel," she said, and now her smile drew itself tight at the corners of her mouth, "seems likely—doesn't it?—that eventually you've got to be right in your dreams about *something.*"

Maybe so, Karel thought now, but not about this. Sophie was carrying all her weight up high, and he'd seen it before, twice in three years, and he knew what it meant. He took a last sidelong look at the coming clouds, spat some loose strings of tobacco from his tongue, swallowed the grainy dregs of his coffee, and then he went to work.

40

In the cattle pens, he ran his hands up under the knotted tails of each red heifer, checking for inflammation or bloody show, and, finding none, cursed them both for being slow. They lowed and switched their tails, their dark eyes unblinking up high on their white faces. They bent and took in more hay, and Karel was thankful at least for this. The youngest of these girls had proven herself vengeful, an unusual characteristic for a Hereford, and he still wore a bruise on the side of his belly from her antics the week before, a dark stain of blue ringed in black scabby stitching where the teeth had drawn blood.

"You're whores, the both of you," Karel said, slapping hard on her flank the young little bitch who'd put the bite to him. "Slower than Christmas, too."

He shoveled the shit from the pens and wheeled it out back to the compost heap, which stank of rotting eggshells and chicken heads. He slung feed to the pullets who'd been thus far spared Sophie's strong hands and sharp blade. He hung pails of sweet feed in the stables for the horses, then he walked out east of the barn to the smokehouse, added some pecan chunkwood to the embers, and pulled a strip of glistening fat off one of the hams he'd strung up two mornings before. He popped the fat into his mouth and held it there in the hollow of his cheek without chewing, sucking the salt while he made his way back to the barn.

As an afterthought, he grabbed his toolbox and went out to grease the windmill bearings, which were scored badly on their races and would soon need replacing. He loosened the shaft collars and worked the bearing puller onto the housings. Once he'd pulled them free, he popped the bearings from the housings and lubed them well with a finger dipped in grease.

This was the kind of morning work Karel liked, simple little tasks he could complete without calculating figures or opening his wallet or asking his wife for help. If the world were made of only such chores, he thought, he wouldn't fret so about being without a son.

He wouldn't have to keep Sophie on her back every night in March so that, come next December, after the bulk of the year's work was done, she might finally get it right and deliver a boy. If all his work were this easy, he could spend his time thinking instead about the Novotny girl, the way her skin shined dark as a polished penny, the way her arms and shoulders rippled with ribbons of muscle from years of working at her father's feedstore, the way she hadn't grown heavy in the hips or sharp of the tongue. The way she never said no.

The wind was picking up out of the west as if bent on keeping the sun on the morning horizon, and when Karel got the bearings remounted and the drive shaft engaged, the mill began pumping furiously.

Out in the pasture, the jackass lolled its heavy head around while lumbering along, chasing the new calves in circles. The dumbest animal on earth, Karel thought. Dumber even than a cow, but just as useful. Too dumb to fear coyotes, and stubborn enough to keep them clear of the calves. Karel swallowed the pork fat, put his fingers in his mouth, and whistled loudly. The jackass stopped in place, its ears standing forward. The air was ripe with the smells of cattle and smoke and winter pine. Stray wisps of cotton swirled in the wind, and Karel couldn't help but see the waste in it, couldn't help but imagine the three or four bales his hired Mexicans had left in the fields. The ass was still motionless amidst the herd, waiting, and as Karel walked back to the barn to check on the kegs of beer that had arrived overnight, his guts stung with the recognition that he couldn't command much in the way of obedience from anything but a half-wit animal.

The week before, when the heifer had bitten him, he'd kicked her hard down in front of her udder. She'd shuddered and stepped backward, just keeping her feet, and her great white face turned away from him in a way that reminded Karel of the hiding game his youngest daughter, Evie, had taken to playing in recent months, covering her eyes with a blanket, certain that if she couldn't see,

42

she couldn't be seen. Karel had looked down at the scuffed toes of his boots, inflamed with anger at himself, worrying over the money he'd lose if the heifer took to bleeding inside and couldn't calve. Then he spat into the soiled hay and waited for the cow to turn her face to him. When she did, he kicked her again, this time harder and higher, just back of the brisket, where it would be sure to sting her like fire without costing him so much as a cool penny.

UP IN SHINER at the Spoetzl Brewery, the young brewmaster Kosmos made most of his living these days by ruining the strong pilsner he'd become known for in half a dozen counties. The Texas Senate still allowed for near beer, an all-but-tasteless concoction that could get a man drunk only if a man's definition of drunk involved a dull pain above the ears and a near-constant need to piss. By state law, Kosmos was to brew his Bohemian recipe and then boil off the bulk of the alcohol, but he could be forgetful sometimes, especially when Karel Skala paid him to forget. To be a Czech farmer in south Texas was to be always thirsty, and it was a well-known joke among the women of Lavaca County that if their men were made to choose between their pints of pilsner and their peckers, there'd be a premium on good sharp knives and coagulant salts at the general store in Dalton.

In the loft, amidst the stagnant smell of still-damp hay, Karel pulled back the square bales near the northern ladder and stepped into a long corridor of secreted beer, a single oaken row of kegs stacked two high that ran the length of the loft. From the ground level of the barn, all anyone could see of the loft was a wall of hay bales, but for four years now Karel had kept a hollow between the back row of bales and the wall. In the winter months, the kegs would stay cool for several weeks, long enough to find buyers for them but not too long to keep them hidden before the hay needed to be put out for the cattle.

44

The Praha Jolly Club would be good for at least three, Karel figured, and if he had to make the long trip out there today, and sit in church besides, he was damn sure going to turn a profit doing it.

He lowered the kegs one by one from the loft with a rope hoist, rolled them out to the Dodge truck he'd bought last year, for five bits on the dollar, from old Lad Dvorak's bank in town after it foreclosed on the Slovacek place over in Weid, and by the time he got the kegs loaded up and the truck's wheel bearings greased, the fast fat clouds were blowing past overhead without turning loose even a misty bit of their burden.

Inside, after a long hour spent tallying earnings and costs in his ledger, Karel shaved and changed into his suit, then he sat sipping coffee at the kitchen table, rolling sixteen cigarettes and lining them up in the silver case Sophie's father had given him for a wedding gift. The house was warm and fragrant, the milky-sweet yeast dough of kolaches browning in the oven, and when his cigarette case was full, Karel spent a few minutes chasing the girls around the house, growling like a bear while they squealed and laughed and Evie hid behind her blanket. In the living room, Karel plucked his youngest off the floor and nibbled behind her ears until she giggled and buried her face in the collar of his shirt. The oldest girl, Diane, ever hungrier for attention these days, stood below, tugging on the leg of his trousers. Karel put Evie back on the floor, squinted up his eyes and made his fingers into claws before crouching down beside his oldest. "Deenie," he said, "when I catch you I'm going to pull off your toes and eat them with mustard."

The girl, at three, was as fast as she was loud in her escape, and Karel couldn't help but laugh. "Let's to it, all you good-looking women," he said. "If we're going, we're going now."

This was a trip that gave Karel fits, that slicked his guts with a hot mix of envy and resentment and lust, and he tried, mile after slow mile, to keep his eyes only on the road, on the out-flung fencelines blurred by the dirty haze of the truck's front glass. Had it been a stranger at the wheel, someone from northern Fayette County or down near the Gulf Coast, that man would likely have taken note of the name on the passing cattlegates and assumed that he was rolling by one man's expansive spread of property. But the men of Lavaca County knew different. The land between the south and north forks of Mustang Creek, with its wire-fenced stretches of pastureland and black-soiled cotton fields, was the original Skala parcel, some of it bought and some of it won—all of it amassed by old man Vaclav before his sudden death and then deeded to Karel. Everything north, for six miles beyond the Shiner town limits, was the property of the older three Skala boys and their families. The northernmost plot, nearly four hundred acres that lined both winding sides of the Shiner-Moulton road, was the one that most made Karel wish he could drive blind.

Even with sweet little Diane in his lap and Sophie up against him, hip to hip, holding their two babies, one on her knees and one yet curled up and floating tethered in the soft and murky insides of her—even with all this family pressed so close to him—Karel couldn't keep his eyes from the stand of blackjack oaks about a mile up the road, from the farm road that ended at the gate amidst those trees. Nor could he keep his imagination from winding up that road to the house that sat, just out of view, a quarter mile from the gate, nestled among a grove of peach and pecan trees, its back porch steps leading up to the door that opened into Graciela's kitchen. Just last week, he'd seen her out front of the mercantile in Shiner, walking with her children, the little girls dressed in gingham and hair ribbons and clean white stockings, and for once he hadn't crossed to the other side of the road to avoid trading pleasantries with her. The truth was, talk or no talk, it took less than the sight of her to take him back all those years, to the wonder of her dark hair and the taut swell of her calves below the hem of her dress, to the sweet, earthy smell of her he'd taken in some fourteen years back, and to the desire that he'd begun to imagine he'd never again satisfy or suppress, either one.

It was a long trip, just shy of thirty miles to the church in Praha, and the unkempt road made the driving slow. The truck bounced and lurched, slipping into and out of the hard ruts, throwing packed clods of dirt and rock against the undercarriage. Karel steered with one hand and put his eyes back on the northernmost horizon and pulled his cigarette case from his shirt pocket. He flipped the top open with his thumb and pulled a cigarette out with his teeth.

"Time we get home," he said, "it'll be twice as much driving as praying."

Sophie turned the baby, who'd already taken to sleep, so that the little girl's cheek was against her chest. "It's always a ledger with you, Karel. You could pray now, I suspect, if you want so bad that things end up equal on both sides."

"I been doing just that," he said. "Ever since we left."

An hour later, up past the Columbus Road and into the slight swells of forested hills that rose up near the county line, Karel had yet to free himself from the thoughts of his brother's wife. He had yet to strike a match, and his cigarette still hung there, unlit, from his lips.

JUST OVER THE Fayette County line in Praha, there was medicine more than Mass at St. Mary's to be found, and by the time they arrived, both Karel and Sophie Skala were in need of one sort or another. A cool, parched wind had crept in behind the morning's clouds, evening was coming on, and Karel steered the truck behind the church and set the brake beneath an old live oak whose bare branches spanned the twenty-yard gap between the church itself and the adjacent hall, a new, two-story construction of stone and red brick where the dance would be held after Mass.

The long ride had been a rough one, rough enough that now, climbing from the cab, Sophie could tell the moment her feet touched the earth that her third child would be born in Praha, and on the day of the Feast, no less. In the shadows, the air carried a new chill, and Sophie was thankful for the warmth of her body, for the warmth of the body curled up within her. Resting Evie's sleeping weight on her hip, she pulled her shawl up to cover the back of her neck and then cupped her free hand beneath her belly, exhaling sharply.

When Karel made it around the truck with Diane, his mind still miles back on the road in his sister-in-law's kitchen, Sophie took her oldest girl's hand and, before leading her around to the front church steps, said, "I'm needing to sit, Karel. We'll keep a place for you inside."

Karel rubbed his arms against the cold and, as an afterthought, went back to the cab for his suitcoat. Stove smoke came swirling up from the houses hidden amidst the trees to the east. He wanted to clear his head, so before he rolled the kegs of beer into the hall and discussed price with old man Novotny, he walked out back of the church to the parish stables and smoked a cigarette there among the four horses and the smell of tack oil and oats. In the nearest stall, a roan gelding looked up from its bucket of feed and blew, blinking its eyes slowly, and Karel wished there was some immediate need that might keep him here—a hard foaling or a hay fire, either one—anything to keep him out of that church where he would have to sit in the gleaming pews and try to find a place for his eyes to fall without causing him pause or regret or something less forgivable.

Now he held his cigarette in his mouth and scratched the horse behind its twitching ears before turning to watch as more families arrived, most in automobiles, a few yet in wagons, all wearing their finest clothes and tempered smiles.

St. Mary's was one of the three "painted churches" in the surrounding countryside, the ceiling brushed brightly with vivid images, the most unsettling of which was a gold triangle that framed a single unblinking eye, an eye that stared down on a full congregation or on empty pews with the same unflagging and illegible gaze. Even so, Karel thought St. Mary's handsome—from the outside, at least. Erected the year of his birth, the church stood unassumingly enough between the clusters of white pine and moss-veiled oak. Trimmed in marbled stone and planked with simple whitewashed pine siding, the structure's only exterior embellishment was its tall steeple, on top of which was a burnished bronze cross that the townsfolk had paid a young bohunk a keg of beer to mount in its lead pedestal.

Karel had heard the story as a boy, had marveled at the man's bravery. By all accounts, the week before Easter, he'd climbed out the topmost steeple window and shimmied up so that, perched with the toes of his boots on the windowsill, he could steady himself such that he might raise the cross high enough to slide the bronze

49

tenon into the pedestal's mortise. The parishioners stood below, calling up to him with encouragement and advice. Overhead, the sun flickered between passing clouds. When the young man raised the cross, one of its arms snagged on his shirt collar and, just as he worked it free, a gust of wind sent the leaves skittering across the rooftop from the nearby trees.

More than one hundred feet above the ground, the man braced himself against the wind, leaning into the steeple the way a child will lean into his mother for the shelter of her body, but there was nothing of help to be had. With one hand on the cross, the other trying to take hold of the steeple, he pressed himself against the structure, swaying there until he looked down and his boots slipped from the sill.

He fell to the rooftop, sliding on his belly down the steep pitch with the cross gripped in one hand while the fingernails of his other raked over the cedar shingles as he slid. He flailed and kicked, his boots scraping, in search of purchase, as he descended toward the eaves.

This, the onlookers would say, was a malediction, evidence more than ample of evil's due influence in a world of fallen men, and when the young man flipped himself onto his back, planting his heels and stopping himself just short of falling, and lay there pumping hot breath from his lungs before crawling slowly back toward the steeple to complete the job, the cross leaning against his shoulder, the parishioners cheered before they fell silent in solemn recognition of the Lord's intervention. They whispered, as they still did, of this act of grace, of the vision that had brought before their eyes and renewed in their hearts the savior's struggle beneath the weight of his own glorious burden. An Easter miracle, a new testament of their faith, and all for a few gallons of beer.

Now, as Karel ground the wet tip of his cigarette into the earth with the toe of his boot and walked back to his truck, the cross stood glistening against the darkening sky, and dulled only slightly by weather and time. Beneath it, inside the church, Karel's wife was forcing smiles at the other wives from her pew while the painted eye gazed down on her, bearing muted, candle-lit witness to her own struggle against the onset of a hot and cramping wave of contractions. On Sophie's shoulder, little Evie still slept, a thin ribbon of saliva strung from the corner of her mouth to her mother's shawl. Beside her, Diane sat gazing up at the ceiling and the stained-glass windows, listening to the whispered prayers and conversations of the growing congregation. The youngest child, suspended head down in the red liquid glow of its mother's womb, tucked its knees up against its chest and rolled the back of its head against the hard rope of its mother's spine.

The altar boys appeared quietly from the nave, genuflected and lit the altar candles while, in the sacristy, Father Petardus slipped into his fine white vestment. Outside, Karel rolled three kegs of beer from his truck into the hall and stood laughing with the men of the Jolly Club, taking Novotny's flask of corn whiskey when it was offered, folding bills into his pocket. Novotny's daughter, Elizka, wearing her Sunday dress and white stockings, managed a discreet fingertip wave from behind the bar where she was readying the glassware. Karel gave her a nod, his insides alive with a potent mash of whiskey and desire. He took another pull off the flask, swallowing with a grimace, while in the pews Sophie breathed hard through clenched teeth and thought, with a kind of willed determination that never fully blotted out the fear, of what lay in wait for her. She'd had hard labors with the first two, but this would be another thing entirely. The child would come from her, and she would survive it, but it would be hours yet, and the back of its skull would grind against her spine as it came.

It had begun, she knew that, but she couldn't know that it would progress in the way that it would, that the baby would be rendered from her in a fashion as protracted and inexorable as the way stones are tumbled, turned smooth by years of rushing water, and men are eroded of kindness by the slow, interminable friction of their unrealized desires.

HER WATER BROKE at the kneeling rail.

The church was quietly alive with the flickering of candlelight and the swirling haze of incense smoke, and Karel was on his knees beside her, amazed as ever by the serenity that overcame his wife's face when Father Petardus placed the Eucharist on her tongue. Holding Evie, who stirred now on her shoulder, Sophie kept her eyes shut, bowed her head, and when the altar boy moved the communion plate beneath Karel's chin and the priest held the sacrament before him, saying, "The Body of Christ," Sophie inhaled with a plaintive gasp and whispered, "Oh, Karel," as if begging her husband to accept what he'd been offered.

He did not.

His hearing, after these five years of marriage, was attuned to her voice in the way common only to husbands who adore their wives and those who lie to them with regularity. To Karel's mind, he practiced the latter because of the former, because Sophie was a good woman, kind and hearty and generous, so much so, in fact, that he suspected she knew when he was less than honest, less than wholly hers, and that she endured the indiscretions the way a good horse will endure shoeing and hard harness work, blinded to everything but the promise of brushstrokes and oats, of kindness and comfort. With eyes affixed only to a future worth forsaking the present for.

Now, because Sophie was speaking at the communion rail, speaking to him in an attitude she would normally reserve for her queries of God, Karel turned from Father Petardus's offering. He leaned toward his wife, his hand reaching down to support himself, and, in doing so, touching the wet hem of her skirt.

When, for years afterward, he told this story to his child, he would say that the birth had begun at the precise moment that the body of Christ had touched his tongue, that it was as if the sacrifice of one son had allowed for the arrival of another.

This was to become Karel's way, the stretching of truth in an effort to instill in the workaday the wonderful, and this was especially true in the stories he would come to tell his children. His own upbringing had been one of quiet exclusion, his father moving through the rooms of the house and the rows of the cropfields in what seemed a determined if not wholly unnatural silence. Year after year, the rain would batter the cedar shingles overhead, the sun would bake the black earth to a hard ceramic sheen around the rigid cotton stalks, the quail in the pastureland would covey and nest and hatch and fledge, each season born naturally of the one before, but on the rare day that Vaclav Skala would gather his boys behind the barn or on the tree-lined banks of Mustang Creek with fishing rods and tin pails of grubs, the very earth would cease, in the boys' minds, its slow, secretive turning, and they'd stand eager and mute, dumbstruck by the anticipation of their father's words.

Usually the stories were brief, meant to impart some lesson, and while Karel might laugh or grow solemn at the stories his father told – of his stormy voyage over high seas from the old country to Galveston, of the wolves he'd hunted alongside his brothers in the hills of Bohemia, lessons about hard work and fields sowed with stubbornness and sacrifice – he never found in these moments any new revelations that could dispute what he'd been told, since he was old enough to comprehend, by his brothers: That he'd killed their mother; that their father despised him for it and had refused, on the day of Karel's birth and thereafter, to hold him.

Now Karel realized that Father Petardus was still extending the Eucharist toward his lips, and Sophie was holding Evie in one arm while she clung to the kneeling rail with the other, her cheeks flushed and running with perspiration from her hairline. Karel brought his wife to her feet and turned away. The priest took a step back with the host yet in his hand and looked down at the couple rising from the rail. The altar boy stood blinking, a frightened grin focused on his own shaking hand and the polished plate held under the host, wondering, no doubt, just what under heaven to do now.

Karel, with whiskey and smoke still on his breath, led his wife down the center aisle of the church toward the doors, a hand in hers and another around her waist. In the pews, Diane met her father's eyes with her own. He nodded toward the door, and she rose to join her parents in the aisle.

Sitting back from the kneelers, making way for the girl, the congregants were pulled from the downcast gazes of their prayers by this unexpected procession. When he'd brought Sophie to her feet at the kneeling rail, Karel had inadvertently stepped on her hem such that now, as they made their belabored way out of the church, the back of Sophie's skirt dragged the floor and streaked the hardwood with her water.

Outside, in the gloaming, the trees lurched and swayed, animated by the shifting winds, the air chilled and sharp with dry pine and chimney smoke. Karel breathed in deep through his nose the way he did when he butchered an animal or kindled a fire, and he laughed as he held his wife around the waist. "It's turning out about how you wanted it," he said. "Ain't it?"

Sophie forced a smile between grimaces. "Not if you're meaning to let me labor in the back of that truck all the way home to Dalton."

"Why, hell no, I'm not." His pale eyes gleamed with mischief, and Sophie recognized the look as the one, more than any other, she'd found irresistible when he'd courted her with dancing and dandelion wine, with kisses and wandering hands among the hay bales up in his loft, she the eighteen-year-old daughter of a father soured by his own determined and ill-humored devotion, Karel the wild-eyed and tough-skinned owner of a vast and growing, if begrudged, fortune in Lavaca County. He was irresistible then as he was now—prone to recklessness, yes, but thoughtful enough to touch her with only the backs of his fingers so as not to rough her skin with his leathery calluses. And he was wounded, too, as anyone could see, and his afflictions opened something wide in her that only caring for him could fill.

When he looked into her eyes, he put the flat back of his hand smoothly against her cheek and pushed her face to the side so her head would match the permanent cant of his own, and in this way he seemed both to acknowledge and soften what his father had done to him with plow and harness and neglect. His smile was forever bent with a hint of impertinence, and he made it his way to say, always, any damn thing he felt like saying, as he did now when he pulled open the church door and called in to the congregation, "Is it a midwife on her knees in there somewhere, and someone to look after my girls? It's a long way back to Dalton, and my wife's taken a mind to farrow out here on these steps if she's not lent a bed instead."

Inside there was the turning of heads and the scuffing of shoe soles on the hardwoods as the parishioners looked away from the sacrament before them and toward the voice at the back of the church.

"Karel," Sophie whispered, pleading with her eyes.

Little Diane was tugging his trouser leg, and he smiled down at her and widened his eyes in such a way that set her to giggling. He looked into the church, caressing Sophie's swollen belly with the backs of his fingers while he called, "Make you a deal, gentlemen. You tend to my wife, and I'll dance with your daughters."

COME NINE O'CLOCK, in the front bedroom of her squat, lamp-lit house, the old widow Vrana had set her mind to it that they would not lose this child. She moved birdlike, shuffling about the room on arthritic bare feet, wringing cotton rags in a basin of cool well water and folding them onto Sophie's forehead as the poor woman labored beneath a single sheet.

The children had been lulled to sleep in the widow's bedroom where, sixteen years before, her husband had coughed blood so violently that it had misted the walls, and where he had died when he'd coughed his last. She had checked on them, these two darling little girls asleep in the bed of her long and fruitless marriage, and the traces of moonlight through the windows reminded the old woman of the nights of her own childhood, nights nearly seventy years gone when, wintering for the first time in this strange new country, in the one-room shelter her father had thrown together when it got too cold to sleep in the wagon, she'd awoken long before morning to the sounds of indecisive winds and coyotes and her two sisters' breathing to find their faces graced by ribbons of light that found their way in through the joints of the hastily hewn roof timbers.

But that had been so very long ago, and they were all buried, father and mother and sisters alike, in the St. Mary's cemetery, not a quarter mile from this house with nothing but densely clustered trees and a narrow footpath of fallen leaves and the indeterminate remainder of her own mortal life between them, and she could make that short walk through the little thicket with a pail of sudsy water and wash their headstones with these same cotton rags, and she could do so any time at all that she liked, excepting now, when both she and the rags had a more pressing purpose.

This baby wasn't turning, and Sophie Skala was one of Praha's own. As a girl, before her father moved the family south into Lavaca County, Sophie had run ponytailed and sun flushed through the thickets and creekbeds of Praha, and a much younger Mrs. Vrana had often taken note of the girl at Mass, sitting so prim and fair, that ponytail tucked up into her Sunday bonnet like a sweet, if poorly kept, secret. Widow Vrana, who now sat on the edge of the bed whispering Hail Marys with the woman that girl had become, helping her pray her way through these violent contractions — strong but unproductive these last two hours — this old woman, she'd pined in those long-gone days for a little girl like the one Sophie had been, one so sweet and well mannered, one so at home all the same in her best dress or in the little smocks she wore while traipsing barefoot around the countryside. It had not come to pass, and it had tested Mrs. Vrana's faith more than even she believed it was meant to be tested that, over the years, in a land of farmers and tradesmen whose wives had little money for physicians and even less faith in their science, she had attended to perhaps four hundred births, and still, no amount of her garden's herbs or store-bought tonic or time spent splay-legged and praying beneath her husband's weight had yielded so much as a short pregnancy, much less a child of her own.

And so, by her will, if not by God's, this child would live. The water had come hours ago, and she'd seen both babies and mothers lost to less dangerous labors. Already she'd applied onions to Sophie's feet and a poultice to her lower back to calm the spasms. She'd purged her with a tea of mugwort and sorrel, and now, to her mind, time was a creeping and persistent rival. The widow knew well, as did all the midwives in three surrounding counties, of the death, nearly thirty years back, that had taken Klara Skala, and needlessly so, she thought. Edna Janek was an able practitioner, and it would not have happened, she believed, had Klara been attended to sooner.

Now, after a final prayer together, she sopped Sophie's face with a new cool rag and pulled back the sheet. She checked between the suffering woman's legs, and then she struggled onto the mattress and positioned herself with her hands cupped on either side of Sophie's belly.

"I've waited as long as I'm willing to wait," she said. "Catch your breath, dear. I'm afraid this is likely to pain you something terrible."

AT THE PARISH hall, during the two further hours of the old widow Vrana's ministrations, and an hour longer of Sophie's grunting and pushing to expel this thing that had so beset her, Karel Skala would unhinge himself with drink.

It had gone full dark by the time he'd gotten Sophie and the girls over to the Vrana house and settled the little ones into bed. He'd kissed Sophie on the forehead, and the old woman had ushered him out the door as if he were no more welcome there than would have been a common cur. On the path through the thicket, without a lantern, he'd been grateful for the emerging moon, swept clean of the day's clouds by the push of cold weather from the west. It was too cool out for tree frogs, and Karel felt their absence. He'd grown up with the throaty urgency of their chirping, and a walk through woods with only the sounds of nested birds and insects was a fresh reminder of all the little disappointments that conspired to set a man to thinking about greater ones. He stepped quickly, wishing to rid himself of this thicket, and his boots crunched in the brittle leaves and pine needles underfoot until he emerged into the unhindered moonlight.

He was grateful, too, for the sight of the cemetery at the end of the path, for the muted animal sounds within the parish stables, then for the gleam from the hall's lighted windows and the muffled, brassy half step of the music that could be heard as he approached, all of which brought him closer to the promise of soft skin and hard drink.

Just outside the hall doors, Bohumil Novotny stood laughing and passing a half-gallon jug with a pair of boys who, but for the work a blade had done to one of their cheeks, could have each passed for the other. Karel stopped behind the trunk of the giant live oak so he could study them awhile. Judging from their caked work boots and oilcloth coats, they hadn't come for church, and Karel would have bet a dollar against a dime that they weren't yet sixteen. Still, here they stood, running their hands through their dark, closely cropped curls and taking seasoned, deliberate pulls on the jug. They made a habit, these two, of hooking their thumbs in their trouser pockets when they laughed. Karel noticed that they held themselves in the same way, upright and rigid as if they'd been skewered with cedar posts, but when they moved they did so leisurely, with loose-jointed gestures.

As for their company, he was about as complicated as cornbread. Between his feedstore and rail interests, Novotny had amassed as much of a fortune as one could in a town so small as Praha, and he was as well dressed as he was red-faced and overfed. Beneath his tailored and unbuttoned black suitcoat, his shirtfront had been freed from his trousers by the protrusion of his belly, and when he took note of Karel approaching from the shadows, he fell silent and scratched the underside of his down-slung stomach while the young fellows beside him toed the dirt and nodded their greetings.

"Damnation," Karel said. "You men so scared of touching a woman that you'd hide outside in the cold rather than take a turn around the floor?"

Novotny raised his brows at the others and took his handkerchief from his vest pocket to clear his nose. Then he took a pull from the jug and held it up as if raising a toast to something no less impressive than the moonlit sky itself. "I'd let you a drink of this corn here, Karel, if I thought it might quiet you down. Thing is, given your communion-time proclamations, I don't believe the last few drops I give you had that effect."

Inside, the band held the last long note of a schottische, and then came the vigorous applause from the dancers. "A few drops just ain't enough to do the trick is all," Karel said, "but I see you found a bigger portion now that the sun's not out to lay light on it." He nodded at the hall door. "Orchestra sounds lively tonight."

"Whole town's lively on account of that near beer you brung." Novotny winked at the boys and handed the jug to Karel. "You know these boys here, I believe, or did once. Villaseñor bought their pop's land down your way."

Karel bubbled the whiskey and took a cigarette from his case. When he lit the thing, the first pull of smoke fell slowly, as if of its own weight alone, from his nostrils, and then he gave these boys a look, one they didn't manage to return, as they appeared intent on studying the scuffed toes of their boots. Good-looking fellows they were, broad across the shoulders and bright in the eyes the way boys tended to be when they got the first scant sniff of their own manhood. If they had a whisker between them, Karel couldn't locate it. "Son of a bitch bought a passel of folks' land," he said, passing the whiskey back to Novotny and putting a hand out as the band took up a new number inside. "Only twins I recollect was the Knedlik boys, and they were still on the tit last time I saw them."

Now the boys turned their attention upward in unison, and the one with the scar stepped forward, smiling, and shook Karel's hand while indicating his brother with a tilt of the head. "Joe here ain't got off it yet," he said, a statement that earned him a hard elbow to the shoulder and smiles all around. "Name's Raymond."

Karel took note of the mark the boy wore, a thin and winding line of poorly mended flesh that ran from the swollen underside of his left eye to the corner of his mouth. "Someone mistake your face for a beefsteak, did they, Raymond?"

The boy put his hands in his pockets and gave his brother a glance through the corner of his unblemished eye. Novotny said the Knedlik troubles had made the paper more than once, and wondered how it was that Karel always knew the market prices of hay and cotton if he never unfolded the *Gazette*.

Karel shrugged and kept his eyes on the boy to let him know he was still awaiting an answer. Before they went inside, with the moon flickering between a few remaining wisps of clouds, Raymond Knedlik worked his tongue around in his mouth awhile and spat between his front teeth. He took a step sideways to square his feet with his shoulders. "It was a family matter," he said.

Karel nodded and turned for the door, but the boy took hold of his shoulder and stopped him short.

"Seeing that we're talking appearances, Mr. Skala, I'm wondering who it was what nailed your ear to your shoulder and left it there until your neck growed that way. A family matter, was it?"

Karel held his cigarette between his teeth and shot Novotny a look that had both amusement and wonder in it. *Who in hell is this little green-ass?* he wanted to say. *And why is it that I want to kick him in the ribs and slap him on the back all at the same time?* Instead, he took a long pull from his smoke and did something he rarely did, something that had always proved as useless as sowing seed in September — he tried to straighten his neck so he could look this boy level in the eye without leaning.

He couldn't any better than he ever could, so he spat his unfinished cigarette from his lips and ground it asunder with his boot heel instead. "I ain't got a family no more," Karel said, "excepting my wife and girls."

"*Excepting?*" Raymond said. "Hell, you can feed me shit on a biscuit if you ain't got me beat. All I got left is Joe here."

"That a fact? Last I heard, your pop had bought a parcel up county from Flatonia."

"Yessir. And me and Joe here just sold it. Which, so long as we're on the subject of commerce, you reckon it's some of that beer left for sale inside? We wouldn't mind drinking one to your family, Mr. Skala. We hear it's getting bigger presently."

"It damn well better be," Karel said, opening the door. "On both counts."

THERE WAS BEER left aplenty, and Elizka Novotny there to pocket Karel's coin and hand him the glass, making sure, each time, to brush his fingers with hers when she did.

The only child of the wealthiest man in town, Elizka had made use of her advantages. During the war, when enrollment fell and the University at Austin had opened its doors more readily to women, Elizka had left Praha for three years of book learning. When her mother fell to a crippling stiffening in her hands and feet, she came home before graduating to assist in the woman's care and ended up managing her father's business interests instead. She had a knack for numbers and negotiation, and once, when Karel had asked when she planned to settle down, Elizka Novotny had pulled a wisp of curls from the corner of her wet mouth and said, "I am settled. I didn't grow Daddy's business just to marry some dirt farmer who expects me to hand over the reins so he can make a wreck of it."

Now Karel gave her a wink, handed beers to the Knedlik boys, and turned toward the music. On a stage of pine planks laid over railroad ties, the five-piece band had come out of their suitcoats, and there was sweat showing beneath the arms of the bandleader's shirtsleeves and wicking into his vest as he kept time to the music with his foot. He handled his accordion with an oddly orchestrated violence, and when he stomped his boot heel sharply through a three count, the horns and drums met him on the third beat, striking up another polka.

Bohumil Novotny buttoned his suitcoat and made his rounds, shaking hands with his fellow townsmen before begging their pardon to carry a plate of food home to his ailing wife. When Father Petardus rose from a table in the back and raised his empty glass, wishing the parishioners a pleasant night, the band kicked into a droll march as the pastor walked for the doors to make his exit. The onlookers hooted and slapped at their thighs, the older among them throwing themselves forward until the laughing turned to wheezing and hacking.

Karel, for all his talk, spent most of the night on the perimeter of the dance hall, moving with the Knedlik boys in tow between the long tables, introducing them to the folks he knew while young suitors reached for the hands of their sweethearts and husbands danced with their wives, stirring the baby powder that had been sprinkled on the hardwood flooring to make shoe leather cooperate with the slide steps of the occasional waltz.

The hall had gone ripe with the smells of spilled beer and sweat and the lingering, fatty spices of the sausage and onions that had been served before the band had tuned up. Throughout the hall, between songs, rose frequent outbursts of laughter and the ivory clicking of dominoes being shaken between hands, but it was the music Karel wanted, and the band kept it coming while he drank and smoked and took a seat across from the Knedlik brothers near the door.

The boys took long drinks from their pilsners, but only Raymond studied Karel from over the rim of his glass. Joe kept his eyes on the table, his mouth pinched up between drinks like he'd been trying the whole of his short life to wash one bitter taste from his mouth with another.

Karel tapped his toe in time with the music and sat back in his chair with a groan. He hadn't found time to eat, what with all the commotion, and now his stomach was a sour swirl of beer and corn whiskey. "So, you boys in need of work?" he said.

64

Raymond smiled and licked a trace of beer suds from his upper lip. "It could be. You in need of help?"

There was a commotion on the dance floor, and Karel looked out to find a young girl sprawled out on her back beneath her red-faced dance partner, who was struggling to bring himself back upright after their tumble. *Hell, boy,* someone called out. *It's a dance, not a circus!*

Karel turned back to the twins, who were chuckling into the foam of their beers. "I might could use a hand or two," he said. "Your folks is gone then? I didn't hear."

"Ashes to ashes," Raymond said, and then his smile turned in on itself at the corners of his mouth. "Mother was a good woman. Deserved better than what God gave her. Died of the typhus last winter. The old man, he burnt up in his bed when the house caught fire. Just after the last cut of hay."

"God bless," Karel said, feeling, at the word of the mother's death, some old, buried connection to her clawing at him like a blind, burrowing animal awakened to find its den collapsed around it. His words, he suspected, had betrayed nothing, and when Joe looked up at him, his bright eyes glassy and red with whiskey and fatigue, did Karel think how halfhearted it must have sounded, the invocation of God coming, as it had, from a man who'd not two hours ago interrupted a sacrament. "What I mean to say is, that's a sorry lot, boys. It was good fortune you managed to make it out."

Now Raymond traced his scar with his thumbnail. He finished his beer and kept his lips closed while he held his stomach and muffled a belch. "We wasn't ever in anything what needed getting out of, Mr. Skala. We don't believe in fortune. Nor accidents neither."

Karel frowned and lit a cigarette. He started to say that a man ought to watch how much he said, and when, but he thought the better of it, saying instead, "How about work? You believe in that?"

"We ain't interested in farming, if that's what you mean. Joe here's good with animals. Sits a horse good as any. I can butcher damn near anything born with blood in it. But we don't tend to crops. We got enough money to get by a good while. Got a new truck. Got no use anymore for planting fields and mending fences. If we had, we'd have kept the land up county."

"I expect you would have," Karel said. "Anything else you won't do, assuming there's good money to be made in it, of course?"

"Just that. Crop farming. I reckon that's the whole list right there."

Karel polished off his beer and grabbed the boys' empty glasses from off the table. And then, before heading toward Elizka at the bar, he clinked the glasses together and squatted down such that his haunches rested on his heels. Now that Sophie was laboring, they'd have cause to stay put in Praha for another day or two at the least, and he'd need someone to look after his heifers and smokehouse, and there were at least four kegs of beer that needed delivering to Hacek's Ice and Coal in Moulton, but first he wanted to see how much doing it might take to spook these boys.

The orchestra held one last, long note of a polka, and when the dancers had spun to a stop and turned toward the stage to applaud, Karel put his cigarette to his lips and held it there burning orange at the ember while he leaned in close to Raymond Knedlik. "Set a house afire, would you, Raymond?"

The boy glanced at his brother and then looked hard and without blinking through the rising smoke into Karel's eyes. His bad eye twitched, its bottom lid pulsing with the measured beating of his heart. Then he pushed his chair back and stood up, his brother following suit. They hooked their thumbs into their pockets and laughed while Karel came to his feet with the beer glasses still in his hands and his cigarette hanging from his mouth.

"If what folks says is true," the boy said, "it's more than me and Joe here that's helped his old man into the hole he deserves."

It had been a long time since anyone, friend or otherwise, had dared to mention Karel's father within earshot of him, and Karel noticed that his fingers were gripped around the beer glasses so forcefully that his veins bulged beneath the tanned skin on the backs of his hands. What I ought to do, he thought, is take you little shit-asses outside and stomp some sense into you, but the brothers held their ground, moving together in such a way that their shoulders nearly touched, and Karel found himself thinking of the days he'd been harnessed with his brothers to the plow. It had been hard work, but they'd suffered it together, shoulder to shoulder, and now there was something cool bubbling up inside him, working its way through him fresh and clean the way the waters of the cold springs out west bubbled up through stone to feed the winding rivers in the hills.

Karel let his cigarette drop from his lips and ground it into the floor with his boot before moving close enough to the boys to smell their sour breath. Onstage, the bandleader pulled a red kerchief from the back pocket of his trousers, mopping his forehead and the bridge of his nose before he announced an intermission. Karel found himself whispering: "If what folks says is true, then we'd all three of us be waiting for a turn in that new electric chair they got in Huntsville, sure enough. So either it ain't true or we ain't been so goddamned mindless enough yet to go flapping our gums about it at a church dance of a Sunday night. Besides which, there's a difference between killing a man and letting one die, so why don't you just take your seats there and let me buy you another beer and listen to what I'm wanting to ask you."

HALF AN HOUR later, after the Knedlik boys had agreed to look after the Skala place for a day or two, and to stay on after that if they could agree on the terms, Karel saw them out to their truck and shook their hands, their breath steaming in the growing cold as they said their good-byes.

And then he took to drinking in earnest.

The beer did its work in much the same way he knew river water did, running through him and carrying away, grain by grain, the sediment of ill will that had embedded itself within him over the past year of hard work and worry. What was left now, he thought, as the night deepened and the hall thinned out, leaving only the most vigilant of dancers and drinkers, was nothing less than the very bedrock of him, deep and compacted such that neither plow nor music nor drink could unearth it.

Karel's earliest taste of the bottle had come eighteen years back on the night of his first race against the Dalton boy. That night, beaming with victory and the whiskey his brothers had smuggled into their room from their father's stash, he had stirred in his bed, flushed so fully of his usual thoughts that it seemed to him there was nothing left of him but skeleton and skin and the tingling thereabouts that came from having done something his pop might praise him for and from having drunk something that might send the old man reaching for his strap.

At first he'd kicked the sheets away and marveled at the novelty of it, of a night freed from the knot of longing he'd had cinched in his gut as long as he could remember, but then the room had begun its slow, almost reluctant turning, the way a windmill did sometimes when a trace of breeze crept up so softly overhead that it didn't even register on his sweat-glazed skin. He'd sat up in bed, alone in a room alive only with the sounds his brothers brought forth from their dreams, and though he couldn't have put it into words, what he knew somehow was that he'd been scooped clean inside of more than he might be able to do without, reduced to something so thin walled and brittle and hollow that it felt, any moment, like it was sure to cave in on itself if he didn't find some way, or someone, to fill it.

He'd discovered on that night, and many like it afterward, that he could manage to stay upright on horseback even when he'd drunk himself incapable of walking a straight line between the back porch and the outhouse. Fumbling with the straps, he'd grabbed the saddle by the pommel and set it aside in the hay. Then he mounted the horse and rode with only a bridle. He cantered out past the cattlegate and slowed to a walk while crossing the south fork of the creek, and when he came up the far bank he gave the horse a heel and marveled at the solid resistance of the animal, that and the surging response that leveled off into a ride so fast and smooth that he could hardly tell himself from the animal or the animal from him. There was the controlled violence of the muscles rolling beneath him, the vibrations working through him so fully that the roots of his teeth tingled in the hard bone of his jaw. In the distance, mesquite and pecan trees cast their erratic black shapes against the bruised sky that hovered over the solid line of the horizon. It was a wonder, and Karel relished the mystery of it—all these acres, so familiar beneath the bald sun, now rendered foreign as provinces in the Bible. All he needed, it seemed, was night air made fast in his hair by an animal run hard in the night, and he could find the loud landscape of his father lulled quiet by something so simple as the absence of light.

In the end, such a ride had only once failed to right him, to restore in his echoing hollows the weight of all the worry he couldn't seem to feel whole for long without.

Now, near midnight in the parish stables, a soft diffusion of moonlight found Karel leaning against a stack of square hay bales and listening to the idle tramping of the horses as they shuffled and sighed in their sleep. Outside, the thicket was loudly alive with the work of insects and wind. When Elizka Novotny came to meet him there, as she'd done twice before in the course of the last year, Karel tried to stand upright and, in the attempt, lurched forward in a fashion so sudden and awkward that at first he imagined one of the horses had worked its way free and come up to nudge him between the shoulder blades. He swung his arms back to compensate, sliding around in the loose hay underfoot before falling back against the rough bedding of the bales.

Elizka pulled the long curls of her hair back over her shoulders and moved toward him past the stalls. "If you were wanting to dance," she said, "you should have asked me an hour ago when the orchestra was playing."

He shrugged and sat up. She held his head in her hands, pulling him toward her, and he could smell her there in the dark, the bitter tang of perspiration and sour malt sweetened by the earthy, animal scent of her. Karel leaned forward and breathed in sharply through his nose. "You smell something of a horse," he said.

She went to work on the buttons of his shirt and shushed him, pushing him onto his back atop the hay. Above them, hung from nails in the joist timbers, was the old weather-checked tack that the parish had forever mended rather than replace. Elizka pulled a rusted martingale ring out so Karel could catch sight of it. "You imagine it has anything to do with this fancy inn you keep inviting me to?"

Karel held his tongue and kicked off his boots. After she'd gotten him out of his trousers, she worked her underclothes down over her hips and pulled her dress up around her waist to reveal the chill bumps rising there on the tops of her thighs. When she straddled him, he looked down as the soft cleft of her yielded to him in the shadows, and then he smiled at her with his eyes closed while she worked the slick and fragrant heat of herself against him. "No," he whispered. "I'm near certain it's you."

Elizka moved atop him for a long while, her hips shifting up and back in the smooth, rhythmic cycle of a seasoned horsewoman posting in the saddle. Karel lay there with his eyes clamped shut, remembering another astride him, the lather of her tracing cool trails down his thighs, until he could scarcely tell what among all this forgiving flesh was hers and what was his. The horses twitched and switched their tails in their sleep. Outside, the wind threaded its way through the thicket and swept leaves from the roof timbers while Elizka's breathing gathered into its own urgent cadence.

And then it was upon him, the same irrepressible breed of desire that he'd felt the night he left his father to expire in the mud after falling beneath the weight of his horse. A longing to turn loose of every damned handhold the earth afforded a man, a longing he'd managed, until then, to defy long enough to unlearn.

When it was time, he pushed himself into her and he held her hips as steadfastly as he was now held by this intoxicating urge, one stronger than the alcohol, one which compelled him to surrender to what beckoned him simply because it beckoned and he heard it. A summons as vital and insensible, Karel felt, as the one the very pull of the earth had on the unborn, that unanswerable force that landed foals and calves and infants alike in the world with the intention to let them fend, in the end, entirely for themselves.

When his body shuddered, Elizka stopped all at once and leapt off to find him smiling at her, his eyes wide with the kind of self-satisfied mischief his wife so often found endearing. "*Damn it, Karel,*" she said. "*You didn't.*"

He tried to follow her, but he had his trousers and boots to contend with, and by the time he made it to the stable door, she had cleared the churchyard and was pacing up the road, her arms stiff at her sides, toward the room she kept above the store beside her father's house. Karel stopped, and as he turned away there came a voice from out in the cemetery. He scanned the fenceline in the darkness to find the old widow Vrana swinging open the gate. She moved toward him with her shawl pulled over her head like a nun come out of the dark night to chasten him. Her face was creased by what Karel imagined were equal parts weather and contempt, and as she approached she kept her eyes fixed on the feedstore up the road.

When she was upon him, he shivered against the chill of her eyes or the winter air or both, and he looked down to find himself still shirtless, hay dust catching moonlight in his chest hair.

And what was there to say by way of explanation? No sense even in troubling with an attempt. Instead he said, "Evening, Mrs. Vrana," and he gave her a nod and a playful bow.

"Long past it," she said, glancing once more up the road, where now lamplight flickered in the second-story window of Elizka's room. "Your wife is wanting to introduce you to your son, Mr. Skala, if you can spare the time just now."

The wind gusted and then swirled so that it came, for a moment, out of the south. The enormous oak between the church and hall turned loose of a wind-snapped twig so slender and insignificant that it rustled down through the network of bare branches and landed soundlessly on the cool sod of the churchyard. Behind him, one of the horses shifted in its nervous, animal sleep, and Karel moved his toes around in his boots. "My *son,* did you say?"

"I did. Delivered so near on to midnight that I can't be certain which day. But he's a boy, Mr. Skala. I'm confident I've kept the difference straight in my mind."

Karel reached for the woman's hand. She allowed him to take it, and then she took a step back toward the cemetery.

"I'll be goddamned," Karel said.

The old woman let go of his hand, began shuffling along toward the gate, and without so much as turning her head she said, "I can't speak to that, Mr. Skala, but I suspect you can. Either way, your wife's waiting on you, and she's likely expecting you to have your shirt on when you get there."

72

A Sacrament of Animals

MARCH 1910

ALL OF THE COOL afternoon, a steady wind has swept across the brittle pastureland and bristled through the needles of the spindly creekside pines, and now, with the two finish-line fires whipped alive and spitting embers, a sliver of moon flashes behind the low scrim of clouds with all the coy promise of a woman's pale skin showing itself beneath the sheer guise of worn stockings. Near the creekbed, in the shadows beyond the firelight, Villaseñor's men stand watching as the onlookers arrive, the hint of moonlight glinting off the blued receivers of their rifles, which they cradle in the crooks of their arms with a collective if tentative tenderness, the way they might hold their sons, had they any to hold.

In two days, news of the wager has outrun the county mail service, finding its way north to Shiner and Moulton as if conveyed by wire, and when Vaclav Skala leads his sons and his fine snorting stallion out of the darkness of his acreage and through the gate at the pasture's westernmost fenceline, he takes slow notice of the congregation of animals tethered to fenceposts. He reckons there's fifty of them at least, two to each cedar post — workhorses, most of them, with some finer breeding and a few common asses among them. Surveying the ones nearest him, he notes a few in gleaming oiled tack embellished with polished brass rivets and hardware, others haltered in fraying rope and unsaddled, all of them steaming from the nostrils and tossing their heads against the sharp and shifting scents of nightfall. Vaclav stops of a sudden just inside the gate and

75

runs his hand down the twitching flanks of his horse, smoothing the roan hide's confusion of colors as the animal works a hoof halfheartedly in the winter sod and browses the occasional tufts of dried turf. The boys ask wordless questions of one another with their eyes and stand at the ready while their father bites a new portion of tobacco from his plug and works it back into his molars with a finger before spitting a loose string of the stuff from his tongue. Then he turns to them and tilts his head toward the long line of horses tied up and nervous in the night as if staged for some inhumane procession. "If that sight there wouldn't stiffen a horse thief's pecker, boys, I don't reckon any pretty little thing's teats would do the trick neither."

The boys laugh and give the horses a look, but Karel is scanning the shadows for another animal altogether. Two nights in a row now it has worked him awake, the sight of the Villaseñor girl with her knees bare above her fine, polished boots in the stirrups, her hair sweet smelling and black and falling toward him. Stan grips his shoulder and gives him a playful shake, but Karel knows that even his brothers are wishing failure upon him, bearing in their chests, as they surely do, the hot burden of hope.

And they are not alone.

Men are milling about everywhere. Farmers and townsfolk, tradesmen and ranchers, and Karel can't remember a time when he's ever seen so many men he recognizes standing unwarily amidst so many he doesn't, all of them telling jokes and swapping stories and smoking cigarettes, toeing the black earth and warming themselves near the fires. There are better than four dozen, Karel guesses, and there are others he can't see. Out from beyond the stand of pines rise the muffled conversations of those who are newly arrived and as yet planting sixpenny nails in the hard, dark clay of the creekbank with boot heels and securing their jugs of corn whiskey with double-knotted twine and floating them in the cold running water as if fishing for the county drunks.

Just this side of the trees, two squat Mexicans with thin mustaches and expensive rifles stand eyeing Karel and smiling, stubs of cigars planted and smoking in the wet corners of their mouths. One of them winks at him and elbows his partner, who laughs and scratches his low-slung belly and then pulls the cigar from his mouth so he can purse his lips into a mocking kiss that sours Karel's guts and slicks his palms with sweat. And then there's Lad Dvorak, laughing with Patrick Dalton and his boy, the three of them huddled close to the fire farthest from the trees, and when the banker catches sight of the Skalas, he turns and moves toward them with his lips crinkled into a smile and his trousers stiff and creased hard with starch. He makes a point of fingering the silver chain slung from his vest as he walks, and when he stands before them, he pulls the watch from his fob and looks Vaclav in the eye before springing the thing open.

"I've never known you to be early, Skala. That or late, either one."

"Never known you to give a great goddamn one way or the other," Vaclav says, "unless you're carrying a note and expecting payment, which I'll remind you ain't the case." He takes a look around, squinting into the darkness beyond the reach of the firelight and testing the scant weight of the horse crop in his hand. "What's keeping the Mexican?"

Off to the east and well out of sight, roosted mourning doves project the last of their day's lamentations from the dense and tangled stand of moss-draped oaks. Dvorak clears his throat and puts his watch away. "I don't suspect anything is, Skala. Seems to me he's unaccustomed to being kept by anyone other than himself."

Karel takes Whiskey's lead when his father hands it back to him, and then he stands, his feet squared with his shoulders and his stomach fermented by nerves, as his father forces a smile to his lips and scratches the bald and sun-spotted skin of his scalp and then smoothes the fringe of unkempt curls on his head. "Well, hell then," says Vaclav, "I reckon it might just as well be me what accustoms him to it."

"Might as well be you who tries," Lad says, then he locks eyes with Karel and opens his coat to reveal its green silk lining and a folded bundle of parchment secreted there in the monogrammed pocket. "The papers are all in order, boy, excepting your father's signature. You ready to ride?"

Karel spools the leather lead tight around his wrist and reaches out instinctively for the long neck of his father's horse, working his fingers there such that the bristles of the animal's coat prick the tender flesh beneath his fingernails in a way that is both painful and reassuring, and he's about to tell Dvorak that he's sure enough ready when his father raises the riding crop and snaps it sharply against his trousers before handing it over. "He calls you *boy* again, son, you got my permission to sign the family name for me. In welts on his hindquarters."

In the distance, coyotes have found their voices in the damp promise of weather, calling out as if in answer to the inconsiderate onset of cold. Visibly agitated along the fenceline, the horses blow and complain, their hides shuddering violently with the worried work of their muscles. To the west, when Villaseñor's surrey rolls dark and polished as a hearse to the gate, the sky hangs swollen and sickly above the distant horizon as if the whole mass of the heavens has been wounded and gauzed with clouds and backlit feebly by the diminishing moon. The coach rocks on its springs, and when it comes to a stop, the twin carriage lanterns swing in illuminated arcs from their chains. Guillermo Villaseñor ties off the reins and sets the brake. He climbs down from the seat as the onlookers stand casting long shadows in the firelight. Still others emerge unsteady and quiet as spotted fawns from their drinking amidst the trees by the creek. They watch silently as the man buttons his fine otter-skin coat against the growing cold and tilts his unlit cigar up and down playfully in his mouth. The two girls in the covered rear seat of the carriage are visible only as indistinct but animated shadows, and in the moments it takes for Villaseñor to strike a match and puff his cigar lit and take down one of the lanterns and amble to the gate, his men are there waiting, their rifles at their sides, until they exchange some words in Spanish and the two guards cast quick looks over their shoulders at the assembling crowd. They nod, and Villaseñor puffs his cigar and lets the smoke roll from his mouth and swirl out into the night before pulling the thing from his lips. He hands the lantern to one of his men, slides two fingertips into his mouth and whistles sharply.

Out west, a coyote answers and a wet gust of wind scours the pasture and swirls the fires, which throw glowing ash yawing out into the clusters of men. And then the girl rides out of the darkness with her feet high in the stirrups, her black hair roped into a single swaying braid and her face rapt in a solemn beauty that reminds Karel of a memory he can't possibly have, one he's kindled to life since the other night out by the stables. He's seeing his mother, blond and lovely and sitting a horse in the night, and he can't help now but imagine himself curled up and floating inside her, his blood an extension of hers, his bobbing movement a function of her horse's gait, his heart beating only so long as hers refuses to stop. He hears the sharp inhalation of his oldest brother beside him, and then Stan and Thomàs are whispering.

"I believe I've changed my mind, brother."

"Change it all you want. You ain't changing mine."

"I may be of a mind to change it for you, then."

Karel catches himself thinking that he'd just as soon bury them both as suffer the sight of either of them with this girl, and then something heartless and scalding blazes in his chest, and he has to lean into Whiskey's solid weight to keep himself upright. He has imagined yet another unforgivable way to prevent it, one his father might expect of him if there comes the need and the opportunity for it, and he fingers his crop silently and squints against the stinging wind and a blossoming of tears that he wipes away with the oilcloth sleeve of his coat.

The girl reins the horse to a stop beside her father just outside the gate. Their faces flicker in the outermost reaches of firelight, and Karel notices her attire — a velvet riding coat and fine leather gloves, snug trousers tucked into her boots, little shining stubs of spurs rising from her heels — and he doesn't know whether to thank God or curse Him that this girl has come ready to ride to such an extent, that she's left her dress hanging in her wardrobe at the inn back in town. Her father places one hand on her leg and the other on the black neck of his horse, and Karel forces himself to look away, to check Whiskey's cinch strap and stirrup buckles, to ready himself and his animal in such a way that he'll forget, if he can, that he's dreading, for the first time in his life, an occasion to swing himself into the saddle and ride.

IN TOWN, in the candlelit narthex of St. Jude's, Father Carew genuflects and crosses himself and then stands fraught with his own weaknesses. He's spent the whole of the day making preparations for a Nuptial Mass that may never happen, and since the first purple hint of dusk, he's fought the temptation to saddle his bay mare and ride her out past the feedstore and Wasek's barbershop, past the Township Inn and the cluster of houses that stand emptied this evening of their masters. He'd prefer to ride out past Patrick Dalton's diminished acreage in the countryside just north of town, to the Skala place between the forks of Mustang Creek, where tonight, despite the priest's prayers, sin is set either to prevent or occasion a sacrament. To be seen there, of course, would be tacitly to condone that which calls for condemnation, but his curiosity pulls at him like a kind of depraved gravity. He's a man, after all, just as surely as he's a man of God. And there are the boyhood memories, too — his father come home to stand slapping his hands together at the hearth, swaying to the tuneless music of his payday pints, his long evenings spent drinking at the pub, his pockets either loud with coins or empty even of a shilling from his time spent wagering on shuffleboard. Carew's mother would have stood wringing her hands either way. It was better, to her mind, to live on potatoes and turned lard than to buy meat for the pot by sending other men home penniless. Better to live off the alms than to occasion that humility for others.

Carew remembers it all with a shudder. It had all been so many years ago, and now, though his joints creak with arthritis and his skin has grown onionskin thin and crinkled with age, he still longs to be among the men of his parish. It seems to him so often that he's spent the whole of his protracted life trying to care for his mother, long dead, by tending to the women of his parish, by administering blessings and comfort and penances alike to the farmwives whose lives have played out so poorly at the mercy of their hard-willed husbands. And so he prays, and he's thankful for the memory that answers his prayer. He'd almost forgotten. The Knedlik woman has delivered twins, and they've yet to be baptized. He fills a phial with holy water from the font and strings a leather lace through its cork, hangs it from around his neck. Then he snuffs the candles and makes his way out to the stables.

The weather has come to call, and the stable's roof timbers groan as if bearing some immense and unforgiving load beneath the descending cold. His horse, Sarah, an old girl now like her namesake, relents to the tack and blows her hot, rheumy mist as the priest works the halter over her head, and then they're out in the night, ambling down the quiet streets, past the inn and feedstore, past Wasek's place and around the corner where the heavy doors of the bank stand closed behind a gatework of wrought-iron bars. On the edge of town, he rides quietly past the lamp-lit houses, imagining the children sinking into featherbeds and the dreams that await them there, and soon enough he leaves the last house behind and reaches the outlying pastures. A half mile up the road, he rides around the loamy slough tucked in and fringed by water oak and yaupon, and he stops briefly near a young sweet gum just this side of the southernmost fork of the creek. Fifteen minutes in the saddle, and already Carew finds himself shifting the sharp points of his hips in the leather and wishing for the simple, meaningful discomforts of his younger years. Even the years of purposeful self-deprivation at seminary had been better. He'd been able, at least, to keep some weight on his frame and move his bowels daily, to spend time amidst other men without the nagging worry of his influence on the trajectories of their souls.

He gives the old girl a heel, and the horse's hooves clop across the solid and seasoned timbers of the narrow bridge. Carew is grateful for the horse and her infallible memory, for her steady gait on the hard-packed road. Even in the failing moonlight, she knows her way, and the priest laughs and feels the bite of the cold in the worn crowns of his teeth and hunches his shoulders beneath the coarse wool of his overcoat. There's something beautiful in it, he thinks. An animal grown old and indifferent to the darkness. How many men might be able to say the same? Too few or too many?

Up on the farm-to-market road that snakes hoof pocked and wheel rutted beside the trickling of the creek's southern fork, he feels suddenly less alone. Here is the sickly sweet smell of the other horses' droppings growing cold on the road, the well-tended fenceline of the Skala property, the distant complaints of animals come alive in the night. Here, where the road parts ways with the water and turns north as it runs between the outstretched fencewires, he lets the reins fall slack and sits upright while Sarah walks at her own ancient pace and tilts her ears forward when an owl cries out. The wind comes steady from the west, and through the clouds the moon leaks only as much light as might a few long-wicked candles. To the west stands the original Skala plot, land sectioned off into cropfields that have already been turned over into black furrows in anticipation of the planting season; to the east, clusters of cattle stand sleeping and silent in the pastureland claimed from the Daltons over the last several years. A slow half mile up the road, Father Carew finds the distant stand of trees flashing in firelight, and he brings the horse to a stop beneath a low berth of mesquite branches that hangs over the fence to shade the road even of diffused moonlight. From here, he has only to cut through a cattlegate and keep himself unseen as he rides northwest past the Skala house to the Knedlik place a mere mile away.

Instead, he dismounts and surveys the dark encroachment of

clouds to the west. He walks the horse up the road until he sees, a quarter mile away, the impressive line of horses tied to the fence-posts, the dark carriage sitting empty in the distance, a single lantern hanging from its chain and flickering beside the covered coach. In his younger years, his vocation had been such that he would awaken some early mornings with night sweats and a swollen heart and a prayer already formed and half recited, his devotion strong enough to compose itself and pull him from sleep with its silent annunciation.

Now, as he ties Sarah to a post and slips himself between the two highest fencewires, he feels the cool glass of the phial bounce against his slack and hairless chest, and thinks of the Knedlik twins, stained still with the sin of Adam. He walks carefully through the pasturage of cut hay and scrub grass, moving covertly between the sleeping cattle and farther into the darkness, imagining himself no more than another man gone deaf and disobedient within earshot of a divine calling. When he's close enough to get a good view of the assembled men bantering and coughing up phlegm and lurching forward in laughter, close enough to see the two fires ablaze and, between them, Skala and Villaseñor looking down at the papers that Lad Dvorak is unfolding for their perusal, the priest lowers himself onto a half-consumed bale of hay, his hip joints creaking and popping as he settles into his place a safe distance beyond the reach of the firelight.

The men of Lavaca County are less than timid tonight with the use of their shoulders and elbows. They've seen moonlight races before, but none like this, and they jockey for position as they form long lines on either side of the two fires. Dvorak produces a fountain pen from his coat pocket, and the two men steady the papers against their horses while they make their marks. The riders shift themselves in their saddles and look at each other with only quick, sidelong glances, and Father Carew plucks a straw of hay from the bale and works it around in the corner of his mouth, his vocation now but a whisper drowned out by the insistent, anticipatory whirring of blood behind the drums of his ears.

A MILE AWAY, the Knedlik woman peers down into the pine drawer of her dresser where her two babies lie twisted together atop their makeshift bedding of raw cotton sewn simply into a folded blanket. They have slept most of the day, and now their eyes gaze unfocused and unfeeling into the oil lamplight of the room. Beneath her housecoat, her nipples burn, already cracked and raw and leaking with need. She leans to tuck the edges of the top blanket beneath the infants and winces when she comes upright again. She had torn during the birth, and still her husband had come in late from town last night and stabbed himself into her from behind. She'd been sleeping on her side, and when she awoke to the searing pain of him working inside her, she'd bitten her lip until she could hear her teeth grinding together through her own flesh. Now, the rags between her legs are cool and wet with her blood, and he's gone again, out in the night drinking corn mash and cheering for his neighbor's demise.

She'd been but a girl of fifteen when Klara Skala died in childbirth, but she remembers the young family well, remembers Vaclav Skala as a young man, reserved but kind, the gentle way he had with his wife. And now, long without her, the man works his boys like animals, *instead* of animals, and she's beginning to understand how you can come to see in your children only what they've left you without. She recalls the warmth of the youngest Skala boy held against her, taking from her what the child she'd lost never would, and now

85

her own boys, her twins, blink and throw their limbs around beneath the blanket as if impatient already, restless as their father with nights spent at home. She can't help such thoughts. They have his cold, inexpressive eyes, and they look at her with only their own desires in mind. On more than one occasion already, she's found need to nurse them at the same time, one to each breast, and the sharp pull of them working at her and the weighted relief of her milk coming down has been at once reassuring and appalling. It's as if they would take all of her that there is to take, as if they'd willingly leave her drained entirely of herself and offer, in exchange, only cold looks of shriveled brows and quiet, fleeting satisfaction.

"Hail Mary," she prays, "full of grace, the Lord is with thee," and her babies twist and writhe and eye her there in the oily light.

PERCHED ON HIS hay bale and hidden in the night, Father Carew bears unwitting witness as two motherless children get up in their stirrups to do their fathers' bidding. Old Man Skala takes hold of the reins and flashes a blade beneath the nose of his horse, his lips moving in a way that reminds the priest of his most penitent daily communicants, the way their prayers are at once fully formed on their lips and yet unuttered, swallowed with the transubstantiated food and drink. Of course, Carew can't hear the words, can't think what they might be, can't imagine just how calculating and threatening a man can be when he whispers to an animal in the cool, cloud-veiled moonlight of a half-lit winter night.

But Karel can.

His father's words rise to his ears as unmistakably and lucidly as do the imagined memories of his mother's voice. His pop nicks the stallion's nose with the knife tip, and the whinnying horse throws its great head up and around in a furious nod until Karel gathers him back in with reins and clamped knees. The moon flickers above the moving clouds, and Karel steals a glance at the girl sitting horse-back beside him. Her head is canted to receive her father's advice while she faces Karel with her dark brows raised into an unspoken inquiry. And then his father leans in, his face just inches from the knife, the blade all but resting on Whiskey's wet snout. "Get a nose full of that," he says. "You remember that, ain't it?"

Three years back, in the stable, Karel had stood beside the cross-tied horse while his father gelded the colt's sire. It was August, past noon and blazing, and hay dust hung glinting and suspended in the slant of light from the loft window. Outside, mockingbirds called out in all their ambitious imitations, and the cattle protested the heat and ambled slowly, lowing as they went, about the nearby pastures. Inside the horse barn, the two animals stood switching their tails against the nuisance of flies. Just outside the door, Vaclav Skala worked his knife blade into a smoking pail of hot hardwood coals he'd had Karel fetch from the smokehouse, and when he wrapped the handle with wet rags and pulled it from the embers, the blade was steaming and blackened with soot.

The two horses had been tethered nose to nose, the sire cross-tied and hobbled, and Karel watched as his father held the smoking blade to Whiskey's nose. The horse twitched and whinnied, jerked its head in abbreviated motions that seemed, even to Karel, even then, a kind of uncertain consent. "Why not keep him fit to stud?" he'd asked.

His father turned the knife in his hand and smiled as he dropped to a knee just safely in front of the old stallion's rear legs. "Because I've got Whiskey to breed now, and I can sell the old man here for a handsome price, is why."

Karel stood, unflinching, as his father pulled down on the horse's thickly leathered scrotum and spat tobacco juice into the dry hay that had been forked over the dirt floor.

"But we could get more for a stud, ain't it?"

Vaclav worked his tobacco slowly with his back teeth and considered his son without looking at him. "Who's this *we* you're so fond of talking about, boy? This here's my horse, and now that I've bred him I'll be damned if anyone else will. I've gotten one hell of a colt out of him, and I'll breed Whiskey next, and when I'm finished with him, I'll cut his nuts off, too, if it's to my liking. Now hold his head. I want him to see this. And enough of your got-damned questions."

Karel was amazed as ever by the deftness of his father's hands with tools. The man could shoe a horse in twenty minutes, could mend a breached fence in ten. Now it was a matter of a hot, sharp knife and less than a second. The horse screamed and reared against the ropes, stamping the hard earth and clouding the air with blond dust, and then Vaclav stood with the testicles in his hand while the horse streamed blood into the hay. "It's some folks will eat horse balls," he said, "but we ain't them folks," and he threw the whole bloody mess on the ground beneath Whiskey's head. "Get you a good look at that, by God, and don't think your time ain't coming."

Then he turned so that his eyes met Karel's, and they exchanged a strange and conspiratorial smile. "Of course, I reckon we could've had some fun with your brothers. Could've fed them a nice fried-nut supper and not told them what they were chewing till they cleaned their plates."

Karel laughed there in the hot barn with his father, and then it was time to get back to work. "Come here, boy. It's time you learn how to stitch up a gelding."

Even now, somehow, despite the shifting muscles of the horse beneath him and the creaking of the saddle and the brisk air rich with the winter smells of pine and parched sod, Karel is still in that hot stable with his father. It's not unlike the drunkenness to which he's begun, in recent months, to accustom himself. There's a comfort in the distance it affords him from the unrelenting dullness of the present day beneath the weight of hay bale or feed sack or harness or loneliness, and he can feel now, as he does some nights with a belly warmed with mash, the past start to shoulder its way into the present such that he knows, unsettling as it is in its possibilities, that there are moments and days that he'll never outrun, that he'll never bury with hoof-thrown divots of sod nor the forgetting afforded by days and months and years piled up atop the ones that came before them. Now Karel works the leather of the reins in his habitual, delicate way. He'd taken pains today, with boar-bristle brush and knife-tip alike, to get his fingernails clean, and while he'd scrubbed and scraped he'd been thinking of how much approval he'd find in his mother's eyes when he presented his hands for her careful inspection, dreaming her alive and smiling and stricken with a desire to clasp his long, slender fingers in her own.

He shakes his head now, scolds himself for thinking more fondly of a past that never happened than of a future he might occasion with hard work and horsemanship and concentration. There are times, goddamn them, that won't turn loose of you any more than they'll permit you to take hold of them.

Besides which, there's this girl sitting horseback beside him. Her father is standing next to her, leaning forward, his hair slicked back and gleaming such that it might just as well be appointed with butter as with hair tonic. He's whispering to his daughter, giving her instructions in Spanish, likely telling her to stay low in the saddle around the trees, to follow close on Karel's flank until after the turn. To make her move on the final straight half mile back to the fires.

And then he pats her thigh and whistles to his men, who tuck their rifle stocks under their arms and begin walking with the single lantern past the long lines of townsmen and into the shadows toward the stand of moss-strung trees in the invisible distance. The air is sharp with the woodsmoke from the finish-line fires, alive with the nighttime work of animals and the whispers of men, and then Vaclav Skala protests, his knife still in hand, gesturing to Lad Dvorak and Villaseñor.

"Where in steaming hell is them sawed-off Mexicans going?"

The fireside men fall silent of a sudden. Villaseñor's guards look at each other with feigned surprise and smile and keep walking. One of them holds his rifle out without slowing his pace and makes a show of levering a cartridge into the receiver. The air shifts, coming cold from the north, and the fires surge and smoke whips out in gray ribbons and casts the horses and their riders in a dreamlike haze. Karel curses his neck, leans in the saddle to set the world upright so that he can catch sight of Patrick Dalton, who smiles and elbows his son. The red-headed boy stands with his hands tucked into his trouser pockets and nods knowingly, his freckles so thick on his nose that he appears to be afflicted with a single birthmark that bridges his cheeks, on one of which a slight scar is still visible. And then Lad Dvorak and Villaseñor are stepping forward, the latter with a cigar half-smoked and still kindled in his mouth, the banker unfolding the papers and holding them forward for Skala's perusal.

"It calls for witnesses on the course," Dvorak says. "You signed it."

Vaclav waves it away and swipes spent tobacco from his mouth. "Does it now? It say they have to be Mexicans with loaded guns, too, or is that part just something you gone and dreamed up in that corn-popper mind of yours?"

Whiskey sidesteps and Karel wedges the toes of his boots into the stirrups and reins him back in line. When he glances to his left, the girl has tucked her crop handle into her boot and is running her gloved fingers through her horse's black mane, looking at Karel with eyes half-open, as if she's only now awoken to find herself sitting in a gleaming saddle with a boy's eyes on her. She wets her lips and smiles, widens her black eyes at him, and then she pulls her crop from her boot and levels it across her horse's shoulders.

Villaseñor steps in front of Lad with his hands open and his palms out in an unthreatening and diminutive way that reminds Karel of the other day, of the first time he'd seen the man and his daughters. It's off-putting, this gesture, and Karel reckons there's not another man in the county who would configure himself so in the presence of other men. There's something almost womanly about it, too forgiving and soft, too vulnerable, and still Karel finds himself beset by a soft pull in his chest, a sympathy that threatens to well into something not unlike kinship.

His father is having none of it, and he turns now to his older boys. "Stan," he says. "Get on up there by them trees. And take one of your brothers with you."

Stan straightens himself up into the best shape of a man he can make, a man with oilcloth trousers and hair wet combed and parted neatly on one side despite the turbulent weather, a young man with a neck bent to match his brothers' and the will to walk farther away from his father than he's been instructed to walk. He nods at Thomàs and, as the two move past Karel, Stan runs his wind-chapped hand along Whiskey's side and, ever the eldest brother, slaps Karel's boot from the stirrup.

The onlookers fall back to drinking and placing whispered wagers as the two boys trail Villaseñor's men off into the darkness, and Karel works the toe of his boot back into the stirrup and readies himself to ride.

And then his father is beside him, and Karel catches a sour whiff of the man's chewing tobacco. Vaclav grabs him by the coat pocket and pulls him down so he can whisper in the boy's ear. "I expect you think you can cozy up to little Mexican heifers out back of the grove nights and keep it a secret, is that it?"

Karel looks his father in the eye like he's been taught, but he's so stung by surprise that he can hardly breathe or swallow, much less speak.

"As per usual, I expect you're wrong. But I'll make you a deal. Win this race and you can run off with her and sire a whole houseful of little half-breeds if she'll have you. You ain't good for nothing but riding any-damn-way, but I'll tell you this, boy—you lose and you'll never ride that horse for pleasure again."

FROM WHERE FATHER Carew sits, the whole affair might just as well be conducted in silence up until the moment when, with the papers made legal and the witnesses dispatched into the shadows and the riders prompted, Lad Dvorak steps beyond the horses and off to the side a few paces and raises his little pistol overhead. Carew sees the testament of smoke from the barrel before he hears the sharp crack of its report move over him as if ushered by the breeze, and he considers, as the horses plunge forward and the riders go to work with their whips, that this may well be the fashion in which the souls of men rise from their bodies — discreetly, soundlessly, yet all at once, as if cast forward into their everlasting fates without any outward indication to the temporal world.

Carew fingers the phial of holy water through the rough wool of his buttoned coat as the sound falls over him in such a way that he finds his senses, long stunted, have been triggered as violently and unexpectedly as by the onset of seizure or epiphany. The night now overtakes him — the wild, leering cheers of the townsmen; the chill of the breeze so damp and strong with the odor of smoke and manure that he imagines it adhering itself to his exposed skin; the gritty, broomstraw taste of the hay between his lips — all so wonderfully alive with the compulsory if tainted enticements of a fallen world.

The moon, just as surely, is overtaken again by the clouds. The horses are throwing turf, bearing their riders out of the firelight and toward whatever awaits them in a darkness so dense that, if Father Carew weren't compelled by it all so viscerally, he might liken it to the irremediable and uncomprehending darkness of which St. John wrote, to the wholly unintelligible nature of light to a world gone black.

Instead, the priest springs to his feet with a youthfulness he hasn't known in more than two decades, a sound rising from some rarely plumbed depth within him, something akin to the chants of a High Mass. But there comes, just overhead and not a yard off his shoulder, a silent and startling black flash of something winging by, fast and fleeting as the peripheral arrival of the conscience in sinners. A horned owl, banking now with a wing dipped vertically, arcing across the pasture and leveling off again, gliding out toward the running horses in search of field mice or nesting coveys of quail or a young opossum lagging too far behind its mother. Carew tracks it until it vanishes into the trees assembled just this side of the creek, and then he looks around at the congregation of nightfall and desiccated pasture grass and sleeping cattle. He had almost called out, had almost cheered the riders, and now, as the relief of the undiscovered culprit courses cool within him, he turns his attention back to the race, watching in silence as the horses carry their burdens into the indiscernible distance.

KAREL HAD EXPECTED that she would hang back before the turn, that she would test his flank and work carefully alongside him in anticipation of a final sprint back to the finish. Instead, he is trailing her from the start, her long braid whipping back at him as the ride smoothes out and he finds his balance, crouching forward and low over the horse's rhythmic exertions. Out of the firelight's reach and swallowed by the darkness, he squints against thrown dirt and the sharp gusting of the wind, and when his eyes adjust to the scant moonlight, when the slow, familiar muscular burn flares and creeps beneath his skin like a hot wicking of oil up his calves and into his taut hamstrings, he considers his options. He could do as the Dalton boy had done those four years earlier, biding time until the last moment, waiting to see which direction the girl takes around the trees and then veering the other way. Or he could follow her and hope for an inside opening as they break into the straightaway. A hundred yards from the oaks, Karel crosses the crop in front of him, applying it to alternating sides of the animal's hide until he gains some ground and is riding hard just off the girl's right flank. He has learned in these years of riding that properly sizing up the opposing rider trumps any impressions he might have about the horse. But this is something else entirely. She's fast, unyielding with her crop, but her true advantage, and one he finds himself helpless against, is that, even now, he can't keep his eyes off her. Something about the smooth and easy flexing of her knees, her backside cocked back and shuddering with the vibrations of the ride, her riding pants tight enough to reveal the swell of her hips and the sweet crease between them, the whole thing bobbing like a firm, just-ripe peach hanging from some wind-worried branch.

God bless, Karel thinks, and he whips the horse soundly.

It's been three weeks since his fifteenth birthday, and as he urges Whiskey on, hoping to gain enough ground to afford him a look at this girl's dark eyes and swollen lips, he finds himself wishing that he had a father like this girl has, one who would risk his own wealth and pride for a chance at earning, for his children, the pleasure of a lifetime of nights spent in the company of someone they might come to love. As it was, this year Vaclav had given Karel a birthday free of chores and two extra eggs at breakfast, that and a dollar that Karel spent the better part of buying bottles of beer for himself and his brothers at the icehouse. Hell, next year might warrant two dollars, but not if he didn't quit himself of all these got-damned thoughts and teach this girl and her bouncing round hams a thing or two about horse racing.

Just before the stand of oaks, where he takes note of the surprisingly loud and mechanical sound of the insects at work there in the tangled berths of the branches, Karel shifts his weight farther forward over the horse's shoulders and blisters its hide with a flurry of right-handed encouragements. Circling the trees to the left, the girl stands a bit in the stirrups, bringing Karel fully square with her on the outside while she turns her face his way against the spiderwebs and willow-thin branches that reach out from the treeline's perimeter. Karel eases up on the whip and, though he means to look blankly at her, finds himself smiling the way he has some nights when he failed to disguise the joy of holding a strong hand when he and his brothers played cards around the kitchen table for pennies.

The girl crouches and rides and averts her eyes, and halfway around the turn her forehead crinkles into delicate little ridges. Karel follows the direction of her glance to find, off to the right and some thirty yards out from the horses' determined path, the flickering glow of lanternlight and his two brothers standing side by side with one of the Mexicans, lit cigars smoking and orange tipped in the upturned corners of their mouths. To Karel's mind, though he might have expected it, though he wants as surely as do his brothers his own land and an easy life spent freed from the hard grasp of their father's hand, there's still no way to make this right, his brothers standing there in the flickering diffusion of light, smoking cigars as if they've been smoking them all their lives, filling their mouths with a foreign, sweet smoke that Karel knows they've never before had the pleasure of tasting, cigars that have all but surely come from the Mexican who stands smirking here in the shadows, his boots dusted with the topsoil of his father's land and his heart darkened with the desire to take it from him.

Casually, as if occasioned by afterthought, the man raises his rifle, swinging it level toward the oncoming horses for a moment just long enough to give Karel pause and cause sour questions to rise like bile in the back of his throat. Where in the devil, he wonders, is the other one?

Instead of steadying his aim, the man moves the gun in a continuous, sweeping motion, as if practicing for a shot at a low-quartering quail, and there's a pinched grin on his lips when he drops the barrel and holds the gun again crossways and harmless against his waist. He nods, and Karel strains against the stiffness in his neck, shifts his eyes to catch sight of this girl as her lovely face is graced by the hint of a smile, by a slight and silent and nodded reply. And then Karel is leading, if only by half a head, his crop gone cold in his sweat-slicked hand. He thinks of his father, the stink of tobacco on his breath and the bloodshot eyes, his promise and his threat, and Karel wonders if he could bring himself to strike this girl. He has her within reach, his whip in hand, and the idea works itself free in his mind the way a deep cedar splinter from a hard week of fencework will sometimes slide, as if tweezed by a ghost, from beneath the calloused skin of his hands: If he can just get her off that horse so he's sure to win, then he might do as his father has said he might and keep her for himself. Beside him, running hard and just trailing, her horse is lathered at the mouth and steaming from the nostrils, and the girl's faint smile hangs on her lips like a forgotten flirtation. Karel squeezes his crop, imagines the astonishment registering on her face, those lovely, swollen lips fallen open into a pink wet ring of wounded disbelief. And then later, after he'd won — and won her in doing so — he'd sugarcoat it so she couldn't help but understand, and she'd forgive him, and she'd close her pretty lips and put them to good use against his.

He adjusts his weight backward over his stirrups, his stomach alive with the work of rendering conviction from uncertainty, and just as he's convinced himself to swing at her comes the moment Karel will study in his memory for better than a decade, searching in hindsight for the details that might help him discern the difference between an occurrence occasioned by accident and one born of calculation. When a blast of damp air incites the trees to a violent bewilderment of leaning and lurching, the girl's boots come out of the stirrups, and she's pitched off balance and lashed forward and up and free of the saddle such that she's clinging to the neck of her animal, her crop still clenched with the tangled hair of the horse's mane in her gloved little hand, both legs flying wildly and slapping against the outside flank of the horse. Karel locks his knees and stands in the stirrups, feeling the hot wash of fear in his chest, his guts strung slick and tight as greased cordage beneath his first rung of ribs. Whiskey reacts with a tossing head and the jerking steps of a horse pulled up short and against its will into a trot, and Karel digs a heel into the animal's side to swing him well out and away from the girl so that she can come off the horse, as he is sure she will, without being trampled by another.

It's curious, though, or it will seem so later when he plays it all out in his mind, that *her* horse never breaks its stride, and with Karel lagging behind, allowing her a wide berth, the reins cool and damp in the palms of his hands, she hugs the horse's neck and relaxes her legs so that they hang insensibly toward the ground. And then, as she passes Karel's onlooking brothers and the Mexican they seem all too eager to stand beside, the girl arches her back, limber as a bottomland cattail, and kicks her feet back. For Karel, long accustomed to the gangly and lumbering company of men, her graceful and long-practiced ascent to the saddle seems occasioned all at once by a singularly feminine and fluid motion, but when he remembers it later, when he tries to duplicate it on his own horse out in the coverts of a new-moon pasture, he'll think on it hard enough to see then what he's seeing now without knowing he's seeing it — the tandem backward swing of her legs, the perfect curved line of her spine as her knees float back over the horse's thundering haunches, the slightest cant of her hips and the scissoring of her legs that returns her smoothly to the shining leather of her saddle; her feet coming forward, the toes sliding into the stirrups just as she leans forward into her crouch and, with her backside hovering above the saddle and her knees bent and absorbing the plunging force of the ride, her head turning back so that, just as she brings the whip down hard on horsehide, she's smiling back at Karel from three full lengths ahead.

And then she's running hard and away, hugging the perimeter of the trees as she widens her lead and whips her horse, her braided hair flung back and black and dancing playfully in the air behind her shoulders.

Alive in Karel's mind is only a whisper of suspicion, one muted by the astonishing beauty of what he's seen, and he smiles at the fortune of having borne witness to something so graceful and yet so capable and strong, to a girl turned woman before his eyes, to that woman flashing her white teeth at him, smiling because, for her, as for Karel, there is nothing quite so thrilling as a race run on horseback, nothing filled more with wonder, nothing so able to convince you that you are flesh and blood and alive in the world that offers so few joys other than this running.

Instinctively, he whips his horse and gives chase, angling the animal back into a tight, sweeping circle around the trees, but then it's as if a leafless branch reaches out for him from the stand of twisted oaks. He catches it out of the corner of his eye the way he sometimes notes the flash of a diving hawk in a distant pasture while harnessed to his father's plow. He leans instinctively away, but his neck is locked in its perpetual cant and the thing rakes him hard across the scalp and face. There's a flaming pain where the hair snags and rips from its roots, and he knows, from the taste of warm iron and the hornet's sting of it, that the tender skin at the corner of his mouth has been torn. He's knocked off balance but manages to keep his mount, holding the reins a little too tightly for good riding and grinding the serrated enamel of his teeth until the horse takes note of the boot heel digging into its side and resumes its running. A gust blows cold, biting at Karel's wounded lip, and he's as certain that he can still ride as he is that even the most violent of winds don't stretch tree branches outward from their trunks into the paths of riders. He looks back over his shoulder to find the branch retracting into the mossy veil of the trees, and he's still cursing when he breaks into the open pasture and spots the distant fires burning as if in self-consuming anticipation of his arrival. The missing Mexican, he knows, was up to nothing so innocent as relieving himself in the shadows, and Karel runs through a few quickly imagined scenarios of how he will take his revenge, none of which, he realizes, is going to help him gain enough ground to win this race.

The girl is running hard out front, and he swings his crop and nudges Whiskey to the left to avoid the stinging draft of dirt and dust thrown back at him by the horse he's trailing. Still, he can't quite let loose the image of the girl, of her body willing itself back onto her horse. And what to make of his brothers? Of their easy way of standing, hips cocked and arms crossed, those cigars aglow like smoking punctuation marks to all the sentences they've thought but kept themselves from saying. He knows it shouldn't, but still it surprises him—they want him to lose just as surely as he wants to win, but wasn't there supposed to be something more binding in brotherhood than that? Wasn't there something written by common blood or by God or by what Karel imagines as the fine, looping script of their mother's unwritten will that should have kept them from standing idly by, grinning and sucking on cigars afforded them by the very men who had tried to take his head off at the roots with an uprooted timber?

Karel is running five full lengths behind but holding when the moon slips out brightly from the clouds just long enough to oversee the goings-on below, and when it ducks back under cover there comes, from out north in the pastures beyond the creek, a sound like slow-tearing parchment that grows steadily louder in its approach. This is a rainfall that will defy the almanac and swell the creeks beyond their banks, a four-day flood that, before it relents, will level the furrows and float topsoil from the cropfields and drive the county's cattle to huddle loudly together beneath the shelter of mature oak and pecan trees. It will prove a nuisance to nuptials and make it all but impossible to dig a respectable grave. It will reduce the finish-line fires to soft and steaming black stacks of drenched timbers, but for now, to Karel's way of thinking, it is a welcomed relief. It's been a long, dry winter, and soft soil makes for easier labor. The cold water wicks into his clothes and numbs his scalp and face. Besides which, Karel has spent the larger portion of his life waiting for simple changes, for the sun to come out or the rain to fall, for the school bell to ring and release him to the outdoors, for the cows to show in the swollen gashes beneath their tails the bloody discharge and the hard edges of hooves that signal the onset of calving.

For now, he's simply thankful for the sudden turning of the weather, for the chance that the rain might fluster a girl who's likely been kept under roof when the weather sours, who's grown up riding only on ideal days at ideal times. Once the sweeping sheet of downpour reaches them, he feels the cool renewal of confidence at work in his blood, in the quieting of his heart and the stillness of his hands. The horse is all speed and momentum, a rolling and muscular extension of Karel himself, and the steam from the animal's breath breaks over him like windswept fog. His hair is soaked and streaming from the teeming weather. He imagines Stan and Thom, wringing wet and walking all this way back, the comfort and easy confidence washed from their faces. He pictures each brother with his shoulders hunched against the rain, walking and frowning, looking at his sad and sopping cigar with all the puzzled dejection of a man come home from his fields to find his wife run off and the breakfast dishes still stacked in the sink, hard-caked with the reminder of all she was to him besides cold hands and warm legs in bed.

He's gaining now, but not nearly enough, and they're close enough to see the lines of men hunched forward beneath the downpour, cheering with their hands on their knees as the fires fail in the pouring rain and shoot steam outward as if from the undersides of braking locomotives. He makes one last push, one of both desperation and obligation, swinging his crop and urging the horse on with sharp, vocalized exhalations — *"Haa, boy! Haa, got-dammit."* Water seems to erupt from the hoof-struck ground, and the animal's ears twitch and fold backward. Karel pulls within two lengths, but the girl is riding with ease, streaming water from her hair and rocking forward and back in smooth, effortless revolutions, and when she senses him making ground on her, she flips the crop around in her hand and waves the knot just in view over her horse's eyes.

And that's all it takes.

The animal lengthens its stride and drives forward with such immediate comprehension that even Karel can't help but think it beautiful. Well, hell, he thinks. Would you look at that. She didn't even *touch* him.

Now he might as well sit back in the saddle, and he knows it, knows it's too late, knows that his mind, this last half mile, has been too damned often clouded with matters other than the race. Still, he puts the whip once more to the horse and holds his crouch, feeling his eyes flood with saltier stuff than rainwater as he reaches the first of the onlookers.

The Dalton boy is smirking, standing straight despite the rain, shouldering the affectionate weight of the arm his father drapes over him, the scar on his cheek faded into the slightest line and visible only because it stands pale on the boy's wind-flushed and freckled skin. Dvorak has turned from the race and is walking back toward the cattlegate, against which Villaseñor leans with his hand cupped over his eyes and his dark brows raised in appreciation as his daughter crosses between the smoldering fires and comes upright in the stirrups, swinging her animal out into the pasture past all the horses roped to their fenceposts and bowing their heads against the rain.

When Karel finishes, he avoids his father's eyes as he passes him and reins his horse in the other direction, circling out toward the creek and the canopy of the treeline. His father looks his way with narrowed eyes, pinching his lips together and shaking his head as the townsfolk gather around the Villaseñor girl and her horse, slapping her father on the shoulder and shaking his hand. Beneath the shelter of trees, Karel sits the horse and marvels at how quick these men are to shift their allegiances, at how little it has to do with their admiration of these strangers. He's known all his life that his father was the envy of his neighbors, that he was seen around the county as cold and self-interested, and now it comes so naturally, this celebration of his comeuppance. Hell, Karel thinks, if coyotes took every last one of our calves, these bastards would gather at the fenceline cheering the slaughter.

Shifting his weight in the saddle, Karel turns his face up to the cold drops of rain that find their way through the pine boughs above. His mouth burns with its wound, and he runs his fingers through his wet hair, fingering the swollen knot on his scalp. The wind shifts, and out in the distance the falling rain sways and tosses all at once like sheer drapery hung from an open window on some moonless, gusty evening. The townsmen drift about, pushing their hats down over their ears and hugging themselves against the cold, moving in small groups toward the road and their horses, back toward the creek to fetch their whiskey. Karel watches Mr. Knedlik, wiry and weaving with liquor already, labor himself into the saddle with a groan. He's a mean old son of a bitch, one whose wife has been seen about town for years with yellow bruises on her arms and eyes shot red with his handiwork. And now the poor woman has delivered twins, and it strikes Karel as telling that the man turns his horse for town, with the hope of finding the icehouse open late, rather than out through the western pastures toward home.

From out of the crowd, Eduard comes beaten looking and sloshing through the mud, hunching his shoulders as if gravel rather than rain has been turned loose by the sky. When he stops beneath the trees, he wipes the water from his face with his coat sleeve and takes hold of the horse's reins. He offers a conciliatory grin and says, "You reckon it'll rain, brother?"

The horse blows and sidesteps, and Karel leans back in the saddle, supporting himself with flattened hands reached back against the animal's haunches. He's quite certain he could go a week without saying a word and not miss the sound of his voice in the least, but somehow he manages. "Supposed to mean good luck for weddings."

Eduard studies the sod at his feet for a moment and makes a show of wincing, as if he's grown cold to the idea he'd been so ready to banter about two short nights before in their room. "Just so you know," he says, "it's nobody here who thought you would lose," but there's something sidelong and searching in his eyes that doesn't cotton to his words.

Swinging down from the saddle, Karel takes the reins from his brother and looks out to the east where the distant stand of trees is masked by the darkness out of which his other brothers will shortly emerge. "It's sure as shit some who did," he says. "It's some who were celebrating with cigars before the thing was half run."

From the overhang of pine boughs, rain spatters down onto the horse's hot hide and steams there as the animal signals its impatience with sidesteps and quick tosses of its head. Eduard studies his brother. "I wouldn't know about all that," he says, then he points at the corner of his own mouth by way of indication. "You're bleeding."

"Deserve to be," Karel says, nodding his head out toward the oaks in the black distance. "It's a Mexican up there with a tree growing out of his arm, and he ain't bashful with it."

Eduard offers a confused look. The gray rain comes down as if flung from feed pails, and the pastureland looks to be sheeted in roiling water as the puddles are splashed by the new torment of drops. Some of the townsmen have short words for Karel, but most either touch the horse lightly and nod at him or pass without any acknowledgment whatsoever.

Karel inhales hard through his nose and works the bitter result around in his mouth awhile before spitting it into the muddied earth. He matches eyes with his brother and plays down the whole thing with raised brows and crimped lips. Then he stands beneath the pines and looks around at the dispersing crowd of shadows as a few begin to unknot their horse leads and amble out into the darkness. Whiskey stamps and whinnies, and Karel settles him by slackening his hold on the reins and rubbing a flattened hand up and down the broad slope of the animal's neck.

Out toward the road, just this side of the cattlegate, Villaseñor is still huddled in congratulations with his daughter, the other two girls as yet sheltered from the rain in the backseat of the surrey as their sister sits wringing wet and smiling in the night while her father shakes her playfully by the shoulders and squeezes the top of her thigh and cups her cheek in his hand. And then, instead of heading through the gate out to the road, she turns the horse into the night-masked pasture and glances back at Karel as she goes. She gives the horse a nudge and walks it into the darkness of the rain and cut hay to the south. Her father lifts up on the gate, unlatching it, and steps out toward his carriage, nodding to Karel's father as he goes. Vaclav moves his head in acknowledgment without meeting the man's eyes. They're barely visible now except for the single carriage lantern throwing a pale halo behind them, and Skala stands there in the tumult of weather, leaning casually against a fencepost as if the sun and good fortune both were shining down on him. His face flushed by the weather and anger, he draws his knife from the sheath on his belt and busies himself cleaning his fingernails while Dvorak and the Daltons stand talking in the rain.

The fires, burning hot and blue just minutes before, are smoking and black, and Karel catches a glimpse of his other brothers and both Mexicans walking with the lantern out of the distance. Karel studies Eduard for a long moment, watching him watch the girl as she canters into the shadows. "Where you reckon she's off to?"

Eduard shrugs. "It ain't no telling."

Karel watches as the girl moves slowly into the dark downpour, and when Stan and Thom come sloshing up with the Mexicans, he makes a point of looking them each hard in the eyes. Stan doesn't seem willing or able to hold his gaze for long, so intent is he on studying his muddied boots. But Thom, ever the most brazen, smiles brightly and slicks his wet blond hair back on his scalp with a flourish. "What say you make me a loan of that horse," he says. "It's time I go introduce myself to my bride."

Despite the weather and the wound, Karel finds his mouth inexplicably dry, so he parts his lips and gathers blood and rainwater on his tongue so he'll have something to spit at Thom's feet. But when he notes the men standing silent and armed behind his brothers in the dancing light of the lantern, he swallows the water and, with it, the impulse to ask why any man with a perfectly good rifle would have to secrete himself behind oak moss taking potshots with tree branches. Instead he shields the rain from his eyes with one hand and takes an exaggerated look out to the south where the girl has ridden into the night. Then he glances west to the cattlegate. Just this side of it, their father has put his knife away and now comes slopping through standing water with his fringe of curls hanging wilted about his ears. Karel turns toward Thom and mocks his vanity with a slow swipe of his own rain-slicked hair. "Ain't my horse to lend," he says, "but go on ahead and ask Pop if you want. He's likely in a giving temper."

When Skala joins them there beneath the pine trees, the man lets fall from his lips a thick glob of tobacco juice. Fishing his handkerchief from his pocket, he studies the boys with a stern silence that dares them to speak, and when he looks toward Karel, his eyes narrow and he makes a low, deliberate sound in the back of his throat while he wipes his face dry. He takes the boy's chin roughly in his hand and tilts his head back. "The hell happened to your mouth, boy?" he asks, but he turns his attention to the others without waiting for an answer. He scans their faces, stuffing his hands into his coat pockets and baiting them with his gaze, and when he takes sudden notice of the men keeping close company behind them, armed with their lit lantern and rifles, Skala snarls, his face deep-creased with disgust. "Oh, *Jesus.* Ain't this rich," he says. "I knew you boys had taken to Mexicans, but I didn't expect you'd favor the ones wearing mustaches! Hell, what next? You all pull your peckers at night thinking about those darkies they hired on at the wire works in Shiner?"

Stan fidgets and can't will his eyes upward, and when the sting of his torn lip throws a shiver through him, Karel realizes he's smiling. His oldest brother has never fit his role, though he's never stopped trying. Ever the peacemaker, ever the one who would relent to kitchen chores and hard labor alike rather than listen to the rest of them squabble about whose turn it was to shuck the corn or scrub the floors, Stan is a born mother hen. At nearly twenty years of age, he's been marrying age for better than two years, but he's never so much as mentioned leaving home, leaving his brothers, and he's never once outwardly crossed his father.

"Ain't no one leaving until one of you little sugar tits tells me why this boy looks like he's been chewing barbwire."

Stan swallows, shifting his weight on his feet while the Mexicans eye each other with wry looks. Eduard shrugs awkwardly, his neck as bent as his brothers', and in his gesture is a hint of relief and resentment. He'd been left behind to stand in wait with his father by the finish-line fires, and if something happened out on the course behind those trees, he damn sure hadn't had the privilege of seeing it. As for Thom, he rolls his eyes and casually plucks a string of tobacco from his tongue before speaking up over the rain. "I reckon losing gives him an appetite."

Something twitches in the ropes of Karel's guts, and Stan jerks his head toward his brother in disbelief, his head cocked sharply on his cambered neck, his brows up and his jaw locked like he's taken the tetanus. If Thom has astonished himself, he doesn't show it. He squares his feet with his shoulders and stands there pleased with himself, his arms crossed smugly across his chest. Vaclav feigns amusement, holding the buckle of his belt like he's just pushed back from a Sunday meal, nodding in mock appreciation of the boy's wit.

When he stops smiling, he hurls his arm backhanded across his body and drops the boy with a single blow that crashes into the side of Thom's face with the sharp sound of dry kindling popping in the woodstove. There is a frozen moment of adrenaline and traded gazes while Thom slops around in the mud on all fours, and then he's up on his knees, pulling a hand from his face. The chapped skin is split open along the cheekbone, blood running thin with rainwater and streaming from his chin. He studies the flat of his hand with the confused look of a lost traveler, studying the map-work of blood in the lines of his palm. Karel recognizes the look on his brother's face, knows that the shock will be short-lived, that the disbelief will sink fast beneath a blank and impenetrable gaze, his expression hardening over like the frozen surface of a pond until there's a whole undercurrent of dark and teeming things at work beneath a frigid skin that deceives as surely as it obscures. Beneath Thom's feet, a gnarled and twisting tree root juts from the wet sod like a fossilized cottonmouth. Soon enough, the boy begins to right himself, planting the toe of his boot against the thing for leverage.

"You rotten son of a bitch," he says, and he lunges, throwing himself forward, driving his head into his father's ribs and hooking a hard, stray fist into Skala's nose. A mist of blood sprays down across the man's lips, over his chin and into his son's hair, and then they're both going down, falling until the boy lands atop his father. When they hit, a rasp of hot air kicks from their lungs, and they gasp and flounder there like angry conjoined fish until Thom finds his breath and steadies himself with one hand on the ground, cocking his elbow to throw another punch. It never lands. Before it can, the man rears back and throws himself forward at the waist, his forehead slamming into his son's mouth.

Now a roar goes up from the townsmen as they rush from their idle banter, pulled by some irresistible gravity to circle around the action and cheer this perverse spectacle of a family's hell-bent dissolution. As if cued by these new, loud encouragements, Thom rolls away from his father and sits up to reveal a grimace of torn gums running dark with blood, his top front teeth folded back toward the roof of his mouth.

What happens next comes so naturally that, later, Karel won't be able to recall dropping the horse's reins, won't know if his actions were driven by some innate if misguided compulsion to protect his father or by some long-stabled animal urge toward violence, won't remember even if he lashed out first or was spurred into the fight by a blow from one of his brothers. What he will summon in his mind is the way his brother puts a hand to his own mouth and, feeling the damage his father has done there, rolls onto his side, screaming and kicking back at the man like a branded mule.

Faces aglow with amusement, the Mexicans step backward to dodge the flailing limbs, and the moving lantern throws an erratic tide of yellow light over the fight while Eddie and Stan rush in to put an end to it. They reach down to haul their father up, but Skala is having none of it. He comes up in a blind, swinging rage and catches Stan in the neck with an elbow that drives the boy staggering backward and wheezing, clutching his throat.

Beyond the cattlegate, Villaseñor finally takes notice. He rises from his seat up front in the surrey and pulls his coat tight across his chest. The wind stirs the carriage lantern, and he shields his eyes with the awning of a flattened hand held above his spectacles, then he peers out at a night of gaming turned fierce. Out in the pasture, even the girl takes note of the sudden cheering, turning her horse to give this new, disquieting diversion her audience.

A little better than two hundred yards beyond her, the priest stands on his toes atop his hay bale, and for a moment he struggles to grasp the meaning of this boisterous new encirclement of men. His coat is soaked and the wind is needling his face with raindrops, and still he remains, leaning this way and that to find a better vantage point. He can't see a thing, and then, in the irregular yellow lanternlight and haze of woodsmoke, the ring of men swells and constricts like some jaundiced heart pulsing in a miasma. Stumbling backward, one of the onlookers opens a gap in the circle such that Father Carew catches sight of what's at work inside, and he would swear—if he swore—that his lungs have forgotten how to take air just as surely as he's forgotten, this last half hour, how to pray. He has seen father and son both spilling blood, the exuberance of the crowd around them—he is bearing witness now to something far more regrettable than a race for land and bridegrooms' hands. This is the bloodlust of brothers, the vengeful rage of the father, all of it born out and somehow flawless in its wickedness, like some depraved reenactment of Genesis staged solely for the amusement of reprobates. How far? he wonders. How far may we follow one illchosen and descending path?

In the meantime, Skala has gotten Eduard by the hair, and before he drives the boy's head into a raised knee, he catches Karel's eye. The old man wears the twin puncture wounds of Thom's teeth deep in the sun-spotted skin above one eyebrow, and he nods at Karel with a satisfied look on his face that suggests he's been waiting for this since the first of his sons slid wide-eyed and helpless out of their mother and into the world.

Thom is struggling to stand, his boot soles slipping on the muddy sod, and Karel watches him with the same cool patience he feels when he's hidden behind a tree some mornings, leveling his rifle as dew glimmers in the tall grass all around him and a buck walks proudly out into the clearing, all but begging to be shot. And then it all churns sour in Karel's mind—the lost race and his father's bloodied, contented face; the cold rain coming down, numbing everything but the hot swell of desire that he carries for the girl; the vision of his brothers and their goddamned cigars; the smell of smoldering fires and wet cow shit; the hot hollow in his guts he doesn't figure he'll ever fill up; the metallic paste of his own blood on his tongue—all of it rendered clear by the electric spill of adrenaline into his veins. He recalls the quiet thrill of a morning spent hunting on his father's land, the trigger of memory cold against his finger, imagines squeezing it back, and while his father and Eduard exchange blows, Karel drives a boot heel beneath Thom's ear before he can find enough purchase to stand upright. Karel feels the shock of the impact in his hipbone, an abrasive jolt that makes him imagine his bones as sandy stones crushed together underfoot. Thom drops to the ground for a third time, facedown in the muck and standing water.

And then Karel shoulders up to his father, and they're all at it with fists and feet. Eduard rears back, landing a shot to Karel's temple that blazes in blinding light across his field of vision such that he mistakes it at first for a flash of lightning, and he's throwing blind punches as he awaits a rumble of thunder that never comes. When Stan leans over and drags Thom to his feet, the two of them come wildly and unwarily forward. Dazed and unyielding as a drunk, Thom still wears a look of serene release on his wrecked and swollen face. He draws back, twisting at the waist, and when he uncoils, swinging with a scream, he doubles his father over with a blow to the kidney.

Karel gasps as if he's taken the punch himself, and then Eduard and Stan are on him, crumpling him beneath their weight. They yank him up by the arms, twisting his wrists behind his back until he thinks his shoulders will come clean from their sockets. He flails and kicks back at his brothers' shins, sliding in the mud and held upright by the same muscles that restrain him as he watches his father holding his stomach, grunting under his own weight and attempting to stand. Hovering over him, Thom flexes his hands at his side, waiting for more. When Karel calls out, cursing his brothers as he stamps at their feet, his arms held fast behind his back, Thom turns and avails himself of the easy opportunity. "I'm fixing to give you your druthers, little brother," he says, showing Karel a fist. "You rather eat tomorrow or see?"

Karel hurls his body forward, trying to shrug free of his brothers' grasp, but they torque his arms harder behind his back and it burns in his shoulders enough to bring tears to his eyes and flood his mouth with saliva. He tries to spit, but the stuff catches on his swollen lower lip and rolls down his chin like drool from a toothless dog. "You ought to see yourself, Thom. Face like yours would scare a whore off a five-dollar dick."

Thom spits blood and opens his mouth wide, making a prideful show of his injuries. "I got no use anymore for whores," he says, smiling. "I'm the marrying kind." When he swings, the night flashes hot white before Karel's eyes. As the light wanes, it is replaced by a blackness overlaid with crimson. A tide of nausea crests in the hot swirl of his stomach and all the starch drains out of his knees. His brothers yank him back to his feet, his pulse throbbing hot in his blind eye, the welt over his cheekbone swelling until he can feel it buoying the tender skin of his lower eyelid.

The wind shifts again and plays hell with the trees such that out by the creek comes a clattering racket of snapped branches and fallen pinecones. Over the commotion of weather, Vaclav is shouting, "*Turn him loose*," and when Thom spins around with his fists up he finds his old man on his feet with his knife drawn, waving it there in front of him, the honed blade wet and shimmering in the flickering light.

When the gun goes off, even Vaclav startles. The blast is sharp and short-lived, the sound of an errant hammer striking milled white pine.

Karel freezes, half expecting to hear a body splash against the waterlogged earth. Startled, one of the Mexicans swings his gun up and leans his cheek into the smooth walnut of its stock, stepping back and readying himself to return fire while his partner waves the light above his head, searching the darkness to locate the shooter.

"Put that damned knife away!" Lad Dvorak shouts, stepping forward with his pistol raised and smoking above his head.

Karel shrugs off his brothers, and they turn him loose and step warily toward the safety of the armed guards as their father turns one way and then another, slashing the air in front of him with his blade, squinting into the shadows until he locates Dvorak. "Best mind your own business, Laddie," he says.

"I mean to," Lad says. "I'm going to make it my business to ride clean into Hallettsville and collect Sheriff Munson if you don't put that thing back in your belt where it belongs."

Skala grunts and shakes his head, wipes his face with the sleeve of his coat. "Put that sorry excuse for a gun away, you son of a bitch. This whole thing stinks to high hell. I ain't putting this knife anywhere but in your gut unless someone can explain to me how a boy runs a horse for a mile and comes back bloody."

Without shouldering forward from his place in the ring of onlookers, Patrick Dalton lets out a disgusted laugh. "Lord-a-*mighty*," he says. "Listen to yourself, Skala. Just look at my boy's face and listen to yourself."

"Hell, Dalton. All these years and your cunny's still sore? Why don't you limp back home and have your boy rub some salve on it if it's all that bad."

There comes a chuckle from the crowd, and then there's whispering and jostling as the circle widens and breaks open to admit Guillermo Villaseñor to its center. The man walks with his hands in his coat pockets as if he's strolling around town of a dry Saturday evening, his wavy hair as yet oiled and orderly despite the blowing rain, and when he gets within a few feet of Skala, he motions to his men with a tilt of his head and a clicking sound he makes with his tongue. They nod slowly, in unison, and only once, and then their boss brings his hands from his pockets and holds them out as if he's come down from his surrey with no business other than that of collecting rainwater by the handful. The wet lenses of his spectacles throw slanting reflections of lanternlight from their surfaces, and before he speaks he makes a sound of paternal disappointment and impatience, half clearing his throat, half sighing. "I must confess," he says, raising his voice above the din of rainfall, "that I had hoped I might afford my daughters the luxury of unblemished bridegrooms, Mr. Skala. As I had hoped you'd be a man whose word proved worthy of his wealth." He tilts his head and arcs his thick brows in a look that indicates regret and resignation both. Returning one hand to its place in his pocket, he flips the other palm down, working his fingers in a dismissive gesture one might use to give an idle servant leave from the room. "Please, let's be reasonable. Put the knife away."

Skala lowers the blade, but keeps it in hand at his side. His forehead is deeply bruised and swollen above the twin toothmarks, his speech dulled by a split lip, his shoulders thrown back as if he were bragging of an evening at the icehouse about cotton yields or bale weights. "It's been some shenanigans during the race, I'm betting. And that's got to be answered for," he says. "It's raining to strangle toads, sure enough, but not hard enough to break skin." He points to Karel with his knife. "I want to know how the boy's mouth got bloodied of a horse ride."

Karel hears his father speak the word, and he's suddenly aware that he's lost track of Whiskey. He gazes one eyed toward the creek, scans the line of trees back toward the cattlegate. When he reaches up to feel the swelling beneath his eye, there flares a searing pain beneath the skin that Karel would swear begins burning before he even touches the wound. He wonders if the worst of pain lies in the anticipation of its arrival. Wincing, he turns back toward his father, squared off and awaiting an answer from Villaseñor. The horse is nowhere to be seen.

The man nods slowly, shifts his attention from Skala to Karel, from his future sons-in-law, who now stand battered and serious and shouldered in front of his guards, back to Skala. "Well, sir. While I can't say that I appreciate the tenor of your curiosity, I certainly do recognize your right to its satisfaction. Thankfully, despite all your pleasantries here, your boys still appear to be conscious. Shall we ask them if the race was run fairly?"

"I told you at least once before, stranger, that *we* ain't doing anything. Besides, I already asked them twice — once with words and once with an ass whipping."

Out west, the moon slides into view, washing pale over the landscape for a slow moment before ducking back behind another jagged-bottomed line of clouds. The rain slackens to a drizzle, and Karel feels the hot throb of his pulse in his swollen eye. Grown suddenly impatient with all the chatter, the townsmen take to groaning and whispering, shuffling around in the mud and waiting.

"It don't look to me like you got that much the better of it, Skala," Patrick Dalton says. "Besides which, if you choose to lay licks to your witnesses, then it ain't nobody's fault but your own if they won't vouch for you."

"Dalton," Skala says, an angry blue vein snaking up his throat from beneath his shirt collar. "I believe I already invited you to leave. Ain't a man here who doesn't know you sit down to piss, and not a one who'd take two steps out of his way for your fool opinion."

Villaseñor holds a hand up to the crowd. "This is my business, gentlemen, and as much as I might appreciate your interest, I'll kindly ask you to hold your tongues until I can effect a solution." He motions to Stan, and his guards push the boy gently forward into the circle. "You are the oldest, is that correct?"

Stan's nose is bent opposite the cant of his neck, a black plug of dried blood protruding from one nostril. What surprises Karel is that his brother wears his welts with a prideful posture. He stands straight and nods immediately, then he clears his throat and says, "I am."

"Very well. Then would you tell me, as your father's witness, if there's any reason to doubt the result of the race."

Stan glances at his father, who turns the knife in his hand at his side while he returns the boy's gaze. "The girl was out front the whole way, best I could tell. She damn near lost her mount out back of the trees, but even then she was leading."

"What about your brother's face?"

"Can't say for sure. Wind came up mighty strong before the rain blew in. Gusted through them oaks pretty good, and they were riding right up tight against the treeline. I expect he took a branch to the face, but if he did it didn't look to hinder him much."

Villaseñor turns to Karel, swiping beads of water from the smooth skin of his coat sleeves. "That sound accurate enough to you?"

Karel glances one eyed at his brothers standing three abreast, their backs straight, knees locked in anticipation. In the corner of his vision, Skala weaves on his feet like he does some nights when he stays late at the icehouse. Turning the knife at his side, the man coughs phlegm and spits, and it occurs to Karel that, in all these years, he's never thought to imagine that this wiry and unforgiving man was once the very one his mother had loved. When he imagines her, dreaming her alive daily in his mind, manufacturing memories, forging connections with her that he'd never known, what he sees is a woman sitting horseback with a swollen belly, a woman pale and lovely and comforting her youngest son, stroking his curly hair and pressing him to the warm, faintly perfumed comfort of her bosom. Only now, with the wind's murmuring in the pines akin to the hushed sounds of graveside consolation, does he shiver with the notion of all she's lost, all she'll never know of the family she's left alive and discontented in the world from which she must always have meant to protect them.

"Well, boy?" Vaclav says.

"She was too far gone from the start," he says. "Tree or no tree, there wasn't any catching her."

AFTER THE TOWNSMEN break away from their tight-huddled circle, murmuring at the disappointment of a fight brought so abruptly to an end, recounting the most staggering blows and arguing light-heartedly about who got the best or worst of it, Karel dodges his father's attention and goes in search of Whiskey. The horse has wandered from the dry shelter of the trees and is nibbling at the short remains of wet hay on the fringe of the southern pastureland. Beyond him, the girl has turned her horse out into the dark field and is walking the animal slowly, looking back over her shoulder as she goes.

Trudging out to collect his father's animal, Karel hears his father getting in the last words, warning his brothers, telling them that they have one hour to collect a change of clothes and get the hell out of his house. They can sleep at the inn, by damn, and on Villaseñor's nickel, too. That or they can sleep out in the rain or go cuddle up in some hayloft with the mustachioed Mexicans they've taken a fancy to. And then the man is swinging open the cattlegate, stopping to bite a new portion of tobacco off his plug, spitting and shaking his head, a hand clamped to his side as he heads out across the dark stretch of acreage in which, at least outwardly, he's always taken greater pride than in his boys.

As for Karel, he comes up slowly on Whiskey, works a flattened hand down the horse's smoothly muscled shoulder, stroking cold rainwater from the horsehair and reassuring the animal for a few moments with his voice. "There you go, boy. That's it. It wasn't your fault, now was it?" Taking hold of the pommel, Karel slips a boot into the stirrup and swings himself into the saddle, nudges the horse around with a heel and a clicking of the tongue.

What Karel knows, as he rides into the darkness to the south, is that he has nothing more to say about this night, no desire to go home and meet the silence of his father or the whispering exodus of his brothers. He'll ride the horse fully cool out here in the weather, let his stinging lip and his swollen eye and the reassurances of nightfall and drizzling rain convince him that it wasn't only his distracted riding that cost him the race. When he makes it home and gets the tack put away and the new hay forked into the stables, maybe he'll bed down out in the loft until morning. But for now he'll ride south until he finds the lower fork of the creek, and then he'll follow it around to the house. Out there somewhere in the darkness, he knows, is a girl astride her black horse, the both of them streaming rainwater, and it is toward her that Karel rides out into the night, a failure on his father's horse.

ON THE BANKS of the creek, where the remaining men stand winding frayed wet twine around their wrists, reeling in their jugs of corn mash and laughing and passing the wet coins of their wagers between them, the horned owl perches amber-eyed and ruffling rainwater from her feathers, watching from the sheltered lower branch of a sweet gum tree. Across the creek along the far bank, near the tangle of water oak and pine roots and the deep impressions of boot soles in the wet silt, she discerns the slightest distinction in the clustered dancing of bluestem spires, knowing by some sharp and instinctive insistence in the grainy fibers of her muscles that rain and wind bend the uppermost inches of grass blades while the scuttling of prey and the dragging of a tail will set the reeds to shivering upward from the tillers.

And then she's aloft and diving, her wings thrown back and rippling as she descends across the water and meets the ground with outflung wings and extended legs. The men turn their heads in the darkness, sensing amidst the drizzling rain and uncertain wind her silent and feathery slice through the air and across the creek.

Then the little opossum shrieks and writhes as the hard points of talons break the skin and dig deeply in.

A moment more and they're airborne again, the prey fighting its useless clash of twisting tail and snapping teeth, knowing in its thoughtless and animal intuition that to effect escape by the instinctive feigning of its own death is as unlikely as is this flight itself of a wingless creature over treetops.

There's the confusion of the dreamed and the dreamlike. The dying animal, only two weeks weaned and shunned from the pouch in the colder months, is shot through with a searing internal heat, the distinction blotted out between its normal downturned sleep and this new, impossible reality of hanging high above the earth without its tail coiled and clinging to tree bark.

The owl dips a wing and veers west. She clears the trees and glides over the pastureland toward the far southern fork of the creek, toward her hollowed oak and the three fledglings waiting there with eyes just newly keen enough to know the approach of trouble but helpless in all other faculties to defend themselves against it.

Riding the familiar line of fencewires beneath her, she streaks low and level as she works her wings against the downward push of the rain and follows the mile-long fenceline toward home, squeezing her claws into the hot meat rhythmically with the upward pull of her wings. Beneath her, just to the east, there's the dark movement of a horse and, with another hundred yards of wind and rain run through her feathers, another black and cantering shape, an animal too large for her consideration and too earthbound to trigger the panicked reflexes that urge escape.

The wind gusts and propels the rain horizontally out of the west. The owl angles her coverts to the wind and gains loft, vectoring out and up toward the hardwood tops before her in the distance while below, weighted by the wet wool of his coat, Father Carew flails ineffectually, ensnared between the two barbed and topmost wires of the fence. His old bay shudders and sneezes, turning her head against the windblown rain in such a way that it appears, to the priest, as if she's avoiding sight of him, of a man who is her master and yet so powerless against feebleness and gravity and fence-wires and the simple predicaments they occasion. Struggling to free himself, the priest folds himself over at the waist, reaching out to the gritty mud of the road before him as he works his legs and his boots slide in the rain-glazed weeds and cut hay underfoot. He feels the points of the wire prick through his clothes into the aged and thin and tender skin of his belly, and as the owl alights a half mile away, unnoticed to all but her waiting young, the priest digs the toes of his boots into the soft, yielding earth and finds purchase enough to propel himself through the fencewires, tearing his coat and shirt as he goes.

And then he's facedown on the rutted muck of the road, and by the time he gets his boots free of the fence and works himself slowly to his feet, there's a pointed pain in the loose skin over his ribs. He leans against Sarah, gathering his breath with his back to the weather as it hurls itself against him. He unbuttons his overcoat and shirt and finds there against his chest the hanging shattered glass of the phial and the burning laceration from which issues a cool and uncongealed stream of holy water and blood that slicks down his sternum and runs thin until it gathers at the cinched waistline of his trousers and pools in the shallow whorl of his navel.

KAREL LETS HIS horse find the way, this landscape he knows so well grown foreign, his whole field of vision reduced to the opacity of black sackcloth. The rain comes on lightly but steadily, running beneath his clothes and down the ridge of his spine and into his britches. The horse moves slowly, following the scent of the animal it has spent the night trailing. Out west, a flash of lightning wicks into the low ceiling of the clouds and washes the plains in a muted glow that lasts just long enough for Karel to see the girl and the haunches of her horse out some seventy-five yards and closing on the creek. But this he expects. What startles him, illuminated in the short second of eerily white light, is the appearance of a man on the flooded road beyond the fence, a man with his arms thrown around the neck of his horse and a face weathered by time and weighted by a cross between sorrow and surprise. His eyes are pale and wide, the skin beneath them slung low and discolored. Here's a man who, as if by intuition, turns toward Karel to reveal a muddied and open overcoat, a shirt unbuttoned and stained, something glinting and jagged hung round his neck. Unlikely and inevitable as the rising of the dead in one's dreams, here stands the old priest, bleeding and clinging to his horse in the rain, and when Father Carew parts his lips to speak, the world is cast again in black.

Whiskey takes no notice, moves forward, his hooves splashing in the standing water of the pasture, and Karel shudders against the cold, against the unexpected rise of penitential guilt. He has seen, he knows, something he was not meant to see, and on a night when all but the nocturnal are deprived of sight, and on the skin of his arms he wears the prickle of conscience-laden exhilaration, the same as he'd felt when, as a boy skipping rocks on a summer Sunday, he'd stumbled across three bathing schoolgirls in the swollen creek, their sun-flushed skin appointed with beads of water and a smooth newness from which Karel couldn't pull his eyes – the arc of their spines when they bent to splash water onto one another, the dark mystery of their nipples, so different from his own, wind kissed and erect and upturned on their budding breasts.

Karel smiles and shakes his head. How is it that seeing the priest who baptized him could occasion memories of naked girls? How is it that anything ever gives rise to what it does instead of what it should?

After half a mile spent all but blind on this horse, when the rain lets up further without stopping altogether, Karel's eyes find some discernible depth in the darkness. Whiskey blows, his hide rippling beneath the saddle, and Karel breathes through his nose, inhaling the sweet, musky smell of wet horsehair. His eye is puffed up near to closed, aching still, but only as a muted throbbing deep beneath the skin. There's something to be taken from this, he thinks. Something about the body, something about the eyes, about the flesh and the bones and the heart. About how they want to adjust, to heal, to see and feel. And they do, he thinks, if never entirely.

At the southern fork of the creek, he makes out the girl and her horse silhouetted against the trees rising out of the slough. When he pulls the horse up a few yards from her at the water's edge, he hears the swollen rush of the current over stones and the rain draining like endless handfuls of sand let fall between clenched fingers into the water. Just off his right flank there comes the creaking of the girl's wet leather tack as she shifts her weight in the saddle. Karel points his toes downward in the stirrups and breathes only through his nose while he strokes his horse's long neck. She's near, and then she's speaking, and at first Karel feels a pinch of guilt, thinking he's

124

come unbeknownst upon a girl telling private thoughts to her horse beneath a pall of unrelenting clouds and nightfall.

"My father knows where I am," she says, her voice nearly inaudible beneath the rainfall.

"I suspect he does," he says, but he wonders how this is intended — as a warning? As a simple, startled declaration?

"He does."

"Doesn't seem the sort who abides not knowing things he just as well might."

"Yes," she says. "That's right."

"He know the priest who's set to say Mass at your nuptials is out on the road getting fresh with his horse?"

She turns her head sharply toward him. "Please don't speak that way."

Her voice comes at him so softly, but Karel can't see her eyes clearly, can't figure if it's some tenderness in her or the faint sound of the rainfall that makes it so. Another strobe of light brightens the horizon and outruns its thunder. They wait it out and sit there awhile, watching the electricity do its work out west, and when Karel looks over at her again, the girl is sitting the horse with the reins in her lap and her hands reaching back over her shoulders, unplaiting her wet hair. Karel can see rising from her collar the delicate slope of her neck. She's squinting against the rain, looking away from him toward the creek while she works, and in another instant it's full dark again and the thunder shakes the earth beneath them. The horses stamp the ground and voice their concerted complaints. Karel moves Whiskey forward toward the sound of running water and then stops when he feels the warmth radiating from her horse.

"He may know you're out here, but he'll wish you hadn't been all the same when you catch cold and can't make your own wedding."

She turns her head and laughs, and Karel bites the inside of his cheek against the disappointment of not seeing clearly the wideness of her eyes when she does. "We've seen greater danger than rain," she says.

There's a certain superior curtness to her speech that Karel can't reconcile with the smooth sweep of her voice, and all at once he supposes that she's talking down to him, the winner of the race making light of the rider she's outrun. He recalls her fall, feigned or not, the ease of her ascension back into the saddle, and it is this memory that worms itself around in his mind with enough torsion and convolution that he's somehow firmly and unexpectedly sure of his suspicions. "I don't doubt it, but then again I don't reckon much of anything seems dangerous to you, Miss. You make falling off a horse look like a game at a play party."

The rain surges with a hard gust of wind and then falls to a sprinkle again. Karel combs his fingers through his tangle of wet curls. A nervous muscle pulses in the crook of his afflicted neck, and he shifts his wet weight in the saddle to have a fruitless, squinting look overhead. The rain needles his good eye, and the sky is dark enough to suggest that the moon has orphaned the heavens. She shivers beneath her wet riding coat, and now Karel feels the cold so suddenly that he thinks for a moment that, but for distracted riding and misfortune, it could be this way with her, that he could spend the rest of his life noticing his surroundings only as they pertain to her. He waits for her to speak, for whatever's coming next of her cleverness to find words for itself, and when she sits silent for a long minute, before he can stop himself, he hears himself ask, "What's become of your mother?"

Lightning streaks silently across the distant sky and, before he can recognize it for what it is, Karel flinches at what he sees coming toward him—her hand, pulled from its glove and dripping with cold rainwater, cups the back of his neck, and there's a shuddering of electricity in him that has nothing to do with the weather.

"You're asking if she's alive?"

As if in answer to her question, he leans his neck further into her palm, which is already growing warm against his skin. In part, his vision comes back to him, and he can see her there in the shadows, the taut line of her arm strung between them, bridging their bodies above the indifferent loitering of their horses.

"My father says that if we look for ourselves in others, we're likely to find someone we don't recognize."

Karel stirs slightly in the saddle, uncomfortable but unwilling to pull away from the softness of her touch. He considers what she's said, the meaning of which flits in and out of the limits of his comprehension the same way a flushed bobwhite will weave itself into a stand of trees to elude his shot. "I'm thinking there's easier riddles than that one in the Bible," he says, and her face, leaning toward him, is visible but illegible—bottomless black eyes weighted with sadness, lips curled into a smile—the whole of it more confusing than consoling.

"It's Graciela," she says.

"Do what?"

"My name. It's Graciela. And my mother is alive to everyone but my father. Now follow me," she says, pulling her hand away and nudging the horse out into the creekwater.

"Follow you? Hell, I *have* been."

Without turning in the saddle, she clicks her tongue loudly at the horse and calls back, "You ought to be accustomed to it then. Come. We'll get the horses out of the weather."

ON THE EDGE of town, three poor horses stand tied out front of the icehouse, shuddering in their sleep. The building is the size of a modest barn, cobbled together of rough-hewn, unpainted pine. From the rooftop stovepipe coughs gray smoke, and the fogged windows glow with lamplight. Karel and the girl ride the horses by at a walk, keeping to the other side of the road beyond the meager reach of the light. Fifty yards into town, just beyond the druggist and the tack-and-saddle shop, they stop and secrete themselves beneath the eaves of the feedstore that stands next door to the Township Inn. The girl's horse takes the opportunity to lift its tail, shining and black as blued gunmetal, and leave a steaming heap on the hard-packed road such that the night smells, to Karel, of home, of the outdoor comfort of woodsmoke and horse dung.

With a hand held back to keep Karel still and quiet, Graciela peers around the corner and down the alley toward the inn's stables. Toward Dalton's town center, something moves slowly across the road, and Karel squints his working eye until he can make out the shape of the old priest, who glances back over his shoulder as he walks his horse around the corner of the church toward the parish stable.

Turning back, a hand on the cantle of her saddle, the girl says, "Father and my sisters are indoors, but the inn's stable boy is still tending to the carriage horses. It won't be long."

While they wait, Karel runs his tongue along the jagged wound at the corner of his mouth, feels the cool seep of fluid down his cheek from his engorged eye. He watches the girl leaning forward over her horse's neck, her hair falling crimped in wet ripples down her back. Even on a stationary horse, her weight is centered over her bent knees, her spine held straight. There's a seasoned confidence to her, he thinks, and she carries it in her body, in her upright and unflagging posture, a solidness in her legs and shoulders that is almost masculine. But then there is the breathtaking taper of her back, its sudden slope into a waist so slight that Karel feels certain it's smaller around than a man's hatband. There's the wide, smooth flare of her hips. If she were reclined such that you could run a finger along the side of her body from ribs to thighs, it might put you in mind of a single, perfect valley found in a landscape of irregular, rolling foothills, of a horizon you'd gladly ride all day to reach. Sure enough, she's her father's child. She has his olive skin, his dark hair and eyes, his easy assuredness, but one look at her would make any man wonder how lovely was her mother. As Vaclav Skala would say, she may have her father's features, but she sure ain't got his fixtures.

They wait there a solid fifteen minutes, and when the girl swings down from her saddle, she holds a finger over her lips and tilts her head toward the small stable set back from the road behind the inn. They walk the animals down the alleyway, the hollow sound of the horseshoes on wet stone bouncing between the brick walls of the inn and the solid planking of the feedstore. Slowly, Karel slides the stable door open and inhales the smell of animals and dry hay. The girl hands him her reins and slides beneath his arm as she slips inside to light the lantern.

When they get the horses inside and dried and curried, she scoops oats into the feed buckets and they hasp the horses into the two empty stalls. Only then does Karel get a good look at the other twin black animals, warm now and switching their tails in the opposite stalls. If anything, they are more impressive than the one the girl has just stabled, taller and hard-ridged with muscle, painted with the same distinctive and shockingly white blazes, and Karel wonders how any man could bear to harness such a horse to a carriage. He turns to the girl, who sits beneath the lantern on a farrier's stool, blond hay bales stacked two high behind her. She's removed her riding jacket, hanging it from a crossbeam to dry among odds and ends of tack. Her white blouse is buttoned to the throat, pleated and blooming across the rise of her breasts, and thin enough that Karel can see, beneath it, the lacy filigree of her camisole. Her hair falls over her shoulders, and it calls to Karel's mind shallow black water running over a gentle outcropping of stone. She's smiling up at him, her skin dark and damp still with rainwater and gleaming in the dancing yellow lanternlight. There's a pinch at the scabby hinge of Karel's lips, and he realizes his mouth is open. "Graciela, huh?" he says, and she laughs a little and nods. "You ever ride those monsters yonder?"

She shakes her head.

"Your father, then?"

"Not anyone. They're carriage horses."

"The hell they are," he says. "Just look at them."

Outside, the rain is still coming down sparingly, but the wind throws itself in dithering gusts against the cedar shingles and whistles loudly beneath the eaves. She stands, stray wisps of hair strung in wet threads about her cheeks, her eyes deep and studious, moving up and down the length of him, settling back on his eyes as she approaches him. "I've seen them, Karel," she says, and his name on her lips sets loose something warm and liquid beneath his skin, a rush of comfort that seeps into him and swirls around his bones. "I saw them born. All of them, and the best of the stable are boarded over at the Dalton place. But tell me, if horses are only ever used to pull a carriage, how are they anything but harness horses?"

Karel gives that some thought, and it reminds him of his least favorite arithmetic lessons at school, the long and pointless story problems Miss Kubek always asks last, knowing that even the brightest among her pupils will puzzle over them. But these are horses, he tells himself, not numbers, not something dreamed up to exist only on slate or paper. "Because you can look at them and tell," he says. "It's that damned simple. You can tell within an hour after they're foaled. The second they can stand without a wobble. There ain't but three kinds of horses, Miss. Those made for the harness, those made to run, and those made so poorly that you know how lucky you are if you own one of the first two kinds."

She's standing so near to him that he can smell her breath, not sweet like he might have expected, like her hair, but earthy and clean, slightly metallic, the scent of wet, mineral-rich soil at the edge of running water. As he breathes her in, she touches him again, this time with both hands cupped about his neck while she brushes her lips against the swollen mass of his wounded eye in a kiss so light that Karel thinks it either accidental or imagined.

It is neither, and when she leans back to show him her smile again, he feels as he had as a young boy when, on some rare occasion, a woman had shown him affection. What he wants now, as he wanted then, is to take hold of her, to hide his eyes in the curve of her neck and feel her fingers in his hair, her arms around him, and in this way lay claim to the moment so that it cannot be taken from him. What he wants is to accept and possess the tenderness all at once. Instead, he stands with his arms at his side and wills it to continue. Overhead, the rain spatters on the shingles while here, inside, the lamplight flickers against the rough woodwork of the stalls and crossbeams while the horses switch their tails and empty their buckets of feed.

"You may be right," she says, blinking slowly, one time, as if for emphasis. She pulls one of her hands away, traces a finger down the unnatural curvature of his neck with the other. "But how will you ever prove it to me?"

It is part beckoning, part challenge, and then his lips are on her, the warm, loamy taste of her surprised exhalation rushing across his tongue as he holds her by the hips against him. There's a pinched pain at the torn corner of his mouth, a little lick of fire come alive from

131

stirred embers, and when she pushes him away, he drops his hands into his trouser pockets to obscure the extent of his excitement.

"Wait," she says, pulling her hair back over her shoulders as she crosses the stable toward the lantern hung from the raw timber framework of the nearest stall. When she retracts the lamp's wicking, a horse blows, and Karel knows without question that it's Whiskey, fed and dry now, and warm, but awake and restless nonetheless, disquieted by the sudden onset of shadows. Working his hands from his pockets, Karel watches the girl, steadying himself against the hot work of his own musculature, against the rolling spasms in his lower back and abdomen, the arousing arc of energy that surges from his tailbone up into the blades of his shoulders.

Her silhouette is cast against the pale remnant of light behind her, and when she approaches him, walking in slowly measured steps, Karel's breath catches, and then it comes all at once. Her hands, he sees, are at work on the uppermost buttons of her blouse.

Meander Scars

MAY 1898

NOT YET NINE in the morning, and Vaclav Skala had broken a hard sweat out in the western cropfield. He was thankful for it, for the cool slicks beneath his arms and down his back, for the ring of relief afforded by the wet band of his wide-brimmed hat. If you took the time to read the *Farmers' Almanac,* which Vaclav did, though he had recently begun to wonder why, you'd expect these May skies to be crowded with clouds, but when he whoaed his shabby draft horse and removed his hat, wiping the sweat from his face with his shirtsleeve, he looked overhead and studied the unbroken blue of it while he fished his new plug of tobacco from his pocket and unwrapped it and bit off a portion. Whatever fool it is writes that rag, he thought, probably ain't ever once set foot in Lavaca County. He was going to need plenty of dry heat in time, but if he spun all this cottonseed into the soil only to have the sun bake the earth hard before it could take, then he'd have to suffer the first poor yield since Klara had died. Just the thought of it went to vinegar in his blood. He'd have to wait another year until he could afford the lumber and shingles he needed to finish his stable, and then what would he do? Old Man Kaspar had a fine roan mare coming in season, and when Vaclav had unfolded last week's *Shiner Gazette,* he'd seen an advertisement for a monster of a horse named Arasmus, a giant stallion shipped over from Italy, of all goddamned places. He'd never seen a stud fee so high, nor a horse so imposing. After all these years, he was fed up full with all the red-faced bragging his neighbor Patrick

135

Dalton did about his stable of racehorses, and Vaclav had folded the paper and tucked it under his arm before pushing back his chair. He left his coffee steaming on the table, told the older boys to mind Karel and their chores, and he'd ridden straight away to see Lad Dvorak at the bank.

Two days later, for thirty dollars up front in boarding, feed, and stud fees, the whole thing was arranged. Another thirty would be due after the foal survived a fortnight, and he'd keep Kaspar's horses in hay for a year thereafter to pay off the mare's share. The mere thought of it set Vaclav to tingling with anticipation, and now, as the tobacco did its work on his nerves, he studied the straight furrows of his fields, marveling at the sound results of his own able work. He looked back toward the house, over his shoulder and into the glare of the sun. He'd kept the older boys home from school, and he'd have to tan them if they hadn't fed the hogs and chickens and gathered the eggs by lunchtime. Or if they'd let the youngest boy soil his britches again instead of coaxing him into the outhouse.

Now he snapped the reins and clicked his tongue at the ragged old horse, one that deserved nothing more than hard work and a bucket of dry oats and another day above ground, and he engaged the planter. If a man put his mind to it, he could single-handedly seed half an acre in an hour. By noon, when Skala will find his boys by the creek and slap the oldest one hard across the cheek, he will have exceeded that pace by nearly a quarter acre, and then he will come furiously back into the fields without eating, and he will work the horse into a half-lame lather, and he'll let himself cry for one last time in his life.

Fifteen years before Vaclav Skala bought his land, a storm had uprooted a hollowed-out red oak and blown it across the northern fork of Mustang Creek so that its crown splashed down in the slough on the opposite bank. It was the worst weather the residents of Lavaca County would see until the winter flood of 1910, four straight days of wind-driven rain that left the furrows brimming with water and the farmers sitting in their kitchens, watching from the windows, weathering, at once, the storm and the apron-wringing worries of their wives. As the fruitless windfall of twigs and foliage swept downstream, lodging against the downed oak, the water dammed up behind it and rolled, roiling and thick with sediment, into the slough, carving from the soft loam a deep new trench that would circumvent the fallen tree, that would last beyond the storm and the return of the sun, that would bend northward and loop back around to rejoin the stream, leaving the old creekbed dry and richly fertile and, by the time the Skala boys found it, lushly overgrown with a bed of little bluestem that made for comfortable sitting with fishing poles and lunch buckets and the collective desire to pretend, beneath the ribbons of light that slanted through the treetops, that they were not bereft of the feminine tenderness that, to young boys, is nothing shy of sustenance.

And so just before noon, with their morning chores complete, they played, today like so many days, beside the trickling of creek-water. Their feet were tanned and bare, their faces soiled with the congress of dust and sweat. Stan stood on the bank, throwing twigs and clods of dirt into the moving water while Eddie and Thom took up makeshift arms, dueling with the swords of fallen branches. The youngest, Karel, sat where the creek had once been, pulling shoots of grass from the soil and, with full fists raised above his head, letting the blades flutter down on himself, laughing with delight, shaking his head and sputtering loudly when the falling grass stuck to his wet lips. He stood, fetched a stick, and, when shooed away from his brothers' play, slapped it against the trunks of trees and then squatted on the bank of the creek to swirl it in the water, as entranced by the cloudy rise of silt it occasioned as he would be one day by the reaction a swung crop could affect in a horse. And then it struck him, the sudden constriction down low in his bowels, the gurgling urgency against which he tightened his muscles, locking his knees together and shuffling his feet with his back straightened, a cold panic shivering through him as he imagined the close, foul shadows of the outhouse.

Stan bent to find another clump of dirt to hurl into the water, and he took note of Karel there, doing his rigid little dance. "Don't you mess your pants again, Karel," he said.

Karel looked up at his oldest brother, his arms swung back and his hands cupped over the seat of his dungarees. "I won't."

Stan sighed and shook his head. "You will, too, if you don't go now," he said. "Come on. I'll go with you."

Off to the east of the house, just beyond the smokehouse and the new, half-framed stable their father was building, Stan stood with Karel, the door to the outhouse swung open on its rusty hinges, the smell of it rank and intensified by the heat and washing out over them. Little Karel stood there balking with his face bunched up like he'd licked a lemon, shaking his head. "Just get in there and do your business," Stan said. "Pop will be coming in for lunch soon, and we'll run out of time to play."

Still the boy wouldn't go. "I want Mama," he said.

"You get in there and go," Stan said, "and I'll go fetch her. Okay?"

"You promise?"

"I swear. You can leave the door open if you want. Just go, and don't forget to wipe good this time."

Inside, Karel sat holding his nose and trying to convince himself to unclench his muscles, his little, dusty feet dangling in the angle of light that widened and narrowed as the breeze swung the creaking door back and forth. His brother Thom had told him that there were snakes down in the hole, slithering around in all that filth, biding time and waiting to bite a boy's backside. Karel didn't believe it. He'd asked his father, who'd wanted to know why a snake would choose to spend its time wallowing in shit if it could just as easily do its swimming down in the creek. This made sense to Karel. His father usually did, but he still couldn't shake the vision of water moccasins coiling in wait down there, their forked tongues flicking fast in and out of their mouths. Besides which, he himself had seen the thick, leathery tails of rats sliding beneath the rough planks of lumber where the walls of the outhouse met the ground. Rats were hardly better than snakes, and just sitting perched over the hole stiffened Karel's muscles with panic. It was worse than mere darkness, worse than his fear of falling from the top fence timbers of the cattle pens where his father sometimes perched him in the sunlight to keep him out of trouble while the young bulls were castrated or dehorned. Now Karel felt the onset of movement within him, and, as much as he wanted to finish and escape the sour, confined heat, the boy found it difficult to reckon how he could let so much of himself fall from his body and still emerge squinting, just minutes later, into bright sunlight to find that there was nothing of him missing, that he was still the same boy he'd been when he'd gone in. Now he closed his eyes tight, let his muscles go, and listened for the sick splash down below. Then he tore two pages from last year's almanac and wiped himself clean.

When he emerged into the fresh air, into a light so intense he had to clamp his eyes shut and stand blind for a few seconds against the white glare of it, he found his brother standing there, the old handmade picture frame in his hands. Stan stood looking out to the west, keeping watch for his father, and then he wiped the glass with his shirtfront and gave the photograph a look before handing it over to Karel.

"Be mindful with it," he said. "We'll have to get it back into Pop's room after lunch so he don't find it missing."

Back by the creek, the other boys pulled biscuits and bacon from their pails and sat with their feet in the cool push of water while they ate. Karel crouched in the shade beneath a pine tree, gazing at the mother he'd known only this way, as the two-dimensional woman standing in white, her fair hair smooth and long, falling back behind her shoulders, her wedding dress white and high necked, fringed with lace and beaded smartly about the bodice. Her shoulders square and strong, her legs long, her hips full and round and tapered up into her narrow waist. But it was her face that Karel sought, and though he had no words for it, he could imagine those bright eyes on him, softened by kindness. He could picture her hair falling over him as she knelt facing him, his face pressed into her while he said his prayers before bed, her lips brushing his forehead after she'd tucked him in. Looking at the photograph, it was all too easy to forget that she was one of two people in the image, that his father, too, stood in the frame, his dark suit crumpled and his starched collar buttoned to his Adam's apple. His face young and clean shaven, the sly hint of a smile on his lips. They stood together, her arm in his, and there was a stand of trees behind them, hazy and out of focus, that Karel didn't recognize. What Karel saw was only the woman, only his mother, and though he'd done so before, only to lapse into sadness and tears, he couldn't help himself: He tried to touch her. He put his fingers to her face, her ankles, her fancy dress, and what he felt was only the frame's glass, only the flat cool of her absence.

Then came the onset of an emptiness that, at three years old, he could already feel but not explain, and when he stood with the frame held loosely in his unsteady little hands, he walked without taking his eyes from the ground to where his brothers sat eating lunch at the edge of the water.

When their father found them, the damage had already been done. The boys had tried to remove the picture from the frame, but the water had crept between the photograph and the glass, adhering the two, and when they went to pull one from the other, the clarity of the image was lost to a broad gray smear that obscured both bridegroom and bride, rendering them both as sullied and indistinct as the trees behind them.

Now Vaclav stood over them with his hat in his hands, his face sun flushed and running with sweat. The three older boys were huddled around the ruined photograph, whispering accusations, and Karel was collapsed at the bank of the creek, his head buried in his out-flung arms, quivering with his crying, his tanned little hands clinging to the grass that grew in proud clumps right up to the water's edge.

"This don't look like chores or lunch, either one," Vaclav said. "Don't recall giving you boys permission to do anything else."

The boys rose, their eyes on the ground. Not one of them had been brave enough to stand with the evidence of their failure in his hands, and now their father stood chewing his tobacco and wiping perspiration from his forehead, shaking his head and gazing down at the boys' feet where the photograph and its dismantled frame lay in the grass.

"One of you little shitasses better start talking," he said.

Eddie and Thom moved together behind their older brother, and Stan avoided his father's eyes and glanced down at the picture frame, twisting his hands in the hem of his shirt, bouncing nervously on the balls of his feet. "Karel wanted to see it," he said.

"Well so did I, goddammit. Wanted to see it about a hundred times this morning, but I didn't leave my work to go get it, did I?"

"No, sir."

The man took a step forward and lifted the wet print from the ground, his eyes squinted and impassive and shot with blood the way they were sometimes when he came home from the icehouse of a Saturday evening and sat at the kitchen table drinking from a canning jar while the older boys played sheep and wolf or spoon before bed. "You going to stand there jittering like you're set to piss your britches, or do you reckon you can tell me why the thing's wet as a dish rag?"

Twisting his shirt tighter in his fists, Stan stopped his bouncing and willed himself to meet his father's gaze. "It went in the creek. Karel tripped over Thom's lunch bucket."

"And so it's his fault, is it?"

"No, sir. It ain't nobody's fault. Not really."

"The hell it ain't. There's nothing ever happens that ain't *some-*

141

body's fault. Even if it's God what made a mess of things, it's always someone to blame. And this time it ain't a three-year-old nor God nor a goddamn lunch bucket, boy. It's whoever took the thing out of my room without any business doing so. Now, who would that be?"

The boy turned his shirt hem loose all at once, and his mouth pinched at the corners as he took a step forward and a tear ran fast down his cheek and fell to the earth. The slightest of breezes played in the pine boughs overhead, and the boy's bottom lip quivered. "Don't strap me, Pop," he said. "Can't we fix it?"

His father put his hat back on his head and looked down at the wrecked image of his wedding day, and when he dropped the thing to the ground, watching as it floated and swayed on its way to the earth like a broad, fallen leaf, he ground his tobacco with his back teeth and then spat. And then he struck the boy square across the wet cheek with the flat of his hand.

Stan's hat flew from his head, and the boy crumpled beneath the blow, dropping to his knees and cupping his face in his hands. He was only down for a few seconds before willing himself to stand, biting his lip to keep from sobbing and looking his father in the eye the way he'd been taught.

"You're too old to strap," Vaclav said. "It ain't going to be that easy for you anymore."

Karel had righted himself on the bank of the creek. Leaf-thrown shadows played across his face, which was caked with dirt and tears and seized with a seriousness that, even for his father, seemed shamefully sad for such a young boy. Vaclav thought for a moment that he might go pull the boy from the creekside and take him into the cowbarn, let him sit there in the cool shade while they took their lunch, but his stomach was soured with anger and he thought about what he'd just told the oldest boy, about how there wasn't anything without blame or anyone blameless, either. He thought of Klara, of how light her body had been and how, even so, carrying her out of the house had been a burden he'd never be able fully to straighten

142

his back beneath. And then his mouth was flooded with saliva, and for a moment he thought he might be sick. His eyes began to water, and when he realized he was about to cry in front of his boys, he pushed the tobacco from between his teeth with his tongue, holding it in the hollow of his mouth while he bit the inside of his cheek hard enough to stop the tears. Then he sucked snot hard through his nose and spit a wad of tobacco-stained phlegm into the now-grassy silt where, twenty-some years before, creekwater had gurgled and surged downstream.

Before turning from the boys and walking back to the cropfields out west, where he would spend the rest of the day away from them, working without relief from sun or hunger or heartbreak, either one, he gave the older three each a sharp look in turn and said, "It ain't no fixing this, boys. She's ruined permanent. Now get back to your chores."

Vaclav took a deep breath through his cleared nose and called out to his youngest. "Karel," he said, "get on your feet, boy. Eat your lunch. And don't you dare shit your britches today, you hear me?"

The Blind Janus

DECEMBER 1924

OVERNIGHT, THE COLD had deepened, the mass of dry air descending as if to make amends all at once for the previous summer's heat, and before the sun was up, when it was yet a glowing, cloud-streaked promise of pale pink beyond the trees to the east, Karel Skala stood beside his truck in the yard of St. Mary's parish, smoking a cigarette and nursing a pain behind his eyes as surely as his wife, over beyond the cemetery in the old widow Vrana's house, was now nursing his child. He'd woken with his boots still on, aching about the shoulders and slumped forward in the overstuffed chair that sat in the corner of the widow's front room. Sophie had been sleeping still, propped up with pillows, the baby silent and swaddled on her chest, and the old woman stood over them, gazing down and sucking audibly at her own teeth, tucking the blankets around mother and child with her skeletal hands.

Karel rose to his feet with a groan, and Mrs. Vrana turned toward him slowly, less startled than expectant, her wispy brows raised to beg questions of him that he felt certain he wouldn't have been able to answer even had he known their content. When Sophie stirred, he told her that he had need to go check on the cattle. He didn't mention the Knedlik boys. Didn't mention the dream he'd had in which he'd arrived back at the farm to find everything in order, even improved, the fencewires strung taut and the Monitor windmill spinning productively and the cattle healthy and fat, ready for profitable slaughter, the entire operation running so smoothly that he'd recognized himself, at once, as wholly dispensable. No, he simply kissed his wife on the forehead and fetched his crumpled hat from the floor beside the chair where he'd slept. He gave the widow two dollars so she could purchase what she might need to provide for his wife and children, telling her that he'd be gone no more than two days, that he'd pay her well for her attentions when he returned, that he'd bring half a nice ham from his smokehouse, too.

Afterward, out in the churchyard, despite the cold, Karel's shirt was soured with perspiration, with the slow leaching of the previous night's beer and corn mash from his body. Across the way, the windows of Elizka's room above the store were dark, and he imagined her in there, lying awake in her bed, cursing him even more soundly than she had the night before. His stomach swirled, and he wished like hell there were somewhere nearby to take an early breakfast. As it was, he'd have to wait until he got back to Moulton, at least. He finished his cigarette, walked back behind the parish stable to relieve himself before the long drive home. When he unbuttoned his trousers to make water, dousing the thickly barked base of an old pecan tree, the smell all but knocked him over—not the diluted ammoniac odor of urine, but a biting, rank fermentation of his and Elizka's congress, the turned scent of her embittered by the hard musk of his own sweat. He finished, buttoned up, and when he made his way back to the truck and got the engine running, he gave his fingers a smell and recoiled, shaking his head and wiping his hand on his pant leg.

Well, hell, he thought, putting the truck into gear. I reckon that's about how fast a woman will turn sour on you.

Out on the road, without Sophie so big in the belly and wincing beside him, without the little one on his lap, he made better time than he had the day before, keeping the wheels in the ruts so that he hardly had to steer. After half an hour, the ride's vibrations and the crunch of gritty, hard-packed earth beneath the tires and the chilled rush of air through the window had all worked well to clear his senses so that now, with the horizon turning loose of the sun, he could sit easily in the brightening light of dawn and smoke a cigarette to mask the acrid, pasty taste of his own mouth. Ahead, the road ran straight out of the little swells of hills, and the miles of well-kept fencelines stretched out, glinting sunlight and shimmering with dew on either side. It was good country, broken black soil, cemented with just enough sand and clay to keep it all from washing away come a hard rain, and Karel thought what a fine fortune a man could make if the seasons wouldn't put an end each year to his industry, if he could take two or three harvests of cotton the same way he could get several cuts of hay.

At least there were other ways, if your spine didn't go soft at the thought of hard work or a risk worth taking, to turn a profit, and Karel smiled there in the cab of his truck, imagining the money he'd make at the cattle auction this spring, doing the arithmetic in his head, tallying his take on the feeder steers and young heifers alike. And then there was the beer, and the chance to outdo his brothers in the growing business of quenching the county's thirst. Karel had an unspoken arrangement with them, one born out of necessity, since he wouldn't exchange so much as a word with them if he could help doing so. He would run Spoetzl beer anywhere in Lavaca County, and he had customers as far north as the Fayette County line, as far-flung as Hallettsville and Yoakum and Moulton. Villaseñor and Karel's brothers did their business over in Gonzalez County, where their facility with Spanish made it easier for them to deal with the growing population of Mexicans off to the west.

Whenever he thought about it, he couldn't help but laugh, thinking that his brothers, born bohunks like all the best men of the surrounding counties, had actually learned to speak that nonsense. Over the years, because their work was so cheap, Karel had hired the same four families of Mexicans to pick his cotton, and they made for strong backs that never wilted in the September sun the way the darkies might. But they sure as fire didn't expect him to speak their language, and they got the hell off his property as

149

soon as the work was done and the pay in their pockets. That was one thing, but speaking Mexican yourself, sometimes even in your own house, and letting your kids speak it, no matter how pretty and brown their mother's skin — well, that was another thing altogether, akin somehow to sullying good polka music with something as silly as a goddamn banjo.

Twenty minutes shy of Shiner, Karel caught sight of a father and his boy in the near pastures just west of the road, walking hedgerows with their shotguns at the ready. His head was clearing, the crisp morning air working cool in his sinuses and numbing the pain behind his eyes, and he pulled the truck over and parked it in the roadside weeds and got out to stretch his legs while he watched the hunt. They were a good hundred yards out, working without a dog, kicking along the brown outcroppings of brush and chokeweed and immature trees as they walked toward the fenceline, the boy out front of his father, turning over his shoulder every now and again to take some whispered instruction from the man. A slight breeze leaned the field of short hay eastward, and Karel thought he'd have better sense than to teach a boy to hunt from upwind, even if it was just a matter of bobwhites. Sound traveled as surely as scent, and if a windward covey couldn't smell you coming, it could sure as hell hear you.

Still, these were days of a generous, ever-yielding landscape, days of bright red wagonloads of tomatoes come summertime, of railcars piled with maize and dimpled, rust-colored sweet potatoes, of dense bales of cotton and hay, of cattle herds that had been spared the foot-and-mouth outbreaks that had so plagued the panhandle way up north, of steers so plentiful that the slaughterhouse pens down county stayed full and the stench of the Yoakum tannery could water one's eyes from a half mile away. And so as much as Karel frowned upon the man's methods, he wasn't in the least bit surprised when a brace flushed low and with the wind, breaking and quartering to the south before the boy shouldered his gun. Karel felt the skin over his forearms prickle into gooseflesh, and when the birds were twenty-five yards beyond the barrel of the boy's gun, Karel found himself whispering, "*Now*. Take them *now*."

By the time the boy got off his errant first shot, the birds were quartering above the hedgerow some thirty-five yards off, the white feathers about their heads and beneath their wings shining like an invitation in the morning light. And then the boy fired again, dropping the trailing hen, its smooth flight stopped so abruptly, the little bird seeming leaden in its plummet toward the pasture, that Karel marveled at both the shot and its result. It was something so simple, something he'd seen hundreds of times in his life, but it was beautiful and hard to believe in a way that he likened to the onset of hard rain, to how astonishing it was that clouds could hold all that water inside and then, as if they'd been waiting for just the right occasion, turn it loose so suddenly, at once, and let it fall to the earth.

The leading bird flittered safely into the distance some forty yards from where the other had fallen, and, just as quickly as it had come up from its hunkering covert amid the hedgerow, it alighted and disappeared into the vast field of brittle hay. At dusk, if it could keep itself hidden from the predators circling overhead, it would find its way back to the covey. As if conducted by the wan light, the cocks would commence with their melodic beckoning, and all the day's dispersed survivors would reconvene. If the boy came out hunting tomorrow morning, he might have occasion to take another shot at this very same bird.

The father held a hand on the boy's shoulder now, shaking him playfully and then pointing out to where the bird had fallen, letting the boy sight down the length of his arm until they'd agreed upon where the bird had gone down. Karel lit a cigarette and thought, That ain't a half-bad shot, kid. Then he waved at the hunters, and, when he had their attention, he tipped his hat. Even from this far off, it was plain that the boy was beaming, and when Karel got back behind the wheel of his truck and steered it loudly back into the ruts in the center of the road, it struck him more fully than it had even last night, once he'd gotten his shirt on and found his way back through the thicket to the Vrana house, where he'd found the baby wrapped in a yellow cotton blanket and sucking softly at his mother, that he, too, had a son.

In the indistinct haze of his drunkenness and the meager lamp-light, the child had seemed unreal to him, even deformed, his little head hairless and tapered into such an unsettlingly sharp point that Karel's first instinct was to take a step backward. But Sophie's face was reassuring, even serene, flushed and beaded with the exertions of her labor, her eyes half-closed with exhaustion but still warm and attentive. She pulled the blanket back so that Karel could have a better look, stroked the baby's hollowed cheek with her thumb.

"It liked to kill me," she whispered. "But just *look,* Karel."

He'd come toward them then, conscious of the sourness of his breath and the unevenness of his steps, and when he sat on the side of the bed, Sophie moved her hand from the baby's face and gently took hold of Karel's wrist.

"He's all right, then?" he asked. "His head looks like its been whittled down near to nothing."

"He's perfect," she said, closing her eyes. "Just wait. He's perfect. You'll see."

Karel sat for a while, wanting to light a cigarette but knowing he oughtn't, watching until the child turned loose of the wet nipple and slept against it such that it dimpled his cheek. Without opening her eyes, Sophie pulled the blankets up close around her child, who twitched and sucked intermittently at air, dreaming already of the breast. Karel waited until Sophie's breathing grew heavy and slow, and then he rose as quietly as he could manage, his hand held on the side of the bed for balance. He moved to the chair in the corner, to the discomfort of hunched, seated sleep and unsettling dreams.

Now, on the road, Karel found that possibilities broke over him as coolly and continuously as did the wind working its way in through the truck's windows. He had his own boy now, one he'd be able, in time, to take out early of the morning, their guns in hand, their breath steaming in the cold air, their stomachs warm and full of coffee and Sophie's biscuits, their voices kept low and their steps careful and quiet as they worked through the tall grass that fringed the creekside trees of his property. He'd teach the boy to work from downwind, to swing his gun smoothly to his cheek with the first fluttering sounds of a covey's flush. And when their work together gave rise to a pair of low-quartering birds, Karel would hold his own gun across his waist and watch his boy do as he'd been taught. Afterward, when they resumed their hunt after retrieving the harvest, Karel would walk behind the boy and muss the kid's hair and smile at the sight of the four little twiglike legs sticking from the boy's coat pocket. And, by damn, wouldn't that be something?

Even before he had a clear sense of what he was doing, Karel was applying the brakes and pulling the truck over once more into the thick hem of weeds on the side of the road, remembering Sophie as she had been the first time he'd seen her, all that sunlit hair spilling from beneath her new straw hat with its wide brim and bright yellow band. It had been a week shy of her eighteenth birthday, and her father had brought her down with him to the cattle auction in Yoakum, hoping to surprise her afterward by buying her a new dress in Shiner before heading home. When Karel saw her there, so at ease among the livestock, so full of light but so obviously not to be taken lightly — scrutinizing, as she was, a promising lot of sturdy black heifers that bellowed and stirred up dust in the corral before her — he lit a cigarette and started the bidding a little higher than he otherwise might have. Here was a girl stout enough to shoulder more than simple housework and easy enough on the eyes to make a man stop to watch her while she did. She'd whispered to her father, glancing at Karel just before she had, and the man nodded at the auctioneer. After sweetening his offer twice more, only to be outbid each time, Karel flashed her father a smile and shook his head, then tipped his hat at the girl. Go on and take the damned cows, then, he thought. I got my sights set elsewhere.

Now, in the truck cab, he lit another cigarette, the last he had with him, and smiled as he blew smoke from his nose and nodded in approval of his own fine idea. He spun the wheel hard to the left, eased the truck out across the road in a wide U, and gave her more gas than he had to as he made his way back to Praha the way he'd come.

By the time he made it back, the small town was alive with the workaday business of its citizenry. He parked in the same spot beside the parish stables that he had left just over an hour before, and after he'd set the brake and worked his hand around inside his hat to tidy its shape, he fixed the thing on his head and made out across the lot and up the road to the Novotny store. Inside, Elizka sat behind the counter working figures in her ledger, a cup of coffee curling wisps of steam into the dark ringlets of her hair. She looked up with only her eyes, keeping her chin tucked down against the ruffled collar of her blouse. "I thought you'd gone," she said.

"I did. Just didn't stay gone long."

And now she raised her head and squared her jaw. "Might have been better for my disposition if you had, Karel."

Karel recalled the smell against which he'd recoiled before dawn. Even this early, with her hair strung in greasy curls from the perspiration of the night before, she was lovely. Her cheeks smooth and tan, a few freckles faint and alluring across the bridge of her slender nose. But this was a trip to Praha that he hadn't made for her, and he was restless now with the desire to see his offspring. "It's just some smoking tobacco I'm wanting," he said.

"Is that so?" she said, rising to her feet behind the counter and smoothing her skirts against the backs of her thighs. "It always is something you're after, now isn't it?" She squatted beneath the counter, and when she stood, she slid a pouch of Bull Durham toward Karel. "Twenty-five cents," she said.

Karel laughed without showing his teeth, weighing the pouch in his hand as he ran his thumb over the black label. "Two bits for tobacco?" he asked. "Is it something rare about it?"

She smiled now, twisted a curl of hair around her finger and looked down at the tobacco on the counter. "There's nothing common in this store, Mr. Skala. You come to Praha from now on, you better come prepared to pay dearly for your needs."

IN THE FRONT ROOM of the old widow Vrana's house, the reception was also one of astonishment, but in this case the surprise was unbridled by contempt and instead strung wide with smiles. Sophie was introducing the girls to their brother, pulling back the blanket so that Diane and Evie could sit on the edge of the bed and run their fingers down the wrinkled red skin of the infant's legs. The girls were wide-eyed in their excitement but they caressed the child gently, and Karel recognized in their comportment a greater comfort in the company of the newborn than he had ever felt when they had themselves been just hours or days in the world. Even little Evie seemed to understand that a well-enough intentioned touch of a loved one could be cause for pain, and with only a single, feathery finger, she traced her brother's leg from the dimpled knee down to the tiny curling toes. Karel stood in amazement of them, his hat still on his head, his eyes shifting from face to face, and when Mrs. Vrana came stiffly into the front room from the kitchen out back, she offered Karel a brusque nod and then shooed the girls from the room. "It's breakfast on the table, girls. Go eat while it's hot, and let me tend to mother now."

Karel helped Evie down from the bed, watching as the girls went barefoot across the worn floors toward the back of the house, and when he turned back toward his wife, Sophie blinked slowly and smiled at him. "We hadn't thought to see you today. Is it you forgot something?"

This was Sophie's way, to greet the uncommon kindness with a teasing question, and Karel had come to expect it with the same brand of anticipated relief as he felt when, after a long day of work and the night's last cup of coffee, he slid himself into bed to find waiting beneath the sheets the cool and calloused bottoms of her feet at work against the tired muscles of his calves. And the feeling that now surfaced in him was a cool one, too, but one that went to work at the hard center of him and swept the heat from his body, a late winter breeze that began in his bones and rustled out through tissue and sinew and muscle and blood to give rise, finally, to a welcomed chill and the gooseflesh it occasioned.

The widow took the baby from Sophie's arms, and his mother threw her hands out instinctively after him as he was lifted from her, this the startled reflex of a mother who's not yet grown accustomed to her child being without rather than within, of all those who have had to surrender from their bodies what they've suffered to bear and nourish, of those who must relinquish from the safe and hot and contracting centers of themselves those whom they long to hold so fearfully in their uncertain arms.

Karel took his hat from his head and tossed it onto the chair where he'd spent the night sleeping upright, then he held his hands out to old woman Vrana, who raised her wiry brows at him and set the child hesitantly in his father's arms. The child squirmed, throwing his arms around in the gesture of falling, kicking his little legs beneath the swaddling blanket, and Karel felt the warmth seep back into him, back into the muscle and marrow of him. "Forgot all manner of things," he said, and when he looked up from the child, Sophie was smiling at him as Mrs. Vrana went to work changing the rags between her legs. "But then I remembered," Karel said, and he pulled the child in close to his chest, marveling at how the whole of the boy was lighter in his arms than a suckling pig, at how the boy's head was already beginning to take its rounded shape, how the eyes were pale blue and unfocused and still intent on seeing what they couldn't just yet render clearly. Karel didn't marvel at the fact that he was doing for his boy, in this, the first full day of his life, what his father had never once done for him. It would occur to him only later, when the boy was older and asked questions about his grandfather, and when Karel realized how few of the answers he could resurrect from the graveyard of memories put so long before to rest.

The widow was still at work between Sophie's legs, and Karel kept his eyes averted while his wife winced.

"Well, Papa," Sophie said. "We going to just call him '*boy*,' or is it you've some other name in mind?"

Karel smiled, bounced gently on the balls of his feet as he watched the child in his arms. He shook his head and looked up at his wife. "I was only thinking girl names. Thought we'd have us a little Klara this time, after Mama."

Sophie's eyes softened and she looked at her hands, clasped as if in prayer atop the sheets. Then, as if she'd cheered herself abruptly with the memory of some childhood mischief, she threw her head back on the pillows and laughed until her body stiffened and she grimaced, sucking in air. When she'd collected herself, she widened her eyes at him and then she raised her brows lightheartedly. "I'm glad you came back, Karel. And so are the girls. It pleases everyone that you did. But if you name that boy Klara," she said, "his first word is liable to be an angry one."

COME THE FOLLOWING morning, on the outlying road just south of Shiner where the farm-to-market snaked away on its unpaved and meandering way toward Dalton, Karel pulled the truck into the drive of the new filling station that had been built by Old Man Kaspar for his nephew after the boy had proven himself unsuited to running figures or machines or much of anything else at the family's wire works. The cool air had persisted all of the previous day, and Mrs. Vrana, though she mostly avoided his eyes, had taken pains to ensure that Karel made himself properly clean for handling the infant. Within an hour of his arrival, she'd drawn him a hot bath out on the screened porch behind the kitchen and set to washing his shirt and underclothes, all of which had worked to refresh his body and obscure in his mind his latest indiscretions. After a half day of thought, he'd named his boy Frank, because it was a simple, solid name, and because it rang sound and plain and honest in his ears all at the same time without sounding weak. He liked the way the Ks stacked up between the two names, like two hard ridges in an otherwise smooth downhill ride, and as he pulled beside the petrol pump, he found himself silently mouthing the name: *Frank Skala . . . Frank Skala.*

Now Karel set the brake, retrieved his hat from the passenger seat, and stepped down from the truck. The clouds had cleared to the east to render the overhanging heavens a burnished blue, and Henry Kaspar stood waiting for him in a stiff straw hat trimmed in Yoakum leather and new overalls, the fabric of which was unblemished by grease stains or scuff marks or any other testaments to actual labor. As he had ever since he'd come of age enough to grow it, Henry wore an ambitiously waxed mustache that seemed to curl around the sides of his mouth like some invertebrate creature that had slithered through cold, congealed oil only to find itself mired on a simple man's face. At this, Karel didn't bother hiding his amusement. A man takes to wearing something that big hanging from his lip, he thought, he surely hangs short inside his britches.

Wiry and pale and almost comically bowlegged, Henry had knees that aimed out toward the peripheries of his sightlines even when he stood still, which he did whenever he had excuse to do so. After a nod, he set himself to pumping fuel into Karel's truck, working his tongue up under his top lip as if curious to see if the roots of his mustache had sprouted through the other side so that he might actually taste how much of a man he was. The biting, clean smell of petrol swirled in the air. He gave Karel a suspicious look, and then he smiled. "Heard you added another little one to the stable, Skala, and I congratulate you on that, I surely do. But just so you know, it's a limit on the free tickets to the picture show."

Karel stretched his legs and worked his boot around in the gravel, pretending to mull that over awhile. "Henry," he said, "it must get terrible lonesome out here on the outskirts of town with only a few folks passing through for a tankful each day. Am I right?"

The man wrinkled his brow, checked the pump gauge, then cocked his head. "We do a steady enough business, Skala, if that's what you mean."

"I ain't doubting that. What I mean is . . . Henry, do you ever find that you're talking to yourself?"

"Pardon?"

Karel laughed, and a gust of wind flipped his collar upright about the whiskers on his throat and sweetened the petrol-laden air with the scent of pecan and mesquite smoke from the smokehouses of farms out west of town. Henry Kaspar topped off the tank and levered the pump off and hung the nozzle back in its place.

"I would have thought by now," Karel said, "that if you spoke to yourself every now and again, you might have come to realize that you make about as much sense to a sensible man as a sermon does to soapstone. A man drives in for gasoline, and here you start up talking about the picture show? You understand my confusion."

Henry lowered his eyes and ran a thumb along the stiff brim of his hat. "I'd think you could find a way to make your point without being so sharp. It must be me who's confused. Given all the gas you bought of late, I just reckoned you were trying to milk us on the promotion. It was in the *Gazette*. For the grand opening? We're giving away a ticket to the picture show with every dollar in purchases."

"All the gas I bought of late? Hell, Henry, you ain't yet been open for business two weeks, and this is the first time I've stopped in."

Henry's shoulders buckled forward a bit with the muscular diminution of a man who's discovered he's been had, of a man who's folded the best hand to a sly bluff or bought some new mail-order tonic that tastes only and unmistakably of watered whiskey and doesn't help to move his bowels or ease his wife's monthly pains, either one. "Check the oil and water?" he asked, smoothing his mustache with his thumb and finger.

"They're fine," Karel said. "Checked the both of them before I headed out this morning."

"It's those hired hands of yours is what I mean, Skala. Couple twins a few years younger than me? Said they used to live around these parts back before Villaseñor bought up all that land. They've filled their truck two times and some fuel cans besides. Said they were tending your business and to put the gas on credit for you. They had your new trailer hitched to their truck, full load of hay strapped down tight with come-alongs, so I took them at their word."

"Hay?"

"Yessir. I reckoned you'd sold some bales and they meant to deliver them for you."

"And you didn't think to send someone to the house, asking was it okay?"

"Knew you wasn't home, Mr. Skala. Heard you'd asked the whole parish up in Praha to dance with their daughters while your wife was in her pains. Only thing I questioned was how these boys had a full load both coming and going."

Karel took his hat from his head, worked his hand around inside to reshape it. "That a fact?"

"It is. Like they'd gone out to sell bales that didn't pass muster and had to turn right around and bring it all back. The quiet one of the two looked to have found some trouble along the way, too. Back of his shirt was dried black with blood yesterday evening, and then they show up again bright and early today, and he looks none the worse for the wear. Just sits in the truck smoking without a grimace and reading the paper while his brother gets out to check the trailer hitch, and I pump some air into the tires and fill some fuel cans he had in the back of the truck. And then they head out on their way."

"Son of a bitch," Karel said. "Which way?"

And now even a man shortchanged in common sense like Henry Kaspar could tell he'd made some bad assumptions. "Looked to turn west just shy of town. Out Gonzales way, could be."

Shouldering past Henry, Karel climbed into the cab of his truck, his face flushed in wide red streams that ran hard down the ridge of his jawline to a confluence of flushed rage about the stubbled skin above his Adam's apple. "Rotten little shitasses," he whispered, and he levered the truck's throttle.

Henry took a startled step backward when the gears engaged and the truck shuddered on its chassis. "You want this on credit then, too?" he asked, his eyes looking off to the side of the truck as if something out on the horizon had been called to his attention by the insistent pointing of his outturned knee.

"That'll be fine," Karel said. "But keep two accounts. I aim to have them boys pay theirs separate."

In the days before Vaclav Skala's death, the drive from the farm-to-market road to the house had been a deeply rutted cause for concern. It ran, as it did now, between the forks of the creek, climbed a slight swell, dividing cotton fields from pastures, and put a good quarter mile between all that belonged to the Skalas and all that did not, between the outlying county road upon which Villaseñor's carriage had all those years ago appeared and the shelter of the house and the pear grove in which Karel had hunkered in his boyhood, watching as Graciela slipped from the stables and swung in the darkness onto her horse until she'd been stopped by surprise and gun barrels both; between where she'd been that night, with her hair falling over him smelling of honeycomb and oats, and where she was now, tending Thom and her children in a solid house afforded by the man who'd been just capable and sharp-witted enough to win the allegiance of another man's sons.

Nowadays, this was a fine road that ran narrow and sure and absolute in its demarcations, but before Karel's improvements it had been bare, hard-packed earth that often went to slurry, deeply pocked and corduroyed with fruitless furrows during the wet spring months such that it proved a torment to wheel spokes and boys' backsides alike. And so it was now that the level, graded earth overlaid with sand and gravel dredged from the Navidad River proved a daily source of pride for Karel. Of a normal day, his satisfaction bloomed within him as surely as the twin forks of Mustang Creek swelled during a deluge, providing a steady reminder of how natural and simple it was to render oneself, with only labor and diligence, straight backed and confident in a world overrun with men beaten down by their own ineptitude and softness — men like Henry Kaspar, the thought of whom leached from Karel the pleasure of riding this road, *his* road, and hearing the solid crunch of gravel grinding beneath the truck's tires.

Atop the swell, once he came round the outcropping of scrub and mesquite that made for a thorny hedgerow between meadows, the whole of the homestead came into view beneath the hard blue sky and a sun so white that it reminded Karel that the blazing thing was a star, just one of some all-but-infinite number. He eased on the brakes, pulled his pouch of tobacco from the breast pocket of his coat, and tugged the pouch's cinch-string tight with his teeth while his hands worked, as if through some half-surfaced memory made animate, to roll a cigarette while he looked at the bright star throwing pure light from the heavens onto his house and stable and smokehouse and barn. He startled with the realization: It was almost Christmas. It was almost Christmas, and he had the kids to think about, his new boy among them, and he'd need to get something nice for Sophie this year, maybe that new Delco-Light laundry machine he'd seen last month at Pavelka's Hardware in Yoakum. He sparked a match and lit his cigarette, exhaling slowly through his nose and squinting against the familiar sting of smoke as he released the brake and drove toward his barn, beside which was a lone rectangular patch of bare earth ringed by a weedy fringe that announced the absence of Karel's new trailer. Henry Kaspar might have been a fool, but he wasn't a liar.

Karel parked the truck out front of the swinging barn doors and again set the brake. Then he sat pulling on his cigarette, watching the smoke as it whirled in thick blue ribbons from his lips and nostrils through the open window and out into the expanse of light and wafting air, as if drawn by some whispered and enthralling promise of its own dissolution.

There was something to be taken from this, Karel thought. Something more than the work of the wind and the fleeting, ghostlike floating of smoke. Something more than the way a dime's share of tobacco that you'd had to spend two bits for turned, in two days' time, to something no more noteworthy than air. No, there was something else to it, Karel thought. There were things other than smoke, he reckoned, that ushered toward their own ends as if they willed it. People, too, some of them, and there was no telling but that these Knedlik boys might be just that sort. If they proved to be filching from him, Karel reckoned he'd have to give them what they must somehow have craved and render them as impermanent in the world as if he had taken them briefly into his lungs only to exhale them through his nose and mouth and watch as they whirled away and flew apart in the breeze until they were of no more consequence than a dry throat and the remaining trace of a pleasantly bitter taste on his tongue.

There was a reckoning of trouble to be found inside the barn, and the first of it was the brim-chipped bowl of blood left coagulating on the old workbench in the barn. The sight of it sank into him like some grainy weight that made him feel in his bowels as if he'd swallowed enough sand to flatten the rope of his guts down into compressed coils beneath his stomach. It wasn't the blood that unsettled him. He'd seen enough of that in his years, his own and others'; it was the sight of his mother's dishware atop the hand-hewn bench his father had made. When Karel was just a boy, his father would serve grits or oats for breakfast, and, while the boys ate, he'd stand watching, a cup of coffee steaming in his sun-chapped hands, and he'd never once failed to remind them to take care with their mother's dishes. After the only photograph of her was lost, the old man had become half-crazed with his protectiveness of the things that had been hers around the house. The dishes. The knitted blanket folded across the back of the wide oak rocker in the living room. The tiny cut-crystal bud vase on the kitchen windowsill into which Vaclav each year had placed the first bluebonnet he found sprung up in the pastures behind the stable. Now Karel seized himself against the downward pressure in his bowels and rubbed the dry skin along the curvature of his neck. He lifted the bowl carefully, hearing his father's admonishments as he did. Inside, a half-dozen beads of lead shot glinted gunmetal gray and smooth in the black tar of blood. Beside the bowl was a torn white shirt, soaked through with blood at the back of the shoulder and yellowed with dried sweat beneath the arms, its hem torn away in a wide strip from beneath the lowermost button around to the opposite buttonhole. On the workbench sat the tweezers and iodine bottle from the upstairs shaving cabinet. Karel picked the bowl up by the brim and tilted it in his hand, watched as the dark liquid oozed grudgingly to the lowered side while the shot stuck in the glue of dried blood at the bottom of the bowl. Not two days by themselves, Karel thought, and already someone's managed to get shot.

And then he looked up into the broad swath of overhead light falling on the hayloft, where the bales he kept so neatly stacked were now set haphazardly to the side in stacks of two or three, revealing the empty hollow where the kegs of Spoetzel pilsner had been. Karel returned the bowl gently to the bench and crossed the barn, climbing the ladder too quickly. When his boot sole slipped from a rung about halfway up, he caught himself with both hands, and his shin hit the rung below with the unforgiving sound of seasoned timber on bone. His mouth flooded with saliva and the pain flared into his hip bone. He cursed between his clenched teeth, got his foot up and found his purchase, then spat down into the hay forked over the floor. He went up the rest of the way in a staggered, half-lame fashion, moving one foot up and then shadowing it with the other so that, with every other step, his boots would come to rest side by side on a single rung. By the time he stood in the loft, the pain was only a stinging nuisance where the skin had been abraded along the flat ridge of his shinbone. Then he stood to prove to himself there above the earth what he had suspected with his feet on the ground:

They were all gone. All twenty-one kegs, and better than a dozen bales of hay with them. Karel sat on a bale and rolled up the leg of his trousers, trying to pry loose from the haze of his memory the drunken conversation he'd had with Raymond Knedlik two nights before. He knew they'd talked about the delivery to Hacek's icehouse in Moulton, and he knew from the past year's business that Hacek would never be good for more than six kegs at a time. That left fifteen reasons why Karel sat rubbing spit absentmindedly into the abrasion on his shin when there was a half-full bottle of iodine downstairs beside a bowl of another man's blood on the workbench, fifteen reasons why he pressed his thumb into the bruised blue flesh around the wound a good bit harder than he had to, hard enough to cause himself to wince and grind the worn crowns of his back teeth together while he thought about how best to find these boys. Wish the little son of a bitch would've been gut-shot instead of winged, he thought. They're young and their truck is new. It'd be easier to follow a wide trail of blood or the stink of a corpse, either one.

By the time he got his pant leg rolled down and descended the ladder, he'd made up his mind. He would check the livestock and the windmill. He'd make sure the cattletank was full, check to see there was hay and salt put out in the near pasture. He'd fetch his rifle from the house and head up to Moulton to have a talk with Hacek, and then, if he had to, he'd cross the county line into Gonzales and see if he could find these boys before someone else found them first and put holes in them that couldn't be mended with tweezers and iodine and bandages torn from a dirty shirt.

He went out the side door and headed between the barn and stable toward the pastures out back of the grove. To the southwest, in the flat field between the stable and the creekside hedgerow, Karel saw that one of the remaining heifers could no longer rightly be called such. And thankfully so. She stood with her head craned back to her unsteady offspring, licking the mottles of her calf's rust-colored hide with her wide pink tongue while the little one turned its head in sidelong suckling. Nearby, the ass rolled its

167

head and gamboled in clumsy circles around the cow and calf, keeping watch like a daft nursemaid, its ears standing forward and its dusty hide quivering. Rolling his sleeves one by one, Karel walked to the fenceline, took note of the windmill overhead, spinning lazily, as if in halfhearted submission to a stuttering breeze it deemed less than worthy of its full attention. Just the other side of the fence, the cattletank was full, the water clean and clear and shimmering beneath the bright skies, his discontented and unshaven face floating on the surface. Everything he saw seemed roughly in order, and still Karel felt the sour torsion of his guts, for it was what he didn't see that gave him pause. He lowered his hat and tilted its brim forward above his eyes as he scanned the outlying pasture, focusing on the hedgerows and mesquite outcroppings in search of movement. And then came a prickling twinge in his consciousness, the work of the inexplicable, all-but-insensate perception that had, on occasion, alerted him to the concerted focus of someone's eyes on his turned back from across a stretch of landscape or a loud and crowded barroom. He turned slowly, expecting someone to be standing behind him. Instead he saw, out east of the stable and barn, four turkey vultures perched on the topmost fence braces of the cattlepen, their faces red and squeezed deep with creases and hideous in their attention to the monstrous, two-headed mass that lay expired beneath them on its side in the sun-bleached hay.

Holy hell, Karel thought. If it ain't one thing, it's two. And then he went toward the mess of mother and child, toward the conjoined remains of cow and calf. Behind the stable, he pried the upturned horseshoe from the rusty nails driven into the framework of the rear door. He planted both feet and took aim at the vultures on the fence. He recalled the day his father had finished the siding of the stable, the way the man had swiped spent tobacco from his mouth and frowned at the suggestion of the boys that they hang the horseshoe there the way they'd seen on other stables, end-points up so the good luck couldn't spill out. He had scoffed at the boys' superstitions, but in the end he had relented. Now Karel, who had, until now, expurgated even this reminder of his father's occasional kindnesses, leaned back and threw the thing hard, watching as it turned end over end and bounced with a reverberating clang, just off its mark, against a fencepost near the hunchbacked birds. They lifted, all four of them, heavy and clumsy and in unison toward the sky, and by the time Karel made it to the pen and swung himself over the fence, the loathsome things were circling overhead with their white-fringed wings casting swirling shadows onto the ground as if their famished, anticipatory flight were some winding mechanism vital to the very turning of the earth.

Inside the pen, Karel removed his hat before he got wind of the animals' decay and placed it over his nose and mouth, breathing in the soured salt of his own musky sweat. The calf was facing south, its visible eye open and filmed with the wilted, chalky remnant of its mother's sac, its body lodged inside her up to the shoulders, its neck collared by the cracked and blistered leather that had once been the swollen and bloody flesh designed to yield what it had failed to yield, to rid itself of this young, animal burden. The heifer was on her side, one eye frozen wide and buzzing with gnats and flies. Karel pulled his hat from his face, gave the air a whiff, and, finding it yet spared a stench, settled the hat back atop his head. He spat at the ground and lit a cigarette, and then he walked around the perimeter of the pen while he smoked, his path moving counter to the revolutions of the vultures overhead, his eyes flitting now and again in perverse curiosity to the heifer he'd kicked out of anger and the unsettling, unnatural thing it had become in his absence.

Unbidden out of his aimless circling arose a thought of his mother.

He shook his head, trying to clear the image, trying to tell himself that he couldn't say why the thought had nested in his mind to begin with. But when he closed his eyes he saw it so clearly – his mother's body cold and blue, her legs splayed, the blond, tangled nest of pubic hair from which emerged, as if hatched from within, his own head and neck, his own pained face slicked with the film of

169

birth. And this was not the face of Karel as an infant, not one that wore the fatty, innocent consternation of the just born; instead, it was the face Karel had seen reflected in the cattletank, one with a day's growth shadowing its cheeks and chin and a jaw set with seasoned resentment. Inside this dead woman, Karel knew, the rest of his body was tucked and tethered and goosefleshed on account of the cold: his forearms softened by thick blond hair; his legs taut with the ribbons of his hamstrings; his solid, round knees held up obliquely against his chest; his slender feet with their yellowed, untrimmed toenails threatening to scrape away at the insides of the body that harbored him. Unmistakable as hunger or thirst, he felt the collapsed void of his lungs, the tightening around his throat, unrelenting and inflamed in its fleshy wet cordage below his Adam's apple, the angry, feminine constriction of a woman who might, even in death, strangle that which she was meant to expel.

Karel threw his eyes open, inhaling hard through his nose, and turned to face the sun while he leaned breathless against the nearest fencepost. He pushed the brim of his hat back above his hairline and forced himself to look unblinkingly into the white flare of the sun, holding it burning in his vision until tears hung glistening in fat beads from his lower lashes and fell onto the sharp ridges of his cheekbones, until he saw, when he closed his eyes, only the circular, phantom dancing of red lights cast against the flat black backdrop of his temporary blindness. Overhead, the vultures tilted their broad wings against the subtle wind. They would fly countless, lazy revolutions. They would not dizzy. They would not tire. They would outlast those who relied upon the living. They would wait.

TWENTY MILES to the northwest, the Knedlik twins reached the outskirts of Gonzales and the icehouse where things had gone so wrong the day before. Raymond drove, smoking a cigarette, and Joe rode silently as ever, reading the local newspaper and favoring the shoulder where, only a dozen hours before, lead had nested an inch beneath the pocked blue skin. It was full daylight, not the best time for what they had in mind, but it had taken the better part of the night and a good bit of whiskey and lanternlight to tweeze the shot from behind Joe's shoulder and get the rest of the beer loaded again into the truck and stacked over with bales of hay secured with cotton duck straps and come-alongs. As it was, they'd meant to hitch the dead heifer to the tractor and drag it out beyond the pasture to the creek, to save Karel Skala the sight and stink of it, but the sun had come up too fast, and they knew better than to dawdle. They might exact most of their revenge tonight beneath the guise of moonlit skies in Lavaca County, but there was a matter here in Gonzales that couldn't wait.

Raymond steered the truck past the slanted shotgun houses that fronted the road and fringed the fields just east of the railroad tracks. There was smoke coming up thinly from the stovepipes and the plain cedar siding was unpainted and warped such that the joints between planks looked each to be some irregular line on a map marking the parched bed of a stream that widened and narrowed along its horizontal path. Beyond the houses, a few Mexican sharecroppers were already out in the early sunlight doing God knows what this time of year, tending to their mules and tilling manure into the sad little garden plots set back of their houses. They looked beaten down and sunbaked even from a distance, and the way they hunched their shoulders against the bald sunlight on a cool morning was all the evidence Raymond Knedlik needed to shore up his lasting aversion to cropwork.

"Poor dumb bastards," he said, nodding out at the field. "Rather be gunshot than a Mexican or a farmer, either one. How's the shoulder?"

Lowering the paper, Joe turned to Raymond and offered a weak smile.

"Don't pain you enough to keep you from lighting a match, does it?"

Joe rolled his shoulder slowly around in the joint, the grin leveling on his lips to a squinting, concentrated expression that was neither smile nor frown. Then he lifted the newspaper to finish the latest serialization of "Judith of Blue Lake Ranch," which had been running the last two weeks in the *Gazette*. His brother ribbed him about his reading, but Joe had always rather read than speak, and besides, this story was a lively one about a horsefarm in northern California, hundreds of head of mustangs and saddlebreds both, and Joe figured he'd prefer to see in his mind the rolling hills of a ranch way out west than this same scrubgrass landscape he'd been living amidst all fourteen damned years of his life. Judith, too, he wouldn't mind seeing, and he wondered if there were women yet walking in the world with keen horse sense and big, pillowy bosoms both. In last week's installment, Judith had up and fired her ranch foreman, Bayne, who'd been robbing her blind, selling saddle-broke horses to Judith's well-to-do neighbor on the sly, and now Joe wanted to see how she'd fare without his help.

Joe liked the idea, as unlikely as it seemed, that a woman could make it on her own out in the scalded, dusty world of men who took their spurs off only to sleep or shit, and he thought how his mother would have turned out if she hadn't married Pa. He suspected she could have done better, and it didn't seem much of a sacrifice to him that he and Raymond wouldn't have been born if she had. She was a bright woman with a strong back and a comely enough figure. If she was hindered, it was only by her unwillingness to part from the literal word of the Good Book and from the conjugal expectations of her father. If she'd found enough room for doubt, enough hard will with which to entomb her selflessness in a cave sealed by a rock too heavy to be rolled away by the meddling or the miraculous, either one, she might have made off on her own, caught a train and gone west. She might have cooked her chicken and dumplings and pot roast and biscuits and tomato gravy at some outfit like the Blue Lake Ranch. She could have saved her pay and opened her own restaurant or saloon, taken men upstairs with her on her own terms at the end of the night. She could have gotten something out of the world instead of bringing a couple of boys into it too late to get them grown in time to save her.

"Put the goddamn paper down and keep a lookout," Raymond said, the scar on his face bending blanched across his cheek and down into the cracked hinge of his lips. "Remember, no shooting unless it can't be helped. And don't forget the rope."

Raymond turned the truck down a dirt road before town and followed it out beneath an overhang of mature oaks lining each side of the road until they reached the Drycreek Saloon where they'd met up with Karel's brother Thom the day before. So far as Joe could tell, there wasn't a creek anywhere nearby, but if there had been, he reckoned it had damn well gone dry.

It had been Raymond's idea to try to unload the remaining stockpile of Karel's beer here in Gonzales. He told Joe they might prove their salt this way, stake a claim to the part of the profits they'd been promised, make themselves indispensable with their initiative. They'd turn two weeks' take in a matter of days. The morning before, they'd done Karel's bidding first, delivering four kegs to Hacek's place in Moulton, moving four others to the icehouses and saloons up and down the rail lines in Weid and Sweet Home, but come lunchtime they still had thirteen barrels in the trailer, and even Raymond knew a trip to Hallettsville was out of the question. Sheriff Munson had taken a fall from the saddle the previous week, the slow encroachments of age and gout making him about as steady on horseback as a bullfrog on a barbed fencewire. He'd be staying put there in the county seat, and Raymond had it in his mind to do their business well beyond the law's reach.

After their conversation in Praha, where with breath that stank of sour pilsner and corn mash Karel had whispered his intentions, the twins knew what was expected of them. Karel had told Raymond that he had all the beer business in Yoakum and Shiner wrapped up tight with Kosmos's consent, that he'd made all those local deliveries the week before, that he'd get to them again just before the holidays when they were likely to need their stores replenished. For now, Karel needed only to keep the beer cool for a week or two and find buyers in the small towns. He'd double his profits if he could sell it all, he said, and he winked and lit a cigarette, offering one each to the boys as he steamed smoke from his nose into the cool night air. And if he did, he'd be more than happy to cut the boys in for a share.

The trouble had begun just a hundred yards down the dirt road the Knedlik boys now traveled, where Villaseñor and his sons by law had outfitted an old barn's loft with floor-to-ceiling hay-bale insulation and enough ice to keep the bootlegged Spoetzel beer cold even in the summertime. On the bottom floor, where once there'd been tack and farm tools and feed bins, they'd opened a saloon. Villaseñor, who grew ever more wary the farther west, and nearer to his old adopted home of Mexico, he got, had put the surliest of the Skala boys in charge of the Gonzales concern, and this was how it came to pass that, on the previous day, Raymond and Joe had come calling, trying to peddle beer to Thomàs Skala, who had fifty kegs of his own on ice upstairs, a loaded twelve-gauge behind the bar, and a merciless, motherless determination to keep fast all that he'd been granted.

To the Knedliks' right, out east, there was nothing but the blond stubble of cut hayfields, the earth gone glossy and dark after the week's rainfall. The saloon was housed in an old horsebarn, one that still had corral posts and a few fence braces rotting along its southern wall, the whole thing leaning on warped beams where the sandy soil had been swept from beneath the masonry piers by years of rainfall and erosion. Out back, a stable had been converted to house stockpiles of coal shipped in by rail. The saloon's siding curled with peeling paint the color of raw cotton, and Raymond steered the truck near the rear of the building, pulling forward and backing such that the trailer would sit broadside behind the sliding doors that had once led to the corrals. When he got the rig situated to his liking, he flicked his cigarette out the open window and set the brake. Climbing down from the cab, Raymond buttoned his vest and rolled his shirtsleeves up to the middle of his forearms as he took a look around. He knew the saloon didn't open until noon just as surely as he knew there was a tack and harness shop out front across the road. From this vantage point behind the saloon, there was nothing in sight and nobody around to take note of them. Nothing but the adjoining hayfields and the barn and granary of the neighboring farm. Raymond pulled his new Smith and Wesson .32 from the seat of the truck and tucked it into the waistband of his trousers so that he could feel the cool of its walnut grips against the knuckles of his spine. He reached around with both hands to see that his vest fell flat in back to conceal the butt. Joe pulled his lever-action Winchester from behind the seat and swung the cab door closed with his foot. Then he lifted the coil of rope from beside the full gas cans in the truck bed and put his arm through the center of it so he could balance the weight on his good shoulder and still keep both hands on the rifle.

The air was still and cool, smelling faintly of coal dust, and the sun hastened its light unobstructed down through the cloudless sky. If it were summer, Raymond knew, he'd have already sweated through his underclothes and shirt, and he was thankful for the cool, as was Joe, who had, as it was, more than enough heat burning beneath the bandages wrapping his wounds. "All set then, brother?" Raymond said. "Let's see is it anybody here what needs tying up."

Joe nodded, but before he took a step toward the saloon's back door, he glanced at the newspaper folded on the dash of the truck. He hadn't finished the serial, and Judith was all dressed up in white boots and a yellow dress, fixing to visit her nearest neighbor who'd been recently widowed. Together, they had over eight hundred acres and just as many broken horses as wild ones. Joe reckoned most readers would want Judith to fall sweetly in love and get married and live a comfortable life as the wife of the neighboring rancher. Most folks wouldn't mind that he'd been buying stolen horses from the wily foreman she'd had to cut loose, but Joe couldn't bring himself to cotton to the possibility of such a wrong given a spit shine and thereafter accepted as right. You could rub a dry turd with a whole can of linseed oil, after all, and all you'd end up with was a mess of shiny shit. As for Joe, he wanted Judith to do the man some fashion of harm, to break his fool heart or swindle him for part of his landholdings and even the score. To bat her eyes at him over coffee while she kept her shawl wrapped tight across her shoulders so he couldn't see the flash of pale skin that glistened there in the hollow of her throat, anything that would cause him even a hot twinge of unsatisfied longing.

Either way, this was no time for reading. He'd have to wait and see. Joe coughed up phlegm and felt pain sear in the stricken meat behind his shoulder. Then he levered a cartridge into the rifle's receiver and followed his brother, who was already trying the back door of the saloon.

KAREL DECIDED to leave the heifer there to rot. He'd have the boys deal with it when he found them, and it warmed his cheeks to imagine what it would look like, the boys hitching the thing behind its front legs with cinched rope, the jerk of the tractor when they released the clutch, the irregular wake the thing would make in the short pasture grass as they dragged it out toward the creek where they could set it afire with kerosene or leave it there to decay beneath the work of sun and wind and vultures and time. He thought it might make for fine amusement to sit on the fence near the cattle-tank, smoking a cigarette and sipping coffee while the boys worked beneath his gaze, while they broke a sweat even in the cool December air. He envisioned the calf coming loose halfway across the pasture, sliding sick and foul from the dead heifer's cavity and giving the twins twice the job to do.

He'd teach these boys more than one thing, and he'd do it soon, and with the tight smile of his imaginings pinching the bridge of his nose, he went to fetch his gun from the house. Inside, there was still the faint trace of sweetness in the air, a hint that the last food to be pulled from the oven had been Sophie's kolaches two days before. In the sink, a single cup. On the table, another sat half full of cold black coffee atop a stack of currency and a page torn from the newspaper with a note scrawled in a childish hand in the margins. *For the trailer,* it read, *and the beer. Can't linger.*

Karel remembered his father's words after he'd hit Stan that day near the creek, words that he'd since coupled in his mind with his understanding of the difference between the trouble that befalls boys and that which comes to call on men. *It ain't going to be that easy for you anymore.* So help me, it ain't, Karel thought. Besides which, what about the gasoline? What about the damned cow? He crumpled the paper and the bills and stuffed them together in his pocket, then he fetched his gun and a handful of cartridges and made his way out to the truck.

As EXPECTED, the door was bolted, and Raymond jerked his head to the side, indicating the northern side of the building. The brothers moved warily around the corner of the saloon and made their way in the shadows to peer into the dusty, double-hung windows. Inside, there stretched a long bar of unfinished pine. Three tables were set with four chairs apiece for cards and dominoes and the swapping of lies, a scalloped glass ashtray in the center of each. Between tables and near the front door, spittoons stood at the ready while, overhead, plywood signs had been affixed unevenly to the rafters beneath the loft. In painted lettering that slanted and curled with enough flourish to indicate the work of a woman's hand, they advised against gambling and the use of foul language. Beside the bar, which was fronted with stools made of sectioned logs, rawhide nailed atop the cross sections, was a long vertical slateboard with prices written in chalk. Above the slate, a tin Coca-Cola sign had rusted through at one corner's nail hole and hung askance from the other. Just the sight of it made Raymond thirsty. At just shy of fifteen, hairless though he was about the chin and chest, he would never admit it, would never drink anything other than beer or whiskey in the company of men whose whiskers had already come in, but *oh*, how he preferred the fizzing thick sweetness of a cold Coca-Cola to damn near anything, clear winter well water and his mother's sweet tea not excepted.

He tried the window, leaning into it such that a long ribbon of peeled paint came loose of the window's latticework and stuck to his palm, and then he caught his brother's eye and shrugged. He pulled his gun from the back of his pants and held it by the barrel, averting his eyes when he reared back and crashed the etched walnut butt through the pane just above the window latch. The sound was one of china hurled against a wall, and for a moment Raymond saw the twisted, fire-eyed snarl of his father come home from a different saloon some twenty miles from this one and many months ago. Joe stepped away from the shadows cast by the old barn's eaves and gave a glance toward the street out front. He shook his head, and Raymond went to work clearing the shattered shards of glass with his gun barrel until there was room enough to slide a hand safely inside to free the latch and lift the window. He tucked the revolver back into his waistband, brushed a few glinting splinters of glass from the shoulders of his vest, and then he hoisted himself up and in through the window with a grunt.

After he'd had a look to make sure he was alone inside, he threw the bolt of the sliding door, gave it a heave on its squealing rollers, and Joe joined him inside and set his gun against the back wall and surveyed the loft ladder that rose against the back wall to a closed trapdoor. Dropping the rope to the floor at his feet, he turned to his brother, indicating his shoulder, and Raymond shook his head there amidst the smells of coal dust and old tobacco spit and spilled beer. Then he crossed the room and shrugged the coil of rope onto his own shoulder and made the ascent in smoothly measured steps. When he pushed the trapdoor open, the cold air fell from above like the settling of an invisible fog that made it feel as if everything his skin contained had leached to jockey for position just beneath the skin, leaving the rest just a hollow strutted and braced by his bones. Inside, there were kegs stacked three high around a column of ice. The floor was sawdust that had mixed with just enough water to make it adhere to his boots. Against every wall, square bales of hay reached to the ceiling. In the corners, more two-foot blocks of ice stacked three high. Overhead, there were three slave-driven fans spinning lazily from the rafters, the metal fasteners of their leather drive belts clicking over their sheaves in regular, reassuring intervals. The room was so cold that Raymond's back teeth ached. These is some crafty sonsabitches, he thought, rolling one of the outermost kegs toward the trapdoor and working a cinch knot into the rope. He looped the rope one turn around the topmost loft ladder rung to act as a makeshift pulley and safety all in one, and then he got the first barrel lassoed and looked down through the trapdoor to find his brother below, waiting with his rifle in his hands and his eyes fixed on the back door. Raymond whistled softly and his brother looked up to find the first keg of beer descending from the hole in the ceiling, the rope humming its braided hymn to friction against the topmost rung of the ladder.

Thirty minutes later, they had ten kegs set sidelong atop the whole stretch of the bar, another centered on each table, and eight others hidden beneath hay and strapped down in the trailer. The exertion had reopened Joe's wounds, and just above his collarbone his shirt stuck fast with blood to the bandages beneath it. Raymond took notice and asked after him with his eyes. Joe shrugged, if only with one shoulder, and then they went to work in earnest, uncorking the barrels until all along the bar and from each of the tables there gurgled amber spills of pilsner. When they'd finished, Joe stood at the back door with his rifle while Raymond removed his hat and knelt down at the nearest end of the bar so he could take a long draught from one of the opened kegs. It fell in a pulsing stream, like a blood spurt or milk sprayed from an udder that was pulled and released by a palsied hand, and when he stood, Raymond's dark curls were drenched and he was blinking the stuff from his eyes. He smiled so that his teeth, yellow but straight, were visible to the gum lines, and Joe had seen this smile only once in the last year, when they'd stood out in the pasture lit by a full moon and the roaring blaze of the house fire they'd kindled with kerosene-soaked curtains in the front room of their father's house.

Raymond leaned forward at the waist and shook his head playfully, a dog come up wet after a deep drink from a rushing creek. "They brew a damned good beer in Shiner, brother," he said, stomping a boot down for emphasis. "I hope these here floorboards is thirsty."

By QUARTER OF eleven, Karel had made the trip to Hacek's in Moulton and found, parked between the train tracks and the storefront, the unmistakable new black Packard of Guillermo Villaseñor, the paint throwing sunlight from its polished surface like the oiled, blued receiver of a fine rifle. Karel's skin went tight around his muscles, and he pulled his pouch of tobacco from his breast pocket and rolled a cigarette to calm his nerves. He sat smoking in the cab of the truck for a long minute before swinging the door open and climbing out, hitching his trousers up and pulling his hat down low over his hairline. The town, less than half the size of Shiner, had been erected in one long row of raised storefronts along the rail line as if its founders, with transient hearts and foresight, expected one day, when a train was made that could bear the load, to roll the whole town broadside onto flat railcars and haul it to some other, more fitting, location.

Between Hacek's place and the nearby dry-goods store stood padlocked rows of slope-roofed bins in which the old man kept the coal shipped in from upstate by rail. From the telephone lines strung parallel to the storefronts, crows gave voice to their grating complaints. There were townsfolk out, walking between stores on the piered pine decking and airing themselves out front of the barbershop and the green grocer's.

Karel tipped his hat to a woman making her way from the barbershop past the icehouse with a young boy in tow, his hair cropped short and parted with a wet comb in a fine straight line over one ear. The woman nodded, pulling the boy along none too gently by his outstretched arm, and Karel remembered the cold fear of being a boy set atop a board laid over the arms of a barber's chair, of the sick smell of hair tonic mixed with the minty scent of hot shaving soap, of the swishing sound of the push broom's bristles on the hard-planked floor. He wondered how old his boy would have to be before he'd need to be taken to Wasek's shop in Dalton for his first haircut. Then he ground his cigarette beneath the toe of his boot and reached for the doorknob of Hacek's icehouse. He told himself to quit worrying over the had-beens and the would-bes and set his mind instead to the business at hand.

Inside, dust hung in the wide slants of light from the front windows, and Villaseñor stood flanked by his two men, who went hatless as children but wore their graying hair slicked back in the fashion of their master. Deep wrinkles stretched from the corners of their eyes. They hadn't missed any meals, and their smooth leather vests bulged out above their rifles, which were held, as ever, across their bodies waist high. Villaseñor leaned against the bar, his hat in his hands, his spectacles low on his prominent nose, and when the bell over the door signaled Karel's arrival, he turned from his conversation and, with a bemused, curious arc of his brows, buttoned his suitcoat and turned back toward Weldon Hacek, who'd found a rag and now busied himself with the nervous work of buffing from the gleaming bar top some blemishes of his own imagination.

Karel stopped just inside the door, made to remove his hat but then, thinking twice of it, left it on and made a show of rolling another cigarette and putting a match to it. He exhaled through his nose and crossed the room with the cigarette smoking between his lips, leaned over against the cant of his neck until his hat brim touched the bar and Hacek had no choice but to meet his eyes. "How about you draw me a beer," Karel said. "You ain't run out of pilsner, now have you?"

Hacek stopped mopping the bar, fetched a glass from the shelf on the back wall and tilted it beneath a tap. The man had a reputation for tasting his inventory at regular intervals, and his nose was a pocked and swollen bulb that hung with such a profusion of brown hairs that they appeared to be the tangled source of the thick mustache that hid the better half of his upper lip. "Was near out after last weekend," he said, sliding the glass toward Karel, "but this here is from a fresh drum I just took delivery of yesterday morning."

"Come by way of a couple boys towing my trailer, did it?"

"Matter of fact," Hacek said.

Villaseñor cleared his throat, set his hat on the bar and removed his spectacles, the lenses of which he studied with a frown before cleaning them with a pressed white handkerchief pulled from his breast pocket. "Well now," he said, keeping his eyes on his work, "if it's a new barrel, then let's all have a taste, shall we? Draw one for yourself, too, Weldon." He pulled a thick bundle of banknotes from his trouser pocket, pulled two dollars from the fold, placed them on the bar with the flat of his hand.

Karel noticed that, after all these years, the man still wore a silver wedding band. "On a first-name basis, are we now, Hacek?"

The shop owner retrieved four more glasses and commenced filling them while Karel tasted his and felt the cool tingle of the froth on his lips. He pulled on his cigarette and flicked the ashes onto the floor while he watched Hacek pour and set the glasses in front of Villaseñor and his men. The latter leaned their guns against the front of the bar and put their hands around the glasses, but they did not drink. Instead, they waited for their boss's prompting, and by the time Hacek filled his own glass, Karel had let the informality of the Mexican's address do its work on him. When Hacek turned all at once to face his vendors and customers, Karel held a finger up before the man could drink while he drained his own glass in one draught. "I do believe I'll have another," he said. "Long as my brothers' keeper here is paying."

"It would be my pleasure," said Villaseñor, holding his spectacles up to the light from the windows before putting them back on. "I was just telling Weldon here that I'd like very much to give you far more than a beer. You're the uncle of my grandchildren, after all, though they barely know you by sight. It's a shame, but it's true." He waited until Hacek put a new glass in front of Karel, nodded to his men, and they all drank together, excepting Karel, who let his glass sit untouched on the bar. "Anyway, as I was saying, Skala, it might be better for everyone if I paid you off your share of the Spoetzel concern. Especially if you insist on hiring boys without manners to tend to your business in your absence. My son-in-law tells me he had to put some birdshot into one of them yesterday. Said they came into our store out in Gonzales trying to unload some kegs and didn't like the reception they got."

"Shit," said Karel. "If you still got Thom running that place, ain't anybody likely to take a shine to the welcome he rolls out. Or have Graciela's better graces softened his temperament same as they stiffen his pecker? How many little half-breed nieces and nephews do I have, anyway? I can't keep track."

If Villaseñor took offense, he didn't show it. He squared his shoulders over his polished black shoes, let out a sigh that seemed occasioned more by relaxation than impatience, and took another sip of his beer. When he set the glass back on the bar, he spun it slowly in the condensation of its own making. Then he smiled at his men and winked at Weldon Hacek. "I was afraid you'd fail to see the sense in a buyout. But no matter. The offer was only courtesy, really. I've spoken with Kosmos. Called on him last night at his home. What a fine wife he has, too. Have you had occasion to dine with them? A woman with a proper sensibility and impeccable taste. We sat in the parlor after our meal and shared some brandy, enjoyed a couple of top-rate cigars I brought with me, and by the time I'd taken my leave, we had come to an agreement that is . . . well, that is somewhat exclusive." He lifted his glass, studied the

186

ring of water it left there on the polished bar, and then he set it back in the same spot and began spinning it in the opposite direction. He looked up only with the corner of his eye, and Karel forced a bemused grin. "Then, just now before you arrived, I shook hands with Weldon here and agreed to take his business at fifty cents per barrel less than you've been charging him, and to deliver it upon demand rather than merely twice per month. I have several trucks, of course. It's all the same to me. And, as a matter of course, I sent Stan and Eduard down to Yoakum this morning, and I trust they are making the same offer to some of your other overcharged customers." The man smiled now, but his eyes didn't shine. They remained dull and black and entirely unamused. "You see, Karel, you can't really expect me to respect our arrangement and keep my business out west so long as you're sending children who carry firearms and make threats into my very own store, now can you?"

Karel took a slow drink and dropped his cigarette to the floor, letting it burn there at his feet without stepping on it. A dry, leathery tightness had begun to creep into the tendons of his neck, one that he recognized as having nothing to do with the cool weather, and he would have sworn it was contracting such that his ear was nearer his shoulder than normal. "If them boys have been out Gonzales way," he said, "they done it on their own. I told them only to make my deliveries here in Moulton, and to call on some others between here and Shiner. Nothing more."

Villaseñor finished his beer, took his hat from the bar, and nodded to his men. They followed suit, setting their empty glasses aside and retrieving their guns before crossing the room to flank the door. "Well, they did a fair bit more than that, it would seem. Spat on the floor of my saloon, one of them did, and used foul language. If you can't trust the men you hire, Skala, then you either hired the wrong men or you didn't make it well enough worth their while to do as you said. Either way, you carry the blame." He nodded, and one of his men opened the door, tinkling the bell overhead. "Do yourself a favor," he said. "Cut those boys loose so you don't end up having to send word to their mother that they've found an early way into the ground doing your bidding."

"They ain't got a mother," Karel said. "And I didn't come here wanting advice."

"You'd do well to take it all the same. Mind your business while you still have some left to mind," Villaseñor said, and then he settled his hat in its place and took his leave.

MEANWHILE, WHEN THE Knedlik twins slid open the back door of the Drycreek Saloon, they found Thomàs Skala perched in the trailer atop one of the square bales, his hat set beside him and his shotgun in his lap, his blond curls catching sunlight and blowing about his ears in a burgeoning wind. They hadn't heard the engine of his truck, which was nowhere in sight. Raymond cursed himself for parking right out in the open, visible from a good distance up the road, where he supposed now that Thom had pulled over and come the rest of the way quietly on foot.

"Good morning, ladies," he called out. "If I'd meant for folks to come up and help themselves to my wares while I'm away, I'd of left a trough full of beer out here in the yard with a canning jar set next to it for customers to drop their nickels in."

Joe ran his thumb over the safety of his gun, making sure it wasn't engaged, keeping his eyes on Thom all the while. Raymond combed a hand through his wet hair and hooked the thumb of the other into the front pocket of his trousers and laughed. "Might should have done that," he said, turning the side of his face to the sun. "Would've saved us the trouble of breaking your window. Broken glass is dangerous, you know. Got me a scar what proves it." Toeing the damp earth sprung through with weeds, Raymond noted the reassuring cool of his pistol against his spine. "It's going to be a rough ride on the back of that trailer. But we'll gladly give you a lift if you're needing one."

Thom nodded as if in appreciation of the boy's wit, and Joe looked the man over slowly. As it had been the day before, his face was cleanly shaven, his back straight and his shoulders squared over his hips, his neck cocked sickly to one side in a way that Joe found to be even more disconcerting than it had been when he'd first met Karel. With the latter, there was a telling, uncompromising plainness to both his appearance and his movements, as if he'd been cast unembellished at birth and couldn't be bothered with betterment. Karel's eyes had gazed, even in the dark of night, with a spare intensity that revealed little if anything of his intentions, and he looked deliberately unkempt, his toughness and humor evident in the way he carried himself and wore his clothes, something askew from hatband to boot heels, and in this way, for him, his warped neck seemed all of a piece. But here was a man with a starched collar and an unwrinkled vest, a polished man with polished boots, a man who wore the makings of a grin on a face that looked like it had been hot toweled and lathered and rid of its whiskers no more than an hour before. Just looking at him, Joe swore he could smell soap. Here was a man who fashioned himself so as to obscure his unsightly twin imperfections, the two top teeth folded back like someone had taken a hammer to them, and then there was that neck, bowed over like a fern blade weighted with dew.

Raymond noticed this, too, had noticed it the day before, when the thought that there was more than one man in the world wearing this affliction opened a damper in his chest and put a red glow to the coals of his kindled anger. Now he freed his thumb from his pocket and traced the jagged scar tissue that fell away into the corner of his mouth as if he'd been made to eat the tail end of the wound he'd sustained. As if the wound itself, then, had for a while sustained him. And then he took note of his brother, the round stains of dried blood showing dull and dark as well-handled pennies through the cotton fabric of his shirt.

"Tell you what, girls," Thom said. "You go ahead and drive off and I'll sit right here, and we'll see if this trailer comes with you or not. I been having a long talk with it out here while you were lost inside my establishment, trying to find your way out, and it told me it didn't like the recent company it's been keeping. It's a Christian trailer, it turns out, and can't cotton to all the sinning it's been drawn into of late. I reckon it might like to stay right here among more honorable, God-fearing folk."

"That so?" said Raymond, his hand still at the corner of his mouth.

"I believe it is. Also, I unhitched it from your truck and let the air out of the tires on the other side. So there's that to consider."

Raymond scanned the trailer, saw that it was so, that it leaned gently back and away from where he stood, that the hitch bolt had been removed and lay, missing its nut, on the shaded bare earth beneath the truck. He swallowed his bitterness along with the souring taste of beer that remained on his tongue. "We been considering a few things ourselves. Spent the better part of the night considering how birdshot finds its way out of your gun when someone turns their back on you."

"And so you came right on back for more, did you? It's even mice that learn, when they lose a tail, not to go sniffing too close to easy cheese. I'm a better shot than to have missed what I aimed at. If I'd of wanted your little sister there dead, he'd of been heaped over with dirt before sundown. A man's got to make his expectations clear. I can't have every sharecropper in town thinking he can come into my place and spit on the floor like what you done. There's spittoons enough in there for whatever tastes too bad to swallow."

"And that's that? You shoot a man because his brother spit on your floor, but now you're just going to teach us this lesson here by stealing our trailer. What's to keep your gun in your lap while we drive away?"

"I had a peek under the hay," Thom said. "And through the side window, too, while you were having your fun. It's you who's been doing the stealing, and I'd call the law if I thought he'd be amused by a mess of real beer being sold around his county. What I get for the trailer will make up for what you've drained onto my floor in there. We'll call it a fair swap, and as long as me or my brothers don't see you anywhere near our property again, then I can go back to selling beer instead of mopping it off the floor and wasting bird-shot."

"How many brothers you got?"

Thom squinted against the sun, and he put his hat back on his head while a gust of wind blew a few loose straws of hay from the bales around him. "It's three of us," he said, "that we claim."

"What if I told you that trailer don't belong to us? That it's on loan to us from the one you don't claim?"

Thom caught a laugh halfway up his throat and squeezed it off. He nodded once. "I'd say you're right about it not belonging to you. It belongs to me. And I'd say a man can count his brothers however he damn well pleases, and that you might should get that truck running and git while your brother still has one left to count himself."

Raymond turned to Joe, pointing at himself and jerking his head toward the truck, and his brother stood with his rifle at the ready. Raymond strode over and got the engine cranked while the wind came up again in a hard gust that seemed both dishonest and point-less without any clouds in the sky to be blown about. When the en-gine fired, Raymond worked the choke and throttle, and exhaust came coughing up from beneath the bed and floated back over the trailer. Thom Skala rose from his seat on the trailer, lifting the stock of his gun up to his shoulder but keeping the barrel down and away from Joe.

Raymond swung the truck wide out to the side of the old barn and circled back around, reaching over while he drove to open the passenger door for his brother before pulling alongside him. Joe slid his rifle behind the seats and climbed in, reaching for the news-paper on the dash before slamming the door shut behind him. And then the truck jerked with the release of the brake, and Raymond Knedlik pulled forward for one last word with the man who made him burn, two days straight, with the knowledge that he'd been out-witted and outtalked, both. "It's going to be a hot one tonight, I'm guessing," he said. "You try to keep cool, now."

Thom fingered the trigger of his gun, the idle caress of a man who's managed to make his point without having to make it loudly. It felt to him better now than it had to have taken aim and executed his shot so well the day before, measuring the distance and the breadth of his shot pattern so he could pop the boy with a few beads while he walked out to his truck, so he could do just enough harm to send a clear and stinging message. And still, it hadn't worked, or it hadn't for long. Maybe this wouldn't either. Who knew? He wondered what had possessed Karel that he'd hire them to do his bidding. These boys were clearly half a head shy on horse sense. After all, the wind had come up again, and out of the northwest, carrying a chill that was as trustworthy a sign as a green, hailstone sky in September. "You need to check the date on your almanac, son. It'll be cold enough to light the woodstove tonight."

"We'll see," Raymond said, winking and clicking his tongue. "Never can tell about the weather, though, and I'm guessing it'll be too hot for good sleeping."

The other boy turned his attention away from the conversation, opened the newspaper and commenced reading. The engine stuttered and then caught with a gray cough of exhaust. While they drove away, Thom stood watching for a while until the truck was clear of his own and out of sight. He had work to do, and a lot of it, the little sons of bitches. The wind came up again and played violently in the upper branches of the old oaks across the road. They were in for some weather, sure enough.

AFTER A LONG DAY in the truck spent chasing those whom he hadn't been able to catch, Karel made it home just before dusk. He propped his gun in the corner of the kitchen, filled the coffee pot with water and grounds and settled it on the stove to brew. In the course of the morning and afternoon, he'd driven to Moulton and Weid, out west to Gonzales, and back home to Dalton by way of Shiner. No one he'd spoken to had seen the Knedlik boys since the day before, when, according to a boy working at the feedstore in Gonzales, the quiet one had been winged with shot as he walked unarmed to his truck out back of the saloon, but it was the sight of the man to whom he hadn't spoken—his brother Thomàs, decked out in his fine vest and shined shoes—that worked cold and sickening in his blood like a kind of distemper. He halved a sweet roll that Sophie had baked two days before from the leftover scraps of kolache dough and folded each half around a fatty hunk of the cured ham he'd brought in from the smokehouse. He ate standing up, wiped his hands on his trousers, scraped a chair back from the kitchen table and took a seat. After rolling cigarettes mindlessly until his case was full, he cinched the pouch of tobacco closed and sat smoking, listening to the growing wind wheeze through the window screens until the smell of coffee brought him again to his feet. He took a cup from the drain board, poured it half-full, then topped it off with whiskey from the jug of mash he kept in the cabinet over

194

the sink and went to sit on the back steps facing the grove while he drank.

It was uncommon, such a wind without even a trace of clouds to diffuse the pink glow of the sunset. Back when he was a boy, there'd been a comfort to the approach of weather come evening time, to the way you could know that something was on the way without quite knowing what. It might blow, it might rain, it might well do both. Depending on the season, there might fall a clatter of hail until it sounded from inside the barn or stable as if there were men doing roof work overhead.

Most often, whether anything dropped from the sky or not, Karel had busied himself in those sunset hours with work about the stables. He'd fill the lanterns with oil so he could leave them lit overnight. He'd muck the stables and shoulder a new bale over in front of the stall doors and break it open there so he could fork it quickly into the stalls. There were extra oats for Whiskey, who could get skittish when the wind blew and he was cooped up inside. Ride him out in a thunderstorm, as Karel had so many times when dark skies slid in fast from the west and caught him too far from home to outride the clouds, and the horse would switch his tail and whinny happily and never break stride. He was spooked only when stabled, and Karel had grown to feel much the same way. He took pride in his home, in the new white paint on the house and the green window trim that Sophie had so wanted, in the graded road and the expanded smokehouse and the new cattlepens he'd fenced in behind the barn, but preferred to see it all from out of doors, where he could lay his eyes on the work his hands had done.

And so it was, though it had been years since there were fine horses in his stables instead of draft animals and spools of baling wire and cans of oil and kerosene and tins of grease, that Karel preferred to be out of the house when the sunlight was failing and some change of weather looming. He liked it better when there were chores to do and the promise of darkness or rain or both became a clock against which he could measure his work, and tonight, when he finished his coffee, he rose to his feet and stretched his sore back with his hands twisted together high above his head, and then he fetched a length of rope and some chain from the stable and carried them out east of the smokehouse to light a small fire beneath the crankcase of his new Fordson tractor so he could get it started in the cool weather.

A half hour later, when he made it around to the cattlepen, he was thankful for the long gray shadows of dusk, for he was sure, by now, that the vultures had made more than one good meal from his losses. He left the tractor idling loudly outside the pen and unlatched the gate and let the wind swing it wide. While he tied the rope like a noose around the half-born calf's neck, he held his breath against the stench and thought of the knowing look on Villaseñor's face, letting himself fantasize for a moment that he was hitching a rope round that son of a bitch's throat. Karel worked bent over at the waist, winding the rope from the calf and then around the front of the heifer's hind legs, looping it in two tight circles from behind the heifer's udder up over her haunches and knotting it along the spine so that the calf couldn't come free from its mother's body when he dragged the whole mess of it across the pasture. When he rose, his hips popped such that he could hear it over the wind, and his back began to throb in deep spasms that felt like steaming water was being wrung upward from the small of his back to the stiffly warped knuckles of his neck. He would bet, goddamn it, that his brothers didn't ache this way, never mind that they'd all once worn the same harness and pulled the same plow. If Thom's youthful good looks were any indication, they were aging handsomely, like their wives' father, who, if possible, was more infuriating now in his polished appearance and disposition than he had been when he'd first come calling in his carriage. His speech was, as ever, salted only by his choice of words, never with the tenor or volume of his voice, and he wore suitcoats and hats that made him stand everywhere in Lavaca County a head above even the wealthier Czechs and Germans. And now he'd rubbed off on his daughters' husbands. Karel tied another two loops just behind the heifer's front legs and pulled the remaining rope tight before looping a cinch knot into the end of it and doubling the chain through that.

When he had the whole affair rigged to the tractor, he climbed into the seat and worked the hand clutch while looking back, easing the slack out of the chain until the cow swung around smoothly in the hay with the calf's head trailing behind. Then Karel throttled it up and steered out through the pasture, straightening his back to brace himself against the jostling ride of the steel drive wheels as he angled between the wide swaths mowed through the old hedgerows. While he drove toward the southern fork of the creek, he pictured his brother Thom as he had seen him from his idling truck earlier in the day just after the wind began to pick up, a man engaged in the deliberate, slow work of the well-to-do, his hair grown longer than it had been the last time Karel had seen him, his face with some sun in it but smooth and otherwise unweathered, his lips held together to hide the wreck of his front teeth, his curved neck carried in such a way that the man assumed a quiet and thoughtful show of satisfaction as he carried buckets full of mop water out to the wide front porch of his saloon and dumped them carefully over the porch railing so he wouldn't splash his shoes or trousers. Sitting in his truck, Karel couldn't help but wonder if his brother still held suspicions about what his wife had done before their wedding day, if she had gone to him seeking to clear her conscience. Karel supposed it wasn't so, saw in his brother an innocence born either of ignorance or denial. And then it occurred to Karel that it wouldn't do him or anyone else any harm to swing his door open and join his brother there on the porch, to lend him a hand. It had been so long since he'd had the company of another man in his work, so long that he now felt almost a longing for those hours and days spent hitched to the plow with his brothers, their boots sliding and sinking in the fine black soil, the sun blistering the backs of their necks where their straw hat brims proved too narrow. It had been enraging and unnecessarily hard work, but at least, linked together by leather, they had felt the common hard resentment, a kind of ill will whose tongue was held in check by fear, for the same man at the same time. If anything, this was what Karel missed about the company of his brothers—their hardness and loathing had shored up his own, given him title to his own hatred. But there was something else: The older boys had also admired their father—his stubbornness and sharp tongue, the way he refused to beckon the help of other men—and so had Karel, and it was this admiration that he couldn't cotton to, the reverence for a man you surely hated, the hard plaque of respect that all the bad blood couldn't scour from your heart. This, too, he and his brothers had shared, and the bile of a common indigestion that rose from the two brands of unsuited feelings had been easier to swallow when there were others around who were burning inside with the same struggle to choke it down.

Karel wondered now, as he neared the line of water oaks fringing the creekbed and the sky darkened to a deeply bruised blue, if it was this aspect of brotherhood that had made it near on to impossible for boys like Billy Dalton to come home from the war, if the mud they had tasted and the gases they'd dodged in those trenches had hardened them together in the same way that countless grains of sand, compacted and fired so long underground, were baked together, in time, into stone. Dalton had lasted only a year back in town before clearing out to take a factory job in Kansas City where a pair of brothers from his regiment overseas had gone to work after their homecoming. Karel had seen him at the icehouse in town some four years back, standing at the bar, drinking alone, young still but no longer a boy. His red hair looked dulled as if by a wash with diluted lye, and the scar Karel had occasioned on his face had faded so that it appeared, in the lamplight, to be little more than a birthmark. Karel had bid him good evening, and the young man had nodded at him, and they'd had a drink together without saying another word, the deep-rooted rivalry of their history buried and smothered by all that had since been shoveled by time over the top of it. Karel hadn't seen him since. He'd left his father and mother and the town that carried his name, this for something akin to brotherhood that probably had no name at all.

Earlier in the day, sitting across the road from the Drycreek Saloon, this was the kind of thinking that had nearly spurred Karel out of his truck and onto the porch to have words with his brother. Each time, though, that he'd found his hand on the door, he'd seen his cigarette burning in his hand, and the red glow of the thing and its smoke had reminded him of Villaseñor's cigar, of all the business he'd threatened to take and of all that Karel had already lost—the girl, Graciela, whose loamy sweetness he could often smell in the air after a hard, cold rain; the exhilarating release of riding nights on a fine horse; the close, stale comfort of a bedroom filled with the loud breathing of brothers; the allegiance, bitter though it may have been, with the father who had staked his final wager with a family that he could never, whether he won or no, make whole. And this was the difference, after all, between Karel and his brothers. They had gone, and he had remained. They had found a way out, or it had found them, and Karel reckoned now that their destination had been one that allowed them to cull all the resentment from their respect just as surely as he now, reaching the creek, slid down from behind the steering wheel and unhitched the dead animals from the chain before climbing back onto the tractor and leaving them there to broadcast in the cool wind their reeking and indissoluble end.

THEY WAITED UNTIL an hour after dark, when the nearby farmers were likely done with the evening chores and gone indoors for the night, and then they kindled a small fire beneath an overhang of sweet gum trees a mere twenty yards from the dirt road where they'd parked the truck. After leaving Gonzales, they'd driven north until they reached the Fayette County line and then turned back east to make their way through Flatonia and over into Praha. There they'd stopped into the druggist's and the general store where, while Joe gathered provisions of potted meat and canned beans and dried sausage and sweet potatoes, Raymond had struck up a conversation with Elizka Novotny. She offered that Karel had left for Dalton that morning, that his wife was recovering still from her labor at the Vrana house, and she wondered what it was that had brought the twins back so soon to Praha. Hadn't she heard that they'd hired on to help out around the Skala farm?

"We run some errands for him," Raymond had said, "over in Flatonia. But my brother there lost his footing beneath a load he was carrying and fell backward into a window. Cut his shoulder to ribbons. We're going to get him dressed up and head on back to Dalton."

"And the food?" she asked, following Joe with her eyes while he made his way around the store, filling a crate. "Won't Karel share meals with you?"

"We don't take liberties, ma'am. We tend to do for ourselves."

Now, with two opened cans of beans warming on flat stones near the fire, Raymond sat on a fallen timber beside his shirtless brother, cleaning his wounds with alcohol and dressing them in clean cotton bandages. When he'd finished and Joe had gotten his shirt and coat back on, they ate upwind of the fire and watched as smoke and orange embers swept up through the branches of the nearby trees. The moon had come timidly off the horizon to find the sky wide and cloudless, a few proud stars already shining.

Raymond fed himself a mouthful of beans, then sat with his eyes on the fire, pointing his spoon at Joe while he chewed. "I been thinking on what you said. If you got it in your mind to go west, that'll suit me fine. One place is as good as another, I guess."

Joe nodded, tilting his can toward the firelight so he could see into it and scraping the bottom with his spoon. When he'd emptied it to his satisfaction, he tossed the can into the fire and tucked the spoon in the front pocket of his coat. Raymond had wrapped the dressing too tight, and Joe propped his arm on his knee to take the weight off his shoulder, which was throbbing at the joint and stinging still from the alcohol. He listened to the gusting of the wind, the rise and fall of it in the tree branches, and he imagined the ocean, wondering if that's how the waves sounded when they rolled up onto the land and slid back down. Somewhere shy of Flatonia, he'd finished the serial in the paper, and now he was glad to have used it beneath the kindling to get the fire started. Judith had let him down, growing soft when the neighboring rancher sweet-talked her, falling into his arms like some pitiful, spoiled, breathless woman in a picture show who'd taken faint upon the sight of approaching Indians or the receipt of a telegram bearing news of her doting father's death.

If he'd been there, Joe thought, he'd have made her look at his shoulder while he unwrapped his bandages and pulled off the scabs where they were stuck to the dressing, and then he'd have squeezed the flesh around the wounds until the blood came up from beneath the skin and rolled down his arm. He'd have accustomed her to the sight of pain and the sounds of danger until she toughened up, and then he'd have told her about the horses her handsome, sugar-tongued neighbor had bought from that son of a bitch, Bayne. After she came to her senses and remembered who she was, Judith of Blue Lake Ranch, not some little ninny who rode sidesaddle, they could have taken a ride together and crossed out to the westernmost meadow of her property. They could have sat horseback together, looking out over the cliffs that fell away down to where the ocean ran up onto the shore below. They could have grown the ranch and found some way to run her rotten neighbor out of business. But he was a long way yet from California, and the damned story was already written, and now it was ashes beneath the glowing kindling of the fire, where it belonged, and it was too late to change it, too late to save her or to remind her how to save herself, and this realization recalled to Joe's mind a picture of his mother, withered down near to nothing after three weeks in bed, the points of her hips and knobs of her knees sharp as sheared rock beneath the blankets, her voice the sound of two dry stones rubbed together, whispering in Joe's ear for water, more water, *just another sip of water, dear,* until, after three late-night trips out to the well, he'd fallen asleep in the chair beside her and awoken to find her dead with an empty glass beside her on the table near her bed.

Raymond stirred the ashes of the fire needlessly with a stick and said, "We'll just do this one thing tonight and then drive north a few days, into Oklahoma, maybe. Sell the truck there and catch a train."

"We could head out now," Joe said. "Drive all night to San Antonio and catch the Sunset Limited. Leave it be. You didn't have to spit on the man's floor, Ray."

Raymond looked up from the fire and then gazed at the moonlit sky, his eyes red and watery from the heat and smoke, his scar irregular and dead white on his flushed face. It was the third time Joe had spoken since sunup, and Raymond wasn't accustomed to his brother being so damned talkative. "I suppose I didn't," Raymond said, tossing the stick into the fire. "I might have spit in his face instead."

Joe hadn't counted on so many horses. In these parts, most of the small-plot farmers kept only enough mules and draft horses to plow and plant their cotton fields. Down south near Yoakum, where there were still sprawling cattle ranches, you might expect a full stable, but not one with horses the likes of these. Near on to midnight, the boys had smothered their little cook fire with handfuls of dirt and driven back south past Moulton until they reached the stand of blackjack oaks on the eastern side of the road, and Raymond swung the truck around so that it was pointing north and parked it in the weeds next to the drainage ditch between the road and the fenceline. Raymond climbed from the truck, tucked his pistol into the back waistband of his trousers, and closed the door softly. Peering up and down the empty midnight road, he walked around to Joe's side of the truck and then lifted the three cans of gasoline from the bed of the truck. The moon was up in earnest now, and Joe thought he might almost be able to read out here without a lantern, and when he looked at the worry on Raymond's face he could tell his brother was thinking too about the light, and not so kindly. Joe left his rifle in the truck and lifted one of the cans with his good arm.

When they'd made it over the cattlegate and walked the quarter mile up the winding dirt road to find the dense grove of fruit trees standing bare between the house and the stable, they stopped and listened while the wind worked the tree branches together and drove the whirring blades of the windmill set out on the near side of the barn. The house rose in fine white siding from the bottom story up to a screened sleeping porch that ran the length of the second floor. Raymond put a finger to his lips, a gesture so pointless, given his brother's penchant for silence, that Joe stifled a laugh and shook his head. Raymond ducked through the grove and slipped between the barn and the new Ford truck that sat outside the sliding doors with Karel's trailer unhitched and empty beside it. Just beyond it, the stable loomed quiet and twice the size of the barn, its new red paint visible beneath the unabashed moon.

Raymond slid the door open one slow inch at a time and marveled at how well greased and silent and true the runners were. The brothers set their cans down just inside the door and Raymond pushed it mostly closed. They stood for a while, letting their eyes adjust to the darkness and breathing the warm air rich with the sweet mix of manure and hay and damp saddle blankets and breathing animals, each scent distinct yet muted, overcast by the strong smell of fine, oiled leather.

Joe lit a match and cupped it with his hand, biting back the bone-deep throbbing in his shoulder as he walked past the loft stairs toward the stalls until he located a hanging lantern and pulled it down from its nail. He got it lit, dialed the wick down low, and then the brothers got their bearings in the new spill of light around them. Before the stalls, a wooden loft chute angled down to the floor from above and hay bales were stacked three high against the wall and beneath the steps leading up the loft. Raymond nodded and they walked down the wide alley, flanked on each side by stalls with brass door bolts and hardwood walls that gave way to polished slats rising from chest-high on either side of the opened feed doors, the horses within breathing and clopping softly in their fresh bedding. A few lumbered forward, blinking their enormous eyes and hanging their heads sleepily over the stall doors to see who had come to tend them in the night and what new comforts they had brought. Raymond pulled another lantern from the beam between two stalls and got it lit, and then they walked two abreast between the long rows, holding their lanterns up and peering into the stalls. Joe counted eight on each side, and only a few of them empty. A dozen horses at least, but really the same horse twelve times. Some mares, some stallions, a gelding or two and, in the last right-hand stall, a nervous little filly that shook her mane and paced within the confines of her enclosure, all of them black from hoof to head excepting their socks and blazes, which shone so white they made him squint even in the dim, oily light of the lanterns. He thought of Raymond's scar, the way it had looked too white to be real in the light of the cook fire, and then he turned to the back of the stable where the wide aisle opened into a wash-down and grooming area with stacks of nested pails on the floor and eyebolts secured in the load-bearing four-by-fours for crossties. On the crossbeams near the wall, an assortment of brushes and currycombs and hoof picks sat waiting for need of their services. Against the opposite wall, fine saddles, many of them strangely lacking pommels, sat atop what looked like wide, varnished hardwood sawhorses. There was tack strung from the rafters and two farrier's stools stacked in one corner beneath a wall hung with sets of new shoes and nippers and rasps.

Mindful of Joe's shoulder, Raymond put a hand flat on the small of his brother's back to get his attention. Joe turned, the yellow lanternlight softening his features so that Raymond saw himself as he'd been years ago before his father put his face through a window the night he'd refused to surrender the pay he'd earned baling hay all one Sunday at a neighboring farm. "Quite an outfit," Raymond whispered, holding his lamp toward the swinging double doors on the back wall. "Crack them doors so we get a cross breeze. I'll go soak the loft."

Joe nodded, watching his brother's wiry frame move between the stalls until Raymond reached the fuel cans, bent to lift one and then rose, enfolded in soft light, up the loft stairs. He gave the filly another look, and she turned from him and pressed her side against the back wall of her stall. He set his lantern on the dirt floor and pulled the bolt from the back door, pushing it slowly outward until a hard gust of wind caught hold of it and Joe found himself going with it, clutching the thing with the wrong hand and dragging his boots in the loose dirt, the back of his shoulder shot through with a deep screaming pain that sucked the breath from his lungs and flashed a blanket of crimson over his vision so that he found himself, when his eyes cleared and he registered the moonlight on his shoulders and the wind whipping the hem of his coat at his back, moaning with a long, throaty exhalation that rolled up into his sinuses until it came out, muted but audible, through his nose. Tears welled up hot in his eyes, and he stood there for a long minute, his forehead holding the door against the exterior wall of the stable, the paddock fenced and well tilled by horse hooves and empty behind him.

When he caught his breath, Joe dug the toe of his boot beneath the door to hold it fast, squatting down as he did to find a stone he could use as a doorstop. He worked with one hand in the sandy earth until he'd convinced himself there was nothing to be found, and, righting himself, he worked a small mound of dirt against the door with the side of his boot and stepped on it to pack it down. Then he retrieved his lantern and listened to the splashing of gas and the soft scuffing of his brother's boots on the floor of the loft overhead.

He was supposed to empty a can in the downstairs hay bales and splash fuel along the walls, but there was something about seeing this little black filly in her stall while his shoulder burned and throbbed, something tender and undeserving of harm, something in her dark, wide eyes and the twitching, tentative way she worked her ears. She was alert and wary, her flanks smooth and well groomed, her legs solid and long, and in her Joe imagined that he could see the many generations of long-considered breeding, the daily vision of her the cause of someone's prideful assurance that, with foresight and honest intentions, a man could see before him all the evidence he needed that he'd made some mark in the world that could not be erased by his own demise.

Overhead, Raymond's footsteps were faint now, approaching the far side of the loft. He'd be coming down soon, ready to put a match to the place, and Joe's feet grew cold in his boots thinking about it, a tingling running up his calves to prickle the hollows behind his knees. Raymond had been born first, by ten minutes or so, and Joe had been following his lead ever since. When their father was alive, prone to all his drinking and the quick ignition of his rage, it had paid to do so. There was something in Raymond, maybe some dilution of their father's hot blood, that readied him always for action, for whatever running or fighting might be called for. Joe had found as a boy that, given the rise of their father's voice in the hall, he would be caught frozen in thought, just lying in bed and thinking, until Raymond grabbed his shirt collar or wrist and dragged him out of his daze toward the window and the long, barefoot run across the pasture to the safety of darkness and trees. But earlier, by the fire, there had been a distant, ponderous look to Raymond's face, an uncharacteristic refusal to look Joe dead in the eye when he agreed to go west. It had been Joe's idea, after all, and he thought now that even his brother's consent was a kind of following, and he didn't know if Raymond's pride would allow him to make good on it.

Outside, the wind threw itself in loud waves beneath the eaves, and from the stalls came the occasional, nervous sound of a horse stamping and blowing. The little filly came forward, tossing her head, and Joe hung his lantern outside the stall and unbolted the door and stepped inside. He reached out for her, smoothing the hide of her neck with the flat of his hand, and whispering, "Shh, girl. It's a way out for you now." He heard a bale come whisking down the loft chute at the far end of the stable, then another, and when he went to meet his brother, he left the filly's stall unbolted.

At the foot of the steps, Joe stood cupping his elbow in his good hand when Raymond appeared, his lantern held low in front of him so that he could see the steps as he descended. When he got down, he narrowed his eyes at his brother and held a palm up at his side. "What is it?" he whispered, stepping into the alley and peering down to see that the opposite door was open wide.

Joe just nodded at his shoulder, shook his head.

"Goddamn it," Raymond said. He'd log-jammed the loft chute with bales, and after they'd hung their lanterns on nails in the nearest stall's siding, he went to work soaking the bottom half of them with fuel while Joe turned the other can of gas over atop the stack of hay beneath the loft stairs.

When they'd finished, Raymond shot his brother a grin and said, "Hope you ain't too pained to run." He fished in his pocket for matches, and Joe stood listening as the stable timbers groaned against the wind and then stopped in a wheezing sigh that sounded to him like the final, raspy exhalation of some infirm animal.

Of a sudden, then, the wind changed directions, swirling hard out of the southeast, and when the paddock door came free from its makeshift dirt stop, it slammed shut so sharply that the horses went wild, crying out in panicked shrieks and throwing themselves against their stalls, this booming midnight sound no less frightening to them than would be a clap of thunder unleashed indoors. "Shit," Raymond said, fumbling with his matches.

When he steadied his hands and threw the struck match, there came a blue flash of flame that leapt up the chute into the loft, and Joe took a step backward as the heat washed over him and he stared up into the blaze overhead, a rush of air roaring in his ears, surging upward as if beckoned by some undeniable and infernal summons above.

And then Raymond shoved past, knocking into Joe's shoulder to get around the blazing chute, running toward the sliding door while Joe went to his knees and looked up, mesmerized by this loud flare of light, the bite of burning fuel and smoke stinging in his throat, the terrified sounds of animals rising until they became for him a disorienting extension of the roar of the fire and the loud rush of blood in his ears. Flames rose from the bales beneath the loft stairs and slanted up the chute, whipping toward the door when Raymond leaned into it hard and slid it open until the rollers banged against the outermost framework of the runners. Overhead, the flames fed a thick clot of smoke that hovered over the chute's opening, and Joe squinted against the blast of heat on his face and shielded his eyes against the thickening swirl of glowing ash. He heard his brother screaming at him from the open door, saw his face flickering and yellow and cast against the moonlight looming soft and unwavering behind him. And then there was a danger looming closer than the fire, certain but inanimate and all but silent, a thought given voice as if from the growing smoke itself, a quiet, urgent voice the sound of which reverberated only beneath the skin, in the sinew of muscles and the soft meat of marrow, in the blood that surged with adrenaline, and when he broke for the door, his brother turned from it, bolting out into the night.

Overhead, fire glowed blue through the joints of the loft decking, and then the fuel that had run through the seams caught in a raining curtain of flame before the door. Joe stopped, pulled his coat up over his head, and even with his ears covered, the stable was just deafening with the screaming panic of animals and the hot rush of spreading fire and the unmistakable approach of hoof strikes. When they were upon him, he turned, ducking and throwing his arms out, to find the filly towering above him, rearing and kicking, trapped between this raining blaze of fire and the door slammed shut behind her at the far end of the stable.

When Joe turned once more toward the door, the horse reared again and fell, its shod hoof hitting just above Joe's calf in the hollow of his knee. His leg buckled and snapped, the sound louder than the popping of dry oak in a woodstove, and he was shot through with a searing pain as he flew forward, the impact kicking the breath from his lungs when his chest hit the dirt, his head snapping forward to slam against the hard-packed earth, and then there were moments of darkness and quiet, of the haunting sound of his mother's voice, of her whispering in the night for water, of a body whole and calm and cool and unaware of fire or animals or the bone splintered and jutting wet through the wrecked skin of his shin.

When he came to, he worked his tongue over a scab of dirt stuck to the spit at the corner of his lips. The filly was still wild, pacing and wheezing beside him, unwilling to break through the smoke and fire that now obscured the front stable door, her hooves shak-

209

ing the hard earth beneath him when they struck. Joe rolled over and the bolt of pain leapt up his leg hot and tremulous and sick until it twisted through his stomach and up his throat, and it all came so quickly there was no turning his head, no stopping it, and Joe's eyes flooded as he wretched into his own lap, the sour spew of beans clogging his throat in abrasive waves until, when he'd finished, he was fully conscious, the heat and smoke and glowing embers falling over him as he ground his teeth and grunted and cried out and kept an eye on the frantic pacing of the horse while he scooted himself back with the palms of his hands and his good leg, working his way to the rear of the stable until he could feel his spine braced against the solid wood of the rear door.

He bent his good knee, wiped the tears from his eyes and a thick smear of blood from his nose and the muddy bile from the corner of his mouth and, with one sharp arch of his back, pushed the door open and felt, all at once, the hard bite of pain that jolted through him in the squeezing of his guts and the shivering skin and the breath expelled with a cry that could only be squelched by biting down hard on his lower lip. The horse came out wildly behind him, and he flinched as she galloped harmlessly over his outstretched legs and circled herself out against the far perimeter of the paddock's fenceline. He found that he was holding his breath, and when he exhaled, he reached back again and clenched handfuls of the loose, sandy soil, feeling the grainy cool of it between his fingers, a sensation so commonplace and familiar that there came into him a startling cold relief. He was out of the stable. It was December. His father was dead. His brother out here somewhere in the night, looking for him or assuming him killed or racing toward the road and the truck. As Joe worked backward, dragging himself over the uneven earth that lay churned up into mounds and pocked with divots, he heard the sound of voices come alive in the night—his name called out like a desperate question in the parched, hoarse voice of his brother; the screaming of trapped animals; the barked, uncompromising orders of a man brought out of his dreams to find the night afire, his family sleeping beside him wrapped in sheets that would burn atop mattresses that would burn in a house made of timber that would burn, all in a world overseen by a god who had long since forsaken water.

Beneath the high moon, with the yellow bone quivering outside of the skin, the blood pulsing up around it and pooling warm in the leg of his trousers, Joe didn't notice the gunshot wound of his shoulder in the least. He didn't any longer curse or scream or call out for his brother. He had to keep himself conscious and moving, and he set all of his mind to the sobering intake of every sensation other than pain, to the slow progress across the paddock, to these handfuls of dirt and the whispering of his mother's voice somewhere inside of him, to the thirst that crept from her dry lips into his own throat, to the hard whipping of the wind and the tingling chill in his scalp and cheeks and shoulders as the blood siphoned down to feed the pool in the leveled leg of his pants, to the reaching and pulling and the gritty soil packing beneath his fingernails, to the sound of the horse blowing behind him and the vision of flames bursting up from beneath the stable's eaves such that the thick, wind-borne smoke thinned smooth and flat into an unrolled bolt of threadbare fabric, doing the work of clouds on a cloudless night, skimming over the near-round moon. It was as beautiful as it was terrible, and a mass of certainty hardened like enamel around the cage of Joe's ribs, and he knew that Judith had changed her mind, that she'd come to her senses and denied her suitor, that she was sitting her horse on this very night, waiting out on the rolling meadows of her Blue Lake Ranch in California, anticipating his arrival, and by the time Joe made it to the far fencing of the paddock and dragged himself groaning and upright on one leg and took the horse by its mane, leaning his chest over her warm hide and squeezing his arms around her neck so he could pull himself up and swing his good leg over her back, he was laughing and crying what all at the same time.

The blood ran out of him now as if displaced by the hydraulics of his own new certainties — he would ride, and he would mend, and he would go for her — and his hands were groping now, and now his vision blurred and narrowed and tinted by the faintest film of red. And here was the filly's neck. And here her mane. And here the splintery fencerail and the thick, draining weight of his boot coming full, and more fence timbers, and the gate, and here the warm undulations of the animal beneath him, the sweet steaming of her breath in his hair, and here the cool cast iron of the latch and the sighing whine of the gate swinging open. And then they were out in the night, only countless outstretched miles of swirling wind and the merging cadences of heartbeats and hoof strikes and the wide black pastures before them.

Testaments to Seed

MARCH 1910

THERE IS OPPORTUNITY enough—whether with hired women in the stale rooms above the Bio Saloon in Shiner or with country girls made pliant by cider in the nearby woodlands on beds of fallen foliage—for the young men of Lavaca County to occasion the satisfaction of their near-constant urges. Over the course of the last two years, it has not been uncommon for Eduard and Thom, their needs strung tighter or their wills wrought of stronger stuff than their brothers', to return after midnight with hushed laughter and drunken bragging to the boys' shared bedroom. When they wake Stan and Karel, as they invariably do, their talk of the flabby, overused whores with whom they've purchased an hour is seasoned with descriptions of living but inhuman things, of animals and ripe fruit. Teats heavy and soft as muskmelons left too long in the field. A backside wide as a sow's. Brisket. Hams.

And so it is that when this girl, Graciela, comes to Karel in the lowered light of the stable, unbuttoning her blouse and then smoothing a saddle blanket on a bed of hay bales, he is struck, as a young man is wont to be in the first fortunate moments of his exposure to the delicately unencumbered wonder of a woman's body, by his own ineptitude, by the inaccuracy and insufficiency of all his feeble, boyish fantasies. Here, with the ticking percussion of rain at work on the rooftop and the unmoving air of the stable cool and redolent of damp horsehair and dry hay, there is simply no way to watch this girl shedding her boots, pulling her camisole over her head, and to see her in terms of anything other than the startlingly novel and incomparable vision that she is.

She sits him on the bales and stands over him, her still-wet hair hanging in front of her shoulders, draping over the gentle hollow of her throat and falling fanned over her breasts, and stops him when he begins to remove his coat. "No," she whispers. "I'll do it. Just sit."

Karel obeys, in part because he hasn't a notion how to defy her, in part because to sit yielding to her will is, in itself, the unexpected satisfaction of a long-untended desire. And so he listens to the rain as the sight of her body gives rise to gooseflesh on the tops of his thighs. He lifts his feet, one at a time, so she can remove his boots, straightens his elbows as she pulls his coat and shirtsleeves from his arms. When she leans over him, kneeling to unbutton his trousers, a breast grazes his knee and he sucks in breath as if in anticipation of some violent submersion.

Then there comes a honing of his senses, and Karel sits naked and marveling at how all his fifteen years in the sunlit world have come to less than this, at how bearing daily witness to outstretched plains and sunset horizons blistered with clouds has taught him no more about the bright surprise of being alive than does the way this girl shifts first onto the ball of one foot, then the other, as she works the waist of her riding pants down over her hips. If he had to, he realizes, he would trade all those years piecemeal, a year of *then* for a minute of *now:* the sight of Whiskey's glossy and frothing and wriggling emergence from his mother for the acute work of his nerves, for his ability to distinguish, in the rough fabric of the saddle blanket beneath him, the coarse, individual threads of the wool's warp and weft; the walks among tall, white-tufted fields of August cotton for this glimpse of the thick, dark hair narrowing down to the proud pleats of glistening skin between her legs; the hours spent imagining his mother's tenderness for the protracted seconds in which this lovely girl ceases to be anything less than a woman, in which she positions herself astride his lap, a cool hand reaching down to take hold of him, to run the engorged tip of him back and forth along her slick folds until she nests him there just outside of her body, until she moves her hands onto the flexed muscles of his shoulders, and, with a pained push of breath rendered low in the back of her throat, takes the whole of him in one slow and shuddering descent.

Karel recognizes, in this moment, that his brothers must be either liars or fools, that there is nothing of the truth in all their lewd talk of creatures and fruit, that there is nothing so common in the sweet heat of this woman atop him, the wet flexing of her muscles taking hold of him, releasing. At the very tip of him, at the deepest point within her, there is a tightening, a hot wire of pleasure that is tethered to the base of his spine, strung from there to his navel and down to his tailbone. His face flushes hot with blood, and then there's a cool prickle on his forehead and cheeks that yields to numbness. The girl works against him, her hands clasped firmly behind his neck, her hips shifting forward and back in their own insistent rhythm, her breath pushing quick and warm in his hair, and Karel is all but helpless beneath her, his injured eye seeping fluid, his hands cupped fast to the tender, rocking tops of her hips, and all the while he watches her.

Not once does she look at him.

Instead, she keeps her eyes shut, fluttering with the intake of breath. Her hair is pasted to her shoulders and breasts, her nipples darker than Karel would have expected, widely encircled by brown bands of skin that he traces with a thumb, the ridges of her clavicle flecked with the faintest little constellation of moles.

He drops his hands from her, bracing them behind his back for leverage, but when he tries to thrust, moving forward with his hips, she drops all of her weight on him, pinning him in place while she breathes hard through her nose and continues her steady and measured undulations. Then a horse blows in the stable, and Karel closes his good eye, listening to the soft play of the weather overhead, to the horses shifting in the stalls, and all the while the wire within him is tightening as if wound by a winch. When he allows himself sight of her again, her head is thrown back past her shoulders, rolling from side to side as if in some makeshift dance for which there is no intended audience. There is the sweet leaking of her body running down onto him, the friction of her work giving rise to a rash down low in the hair beneath his navel.

My *word*, Karel thinks, and he wants now to stand with her still clinging to him, still pressed into the wet saddle of his lap, to take hold of her hips and lift and turn and lay her back onto the blanketed hay, to put his weight on her and feel the solid cinching of her smooth legs around him as he moves inside her. But when he begins to stand, she tightens her arms behind his neck and holds him in place. She centers her weight over him and shakes her head without opening her eyes, and while she increases the speed of her movement atop him, she leans into him and puts her mouth over his swollen eye, sucking at it as if it's her aim to take the whole of it into her mouth, to claim it as her own. Karel's muscles seize and his hands flex hard, his fingernails digging into the flesh of her hips, and a quivering wave shivers through the length of the wire strung hot within him. His eye burns, but her mouth is so soft and wet, her tongue moving in slow circles around the tender skin of his eyelid, and after a while he feels only the remnant of pain, only the heat held in the heart of the metal when a branding iron is dropped hot into well water.

And then it is upon him, the final winding of this unsustainable torsion, and just before the surge of release runs up the length of him, from its origin within her into his stomach, up the switchbacks of his ribs and into the hard buckling knuckles of his spine at the base of his neck, she drops a hand and pulls him from her body. But she doesn't stop, doesn't slow her tempo in his lap, and when his own spasms wane, he pulls his face from her lips and watches as she begins to shudder about the shoulders, her hand working furiously between her legs, her dark eyes sprung wide and fluttering with the perfect, startled bewilderment of something newly born.

GRACIELA LEAVES the lantern low, the stable dimly aglow. She moves quietly, attending to her clothes, her breathing slowed, her actions deliberate and composed, and Karel watches uneasily and wonders what is expected of him. He notes the splotched bloom of flushed skin above her breasts, but then she pulls the camisole over her head and slips into the sleeves of her blouse, her eyes downcast. When she reaches for her boots, Karel is almost surprised to find himself naked, still seated on the blanketed hay. Outside, the light rain announces yet its muted arrival on the rooftop, the horses still clop the hard dirt of their stalls in their animated sleep, and while, excepting the animals and the night and whatever god is attendant upon these shadows, Karel is still alone with this girl, he can't help but think, as he rises from the hay and pulls on his trousers, that this is not the same stable, not the same town, not the same world in which he'd found himself just a dozen short minutes before.

When they are both dressed, Graciela unhasps the nearest stall door and walks Whiskey out beneath the lamp and crossties him there, running her little hands flat against his rippling shoulders, smoothing the roan hide as the horse nudges sleepily at her with his great head and nibbles gently at her hair with his lips. Karel takes the hint and pulls the bridle from a crossbeam hung with tack, and while he coaxes the bit into Whiskey's mouth, Graciela fetches the blanket and places it over the horse as naturally as she had placed

Karel onto it. And then there is the saddle, the bellyband, the cinch straps, all of it worked silently into place and secured with a wordless cooperation that triggers in Karel's imagination a sunlit day in which they might work together in just this way—he out in the fields, manning the planter behind two good horses, spinning the tacky wisps of cottonseed into the earth, she out beyond the stables, hanging laundry on the line, their billowing bedsheets snapping in the wind. And later, with full bellies and the sun pressing itself into the horizon out west, he'd come up behind her and cup his hands on her hips, nuzzle her hair and breathe the smell of her into his lungs. He'd untie her apron and lift it over her head, leading her to the table where he'd sit her down and put a cup of coffee steaming into her hands so that she could rest awhile, enjoying the sounds of calling quail and mourning doves while he finished the dishes. They wouldn't have to say a word, and then, just before full dark, they could walk out into the yard behind the grove and pull the laundry from the line, and they could make the bed and snuff the candles and weave their legs together there between cool sheets that smelled of the floral spring breeze and the clean, broken earth. And then, if they needed the sound of voices more than the sweet give-and-take of bodies, they could talk.

When the horse stands ready for riding, Karel surprises himself as much with the sound of his voice as with the dream he's suddenly willing to share. "Good horses like these, we could be across the county line by sunrise."

She smiles without showing her teeth, finds his eyes with her own. Stroking the long neck of the horse, she wets her upper lip with her tongue. "Which one?" she asks. "Which county?"

"Whichever one you fancy."

"Karel," she says, and the serious, almost instructive turn of her voice muddies his fantasy the way his hand reached into shallow creekwater has so often obscured his own reflection. "I fancy this one. And so does my father. And your father."

"I'm not so attached just now to what Pop wants."

"And still you'll fight your brothers with him?"

Karel feels the cool trail of fluid seeping from his eye down his cheek, and when he wipes it with his sleeve, it sets to stinging again. Only minutes before, she would have done this for him, but she's not touching him now, not reaching for his neck or brushing his face with her lips. Instead, her hands are on the horse, and Whiskey is saddled and ready to ride, switching his tail idly, his great, oily eyes glinting in the low light. "Believe that if it suits you, but to me it felt like fighting for you just as much as fighting with him."

Now she pulls her hands from the horse and reaches forward, buttons Karel's coat for him, every gesture a nudge that seems bent on getting him out of the stable and into the night without her. "You can't fight them for me," she says. "You'd have to fight my father, and you wouldn't win. No one ever has."

"Excepting your mother," Karel says. "If she could get free of him, you could, too."

"He didn't go looking for her. Not the last time. Her going was his doing."

Then, with rain coming down on the shingles above, she tells him about a storm that had moved through the mountains of her father's ranch in Guanajuato when she was twelve, of high winds that had taken down trees, one of which had fallen onto the fencing of her father's corral of unbroken horses. "They ran off into the storm, and by morning they weren't visible even from the southern ridge-line. My sisters liked the comfort of the parlor, liked sitting with my mother and drinking tea and practicing their needlework, but I always preferred to be outside, to be on horseback, to be with my father, and so he came into the house where I was taking my breakfast and asked if I wanted to go with him. Told me to bring a bedroll of blankets and a change of clothes, told my mother we'd be no longer than a day and a half, and by noon we were riding in the mountains with four of his men and four pack horses loaded with provisions and rope. Over the first rise of mountains, my father stopped and chewed on his cigar and dismounted, toed a pile of manure and smiled. He winked at me and pointed out toward the next rise of ridges three hours' ride away. 'Can you smell it?' he asked me. 'The river? The green meadow up the far side of the canyon?' I told him I couldn't. It was twenty-five kilometers off at least. He laughed, the same laugh he always had when we were children, and he would try to balance all three of us on his lap at night before Mother sent us off to bed. 'I can't either,' he said. 'But the horses can. They'll have found it, to be certain.'

"Later that day, when we came over that rise, there they were, grazing in the thick grass along the river that cut through the canyon. Father smiled, sent his men down to round them up, and then he built a fire and I cooked us lunch there in the mountains. We watched while, until nightfall, the men did their work. The next morning, we rode back to the ranch with all but one of the lost horses tied and trailing behind us."

Karel smiles. "Well, then there was one what got away."

She shakes her head. "No. The one had been snakebit. Father shot it."

"It don't make much sense," Karel says. "Riding all day after some horses and not going after your own wife when she runs off."

Graciela strokes the horse and frowns, her eyes downcast and dancing with little filaments of lamplight. "She didn't run, Karel. She never ran. She took up with another man, another rancher. The war was coming, and he promised he'd take her back to Spain so she could be with her family. Father's men found them at an inn together. Father would have forgiven her, I know he would have, but it wasn't the first time she'd gone. There was something in her that needed to live only for herself, to do what her body told her to do. She'd disappear for a day, for a week, and Father would sit nights in his chair, smoking his cigars, and then we'd wake one morning and there'd be three horses missing from the stables, three saddles from the tack room, and when my father's men rode back over the ridgeline, she'd be riding behind them with the feathers of her hat waving at us in the breeze and a smile on her lips. She was no one man's woman, but when the skirmishes started and Father began to speak of moving east, she told my sisters and me that we should go only if we wanted, that we should go only where and when we wanted, that women were only beholden to men if they chose to be. And of course I told Father. He had always stayed with us, had never gone away only to be brought home by men sent to fetch him. I never once thought of leaving him. He never leaves, and he shouldn't be left. He never forgets, and he didn't forget any of the men my mother had been with, either. One morning the horses were gone again, and so was Mother, and so were the saddles. And then the men came back without her, blood on their boots, the receipt from the depot in one of their pockets. They'd put her on a train to Mexico City. Father fashioned a cross from saplings, a tiny thing, just twigs tied together, really, and he planted it on the ridge before we left. He said you didn't always need a body to have a funeral."

Whiskey stands fully alert now, ready to ride, sighing and tossing his head and lifting a hoof repeatedly, dropping it to the hard earthen floor as if to punctuate these hints to his rider. Karel puts a hand on the horse's neck to settle him, and then he looks this beautiful young woman over slowly, from the gentle swells of her calves and the slight rounds of her hips up to her hair, still damp and so dark. Her eyes shine wide, unabashed. Unapologetic. She has some of her mother in her, and she's proud of it, that much is clear. "If your father's so good to you, he would give you what you want."

"I haven't decided what I want," she says. "Not beyond tonight, at least. Until I do, I'd do well simply to take what he offers me." And then she does touch him, but not in the way he wants. She cups a hand firmly on his bent neck, pressing her lips together either in sympathy for his history of harness and plow or for his wounded eye and mouth or to keep some other, gentler words inside. Karel can't tell which. When she turns loose of him, she exhales, the hint of a smile pinching together at the pink corners of her lips. "I've told you about my mother," she says. "Wouldn't you like to tell me about yours?"

Karel turns from her, takes his wet coat from the hay bale behind him and shrugs it on. The cold weight of the thing sets him to shivering. He wraps the horse's reins around one hand and leads the animal to the door. Graciela doesn't follow. He opens the door and the hard, clean sound of rainfall makes it so that he has to raise his voice to be certain she hears him. "You already know all about her. She was just like you. I was inside her, and then she was gone."

ON THE FARM-TO-MARKET road, just across the old plank bridge spanning the southern fork of the creek, Karel nudges the horse into a trot while the rain streams down through his hair and cools the torn corner of his mouth and the swollen wound of his eye. Even in the darkness, it seems to him a strange limitation of sensation to have no peripheral vision on his right side, to see through a single eye into a world that had been reduced to near opacity by the cloud cover and the feebleness of the moon and by the girl's quick dismissal of all his fantastic hopes. The horse whinnies when Karel gives it another heel, moving between the outstretched barbed wire on either side, past the southernmost reaches of his father's land and the occasional squat clusters of scrub and mesquite this side of the fencelines. As the horse's hooves splash down, cantering in the puddled road, it comes clear to him of a sudden that the scant light of the night is narrowing into his good eye with the same concentrated reduction as the hot liquid of his resentment funneling down through his ribcage and into the hardening core of his heart. What kind of woman, he wonders, would give herself to a man only to send him away so that she can get her sleep and marry his brother the next day? What kind of woman brings a boy into the world only to leave him there without the warmth of her bosom or the swirling softness of her skirts or the caressing comforts of her hands and lips and gentle words given voice to rid a boy of the fears that find him wide-eyed and alone in the night?

Loud enough that it reaches him through the rain, the call of a horned owl, low and triadic and hollow sounding in its own solemnity, filters into his thoughts and makes room therein for the sorrow that has so often afflicted him. It is nameless and old, something that has preceded him, that came before his father and mother both, something tireless and bodiless and indifferent to the interminable aching it occasions, and when it sinks into him, Karel feels the stinging salt of his own tears burning within the engorged lids of his throbbing eye, and he lets himself go limp in the knees and jostle there in the saddle while the horse moves on heavily into the night and farther from the rushing creekwater behind them. The owl doesn't call again, though Karel listens in anticipation, waiting for something familiar to make itself known in the darkness. Which it does, but only in the way that wholesome and straightforward prayers are so often met with perverted answers. Out before him on the road, maybe seventy yards ahead, there is laughter and hooting, the clamor of the happily delirious or the drunken, and Karel recognizes the voices at once—his brothers coming to town, leaving the deep furrows and sharp words and burst blisters and leather harnesswork of their father's farm behind them in the wide wake of their elation.

Karel leans over Whiskey's neck, whispering behind the animal's ears, which have come forward at the unfamiliar sounds of men's voices pitched high with joy. "Whoa now," Karel whispers, bringing the horse up short, sitting still in the wet saddle so it doesn't creak, cupping a hand over his good eye and scanning the road ahead to find the pinprick of yellow light swinging toward him, the lantern's flame casting a cold, misty halo in the rain. He angles the reins and presses a knee into the horse's side, coaxing the animal off the road and against the easternmost fence. He slips his boots from the stirrups and lets his legs dangle there against the reassuring warmth of the animal's hide.

When his brothers get near enough to notice him, they quit their laughing, and Stan holds the lantern up in one hand while Thom and Eduard square their shoulders above their hips and clutch the canvas handles of their duffels in front of them with both hands. Thom is smiling despite the blood-encrusted gash on his cheekbone and the gruesome teeth slanted back in his mouth. He cocks the dripping brim of his straw hat back on his head to get a better look at Karel sitting above him on the horse. "Been nursing your wounds at the icehouse, little brother?" he says.

Stan looks down at his boots, shifting his weight from one foot to the other. In the faint light, he appears unmarked by the fight and henlike in his reluctance for any further scuffling. "It ain't too late yet," Eduard says. "Turn that animal round and come tilt one back with us."

Thom clears his sinuses and spits, unable to conceal either the pain in his mouth or the disdain for his brother's peacemaking. He lowers his hat back over his eyes and shoots a look at Eduard, who only shrugs and looks toward Stan for support. When the eldest nods, Thom sniffs the air as if gauging it for some foul remnant of the evening's ill will, and then he slings his duffel over his shoulder and hitches the thumb of his free hand in his pocket. "Hell then," he says. "Why not?"

And here is the moment Karel will recall so often without recounting it once even to the likes of his future wife, the slow seconds of his consideration and the unexpected, fleeting blossom of appreciation that unfolds soft and sweet and delicate within the parched cavity of his chest, the cool drizzling of rain on his hatless head and the expectant eyes of his two braver brothers, the twitching of horsehide beneath him and the weight of his waterlogged boots dangling down beneath the stirrups. The cold. Overhead, a thick quiltwork of clouds gathers and bunches until, pulled forth by the wind, it flattens out as if by feminine hands pressed into its airy batting to smooth it over a mattress. The horse stamps and blows, tossing his head gently against the slackened reins, and before Karel even considers the choice laid out before him, there rises within him a remembered scent of the girl's hair, a recollection of that tightening at the base of his spine that had uncoiled at once and so wonderfully beneath the wet weight of her in his lap. And then he's seeing his brother touching her, their fingers grazing as they pull the sheets from the laundry line, their legs threaded together in bed, the images stamped out as if by some loud machine fueled by envy alone. He sees the girl riding horseback, waving to Thom across their fields. He imagines his mother, round bellied and smiling, her arms full as she tries to balance all three of his brothers on her diminished lap.

Then, what has only just bloomed within him curls brittle and brown at the edges, and he believes now, in the slow seconds of understanding, ephemeral as they ever are, that what lies behind a man in the expanding landscape of his past can never be left behind entirely, that even the blazing, cotton-flecked fields of the summer can't sweat from him the hard, fallow crust of so many winters. He can almost put it into words, but it's fleet and then it's gone, and all that's left is the caustic certainty that there's no moving forward unbridled, that the weather-checked harness will never give, that the weight of all that is dragging behind will know no abatement.

"I ain't thirsty," he says, lifting his feet back into the stirrups. "I been sucking your girl's teats till I can't stomach another drop."

Stan flinches and then looks down again, resuming his studious consideration of his boots. Eduard smiles and shakes his head, his eyes glinting with disbelieving appreciation of his kid brother's gall. Thom gives them both a look, lets his duffel splash to the ground. "I never heard such a steaming pile of horseshit," he says.

Karel stands in the stirrups and locks his knees so that he looms high above his brothers when he spits in the road without taking his eyes off Thom's. "That's the thing about shit," he says. "It ain't something you can hear, but once someone's stepped in it there's no doubting the stink. Give her a sniff, big brother, and you'll know yours ain't the first toes she's squished up between."

When he lowers himself back into the saddle and puts a heel to the horse, he does it harder than he needs to, and when he hears behind him the sound of his brother's voice beneath the splashing of hooves and the drizzling of rain, what he makes out is the anger and weight of it but not the words. A swirl of nausea sloshes around sour in his gut, and when he notes the ache in his jaw, he realizes he's grinding his teeth. The horse is running hard, the cold rain needling them, the speed whipping Whiskey's mane back into Karel's face. Still, it's not fast enough, and Karel kicks the horse again.

He sleeps past dawn and wakes to find hay pasted with dried blood to his mouth, his eye throbbing and his toes clammy and cramped from the night spent wet in his boots. Up in the loft, he sits forward atop the hay upon which he's slept so soundly and listens to the rain and the pained animal sounds below. When he'd gotten home, dismounting at the cattlegate with his stomach turned by a hunger that he had no means to feed and a rising regret of the hasty words he now couldn't unsay, he'd walked the horse the last quarter mile across the brittle stalks of cut hay and found the downstairs windows flickering with the irregular light of the oil lamp. He'd had enough by way of family talk for one night, so he'd come quietly around the outermost fringe of the pear grove to the stable, where he'd lit a single, short-wicked lantern so that he could see his work while he removed Whiskey's saddle and the heavy, rain-soaked blanket and then dried and curried the horse and bolted him into his stable beside that of his seedless sire. Then he'd climbed the ladder and pulled his arms from the wet sleeves of his coat and burrowed himself into the piles of hay straws on the floor.

Now he's come awake all at once from his short, dreamless sleep, and when he plucks the hay from the corner of his mouth, it tears the scab and he finds, even before breakfast, the jolting taste of his own blood on his tongue. His legs have gone stiff, as if his bones have been sunk into mud that's been left to dry overnight, and he works his toes around in the swampy wool of his socks while his head clears and his father's voice rises amid the echo of rainfall on the shingles above and Whiskey's distressed complaints down below.

By the time he gets to his feet and makes his way down the ladder, his father is standing with his steaming knife in one hand and the testicles of the gelded horse dripping blood from the other down into the hay. The horse is thrashing its head about, stamping with two hooves in unison against the ropes crosstied from the load-bearing beams. Just emerged from sleep, Karel has to steady his one good eye on the gore in his father's hand before it registers—the cleft between the two testicles pinching a seam into the horsehide such that it appears as if two heavy peaches have been dropped down into a soft brown cinch-purse made of leather with the hair left on it. On the workbench, just this side of the nearest stall, there's a cup of coffee and an uncorked jug of mash, and when Karel looks up to find his father's eyes on him, shot through with a fine lacework of blood and slowly blinking and glazed over from a lack of sleep or from drink or both, the man just stands there, his back molars grinding tobacco and his bottom lip stained brown from the juice.

"A man ain't no better than his goddamn word, boy. And it don't matter if he gives it to a man or an animal or only to himself. Now sew him closed and put some salve on it. He's a plow horse now, and his day's just getting started."

An hour later, after stripping down to his drawers and scouring himself with a brush dipped in a pail of soapy cold well water, Karel changes his clothes and swabs iodine onto the cut at the hinge of his lips. He sets his boots beside the stove to dry, then he soaks a rag in water, puts it atop the half-melted block in the icebox. He fries four eggs and eats them with a cold biscuit and a cup of coffee. When he finishes, he washes the plate and cup and places them on the drain board beside the sink, peels the rag from the block of ice, and sits at the kitchen table with the ice-crusted thing held against his swollen eye. By the time he gets his boots back on and fetches a hat and heads out through the kitchen door onto the back porch, the morning has darkened further and still the rain is coming down steady and gray onto the distant silhouette of his father, who has gotten the two horses braced to the plow and is trudging through the slop behind them to work useless muddy furrows into the land out west. Karel glances out toward the cattle huddling together beneath the weather in the near pasture, to the sheets of water falling over the sides of the full cattletank, to the windmill shimmying in the desultory wind, its tail whipping from side to side as the gusts shift, the blades churning out pointless revolutions. In the distance, his father slips and catches himself against the handles of the plow, working out toward the farm-to-market road where, just two days before, Karel and his brothers had been working when the carriage had appeared and Villaseñor set the brake and climbed down; when he had paraded his handsome daughters before the Skala boys while they stood sweating and wind chapped, their boots caked with the soil of their father's acreage; when Graciela had parted her lips, astonished at something unknown to Karel in the distance, and he'd seen the pink, wet tip of her tongue. And now, out along the fenceline, with the sun above incapable of mustering even enough light to throw a respectable shadow, Karel's father snaps his whip at a pair of gelded horses he will work until nightfall. Karel reckons there's no sense in helping a man plow a field that will have to be plowed again when the soil dries anyhow, ducks through the grove and walks out beyond the eastern side of the barn and into the field to the south, his boots already wet again and sucking in the mud when he lifts his feet. He's seen enough of this, more than enough of his father and the animals he works toward his own ends, more than enough rainfall and wind. Still, though Graciela has wrung him dry of pride, he can't say that he's seen enough of her. He can't say for sure that he ever will.

BY THE TIME he cracks the side door leading into the narthex of St. Jude's, Karel is wet through once more to his drawers, chilled even deeper than that, and he welcomes the relative warmth of the church and the biting cedar scent of incense hung thick in the air. The narthex is obscured by a long screen that separates this, the narrow realm of catechumens and penitents, from the nave, and Karel eases the door closed behind him and stands listening to the cracked, mismatched voices of the country parishioners who sit singing hymns in anticipation of the nuptials of the town's newest brides. At his feet, dripping rainwater pools, slicking the stone floors, and he removes his hat and runs a hand gingerly over his face to clear his good eye. Before him rise two pillars, flanking the entrance to the nave, and as Karel moves quietly behind the screen to lean against the nearest of them, he struggles to make sense of his own presence here. He's been inside this church so many times, on Sundays and holy days, for the yearly anniversary Mass of his mother's death and for his own boyhood sacraments, but it has felt, on these occasions, like nothing more than an echoing and all-too-orderly indoor auction house, filled only with the improbable hopes of those who sit and kneel within, fashioning of their own desperation a god whose intercessions they rely upon for help amidst all the hardships for which they somehow hold him faultless. Karel's earliest recollection is that of his father's words, the furious, adamant claim that there is always blame, always one upon whom it falls.

When the skin is split, there is ever a whip or a stone or a fist or a knife just as there is always someone behind the lashing or throwing or punching or slashing. Karel's eye throbs and his mouth stings, and when he presses a palm against the smooth, cool stone of the pillar and peers around at the congregation, he finds the chancel glimmering with candles, the altar wreathed in greenery but otherwise empty. Smoke curls in blue ringlets from the censor dangling by its chain against the back wall where, for as long as Karel can remember, overarched by red brick trellised in white mortar, the bloodied Christ has hung suffering.

The singing stops, and there comes the gritty whisk of shoe leather slid restlessly over old stone, the muted knocking of heavy missals returned to the hardwood book racks mounted on the backs of the pews. A few heads turn, and Karel sees that the Daltons are here, as are Lad Dvorak and the Waseks and the Kaspars, maybe two dozen others, all of them seated left of the aisle. On the right-hand side, there is only Edna Janek, her long hair dusted gray by time and the early loss of her husband, her gaze focused on the line of boys she's brought into the world as they emerge now, arranged by age with Stan in front and Thom trailing, from the transept, their best trousers and suitcoats dry and clean but wrinkled, their necks cocked, their faces graced in various parts by smiles and injury. Karel leans back behind the pillar and touches his cheekbone, feels the slightest pressure of his fingers roll through the tender flesh and center itself into a sharp, concentrated point behind the hard sphere of his eye. He grits his teeth and pulls the swollen lid up and holds his breath against the pain, and when he sees the girls and their father emerge with Father Carew from the sacristy into the far side of the narthex, it's as if he is watching them from some submerged vantage point beneath a murky surface of still creekwater.

When he turns loose of his eyelid, his vision narrows again through one eye, and when Father Carew catches sight of him there, shivering and dripping rainwater, the expression on the priest's face

234

is one of confused sympathy, the look of a man who's had his heart wrenched by the incomprehensible sight of a woman crumpled into some mournful posture, undone by tears of joy. The girls are unveiled, their long hair pulled back into braids embellished by tiny dianthus blossoms, their dark skin offset by dresses white and delicate as sunlit dogwood, their calves half-hidden by airy hems of scalloped lace. They are smiling at something their father has whispered to them, their faces blooming with some undisclosed joy and yet still demure and composed, all but absent of the sly pride they'd worn two days before when they'd climbed from the carriage on the farm-to-market road, beckoned by his will and his whistle. But as they near Karel, gathering behind the screen beyond the opposite column, his kneecaps prickle with a chill and the cords of muscle twitch in his warped neck. Father Carew leaves them, glancing at Karel through the corner of his eye while processing down the aisle toward the bridegrooms, but then Graciela turns to whisper something into her tallest sister's ear, and Karel is pierced by the certainty of it — she's wearing a bruise, a dark, upturned crescent fringed with blue beneath her left eye. Karel recalls the sweet pain of her mouth on his eye, and he'd swear his heart has fallen a hitch in his chest, that it's dangling from some fraying wet thread in the cold and constricted insides of him. I ought to be able to return the favor, he thinks, whether she'd want me to or not. When he steps out into plain view, he returns his hat to his head and stands dripping rainwater until Villaseñor catches sight of him and shoulders hurriedly between his girls.

From the nave, the music starts up again, signaling the arrival of the brides, and when the parishioners turn expectantly in their pews, what they see instead of the three virginal girls in white they expect to come in gracefully measured steps down the aisle is Karel Skala in his rain-soaked clothes, his hat on his head in the house of God, standing his ground against the approach of the girls' well-dressed father. And then Villaseñor's men rise from their pews at the front of the church, their hands hung awkwardly at their sides, the thick fingers working in the empty air, unaccustomed as they are to the lack of gunmetal.

Karel glances toward their approach, toward his brothers, who are standing frozen in their lock-kneed anticipation, and then he turns to Villaseñor, who is standing so near him that Karel can smell the clean, smoky warmth of his breath. "Who was it hit her?" Karel asks, nodding over the man's shoulder toward Graciela.

Villaseñor pushes his spectacles up high on the bridge of his nose, clearing his throat and righting his suitcoat on his shoulders by tugging at its hem while he studies this boy before him. When his men reach him, he brings them up short with a single hand held palm down at his side. Inside, the pews are alive with whispers, and Graciela has come to her father's side, her face beautiful despite the bruise, her hair so dark against the feathery white bodice of her dress, her eyes urging him silent with their conspiratorial wideness.

"Who struck you?" Karel asks.

She shakes her head, and her father silences her with a look before stepping toward Karel and issuing him, with a hand behind his shoulder, toward the door and out of the congregants' view. "Come," he says, the promise of satisfied curiosity in the calm, low tone of his voice.

Karel goes with him, his blood pulsing hot in the lid of his damaged eye, and Villaseñor's men follow, affording enough space between themselves and their master for the discreet exchange of confidences. At the door, Karel shrugs the man's hand and plants his feet, stealing glances at the girl, who remains in the aisle between the columns with her groom's eyes and his brother's equally upon her.

"Don't think you can go so easily unnoticed, boy," Villaseñor says. "By day or night, it makes no difference. You've had all of her you're going to have."

Karel's astonishment at such straight talk clots fast into something he can't swallow in the back of his throat, and the nervous resentment of a scolded boy gives rise to an angry trembling in his hands. "But you'll let him have her, sure enough? Marry her off to a man what hits her?"

Villaseñor smiles at such foolishness, pulls his spectacles from his face and produces a pressed white handkerchief from his breast pocket with which to wipe them, though they appear to Karel to be free of even the trace of a smudge or a fleck of dust. "Boy, if he'd struck her he'd be nursing worse wounds than what you and your father have laid on him. He's mostly of a mind that all your talk last night was just that, only talk. I assured him that it was."

"I wouldn't pay a pail of pig shit for what he thinks. I'm asking about her face."

"It's a hard way to go in life without brothers. You'll likely change your mind, and you might see to it that it's not too late when you do."

"It's too late already. You've seen well enough to that. You going to tell me who hit the girl, or do I have to ask her?"

"Your father didn't have to take my wager, boy. It wasn't all my doing."

Karel stuffs his hands into his pockets and runs his tongue over his teeth as if he might taste the bitterness of his words before he speaks them. "You call me boy again, and your men are going to need their guns."

Villaseñor laughs without parting his lips, a half-swallowed dismissal that balls Karel's hands into fists in his pockets. "Well, they aren't far from them if they do. But I've seen you fight, and you don't want to tangle with either one of these two men, much less the both of them. They may have some gray in their whiskers, but there's nothing but black in their hearts. Still, I see your point. You're more man than boy, *Mister* Skala, and I expect you'll act like one. I'll answer your question, and then can I expect you'll take your leave?"

"I ain't much for weddings or church, either one, so I reckon that would suit me fine, long as you don't mean to tell me that she fell in the night or ran into a doorjamb. She's been hit, plain enough."

237

"Yes. Plainly she has. Plainly. And it was the doing of the only man who has the right to do it. The only man who ever will. Now, if you don't mind, I have a wedding to attend to. I've got my guests to think about."

It takes a slow second to sink in, and when it does, Karel's hands come fast out of his pockets. "You're one rotten son of a bitch," he says. "It ain't no wonder your wife up and left every time some other man came sniffing around."

Villaseñor smoothes his fingers over his sideburns and shakes his head as if considering nothing more personal than the antics of some intractable, half-broke colt. Still Karel notices on the man's face the first suggestion of his vulnerability, an involuntary twitch in the fleshy lower lid of his eye, and while Karel focuses in, trying to discern in the arrhythmic pulsing some predictable pattern, Villaseñor unbuttons his suitcoat and, with an exhalation more akin to a resigned sigh than to the breath of exertion, he doubles the boy over with a solid, grunting blow to the stomach.

Felled and gasping, Karel slumps forward on his knees, his throat soured with the rise of bile, the stinging of sacramental incense ablaze in his vacant lungs. The man is standing before him leisurely, buttoning his coat, fishing the handkerchief from his pocket again and wiping his face while his men wrench Karel's arms behind his back and bring him to his feet such that it feels like his limbs might tear loose of his shoulders at the joints. And then he's swung toward the door, his face turned to protect his injured eye as the men use his body to push open the door, his forehead knocking against the seasoned oak with the same muted thud of the parishioners' missals dropped into the backs of the pews. Outside there's the cold, reviving bite of wind, the splattering of rain in the rutted and puddled road, the helpless fluttering in his chest as he's turned loose with a heave toward the slick descent of the church steps. When he lands, his breath comes back to him all at once, and he takes hold of the railing, righting himself, surveying the torn knee of his trousers and the abraded palm of his hand. There's a compacted, leaden weight in his gut, and he imagines that his heart, dense and still throbbing, has been jolted free of its frayed tether and has splashed sickly into his stomach so that it might be consumed by one of the very organs that it has failed with its frailty.

From just inside the doorway, flanked by his men, Villaseñor throws Karel's crumpled hat to the boy's feet and then stands with his arms at his sides, palms up. Overhead, the clouds roll curdled between the horizons, and Karel can make no more sense of the man's gesture than he could two days ago, though it seems now, as then, neither apology nor promise, neither benign nor threatening. He leans forward beneath the weather to pick up his hat, gestures with it at the man, and then sets the sopping thing on his head. "I'm betting it's a lot more of her mother in her than you care to think," he says. "She gets it in her mind to go, she'll be gone for good."

Villaseñor whispers to his men, tilting his head and looking toward the interior of the church, into which they disperse. Turning back toward Karel, he smoothes his lapels and squares his coat again on his shoulders. On his face he wears the impatient disinterest of an undertaker at a late wake. The tick beneath his eye, too, is gone, shed with the mindless, deciduous ease of a single glinting fish scale cast toward the creekbottom by a meandering school. Before he closes the door and the bolt scrapes into its socket, he averts his eyes so that he appears to be looking over Karel's shoulder, speaking to the storm or the Township Inn across the road or some other boy, one he expects might listen. "Boy," he says, "I'd expect you'd have sworn off betting after last night. Besides which, I've heard all the stories, and you don't know any more about my daughter's mother than you do about your own."

THREE HOURS LATER, near on to two o'clock, Karel sits in his still-damp clothes near the blue crackling of the wood-burning stove at the end of the icehouse bar, tracing with his thumb a swath through the cool condensation that has fogged the side of his glass. Excepting him and the new barkeep, the place is empty. Bern Chytka has learned in short order to pull Karel a new pint before the foam of the previous draught slides to the bottom of the otherwise empty glass. And even more to Karel's liking, he's settled into silence and sits behind the bar reading the *Gazette,* keeping a distant vigil over his solitary customer. In the first ten minutes, he'd spoken often enough to keep Karel in his wet coat, to prove himself interested enough in his own reflection to keep the bar polished to a reflective sheen in which he could heed the wet-combed part in his dark hair. A young man who, due either to his pale, willowy physique or his townie temperament or both, Bern has chosen, even before taking a wife, a life spent tending the slurred needs of Dalton's thirsty over the shin-deep frustrations of his family's rice fields out east in El Campo. Karel knows this and more, cares to know none of it, but now there has grown a common comfort in the hot popping of hardwood in the stove and rustling of the newspaper and the bitter cool of pilsner fizzing in his throat. He wonders how it's become so that, at fifteen, he can feel like he's been in the world for an eternity, that he can watch this man behind the bar with the knowing amusement of an old man watching a boy spit between his teeth or stand with a thumb hitched into his trouser pocket, playing at an age the trials of which he can't possibly fathom.

He's far from drunk, but he knows it will only be a matter of time, by damn, so when the swollen door groans open behind him, he shakes his head at the wavering nature of a fate that has rendered him half-orphaned and brotherless only to refuse him a few hours of quiet. He keeps his shoulders hunched forward and his eye on the white rise of bubbles through the amber beer, posturing himself against intrusion, but when Bern says, "Afternoon, there," and the stool next to his scrapes back from the bar, Karel figures it's no use to pretend he's any longer alone. What he doesn't expect, when he turns to bid some rain-idled farmer good afternoon, is to find sitting next to him the quiet, gray-haired woman who'd pulled him into the world.

"Little early for drinking, ain't it?" she says, nodding at his glass.

"No use putting it off," Karel says. "It's late enough somewhere."

Bern has folded his paper and taken hold of his dear bar rag and come with a relieved smile over to a customer he must assume might like to converse. "We don't stock cider, ma'am," he says. "We don't get many women in here. There's some blackberry wine."

She smiles, winking at Karel before she looks up at the new bar-keep and extends her hand. "I'm Edna Janek," she says.

"My pleasure. Bern Chytka."

"Well, Bern, if it ain't considered proper for women to drink beer where you come from, then you might just as well start making yourself accustomed to it now."

Bern tucks his rag into the waist of his trousers and his ears flush red beneath his overtended hair. "Where I come from," he says, "it's a woman's privilege to have whatever pleases her."

While Bern pulls her a beer, Edna settles into her seat and works her fingers through the wet tangles of her hair. Karel reckons he's seen her in town or up county a couple times every month of his life without ever, excepting the occasional pleasantries at Sunday Mass, speaking more than a few words to her. She smells, always, airy and clean, faintly of jasmine and talcum, like a woman half her age and still casting her charms in search of a husband, and now, when she takes a sip of her beer and perches her chin in her hand as if she'd been summoned to meet him here but hasn't yet learned the purpose, Karel clears his throat and widens his eyes at her in a resigned invitation.

"That's a considerable shiner you've got there," she says.

"I've considered it some," he says.

She smiles and her eyes soften, little wrinkles pleating the corners of her mouth. "My boys say those heifers your father sold them last spring paid for themselves already."

"Yes, ma'am. Herefords is good enough stock. Breed them with that Angus bull of theirs and they'll have some nice Black Baldies. Stout enough, and less of a handful than most when it comes time to put them through the chute."

"Well, they claim they like them."

Karel nods and takes a pull of his beer. "Don't know why they sold off them longhorns. It was a nice herd their father had."

Edna spins her glass on the bar, and to Karel it seems an orchestrated act, the feigned idle habit of a woman who has none. "Say it takes too long to bring them to weight. And that's true enough, I guess, but it don't take too much thinking to reckon it was hard for them, working their daddy's cows."

"It's hard working any cows," Karel says, and when he finishes his beer, Bern is already setting a new glass down in front of him. Karel nods his thanks, feels the woman's black eyes on him, and the barkeep retreats to his newspaper. "Keeps raining this way, it might could float all the livestock clear out of the county."

She tilts her head such that Karel thinks at first she's paying mind to the rainfall on the roof, but then he realizes that she's mirroring the angle of his own bent neck, that she's doing what she must to level her eyes on his. And then her hand is on him, holding his forearm, a chapped, working woman's hand with the pale-veined traces of her age strung beneath the skin like rivers on some sun-bleached map. She wears, still, her wedding band, and it squeezes a half-size too tight into the flesh of her finger. "I spoke to Father after the wedding, at the reception at the Township. He wanted me to give you his apologies if I came to see you, said it would have been his druthers to have you there, to have all four of you there. And it would have been for me, too. I tended all four of your births, and he baptized the lot of you. It was something lacking without you there."

Karel puts a thumb to the corner of his eye. Almost numb. The beer is doing its work on him, and he suspects that, after so long on this stool, the floor will tilt beneath his feet when finally he stands. He'd rather not be talking, sure enough. He'd rather sit and drink and draw mindless lines in the frost on his glass, run through his remaining money and drink until dusk and then stumble home through the rain and slop to a father who's spent himself aimlessly in the fields and gone early to snore alone in his bed. Still, there is a comfort in Edna's touch, and Karel guesses there hasn't been a time since he was weaned that he's had occasion to have a woman's hands on him two days running. He wishes his sleeves were rolled up.

"Your father at home? He's going to need a lot of help, Karel. Especially now."

"He's home. Plowing water, last I saw him."

She brushes a damp strand of hair from the corner of her mouth. "I wish you'd have seen him when your mother was still alive. Wish you'd seen them together. He wore a smile you couldn't scour from his face with hog bristles. At the parish dances, he wouldn't give her a rest, had her on her feet for every polka and waltz. Even in church, in the pews, he'd have his arm around her shoulders. She was a handsome woman, your mother. All that pretty blond hair. You've seen pictures."

"No, ma'am," Karel says, pushing back his stool. "Not in a long time, I haven't."

A Reaping of Smoke and Water

DECEMBER 1924

THE WIND HAD broken before daylight with an abrupt and violent certainty. Karel had fallen asleep to the labored groans of the weather raking over the rooftop and rattling through the bare branches of the pear trees out back in the grove, and then, an hour before dawn, he'd come upright in bed when, all at once, the world was beset by silence and stood hushed and bright, coddled by moonlight. He rose, his back and neck stiff from all the jostling of the previous day spent in the truck, and he pulled back the quilt and went gingerly over the cold hardwoods, his feet bare and his long drawers sagging at the seat, to peer out the back window toward the stable. He knew before parting the curtains that there would be no vehicle other than his own parked out there in the drive, no trailer, no twins come to make amends for their time away from the farm and the animals they'd promised to tend. He'd been had, of that he was certain, and without the plaintive wind and the high-pitched voices of children, the house had fallen too quiet even for the comfort of a man who breathed always a little easier when left to his lonesome. He'd wasted a day, and there was no telling how much business he'd lost around the county, and now his pursuit of the Knedliks would have to wait. He'd get dressed and make a pot of coffee. Fry some eggs and potatoes. He'd fill his cigarette case and tend to the livestock and wrap a nice, fatty hunk of ham in paper for the widow Vrana, and then he'd go collect his family and bring them home.

If those boys hadn't shown up by then, he'd hunt them down and make them wish to hell they had.

After breakfast, when the topmost arc of the sun neared the treeline on the easternmost fringe of the Skala property, foretelling its return with a faint flourish swept up in pink streaks from the horizon, Karel straightened his back from his work slinging feed to the chickens and turned toward the sound of an approaching motor. By the time Karel dumped the last of the feed and made it back around the barn with the empty pail swinging in his hands, Father Carew was unfolding his tenuous, ancient body from behind the wheel of his Ford. At better than eighty, the priest had a full head of hair, his brows lush, overgrown tangles that, had he found an outdoor occasion to stretch himself onto his back during the previous day's gusts, would have made for his eyes more than adequate windbreaks. In all other ways, he was an old man, one who hunched and shuffled beneath the mass of his own prolonged history, and for the last year or so it had surprised Karel each time he saw him about in town and, upon doing so, realized that the man was, yes, still very much above ground. Karel tossed the empty pail clanging into the barn and tipped his hat. Carew came slack and sliding his feet up the gravel drive, buttoning his coat with palsied hands and meeting Karel's eyes with a mournful tightening of the lips that had in it, to Karel's thinking, both sadness and suspicion.

"Morning, Father. You're about early."

Carew took a handkerchief from his trousers and hacked wetly into it. "Not early enough, it would seem," he said, studying the product of his cough in the handkerchief before folding it back into his pocket and making the sign of the cross. "There's a dead boy on your property, over where the road crosses the creek."

Karel massaged the curvature of his neck with a thumb and narrowed his eyes. "*God bless.* Who is it?"

"I don't recognize him. You ought to get yourself a telephone, Karel."

"A telephone? They making them now so you can call a dead man and ask his name?"

"He's just a boy, Skala. There's a black filly with him. Looks like one of your brother's animals. If you had a phone, Thom might have called you same as he did me. His stable burned last night. His girl is hurt, bad I think. I was on my way out there when I drove up on the horse wandering just this side of your fenceline near the road. The boy's facedown in your creek."

Karel squinted into the glare of dawn, his ribs chilled of a sudden so that it felt to him like his bones had been left to soak overnight in the cistern. He pulled his cigarettes and matches from his coat pocket, offering one to the priest, who shook him off. Striking the match, Karel looked to the north where, faint but unmistakable, dark smoke haloed with white steam hung above the horizon. He took a pull on his cigarette, saw the girl as she'd been all those years back, the dark hair pasted to her chest and the hips slid each in turn from her pants, the little moles up high above her breasts. He exhaled smoke, which rose white and pluming in the aimless winter air. "Which girl?" he asked. "Graciela? His wife?"

The priest sucked on his teeth and shook his head, his eyes creased with curiosity at the corners. "His *little* girl," he said. "The third child, I believe."

The coldness ran out of Karel, and he took another deep drag on his cigarette, his relief rising within him unburdened for a moment before buckling beneath the dense compression of guilt that found him recalling the recent occasion on which he'd seen the girls following their mother outside the mercantile in Shiner, each of the older two in her store-bought gingham and pigtails, the baby perched on the still-alluring swell of her mother's hip. Over the years, when a chance meeting in town with one of his brothers or their wives occasioned it, Karel had taken to crossing the street, keeping his distance, avoiding even the exchange of feigned pleasantries. There had been times, sure enough, when he'd turned the corner and found himself face-to-face with one of them, but last week there had

249

been nothing unavoidable about their meeting. He'd seen her a full block away, and something about the baby perched on Graciela's hip and her girls all decked out in town made it seem to Karel all the more spineless to dodge something so simple as a conversation. Still, when she smiled at him without showing her teeth, a cautious sadness on her lips, something bitter rose in his throat such that, when he removed his hat, he had to swallow when he would have preferred to spit. "Quite a little stable full of fillies you and Thom got there," he said, returning his hat to his head and reaching for his cigarettes.

Now the smile washed from her face altogether. The two older girls stood at her side, each reaching for their mother's free hand, and Graciela worked her fingers such that one could have the pinkie, the other the thumb. Even now, Karel thought, there's not enough of her to go around. "Is it all still about horses with you, Karel? I heard you sold all your best stock years ago."

"Wasn't anything but geldings left to sell," he said. "Anyway, horse farming didn't suit me. Ain't nothing ever come out of a stable but disappointment."

She nodded while he lit his cigarette, and Karel could see in the dark widening of her eyes that it was a nod of understanding, not agreement. "Well," she said, "it's easy to expect too much, I suppose, out of any animal."

"Expect much of anything with some and it's likely to be too much."

"Too much for the animal, Karel? Or for the one with all the expectations?"

Before she'd guided her children around him and walked down the street, she'd watched him furrow his brow, and she'd laughed with such kindness that he'd wanted to laugh with her. It had been so long, so damned long ago. All of it. And still he couldn't bring himself to cheapen it with a smile.

Even now, when Father Carew spoke of her family, he saw her. Not Thom. Not her father. Not the children. He saw her, felt her long hair falling over him. He couldn't help himself, and then he remembered the nameless boy he'd seen out hunting, working downwind with his nameless father in that pasture up north of Shiner. He saw his own son, just hours in the world, sleeping and sucking quietly at the memory of his mother's breast. "Jesus," he said.

The priest frowned. "Yes. May He help us. I need to go. There could be need of a sacrament. Can you tend to the horse and the body?"

"Better than they can tend to each other, I expect. Tell Thom I'll be there in an hour. I show up unannounced, it's liable to surprise him more than a stable fire. I was heading up to fetch Sophie and the kids in Praha. I'll stop in on the way."

He found the filly nibbling at the fringe of yellow grass along the farm-to-market road just north of the creek's southern fork. Karel set the brake and left the truck idling in the drive while he fetched the rope and harness from the bed and cleared his throat, spitting into the earth that he owned outright. The sun was up in full now, its proud rays striking brightly against the gravel of the drive Karel had so improved since the farm fell entirely to him, and the horse looked up and whinnied when it took note of his arrival, her slender head bobbing in little, anticipatory nods. From her nostrils came punctuated bursts of steam. Karel held a cigarette between his lips, the smoke coming up thin and curling like that which routinely rose from the snuffed altar candles of St. Jude's after Mass. Karel buttoned his coat, left the door of the truck open. He slid his boots as he made his way to open the gate, comforted, as he always was, by the feel and sound of gravel crunching underfoot. With the passing of the previous day's wind had come a distillation of the county's cold-weather fragrances, the sweetness of burning oak from wood-stoves given edge by the mesquite of the smokehouses, all of it over-laid by the cool black newness of the awaiting soil, the sappy hints of sweet gum and pine.

After swinging open the gate, Karel surveyed the horse. She was a flawless, glossy black except for her blaze and socks, and there was no mistaking her owner. She worked her jaw cross-hinged against a mouthful of winter grass, and Karel's eyes followed a trail of bent, blood-painted weeds down to the sick sprawl of the body in the slough on the soft bank where water trickled and gurgled timeless secrets intelligible to the creekbed stones alone. He let the cigarette drop from his mouth and steadied the animal with a hand smoothed down her neck, whispering to her as he did. "Who the hell was it brought you here, girl?"

She snorted as if in answer, and Karel coaxed her into the harness and roped her up short to the corner fencepost. It was an inconsiderate job of horse-tying, a lead too stingy to allow for easy grazing, a half-assed knot, and Karel knew that, had he found her this way, he'd have thought the job done by some prideless, townie fool, by a man who meant to return either directly or never, and who, either way, couldn't be bothered to feel the same way Karel usually did about the importance of doing even the simple, workaday things right.

Down at the water's edge, squirrels were at work in the high branches of the pine and water oak, and when Karel approached the body, a pair of mourning doves launched themselves loudly up and across the creek, flashing the white fringes of their wings in the sunlight as they went. One of the dead boy's legs called to mind a thick and dangling storm-sheared bough. It was broken through such that the trousers creased unnaturally, folding over on themselves at mid-shin, the calf and muddy boot hanging at a tortured angle as if by only the fabric of the pant leg itself. The boy's face was in the creek, the shoulders of his coat darkened with water. It made Karel's stomach sour just to look at it, and he squatted down, picked up a fallen twig and, perching himself on his boot heels, drew a row of imperfect little circles in the wet silt as he considered whether to drag the body or carry it. It was one of the Knedliks, sure enough. From the looks of the broken leg, it was held together by muscle and skin alone, so Karel guessed he'd best lug the boy from under the arms or lift him like some sleeping, overgrown child from bed.

Either way, he'd have to get him out of the water and turn him over. There'd either be a scar on the boy's face or there wouldn't be, and Karel figured he'd know soon enough how at least half of their story had ended. Karel came back to his feet with the groan of a much older man, and when he bent over the boy, flipping his coat-tail up to find that, thankfully, the little son of a bitch at least had the common courtesy to be wearing a belt, he took hold of the leather. The boy wasn't much heavier than a week-old bull calf, and Karel pulled him up through the mud and into the weeds before flipping him onto his back with a grunt.

It was the quiet one, Joe, and Karel stared down at the boy, who stared blindly into the brightening sky. His lips were the chapped, peeling blue of a molting water snake, lips that Karel realized now he'd never heard utter a word, and something about this new certainty prompted Karel to turn, surveying the pastureland behind him for any sign of the boy's brother. Recalling the way the twins had stood together in the moonlight, their loose-jointed confidence and the easy allegiance of those who'd known each other even before they'd drawn breath in the world, Karel couldn't imagine one wandering too far from the other's sight. It would have taken something violent and unforeseen to wreck a leg that way, something even more so to allow for the dislocation of these brothers one from the other. Out two hundred yards to the north, just this side of the nearest hedgerow, a dozen head of Karel's herd stood grazing around two broken bales, switching their tails and paying no heed whatsoever to the mindless, maternal circling of the jackass. Far behind them, smoke churned in the sky like storm clouds. If Raymond was yet around, he was well hidden, but Karel reckoned it was unlikely. He'd heard stories about twins, about the twinge of fear or pain that might vex one if the other, no matter the distance between them, had stumbled into some trouble.

Karel looked into the hard sunlight until his eyes watered, and then he shut them tight and thought of his own brother. He was but a handful of miles away, and his stable had caught fire in the night. If Carew had the story straight, if one of the children was bad off, Thom might be grieving the loss of more than the lumber and tack

254

of his horsebarn. Karel kept his eyes closed and thought hard on it, but he didn't feel a thing. They weren't twins. Hell, they weren't hardly anymore even brothers. Only one of them had ever known his mother; only one had suckled a stranger.

Karel turned and opened his eyes, looking the dead boy over and shaking his head. He leaned over the body, reached down and shut the boy's eyes one at a time with his thumb, the slick, clammy skin of the eyelids no more human to the touch than would be two wilted, frostbitten leaves. He wouldn't drag him to the truck. The boy may have been a thief. He may have been worse. Surely, now, he wasn't any damned thing at all, but it hadn't been even three full days since they'd sat together in Praha, listening to the same waltzes and polkas, licking beer froth from their upper lips and tapping their feet in time to the music. If Karel had found the boys yesterday, he might have broken their legs himself, but by his reckoning you couldn't give the dead any more of what they deserved than they'd already gotten.

He planted his feet and kept his back straight as he squatted beside the body, sliding his arms beneath the thighs and shoulders, and when he came upright beneath the young man's weight, the broken leg swung down with a sick grinding of bone and the boy's boot heel spurred sharply against the side of Karel's knee. "You little shit," Karel said, catching his breath. "All of a sudden you got to have the last goddamn word, do you?" His eyes had come full with tears, and while he waited for his vision to clear, he bent his knees such that the boy was very nearly lying in his lap. He looked him over, noticing now what he had missed before: The blue lips were upturned faintly at the corners. Not a smile so much as the promise of one. "Go on ahead, but you start laughing and you can walk your own dead ass to the truck, you hear me?"

He frowned at his own foolishness, at the fact that he was talking to a dead man, making play threats to the only kind of person who can no longer fathom fear. And then something cracked wide inside him like some parched fissure that opened deep into the baked earth during drought season. His eyes had cleared, the pain in his knee just a twinge of memory, but now he was seeing his father, the blood dark at the corner of his mouth, his body sucking into the mud of the land he'd tried the whole of his adult life to work toward his own ends, his tobacco-stained lips whispering to his one remaining son, the one to whom the land would fall now that he had fallen, the son he couldn't lose because he'd never quite had him to begin with.

Karel looked down at Joe's body in his arms, bore its weight over the very same land where his father had fallen, and when he got to the truck, he lowered the dead boy carefully into the bed. He drove the body to the stable and laid it out on a narrow bed of hay bales against the nearest stall, and then he came back on foot for the horse. It would have saved time to ride the filly bareback up the drive to the homestead, but when Karel untied her and stroked her white blaze, he was still all those years back, staring down at his father, at a man who was talking nonsense, asking, unless the impossible could be done, to be left for dead, and Karel couldn't set himself right for mounting an animal that had so recently carried a dying man toward this parcel of black soil where more than one had found his end on horseback.

ON THE NORTHERN HORIZON, beyond Shiner on the road toward Praha, white steam and black smoke rose together like the
slow wind-borne ascension of a ghost and its shadow from behind
the distant trees, and Karel kept an eye on it above the treeline as
he drove toward his brother's farm with all the lingering, sluggish
reticence of a man beholden to a task that promised to increase
neither his pride nor his property. In the truck, with lips pressed
tightly enough together to flatten the butt of his cigarette, Karel let
the ashes drop into his lap and kept his grip fast on the wheel while
his mind took only occasional note of the road. In the last ten years,
they'd come to him only rarely, these memories of his father, but
once they dug into him they were as biting and stubborn as the
needle-sharp tip of a mesquite thorn embedded and broken off beneath the skin.

He and his father had fallen, in the gray days after Karel's brothers left, into a restless but silent pattern of parallel work. The rain
came on in taunting waves, waning of a morning only to return before the bobwhite cocks began their melodic, eventide beckoning.
During the day, rain or no, his father worked the horses to a useless,
steaming fatigue before the plow while Karel tended to the other
wintertime needs of the farm — mending fences and setting out bales
of hay for the livestock; waking early to sling feed and gather eggs;
milking the dairy cow and breaking, when it froze overnight, the
skin of ice that formed over the surface of the cattletank. In the early

afternoon, he'd come inside to find the cold remnants of his father's lunch on the table, and while he ate with his boots on he'd make a mental list of the chores that remained for him. The laundry, which had to be hung from makeshift lines in the hayloft to dry. The seasoned firewood he had to split and stack to dry in the smokehouse for a day or two before it could be piled into the bins beside the house's two stoves. After lunch he'd move through the day with the same halting, nearly imperceptible progress of the enfeebled sun descending through the begrudging mass of clouds toward the murk of the horizon.

When it was all done, before his father stabled the spent horses, Karel would take a dollar or two from the roll of petty cash his father kept stashed in a tobacco pouch at the bottom of the old milk can set just inside the kitchen door. With a link of smoked sausage or a hunk of bread folded around cold ham or bacon in his coat pocket, he'd make out on foot toward the icehouse in town. Since the wedding, his brothers had been kept busy scouting the surrounding county with their father-in-law for farms they could buy out and, Karel imagined, come nightfall, in the warm beds they shared with their wives at the inn, and he took a resigned, if uneasy, comfort in the knowledge that he wouldn't find them about town after dark. At the saloon, he'd sit apart from the other locals and spend his money quietly, pint by pint, hoping that he'd get home to find the stable lantern out, his father's boots outside the door, and his mash jug corked in the kitchen.

More and more, as the rain kept up and the days began to bleed one into another, this would prove a fruitless hope. His father, after working the animals through all the sunlit hours, had taken to drinking whiskey by twilight and riding Whiskey by night, whipping the gelding and running him hard out near the creek in the moonless rainfall, throwing muddy turf, racing the animal against some phantom rival across the flooded black stretch of pasture, around the leafless stand of moss-draped oaks, and back between the drenched clods of ash in the fire pits toward the fenceline where, absent the agitations of tethered horses, the taut barbed wire quivered in the breeze as if charged by some cold electricity generated by unspoken compunction alone.

Now, on the road between the shimmering, sun-struck fencing, Karel shivered in the cab of the truck. He kept the window cracked despite the cold, and cigarette smoke caught the draught and threaded its way out the window in a fine, unwavering line of white. He was going to see his brother, to see Graciela, to find there some charred remnant of stable and family both. There was a dead boy in his own horsebarn, and in the stall where Whiskey had once found relief from his harnesswork, sleeping and breathing heavily, sheltered from the weather, waking only to nuzzle his bucket of dry oats and blink his eyes slowly before returning to sleep – there, now, Graciela's black filly stood, tired and curried, keeping the company of Karel's sad, underused team of draught horses. It was all the truth of the present, but he had let his awareness of it slouch back into the recesses of his mind the way the guilt stricken, in time, fold their sins into the gray creases of their consciousness, into the musty and neglected shadows of all that is not quite forgotten.

As if supplanted by the present, then, comes a night disinterred from those same rarely robbed graves of memory, and in the short drive from his farm to Thom's, Karel considered neither the bright sky nor the red-tailed hawk riding thermals before funneling down toward some promise of prey to the west nor the face of the boy he'd met only once before carrying his corpse. Instead, there is hard, dark night. There is rain, no longer a downpour, but a sheeting of mist that overlays the landscape in a black, lacy haze, that drips from the lantern he holds in his half-numb hand. There is the cattlegate, swung open and sagging earthward on its worn hinges, the sound of some dull and distant locomotion at work beneath the hissing of the weather. Karel stands with his hat pulled down low on his brow, steadying himself with a hip on the fencepost while he unbuttons his trousers and relieves himself after a dollar's worth of drinking, his head muddled with pilsner, his mouth dry despite the rain, his injured eye yet blue beneath the bottom lid but no longer swollen or tender to the touch.

He's come home to find the stable lantern lit, the back door of the house cracked open, his father's jug uncorked beside an all-but-empty jelly jar on the stable workbench. And now his father, he knows, is out here somewhere on the horse he promised would never again race. Refastening his trousers, Karel looks up to find horse and rider emerging from a night unadorned by moonlight, the animal steaming toward him, churning water up in a wild confusion of spray to meet in midair the persistent rainfall. His father is red-faced and beaming and unsteady in the saddle, his hat brim wilted and streaming, one cheek bulging so with tobacco that he appears to have come directly from some visit to the town dentist gone wrong. When he brings the horse up short before the fence and speaks, Karel can't tell if it's his own drunkenness or his father's that thickens the words with such a gauzy slur.

The horse blows, a gluey froth slung from its mouth, before side-stepping, lurching beneath the weight of days and nights both at this crazed man's mercy. Vaclav reins the animal around and sits there in the yellow haze of rain and the halo of the lantern's flame, his labored breath smoking as he digs into his coat pocket for his watch, which he tents with a cupped hand before springing it open. "Holy hell," he shouts, turning the illegible face toward Karel. "I should've run the thing myself, boy. Even at my age, and in the god-damn slop, too, I can outrun your scrawny ass."

There comes, despite the cold, a hot, crawling wash of blood along the skin of Karel's throat, and he tilts his head the easy way, with the curvature of his neck, and opens his parched mouth to the falling rain. He swallows, his fingers clenching and relaxing around the lantern handle, prickling with cold as the feeling returns to them. "It must be some awful cocksure whiskey you're drinking. You couldn't outrace even Stan, and his nuts turn to mush just *thinking* about running a horse full out."

His father comes off the horse so fast that Karel startles, throwing his free hand up to protect his healing eye while the lantern swings from its handle, casting the staggering man's face and the standing water at his feet in oscillations of jaundiced light and shadow. Vaclav spits tobacco juice and swipes the rain from his face, on which furrowed disgust has displaced the wide flush of pride. "Hell, boy, of course I can't. And neither can you. Ain't no outracing a goddamn ghost. But you look flesh and blood enough." Balling the reins in his fist, he thumps his knuckles into Karel's chest and reaches for the lantern. "Go on ahead then and make me a liar. Show me how fast you are. You sure as shit didn't show nobody nothing the other night."

Now, in his truck and less than a half mile from his brother's spread, Karel remembered little about his own ride that night other than that he'd been prideful enough to take his father's bait. There had come an eagerness, too, to feel the animal once more beneath him, to ride him again while his father was drunk enough to have either forgotten or neglected his promise. And while Karel eased up on the truck's throttle, stretching the short drive even farther, he saw himself handing the lantern to his father, surrendering the only light to be found on the quarter section of flooded meadow. In the memory, the rain is constant, coming down in a mist so fine that the individual drops prove indistinguishable one from the others. Karel climbs, as he has so many off-kilter nights, into the saddle while his father's eyes flash in the oily flickering like twin filaments sunk deep in the sockets of some otherwise insensible skull. Vaclav checks his watch, gives his son the signal, and Karel nudges the horse, feeling the trace of extra give in the overworked gelding's joints but coaxing him forward nonetheless, crouching forward and low over the shoulders of an animal that makes clear, with a violent, steaming snort and the rearward slant of its ears, that it has lost all of the will but none of the instinct to run.

After he circles the trees in a night so absent of animal sounds amidst the sheeting rainfall, he slaps the horse with his wet hat on the homebound stretch, then he stands lock-kneed in the stirrups and watches his illuminated father as the horse circles, favoring now its left front leg, in a half-hobbled, elliptical pattern like some scorched and humbled planet coming timidly round its sun.

When they stop, Karel puts his drenched hat back on his head and strokes the long roan slope of Whiskey's neck while Vaclav lurches forward, the lantern swinging erratically and the watch held out. "The hell'd you even mount the horse for if you didn't aim to run it? You ain't even broke four minutes, and I done that twice tonight already. Done it twice each night this week."

Karel takes the watch and holds it close so he can see the second hand spinning in an orbit of its own beneath the timepiece's primary face, and here he realizes the pointlessness of his father's challenge. Swinging from the saddle, he says, "It's no way for me to tell if I did or didn't, so we might as well just say you won and stable the horse. It's something wrong with his leg, anyway."

Vaclav spits and frowns and pushes his hat down low, reaching for the reins. "Horseshit," he says, handing over the lantern. "If I say you didn't, boy, then you didn't. And I don't care if the animal's ground down to stubs, I'll be damned if I ain't going to prove to you just how slow you are. Just wait until I'm set and tell me when."

Once his old man heaves his weight up into the saddle, Karel nods the signal and shields his face against the splattering of mud slung back at him. The horse jolts forward and then falters, and when Vaclav prods him with two heels thrown back at once, Karel stands in the muck and feels the numbness creep back into his hands. It looks shameful, his father spurring the horse this way, with his knees slack and his backside heavy in the saddle, throwing his feet backward like some moving-picture cowboy gaining fast on some moving-picture Indian so that he can pretend to shoot him with his shiny pretend gun. Karel sloshes his boots around in the standing water, and after a few minutes he holds the lantern high with an extended arm, searching the impervious distance for the emergence of the man for whom he feels a cold flash of embarrassment. He checks the watch, shielding it from the rain, and when five minutes have passed, he snaps it shut, drops it back into his pocket and makes off across the pasture toward the circle of oaks from which pain so often comes unforeseen.

It takes him longer than he would have thought to find them. He had expected to come upon his father drunkenly sulking and dismounted, leading a half-lame horse through the standing black water, the bitterness of his disappointment narrowing his eyes, but when Karel makes it all the way out to the stand of trees without a sign of them, he thinks at first his father has outwitted him once again, that the old man has loped the animal out to the far fence-line and ridden around the perimeter of the pasture in the dark until he's made it back to the stable, leaving Karel out here to drip and shiver in the cold and keep time for a race that was never intended to be run in full. He imagines his father grinning while he stables the horse, chuckling while he warms his hands in front of the kitchen stove and splashes mash from a new jug into the make-shift glass of his jelly jar.

Karel trudges through the mud and the drowning brown grass, holding his lantern out so that he feels the weight of the thing in his shoulder as he circles the stand of oaks. Just audible beneath the rainfall, twigs snap and rattle down through the brittle tree branches, landing in the brushwood below. The red eyes and ghostly mask of a mother opossum peer from within a high red oak hollow at the fringe of the treeline. The rain comes down heavier, and his boots suck ankle deep with each step until, when the light finds the twitching muscled haunches of the crippled horse, Karel stops and feels himself sinking beneath his own weight as if the earth itself were consuming him, little by little. Whiskey lies, slick with mud, on his side, working his rear legs periodically in frantic attempts to render himself upright, and Karel can see the front legs twisted and splayed, one of them clearly broken through above the pastern, a swath of disturbed earth trenching out from beyond the reaches of the lantern such that it appears the horse has dragged himself out of the darkness toward the feeble comfort of radiating light. Karel moves with caution around the horse's rear legs, circling the animal until he can squat, sitting on his soaked boot heels, near its head and run a hand over its neck while he peers into the dark where he knows his father must be. The horse exhales with a shudder, its breath coming in labored bursts of steam, the hollow music of the rain striking its hide like that of a wet-skinned drum played only with the fingertips of children. Karel has never thought of his love for the horse, has never thought of what he felt for the animal as love, and even now he isn't sure that's the word he would choose. But it is certainly something akin to affection, something as fluttering and warm as the fine quivering of the horse's musculature now at work beneath its damp hide. The trouble with animals, with caring for beasts, is that, if you do it very long at all, you have to witness the end of something you've seen born. Karel curses under his breath. He thinks of the rifle leaning by the kitchen door, of the long walk through the rain and mud he'll have to take so that, when he returns, he can do so equipped for a loud and necessary and violent kindness.

The horse, absent the heavy breathing, sprawls so quietly, its pain sustained without much of any outward complaint. Karel marvels at it, at the inborn capacity for such silent suffering. He recalls the crucifix behind the altar of St. Jude's. The way Stan had come to his feet all those years back, biting his tongue and crying unvoiced tears after their father had struck him down by the creek. He considers the countless times he's imagined his mother, the length of her hair, the crinkling pleatwork of her skirts, the soft blue consolation of her eyes. He'd never seen any of it, but now he can't check himself, can't help but think that he might very well have heard her voice, that he might have known the sound of her even from within her body, that she might have sung to her unborn while she went about her chores or cried out in those final moments of her labor pains, and that, though he can't recall it or reproduce it, he's been carrying it around inside of him, the memory of it, an actual memory of her, a real memory, for the whole of his life.

Stroking the horse, Karel blinks rainwater and runs his fingers down the smooth hide between Whiskey's eyes. The horse's ears come up in an attentive gesture of recognition, the only absolution an animal is equipped to offer, and then Karel forces himself to shake off these memories and fabrications, these fruitless distractions, and turns his mind to his father, listening for the sound of his need given voice over the racket of the rainfall. With a hand on the horse's neck for balance, he pushes himself back to his feet and moves forward, the lantern held before him, to discover what he knows he must.

WHEN HE REACHED the bare stand of blackjack oaks, Karel steered the truck onto his brother's drive and rattled over the cattle-guard, bouncing in and out of the deep ruts until he got the tires tracked into them and could drive without even a hand on the wheel. A quarter mile up the drive, when he came around the grove, it looked, for all the automobiles and wagons parked in hasty clusters about the property, to be a barn raising or an auction. Past the grove, between the barn and the cattletank, Villaseñor's Packard stood absent its sheen, the black paint chalked over with dust. Behind it, his brothers' new Dodge trucks and Father Carew's Ford. Black smoke climbed skyward, fringed with steam, from the other side of the barn, and a line of Shiner locals Karel recognized from the brewery and the wire works were busy dragging coupled lengths of hose and coiling them onto the back of the new Speedwagon pumper that the town had displayed so proudly at last autumn's Harvest Day parade. Karel set the brake and climbed from the cab, his sinuses ringing with the bite of cold air, with the tang of smoldering wood and fuel and hay, all of it soured with the foul traces of charred meat and singed hide. He pulled a cigarette from his case with his teeth, struck a match, and stood leaning with a hand on the warm hood of his truck while he let the smoke do its work, scanning the townsfolk for his relations and puzzling at the slow, defeated movements of all the men ambling about while, judging from the dense smoke coming up from behind the barn, the stable still burned.

When he made it around the grove to the pumper, he glanced into the windows of the house, where the soft silhouettes of women moved about behind the sheer kitchen drapes, drawing them now and again to peer out at the progress of the men or the fire or both. Up on the rear deck of the fire truck, catching his breath, Henry Kaspar stood in the center of a muddy coil of hose. If it hadn't been for his bowed legs, which flared out even when he stood still like he'd spent the whole of his life astride a dairy cow instead of some suitable mare, Karel might not have recognized him. His coat was torn at the collar and black as a coalman's, his hat dusted with ash, his new blue overalls left at home in favor of worn hurricane-cloth trousers and a sweat-stained cotton shirt, his mustache untamed by wax such that it appeared the thing had grown down from his nostrils rather than up from his lip. Karel touched the brim of his hat and held his cigarette in the dry hinge of his lips when he spoke. "Didn't make you for the pumper team, Henry. Looks of that smoke yonder, you're quitting a job when it ain't yet done."

Henry's eyes were shot through with the blood of a man who has seen, of recent, too much smoke and too little of his bedsheets. He stood with his boots encircled by the orderly coils of hose and looked down on Karel from his perch atop the back of the pumper, shaking his head at the gall of a man who'd no doubt close the Bible halfway through an early chapter of Genesis and then presume to tell the first of God's subjects how to better go about their begetting. "It's nothing left to do, Skala. We pumped the property dry in two hours. The well and the cattletank both. You want to lend a hand, you're more than welcome to go piss on the embers, see if that does the trick. Maybe resurrect all them horses while you're at it."

Karel bit down on the butt of his cigarette to keep himself from smiling. By damn if Henry didn't have a little salt to him after all. Karel gave the rising smoke another cursory look and then gave the man an appreciative nod. "They didn't get out? I've heard of horses that's kicked a stall door down just dreaming of fire."

Henry shook his head, reached down to pull more hose onto the coil. "Then they ain't dreamed of a fire what burned this fast," he said. "Looks of it, this one went up quicker than most. The men found a couple fuel cans set just inside the door. It ain't a horse one had time to make it out, but it's more damage inside the house than out. Your brother ain't said a word that I've heard since we got here."

Now Karel let his smoke fall and ground it into the damp soil with the toe of his boot as if trying to extinguish the thought that this bowlegged son of a bitch had brought flickering to life with a simple pair of words: *your brother.* It occurred to Karel that this was the way the whole county must see them, as the family that everyone but they themselves recognized as such, and the thought of being the kind of fool who called for fair weather when green clouds folded up in hail-bearing corrugations on the horizon wicked at him until he felt parched and withered and longing, like a cotton plant wilting in a monthlong drought, for the unabated battering of that which might save him. Henry looped another three yards of hose onto the coil and looked up from his work, his tired eyes weighted with fatigue and softened all the same with concern.

"It's one horse made it out," Karel said. "That's for certain. And a dead man riding it. Father Carew said one of the kids was hurt. House looks like it didn't even get singed."

Groaning as he rose from his labor, Henry squared his hat on his head and then put a hand on his hip and leaned backward, stretching his spine. When he'd come straight again, he shot Karel a curious look and spat between his teeth. "Word has it Thom dropped her trying to hurry down the stairs when he saw the stable was lit. Was afraid they'd take on too much smoke on the sleeping porch, I guess. Anyhow, she ain't woke up yet, last I heard."

"Mercy. So he's inside, then?"

"Came out soon as we ran dry of water. Just stood there and watched it burn for a while with the rest of us, then walked round back to the corral. Eddie and Stan gone with him."

"That a fact? Misery loves company, I reckon."

Henry worked his tongue up behind his lip so that it looked to Karel like the man's mustache had come alive and was readying itself to inch across his face. "I don't," Henry said, returning to his work. "I don't reckon misery loves any damn thing at all."

When Karel had circled around the barn, weaving through the automobiles parked in the drive, he noted his trailer sitting unhitched and grayed by fallen ash. Just months ago, he'd been so proud of the thing, of the smooth welds and the sturdiness of the chassis, of the fine black paint of the frame and the wheel wells, of the fine, straight craftsmanship of the bed's lumber. Now it was nothing more to him than an unsettling series of questions on wheels: How had the damn thing gotten here? Whose truck had towed it onto Thom's property? He couldn't imagine that even Raymond Knedlik would have come rolling onto this spread encumbered by a trailer, and so he must have lost it somewhere along the way. He must have surrendered the thing, knowing it wasn't his to begin with, and a boy like Raymond wouldn't have shrugged that off and let it lay. He'd been outsmarted or outgunned, either one, and he'd come looking to retake what he'd lost. For Karel, the questions promised little other than indigestion and the certain prospect that, buried in the unbroken soil of the truth, some stray seed was likely yielding the determined green sprout of his own culpability.

He cleared his throat and spat, reached for his cigarettes, but then, when the wind stirred the fire and its heat washed over him, stinging his eyes, he thought better of it. There was enough burning here, enough flame and smoke, and he turned his attention to what remained of the stable. The roof had caved, buckling the loft beneath it so that the center joists had sheared, splintered in the middle, and now speared jagged and charred into the inflamed confusion of burning stall timbers at the heart of the fire. In the heap of glowing embers lay black ribbons of metal, warped door runners and tack and hardware, all of them twisted amidst the burning lumber like steely tangles of innards within the scorched remains of

269

some mammoth beast that had fallen prey to its own infernal fate. The remaining fuel spat and sizzled, the smoke climbing and billowing, each outward rush blooming so that, from its center, another could rise. Karel leaned against the cant of his neck, trying to puzzle some whole out of all the smoking pieces, but the wreckage lacked any discernible order. The loft staircase had fallen and lay like a colossal and outstretched and steaming accordion, the former rise and run of the steps now inverted and meaningless and forever unburdened by the prospect of footfalls. Twin leg bones slanted up black from the embers like wet, axed forks of a diseased tree rooted and floundering in a steaming and tannic swampland. The stubborn, improbable loft chute still angled upward as if buttressed by some concession of gravity. Karel squinted against the smoke and squared his shoulders over his feet, the senseless remnants of the stable akin somehow to the way it seemed, when he stood in his own cropfields at dusk, that a horizon he knew to be true tilted nonetheless beneath the weight of the sun.

And then the faintest little breeze spiraled the smoke into a hazy tunnel through which he could see, out back of the stable, sitting hatless on the topmost fence brace of a corral meant to contain horses that were nothing more now than roasted bone and greasy ash, his brother. Stan and Eddie were with him, sure enough, standing with hands gripping the fence like it needed holding up, their attention turned to their brother, and when Thom caught sight of Karel, he slid off the fence and took a step forward as if he meant, with his brows furrowed and his hair swept behind his ears, to walk through the fire.

The wind whipped and then again settled, obscuring the view through the stable, the smoke filling the empty space as readily as water found the void of displaced water, as naturally as regret and fear seeped into the fissures of a man's cracked heart. Karel went again for his cigarettes, and this time he didn't stop himself. If the pumper team couldn't put this fire out, if a cistern and a cattletank full of cold water couldn't douse the flames, then there wasn't any harm, by damn, in lighting a little fire that a man could consume and, in doing so, control. He sparked a match, lit his smoke, tucked his cigarette case back into his coat pocket. Then he made his way around the stable, giving the fire a wide berth, wondering as he went how it had looked before the sun had come up, the orange embers drawn up into the sky, the smoke blooming white against the cold night sky. Karel had seen some impressive fires in his years — grass fires sparked by negligence or heat lightning come the parched months of summer, an explosive dust fire once at the cotton gin in Shiner when he was yet a boy — but this would have been different, the panic-stricken voices of animals and men alike rising above the familiar sound of the fire, that loud rush that could all but convince a man that something unstoppable had been set into motion, roaring its way nearer, bearing down on him. Karel wondered how many fires his boy would see in his life, how many he might watch idly before one burned closer to home. Fire was one of so many things that could render a man helpless, and now, as Karel reached the corral fence and circled around to the gate, his brothers' eyes unblinking and tepid and fixed on him, he reckoned that family was another. A man couldn't any more choose which one he was born into than he could will it to stay together when so many things abraded and raveled the fibers that were meant to keep it bound. Try to hold it all together with force, with a harness and a hard hand the way their father had, and it grew so thick with the cordage of resentment that you couldn't even get your hands around it.

Now, as Karel reached the unbolted gate and swung it open, he watched his brothers, the three of them huddled silently, their boots sunk so deeply into the loose soil of the corral that they appeared to be held upright by their trouser hems alone. Behind them, the fire licked and sizzled, the dark rush of smoke issuing from the ruins of timber and tack to sully the quiet blue skies. When Karel stepped into the corral, leaving the gate wide, he studied the lit tip of his cigarette as if he could find there, in the pale glow of the thing, the words to explain his ready proximity to these men after all these years of measured distance. Eddie took a step his way and put a chapped hand on his shoulder, and Karel looked up to find some of the blue gone out of his brother's eyes, which were faded as if from sunlight or submersion and flecked with gray. Unlike Thom, Eddie and Stan kept their hair cropped short, and when Eddie pulled his hat off in the exaggerated pretense of a greeting, Karel noted the weathered crown of the man's scalp showing pink through his thinning hair. Eddie returned the hat, winking at Stan when he did, and then he took his hand from Karel's shoulder, pulling a pint bottle of clear shine from his coat pocket and bubbling it with a grimace before handing it over. "Tastes a trace like kerosene what someone's made water in, but it makes for a warm enough breakfast."

Karel exhaled smoke through his nose and let his cigarette fall to the hoof-pocked earth below. Before him, the flaming loft chute collapsed at last, roaring blue as it fell and giving rise to a loud rush of sparks that launched skyward in the updraft as if of their own hot volition. He accepted the bottle and took a polite, tentative taste of the concoction, just enough to set him to thinking that, given enough fuel, even a man's insides might take to smoldering. When it came right down to it, there wasn't all that much in life that wasn't flammable.

"Don't know that it's deserving of thanks," he said, handing the bottle over, "but it's worse poison in the world, I suspect."

"Oh, it's plenty worse out there," Eddie said. "World is full up to the brim with worse and running down the sides with worser. Get Thom here to say a word one, and I'll give you another sip."

Karel tried to clear his throat again but came up empty. He turned to Thom, who had leaned back against the corral fence like he'd just finished a hard day of working horses and set his mind now to the idleness of a man who'd earned a few minutes of stillness and quiet spent reclined into the solid, reassuring support that only a good tree or fence could offer. Stan stood unkempt beside him, arching his brows and hitching up his trousers with the frustrated effort of one who believed that even the very pull of the earth was out to reveal him in some shameful way. Thom gave Stan a sidelong glance and frowned, and after he ran a hand over his face and sighed, he pushed himself from the fence and stood upright. "You think you were invisible, little brother? Sitting yesterday in your truck up the road from my saloon?"

"Here," Eddie said, pushing the bottle into Karel's chest. "Deal's a deal."

Karel took another, deeper slug of the foul stuff, keeping his eyes on Thom as he did. "Wasn't trying to hide, if that's what you mean. You looked busy. Didn't see any reason to get between you and your work."

"You ain't seen reason to do much of anything within spitting distance of us since Pop died. Now you come around two days running. Something got you feeling lonely all of a sudden?"

"Carew came by this morning. Said one of your horses was on my land, and a body in my creek. I had to make the trip north to Praha no matter what else. I figured I'd leastwise come by to tell you I had some of your property. That it ain't going anywhere and that the boy who took it from you ain't either."

"Which one was it?"

"What's that?"

"The boy. Which one?"

"The mute one, without the knifework done to his face. If it's one of them that deserves a lungful of water, it's the other one that got it."

"Ain't that the usual way? It's rarely the ones deserving that does the getting."

"I reckon that's right. It hardly ever adds up the way it should." Karel had meant to ask after the child, but there came of a sudden from behind the barn the consumptive coughing of the pumper truck, the burst of the engine's ignition and the increasingly urgent rumbling as the throttle was levered up, all of which gave rise to a loud flushing of doves from the grove. The brothers stood watching, turning their warped necks in concert and squinting as the proud-breasted birds came into view above the barn before angling—their wings tipped sharply down and flashing and stroking beneath a blue sky hazed with smoke, their bodies too heavy to be kept aloft absent this constant effort—in a sharp vector around the rising heat of the fire.

Once, so long ago now that Karel had all but surrendered it to the whitewash of forgetting, he had come first to the breakfast table while his brothers readied themselves for school. He must have been four, no more than five, and his father sat palming his cup of coffee, his face running with sweat so that, even at so young an age, Karel knew the man had been out already at his chores, doing what men do before dawn, milking the cows and moving the cattle, startling the hens from their eggs. On the table, dripping clots onto a doily knit by his mother or her mother, either one, sat a congealed pot of gray oats, an oily slick of butter glazed over the surface. Not a week before, Karel's brothers had taught him the game of spoon, and now, to be sure that the final card didn't catch him empty handed, he'd taken to carrying his supper spoon with him everywhere in the bib pocket of his overalls, proudly washing it after meals that called for its use. When he climbed into his chair, he pulled it from its appointed place and set it beside his bowl. His father, who normally rushed through meals and savored his work the way most men did the opposite, sat for a long while before he dished the breakfast into Karel's bowl. Outside, so loud that Karel mistook the windows for open, the crows had begun their shrill, seasonal bickering over the loose kernels of maize left behind after the recent harvest.

"Ain't no reason for them to be so loud, is it, Pop?"

Vaclav didn't startle. Karel never could remember the man startled, but he turned that morning with a look of some stricken, warmed-over fondness in his bloodshot eyes, with an expression too bare and full of remembrance to have been meant for sharing. He dipped into the oats and scooped a second spoonful into his youngest's bowl. "They don't need a reason," he said, scraping his chair back on the hardwoods so he could pull his pouch of tobacco from his trouser pocket. "It's things aplenty like that, you'll see. It's some women who like the sound of birds raising Cain before even the sun's had enough coffee to top the trees. It ain't no reason for that, either, but that don't make it a bad thing."

Now, after the doves had vanished into the distant treeline to the east, Stan hitched his trousers up again and stepped forward. "Was good of your wife to come, Karel," he said, "so near on the heels of her labor. She's a fine woman. It's nobody with any sense doesn't like her. Good of the Novotny woman to bring her, and to bring the medicine Doc needed from the druggist in Praha."

It was cold out, sure enough, but now Karel realized how flushed he'd become standing sandwiched, as he now felt, between his recollections of the past and the diminishing flames of the stable fire. Still, he had the feeling that he needed to pull his coat more tightly across his chest, button the topmost buttons where the air was finding its way to the hollow of his throat. Fever. That's what it resembled, the feeling of being baked and chilled what all at the same time. A shiver ran in ripples down his sides from his shoulders, and he recalled the other night in the stable, the way Elizka's skin was at once covered with chill bumps and hot against his own. He wanted a cigarette, but his mouth was parched, his tongue so dry, and still he knew his brother was awaiting some acknowledgment of his compliment. He wanted to ask how it was that Stan knew Sophie beyond passing, how it was that any of them might. He wanted to ask them if they'd ever, any of them, seen a calf stone dead and staring dumb eyed at the sky without having put a single hoof to the earth. He wanted to know if any of them could recall their mother ever speaking kindly of blackbirds, but he'd learned well enough that there were questions that revealed too much, that sometimes a question showed only that you knew less than you should. "I hadn't realized she was here. I'd aimed to go fetch her before noontime. Go fetch all of them."

"She saved you a trip, then. She's in the house. The kids, too. It's a good looking boy," Stan said. "The baby, I mean."

Searching his older brother's eyes, Karel found only forthrightness and fatigue, a look too worn down by hard work and early rising to be anything other than earnest. "I appreciate that. We're giving serious thought to keeping him."

Eddie smiled, lifted his bottle in a mock cheer, but before he could put it to his lips, as if in afterthought, he turned to Thom, whose pale eyes glinted in the wet corners where the sunlight found the slightest upwelling of tears. "I think you should," Thom said. "We might all ought to keep what's ours."

Karel nodded, and then he turned with his brothers to watch what was left of the fire consume what was left of the fallen stable. There was some burn left in it, but it would dwindle before nightfall, and then there'd be nothing left but the hard work it would take to raise another horsebarn in its place. For now, the four brothers stood there, shoulder to shoulder, as they had on that cold day so many years ago after putting their father in the waterlogged ground, as they had when the photographer Lad Dvorak had alerted to the occasion fetched his fancy equipment from his carriage and urged them to line up, oldest to youngest, to stand closer — *a little bit closer . . . that's some fine fellows . . . and straighten up now, boys . . . What's with the heads leaned so? . . . You missing your pillows already this morning or . . . Oh, heavens . . . of course . . . I beg your pardon* — until Karel could feel the pressed sleeve of his suitcoat touching Eduard's as they waited for the townie with his unscuffed boots to take the photograph, each of them bristling in his church clothes at the uneasy proximity to what he had surrendered out of pride and now refused, out of the same, to reclaim.

With his arms crossed over his chest, Karel watched the low flames lick up from the embers, shook his head at the waste of it all, at all that good, solid wood reduced to ash, at the blackened, twisted remains of animals shrunken sickly there in the coals. And then his brothers were turning, shifting their attention from the fire, and when he followed their gaze he found the slow approach of men in suitcoats skirting the burning stable, walking in Karel's boot prints as if tracking him across whorish terrain. Villaseñor and his men, the latter pair with their shining rifles held loosely across their thick, squat bodies as if they'd been fastened there at birth and had been worn, over the slow course of years that had grayed their sideburns and slowed their steps, slack as the muscles of their shoulders and wan as the skin slung beneath their eyes. As for their master, he led their procession with his spectacles pushed up high on the bridge of his nose, his face shadowed by his dark hat, his suitcoat buttoned and black and unworried as surface water on a still, moonless night. With the wet plug of a cigar planted in the corner of his mouth, he came forward with the smoothly assured gait of a man who'd seen enough trouble to have convinced himself, long ago, that walking toward it was no more taxing than was walking away.

Eddie corked his bottle, hurrying it into his coat pocket while Stan busied himself tucking his shirttail into his pants, and it was then that Karel saw what he hadn't once considered before, that while his brothers had found a way clear of their father, it had led them to this: to farms purchased for them with another man's wealth, to wives given to them only for walking away from what remained of the family into which they'd been born, to lives and livelihoods beholden to a man no more yielding or forgiving than their father had been. It must have been, Karel realized, for them, like waking, morning after morning, from colorful dreams of manhood to find that they were still, all of them, playing with sticks down in the grassy shadows on the bank of the creek.

When Villaseñor came through the gate and the brothers turned to face him, he unbuttoned his coat while his men settled in behind him, their eyes serious and slow to blink, unlit by the lively mischief Karel had come to expect. Then Villaseñor pulled the cigar from his mouth and held it at his side, his mouth working as if accustoming itself to this flavorless new absence. "How considerate of you to come calling, Karel. There must be so much you'd like to explain to my son-in-law here. That or to Sheriff Munson, one."

Karel stole a look at Thom, whose face registered none of the nervousness that his fingers, moving idly at his side, made plain. "There's a mess of things I'd like to explain that I can't," Karel said. "I told you yesterday, I hired those boys to deliver some barrels and watch after my livestock. Whatever the hell else got into them, or why it did, I can't say."

Villaseñor waved the cigar beneath his nose and nestled it back between his lips. Then he removed his hat and slicked a hand through the silver sheen of his well-oiled hair. Before he took his matches from his coat pocket, one eye narrowed in disgust and he extended his hat toward Thom. "Do you suppose you can manage to hold on to this for a time without dropping it?" he asked.

Now Karel noted Thom's fingers curling into fists but held tight at his sides, saw, as he had the night after the race, when Thom had taken his father's first blow rather than hold his tongue, all the hot life at work beneath his icy expression. "I suppose you might could just as easily put the damn thing back on your gray head, is what I suppose," Thom said, his voice steady and controlled, quiet but honed as if by a whetstone.

Villaseñor smiled and played his tongue against the cigar such that it seemed to bob there like a reprimanding finger. He handed the hat back to one of his men and turned to Karel, then made a show of striking a match and twirling the cigar above the little flame until smoke fell from his nose. "I spoke to the padre," he said. "Seems he found one of my daughter's horses on your parcel of land."

"He did. Found a dead boy on it, too, but I'm sure the horse concerns you more than that."

"Please, Skala. You've been sure of so many falsehoods since we first met that I'd think by now you'd have grown weary of sharing them so readily. Quite the contrary, really. I am interested in the boy, who almost certainly had a hand in this fire, and in the injury to my granddaughter. It's just that I'm more taken by where his brother might be. One dead is one shy of what would satisfy me. I need to know where he is. As you're aware, I don't make it my habit to involve the law in my business, but the fire patrol is not bound to such discretion. They have people to report to, and if the sheriff ever gets his boots on again, he'll want some answers out of you. You'd be well served to answer to me first, and I can assure you that I'll vouch for you when the time comes. I need to know where that other boy might be, where he might have reason to go." Villa-señor pulled his glasses from his face and set to work cleaning them with his handkerchief. When he had them settled back in place, he cocked his head toward his men. "They get restless when too much time passes between serious errands, and I intend to give them a chore to keep them occupied."

"If that's the case, then they oughtn't to be restless for a hell of a long while. Unless they're equipped special to track ghosts. Them boys weren't real talkative, and the one laid out in my stable ain't likely to speak up anytime soon. If there's one left breathing out there somewhere, he's likely putting fast miles between himself and here. Check all the filling stations and the train depots and hunt the little son of a bitch down. That would suit me just fine. He took off owing me money, and I don't cotton to setting fires, but you're likely going to need more than two men to hunt him down."

"Two has always been enough," Villaseñor said, sending his men away with a single hand held out to his side, the fingers working as if he were brushing dust from a coat sleeve. "You don't have to know where to look, Skala. You just have to know *how*."

"Stan and I could go with them," Eddie said. "Lend them a hand."

"I hardly see that you have a hand free, Eduard. Seems to me that bottle you keep glued to your palm leaves you shorthanded enough as it is. You go with Stan. He'll have to run the saloon while Thom tends to his wife and children."

"I been in there since the doctor showed up at sunrise," Thom said. "It ain't nothing for me to do but sit and wait like everyone else. I'd be better off at the saloon. The work will keep my mind off it."

"And just why in Jesus' name would you want to keep your mind off of your family? You dropped the child, Thomàs. You *dropped* her. And now you want to go off and leave Graciela alone with all the worry, is that it? You don't leave men above ground if they can harm you, especially if you've given them cause to do so, but you did. You shot one of them when you didn't have cause, and then you let them go when you should have shot them both. You aren't going anywhere except inside your house. It's bad judgment that has brought you to this, and there's no escaping one's own bad judgment. Come now, inside. The rest of you, too. Tell your wives and children good-bye before you go."

Karel stood perplexed by how quickly his brothers fell in line, at how Eddie caught his eye and gave a dirt clod an aimless kick before following his father-in-law out of the corral gate. Stan went, too, hitching his thumbs in his trouser pockets and studying the black acreage and the distant trees to the east with a kind of round-eyed fascination that plucked a string of envy in Karel's chest. How goddamned simple the whole mess of living would be if you could see a stand of oaks a thousand times without ever quite recognizing it or relying on it. Say a single leaf had curled brown and fallen over-night, carried away by the breeze and then rolled along the ground until some animal trod it into the earth. For Stan, that might change the whole tree, the whole treeline, the whole damned county. For Karel, it would have meant only that something he owned had been lessened, even if he couldn't say how, and he thought now, stand-ing beside his brother while the sharp bones of Thom's jaw worked the cud of this most recent humiliation, that the two of them were made of this same stuff, and that it had come to them through their father's blood.

"Jesus," Karel said, "but he reminds me of Pop."

Thom put a hand on the gate, swung it back and forth on its hinges like he was testing it for need of oil. "How's that?" he asked, his eyes fixed only on this invented work.

"Ain't nothing that ain't someone's fault."

Thom swallowed, let his recognition of the words show only in a short exhalation that bore the muffled, wordless sound of his voice. At their backs, the fire had quieted to a hissing bed of embers and heavy, reluctant smoke, out of which rose only the ruined black remnants of the stable's framework.

From out near the drive, Villaseñor called back to them. "*Now, Thomàs.*"

Thom flinched at the man's voice, and now he shook his head until he broke into a smile so that Karel could see his father's work in his brother's mouth. Opening his mouth wide, Thom ran his tongue over his damaged teeth. "I don't need no more reminder than looking in the mirror," he said. "Tough old son of a bitch, wasn't he? Tell you what, Karel. You'd have burned Pop's stable down, he wouldn't have sent someone else to find you. He'd have come to stomp the shit out of you himself."

"I got it coming, I expect."

Narrowing his eyes at Karel, Thom let a laugh and a sigh out in tandem through his nose. "Not from me you don't. I ain't talking about you, little brother."

"Well, all right, then, but I ain't talking about the fire. It's other things that ain't been squared between us."

"You needing to say penance, Father Carew's right up there in the house. But don't say it for me. A whole lot of years have gone by, Karel. Graciela and me been happy together. If something ain't square, I reckon all you have to do is square it with yourself. If it'll help, though, I'll let you do me a favor. You get wind where that other little bastard twin is, don't tell Guillermo. You come to me with it. It's my little girl up there hurting, not his."

"That'd suit me fine."

"All right, then. I need to go see how my little one's doing. You ain't supposed to have favorites. That's what Graciela's forever telling me. Maybe if I had a boy, things would be different, but Tina puts a burr in my heart that won't turn loose. I was only trying to get her clear of the smoke. Anyway, there's about a hundred women up there at the house. Let's see if one of them will pour you a cup of coffee."

FOR THE WOMEN of Lavaca County, the harshest of whispered judgments was reserved for the wife or daughter, not common in these parts, who might be found sitting idly with her apron off in a kitchen, her own or otherwise, and when Karel left his boots in line with a half-dozen other pairs in the mudroom and followed Thom inside, the rich smells of baking kolaches and creamed ham made his insides brew as audibly as the strong coffee on the stove top. Women were everywhere, their hair pulled back into hasty braids and pasted in little wisps to their flushed cheeks, their satisfaction in their work masked only by the seriousness of the occasion that had brought them to service in their neighbor's house. Thom made his way quickly through all the consolations toward the back of the house, where the stairs creaked beneath his steps as he climbed toward news of his little girl.

Karel heard his wife's voice in the parlor, but before he could go to it, a steaming cup of coffee was being put softly into his cold hands. He nodded his thanks and smiled at the tallest of Villaseñor's girls, who'd grown full in the hips over the years and wore her hair in a single rope that dangled past the small of her back. She turned, shaking her head when Stan came waddling in from the parlor, his lock-kneed steps encumbered by two young boys, one straddled around each leg like they were in training for the pumper team that had just rumbled off the property for its firehouse in Shiner. Cinched around his waist were the dark arms of a girl, his eldest—Could she be ten already? Eleven?—who clung to her father with such a fierce affection that Karel knew at once all he needed to know about his brother's inability to keep his trousers from riding down on him.

"You remember Violeta, surely," Stan said.

Karel took her hand, which was softly padded and dusted with flour. "Morning," he said, nodding.

"And these monkeys here is our meal ticket," said Stan, shaking his legs, one at a time, until the boys turned him loose and fell in a tangled, laughing mass to the floor. "Gonna raise them to do tricks and sell them to the next road show what comes through town."

After Stan kissed his wife's cheek and shooed the kids into the other room, he took his hat from the rack near the door and ran his hand around inside to give it shape. "I gotta git. It's nothing says you can't pay us a visit at our place some Sunday, you know. It's sometimes a barrel of beer and a block of ice that find their way from the saloon into my cattletank."

Karel nodded. "Ain't but one way to teach strays like that a lesson."

"That's a fact," said Stan, and with a wink he ducked through the door and closed it gently behind him.

In the parlor, where the dark curtains had been tied back to let the light in, Karel wished, from his first sight of his wife sitting hip to hip with Elizka Novotny on the sofa, that the room had been left awash in shadows. His newborn son slept wrapped in a blanket in Elizka's lap, her sensible blue dress creased between her knees and riding up on her calves so that Karel had to will his eyes from her white stockings. Father Carew sat opposite them in a plush chair the color of August corn tassels, a cup of coffee cradled by his liver-spotted hands in his bony lap.

Sophie came off the couch slowly, wincing as she rose, and Karel put his cup atop the glowing woodstove and opened his arms to her. He would have liked to close his eyes, to smell the comforting confusion of soap and perspiration that, for these last five years had announced to him, every evening when he came in from the fields, that there had been, in his absence, nothing lacking of cleanliness or order or honest work, either one. But now, with his wife's breath warm against his neck, Karel saw Elizka looking from the child in her arms to his father and back again as if there was some arithmetic, some simple ciphering, that might explain how sweetness could spring from such questionable seed.

"Where are the girls? What was I to think if I'd driven all the way up to Praha to find you run off with all the children?"

"They're fine. They're playing out front. Eddie's girls are looking after them." He felt Sophie smiling against his neck. "Maybe you would have thought you'd finally gotten what you deserved, Karel. But I doubt it. You'd have found me eventually, if you looked hard enough."

"I don't know. I'm not much good at finding what I'm after these days."

"How flattering," Elizka said, coming to her feet, the baby held out and away from her body as if she were carrying a bundle of soiled laundry. Sophie turned to take the child, then stood back begging questions of Karel with her eyes while Elizka bent to shake Carew's hand. "Pardon me, Father, I pray the child will heal, but I've got to get back up to the store before Dad forgets we're running a business instead of a charity. Tell Thom I'll have the druggist send him a bill."

"Of course, my dear. My thanks to your father."

Karel had never accustomed himself to the way a woman's joy and sorrow could sound so much the same when given voice. He'd grown up around boys, in the midst of men, for whom pain was weathered in silence and pleasure announced in exaggerated groans of relief. So when Graciela's voice carried down the staircase, so high-pitched and trembling, he found himself reaching for his son, taking him from his mother's arms in an attempt to protect him from the virulent spread of female grief that he felt certain about to overtake the house. In the kitchen, dropped utensils clanged against the stove and the floor as the women rushed into the parlor, their faces lit with expectation, their damp hands smoothing their flour-dusted aprons until Graciela appeared in the doorway at the foot of the stairs, her father behind her, her weight carried high on the balls of her feet with her heels off the floor. Her hands were at her mouth, her shoulders shaking with release, and then Sophie crossed her arms over her chest and embraced herself, whispering, "Oh, thank God."

"She's awake," Graciela said, her dark, dark eyes brightened by a glaze of tears. "Come see. She's awake!"

NEARING NOONTIME, once he'd pulled the truck off the farm-to-market road and onto his drive, the gravel grinding pleasantly beneath the tires, Karel steered with one hand and arched his back beneath Diane's weight in his lap so that he could work his handkerchief out of his pocket and wipe the window glass with it. "Deenie," he said, blowing into her ear to set her squirming, "it's so many of you kids in here now that you're steaming up the glass so I can't see. You're the oldest, so you're going to have to either ride in the back from now on or hold your breath, one or the other."

The girl cocked her head back to find her father's eyes sad and blinking apologies at her. "I can try," she said, taking a deep breath.

Sophie nudged him with her elbow, cradling the infant in one arm and stroking Evie's hair while the youngest girl slept with her feet up on the seat and her head in her mother's lap. "Don't listen to him, Diane."

"Well that's a fine thing to teach a little girl, Mother. It's a Commandment tells you you're supposed to listen to me, Deenie. You just remember that. Don't you let your mother lead you astray."

Karel gassed the throttle through the creekside lowlands and up the swell, where the road came round the hedgerow and mesquite trees, and against his hip he sensed his wife's body tense in a way that told him that she'd had her fill of his teasing. "You want to talk

287

about being led astray right here and now, Karel, or do you suppose we should wait until the kids are asleep?"

Had it been her words that caused Karel to brake the truck hard, sliding it to a stop on the gravel and reaching out with one arm in an instinctive attempt to keep his family where they belonged beside him instead of letting them fly forward to crumple onto the floorboards or crash headlong into the window glass, Sophie might have sat silently staring forward for a long moment, willing her heart to slow and then checking on her children, asking were they hurt. She would have known, by his hot-tempered reaction and by the way she could see, in the grainy flexing of the muscles roped between his shoulders and neck, that he was doing something that he only ever did when he was bewildered or when he was readying himself to tell a lie. She would have known, even if he didn't—and he usually didn't—that his body was asking an impossibility of itself, that it was trying to right the wrongs that had been done to it long before the bones stopped growing and the boy he'd been found himself, at last, in the warped shape of the man he'd become. She would have known that her husband, clutching the wheel so hard that the tendons on the backs of his hands fanned out like the teeth of a hay rake, was working to straighten his neck, and this alone, to her mind, would have settled the issue. Had it been true, she could have begun enduring the weeks of cold nights, sleeping on her side, sliding her hip from beneath the warm weight of his hand, showing him with her body what it meant to be without it. She could have begun punishing him and, in doing so, wrapping her mind, day by day, around the inevitability of their reconciliation.

Instead, she found herself flooded with a cold surge of fear, with a prickling chill in the palms of her hands, her scalp, the bottoms of her feet. Karel was gripping the wheel, testing with some subconscious force the inflexibility of his neck, his sight fixed on their homestead. It had proved such a comfort, always, to Sophie—the house and barn, the smokehouse and stable, all of them rising up clean and orderly the way they did against the backdrop of the pear trees, amidst all the straight furrows of the cropfields and the golden stubble of cut, sunlit hay—but now, as Karel sat with his eyes moving over the expanse of it like he'd seen coyotes slipping between hedgerows of recent and was taking stock of his calves, Sophie knew only that he saw something she didn't.

"Son of a bitch," he said, pulling Deenie, who was holding her breath in earnest now, from his lap. Beside Sophie, little Evie had come out of her sleep and sat upright with startled eyes, a thread of saliva strung from the hinge of her lips to her mother's lap.

"Karel," Sophie said. "What on earth is it?"

As he eased off the brake, rolling the truck down a swath of yellowed grass toward the front of the house rather than following the drive down to the outbuildings, he pointed in the direction of the horsebarn. "In all our years together," he said, "how many times is it you've known me to let the stable door ajar while I'm away?"

Inside the house, with the girls planted in the deep, underused cushions of the front sitting room sofa, Karel bolted the front door and made his way to the kitchen where he found his rifle leaning barrel up where it always had against the backdoor molding. He levered a cartridge into the receiver, and something about the crisp metallic acceptance of the brass quieted the blood in his ears so that he was aware of his wife behind him, her son cradled tight against her bosom, her questions coming out in unpunctuated twos and threes. "Damn it, Sophie," he said, turning the doorknob. "You reckon it was Thom's horses set his stable afire? There ain't a question I won't answer once I've had a look out back, and not a one I got time for until then, you understand?"

Outside, while he wove himself into the grove, tuning out the desperate, wintertime scuttling of squirrels overhead, he kept his finger on the trigger. Still, he couldn't help noting the bellowing of his herd in the back pasture. They'd been neglected, and there was the new calf to check over. They'd need hay set out before long. So often, his days were spent cataloging the need for chores while doing others, and he busied himself with this ingrained list-making even while he kept his eyes on the front stable door swung out a good foot from flush. When he reached the edge of the drive, he tried to step lightly on the gravel, hearing still in the solid friction of the stones compressed beneath his weight the inventory of tomorrow's predawn undertakings. Wood for the two stoves. Milk. Eggs. Cattle to move and ash to collect from the smokehouse. By the time he considered that he'd have to find time to ride the filly back over to Thom and Graciela's, he was peering into the stable where the cold slant of hay-dusted light revealed a vacancy that made him wonder, even while he knew it senseless, if all he'd been taught those long hours in the hardwood pews of St. Jude's had been but a portion of the truth. If there was a Holy Ghost, then oughtn't there to be an Unholy one, one that could bring even the undeserving dead upright and walking and altogether alive enough to swing a stable door open with all the ease of an angel rolling a stone from a cave mouth?

Karel widened the door with his boot, the gunstock cool in his hands, and from the stalls came the indifferent breathing and stamping of the animals. Farm boys in Lavaca County were taught to use a gun the same way they were taught to use a hoe or a baler, and there was nothing more shameful, more deserving of ridicule, than some townie boy stalking imaginary game in the outcroppings of oak and sweet gum just off the road to town, the fancy new .20 gauge his father had bought for him held in his hands like he meant to strangle it. For the boys raised by fathers who fired their shotguns to put dove and quail on the wintertime table, who leveled their rifles to take a deer or keep a coyote from taking a calf, guns were tools, used only when there was no better one for the job at hand. When a boy who'd grown accustomed to the sting of weeping blisters and the weight of caked mud on his boots saw the loaded gun leaning against the back door every morning when he went out to milk the cows, he didn't give it any more thought than he gave the milk pails when he found a cottonmouth in his mother's garden.

Which isn't to say that even these boys ever got over the thrill of squeezing the trigger — *You don't never pull it, boy. Pull your little pud, you want to pull something. A trigger you squeeze. Gentle, like this, when you exhale. You want the shot coming out same time as your breath does.* He never did get over it, never altogether cooled to the importance of what he held in his hands, to what it could do when used well, to the little god it made of him while the rest of the looming world — his father's enormous, hairy hands or the hay bales he couldn't yet shoulder alone or the horizon he could never toe with his boot no matter how long he walked toward it — made him feel so very small.

No, when a boy or the man he'd become had cause to take up his gun, he expected to feel the loud kick of it against his shoulder before he put it down. Karel was no different, and neither, he imagined, would be his boy, his Frank, so when he stepped inside the stable, his eyes adjusting to the shadows and to the fact that there was no longer a boy's body laid out where he'd left it on the four bales of hay before the stalls, he became all at once aware of the nervous slicks of sweat under his arms and lowered his rifle with both relief and disappointment.

Neither of which lasted.

When he'd strode half the length of the stable's alley, he sensed the shadows shift overhead, and by the time he planted a foot and swung his gun up toward the loft, the boy had taken to talking.

"He ain't walked off on you. I got him up here with me."

Karel squinted up at the childlike figure of Raymond Knedlik, who sat swinging his legs over the loft, his pistol dangling from a hand resting on the bottommost brace of the loft railing, his dead brother laid out beside him with his head in Raymond's lap.

Karel sighted down his barrel, centering the bead on the boy's chest. "You got a fuel can up there with you, that or a book of matches, it's fixing to be two of you that's done the last of your walking."

The boy tilted his head back slowly so that a trace more of the scant sunlight shone in his pale eyes, which looked to have lost forever the wide aperture of youth, to have seen more than they could have at his age if he'd slept every night with the both of them frozen open. He shook his head slowly, the way Karel's father had when his sons had disappointed him, and the boy's scar flashed bloodless and white when it caught the light. "I ain't come here to burn you out, Skala. I come to pay you what I owe, maybe borrow a horse for half a day. Walked in here an hour ago to see if it's anything worth riding, and look who's waiting for me but my clumsy little brother here. Any of yours like that? Tell them to run and they fall down crying with a leg snapped in half instead?"

"You don't want to be disappointed in brothers, don't tell them what to do. Where's that shiny new truck of yours? Out rolling around on its own looking for my trailer?"

"It's cash in my pocket is what it is. All I could do. Sold it at sunup to some thick-rimmed son of a bitch at the bank. Wouldn't give me but seven cents on the dollar." He tugged at his pocket, snagging a bit of the dead boy's hair when he did and flinching because of it. "Which, some of it's yours. For the bill up at the filling station. And to put this boy here in the ground proper for me. I can't dally, or I'd dig the hole myself."

"You might as well give it all to me. Otherwise it's just a couple of midget Mexicans with rifles going to take it out of your pockets when they're done with you."

Raymond considered this, his eyes registering no more surprise than they might if he heard church bells ringing of a Sunday morning. "They might. But I'll lay two to one they're heading fast to Fort Worth, thinking I'm on the nine o'clock I was on before hopping off when it weren't no one looking. It was half a dozen folks saw me buy the ticket, and just as many what watched me get on the train."

Not fifteen feet from where Karel stood, the ladder rose up from the hay-strewn dirt to meet the loft where the boy sat, and Karel lowered his gun and held it across his body, his finger still on the trigger, his eyes shifting to the close-cropped curls in Raymond's lap. "The hell'd you haul him all the way up there for? He looked comfortable enough where I left him."

Raymond put a finger in his nose and worked it around as if he might find the answer in there and bring it to light. Then he wiped his finger in the hay beside him and said, "He liked it up high. Used to find him reading way up top of the oak tree out back of the house. All that climbing and sitting way up with the bird nests, and he breaks his leg with both feet square on solid ground."

"He deserved it same as you, Raymond. It's a bunch of dead horses up at my brother's place. That and a little girl who took a hard spill and only just woke up, and you come back here thinking to borrow a horse?"

"I ain't got nothing to do with any little girl."

"That you know of."

The boy cocked his head, sucking at his teeth audibly when he did. "You don't want to loan me a horse, just say so."

"I don't."

"Fair enough. See how easy that was?"

"You can't burn a man's horsebarn down and expect his brother to help you make away."

"You ain't got any brothers, Skala, unless you're talking about me and Joe here. Them others won't claim you. You and me, we drank our milk from the same good woman's teats, and whether you'd like to forget it or not, she never did. The old man never let her, called her a whore for the one she bore when she was yet a girl, said it was God's punishment what took it from her. Said she ought to get used to being treated like what she was, no matter how many rosary beads she prayed."

Karel raised his rifle again, watched the boy tighten his grip on his pistol, thought how good it would feel to shoot the little shit, like scratching finally some old itch that had worked itself down beneath the skin so you couldn't get to it without drawing blood. The Knedlik boy wasn't telling him something he didn't know, but it stung nonetheless to have it come back to the surface the same way it hurt to work an old splinter back out through the hole it made going in. "Not remembering ain't the same as forgetting," Karel said. "Besides which, I been drinking cow's milk my whole life and I ain't once called a bull calf brother. Called a lot of them veal, though."

Now Raymond's face revealed a restless resignation, an impatience in which Karel could detect not even a seed of fear. The boy dropped his eyes into his lap and ran a thumb over the cold blue face of his brother, mussed his hair, slid his own weight from beneath that of his kin, and eased the boy's head back down onto a pillow of hay. Then he rose frowning, tucked his gun against his spine in the waistband of his trousers, and stood wiry and hay dusted and taken with thought at the top of the ladder. "Your wife," he said. "She give you a boy?"

Behind Karel, the little filly whinnied and tossed her head, and it occurred to him that he hadn't yet had occasion to tell most folks about his boy, to walk into the icehouse and buy a round of beers and beam with the pride of a man who'd done what his father had done before him. But then he thought of his own father, of all that a son's birth could cost a man besides a few dollars spent celebrating with neighbors. "Why?" Karel asked. "You take a job with the census?"

"No, but that wouldn't be a terrible way to earn a dollar. Go around keeping count of people, asking men how many little ones they've managed to make." He glanced one last time at his brother in the hay, and then he turned his back to Karel and put a boot on the topmost rung of the ladder so that he was talking all the way down to the ground. "Who knows. You do that job long enough, it might all tally up even. Joe up there does the last of his breathing, but then come to find out it's some other boy born right about the same time. A man could find some sense in that."

Karel took a step forward, keeping his gun down across his waist but balanced in both hands and at the ready. "You can make sense of damn near anything, you look at it cross-eyed long enough."

"I'm just saying," Raymond said, reaching the ground. He turned toward Karel, pulling a roll of paper money from his pocket. "It's better when things even up than when they don't. Here. It's thirty dollars more than we spent up at the filling station, plus another fifty to take care of Joe up there."

"I ain't taking your money. You ain't got enough. There's a stable full of horses up the road you can't afford to square, and you want to stand here talking about making things even."

"Way I see it, that ain't your debt to collect, Skala. Thom can settle that on his own. You want to tell him I'm still in town, then go on ahead. I been in your house. It's not a telephone in there. That's all the head start I need."

"You ain't made it out of this stable yet, Raymond."

The boy smiled, balanced the roll of money on the third rung of the loft ladder, and nodded at Karel's gun. "Not yet," he said, "but to stop me you're going to have to shoot me in the back knowing my momma fed you at the breast."

When the boy turned and took his first careless, loose-jointed steps toward the open door, Karel found his gunstock cold against his cheek, risen without summons like the weeks of nighttime fantasies that would afflict him thereafter, visions in which he'd imagine himself squeezing the trigger and knowing, with the blast from the barrel and the jolt in his shoulder, that he'd set something right other than his pride. Instead, he steadied the gun's sights on Raymond's back until the boy reached the door, and then he called out, "Your mother got paid, did she not?"

The boy swung the door outward and the stable was flooded of a sudden with harsh noonday light. "Not near enough," he said. "Ain't a woman ever been paid enough for all that gets taken from her."

IT WOULD PROVE a wearisome night, all that sleepless darkness coming, as it did, on the heels of a long day that had found Karel Skala answering the questions he'd promised he would after fretting over matters left so long untended on the farm. In the end, the chores and the outdoors, all these years his sanctuary, had failed him, and he'd come inside before suppertime, his socks left on the back porch, salted with the sweat of his nervous work and stuffed inside his boots. For now, the baby was asleep, the two girls playing in the other room, their usual squealing tempered by the charged quiet of the home, by the way in which a house where a newborn sleeps becomes, through some mystery of its own and through the ready, unquestioning complicity of those inside, a series of rooms constructed as baffles against sound so that there, where the infant dreams in the warm heart of them, the silence can incubate the silent.

Karel hung his hat on the rack and lifted the chair rather than scraping it back, suppressing even the groan that usually announced the end of his labor and the beginning of his evening meal. Sophie turned, her apron tied loosely at her padded waist, and poured a cup of coffee, placed it on the table with an ashtray and a halfhearted smile. Karel laced his fingers around the cup and sat for a long minute in appreciation of its warmth against his calloused hands, of the strong smell of it hanging rich in the air, of the sureness of its arrival before him, all of which made him think that, if God had been a woman, she would have sent Adam from the garden all the same, but not without a cup of coffee.

Outside, floating sluggish over the southern fields, a stray cloud carried about its fringes a touch of color so that it appeared to Karel that the thing had made off with some of the unsuspecting sunset. "I know you'll be hard at it awhile," he said, "and you'll need what rest you can get. You strip the bed linens tomorrow, I'll get them washed and hang them on the line for you. Skies look to hold."

She was mixing batter for an easy supper of pancakes, a meal she knew certain to find no complaints from the girls, and when she let the wooden spoon drop against the side of the bowl, Karel closed his eyes and massaged the bridge of his nose. And then Sophie was lowering herself gingerly into the chair beside his, and when he opened his eyes and took his cigarette from the ashtray, she was waiting with her elbows propped on the table and her chin in her hands. "I'd appreciate that, Karel," she said. "But you're giving me butter when what I'm wanting is the biscuit."

And so he had told her, wanting to touch her pale arm while he did but settling for the comfort of the sturdy seat beneath him and the coffee in his hands. He told her about the boys and the beer, about the lost heifer and calf, about the body in the stable and the boy he'd found there swinging his legs from the loft with his dead brother's head cradled in his lap. About the talk he'd had with his brothers while they watched Thom's stable smolder. As he spoke, moving from the story of one day to the story of the next, watching his wife's eyes for the eventual softening that told him he'd said enough, Karel reckoned that she'd stop him short in time, that she'd return to what she'd come so close to saying those hours before in the truck, that she'd want to know, though he felt sure she already did, what he'd been doing out past midnight while she'd suffered their son into the world.

Instead, she sat listening, baiting him on with neither comment nor nod, asking only the occasional question, rising periodically to refill his cup, to feed the stove, to check on the baby, returning each time to lower herself slowly into her seat and set her head in her hands and her eyes upon him, and when the girls came asking after their supper, she set the table and poured the batter onto the griddle and flipped the cakes onto the plates. Then they'd sat together, watching their children eat while the last of the light bled out of the day. When Evie had finished her supper, her pink lips glazed with syrup, the girl hopped down from her chair to help her mother clear the table and stood with her plate in her hands before carrying it to the sink. "That baby is lazy," she said. "He needs to wake up."

Sophie laughed, wincing and pressing a hand down low over her apron when she did, and the sound of her, so unexpected and full of her easy demeanor, brought Karel out of his chair until he was standing behind her, the soft taper of her waist in his hands.

She leaned into him and shook her head. "You'll be hearing all you want to out of him soon enough, sweet pea. He's a Skala, and the Lord doesn't make any lazy ones."

She was up three times with the child before midnight, and when Karel awoke each time from less than an hour of sleep to find the baby crying again, he propped a pillow beneath his head so that he could watch the silhouette of her against the diffused moonlight that found its way between the bedroom's curtains, so that he could watch her bend over the bassinet to change the baby's diaper and then sit with her back against the headboard while she nursed him.

When they'd first gone to bed, Karel had undressed and slid into the cool sheets while Sophie changed into her nightgown, and when she'd fed the baby before joining him there, he'd been heartened by the cool points of contact between them, by the milk-dampened cotton of her gown against the skin of his bare back. Since then, each time the child had come awake, the sounds he made like those of some nocturnal animal who'd grown terrified of the night, Karel had wanted to go to him, to see in his angry little face the confusion of all his needs and to hold him, but he couldn't bring himself to do it, couldn't bring himself to deprive the child of the one soft and able answer for all of those needs. And so instead he'd prop his head up and watch, and at some early hour during the fourth feeding, while the boy suckled, Karel turned onto his side and put a hand on his wife, squeezing the solid round of her knee. "You want me to hold him awhile after he eats?" he whispered. "I'm not in any danger of sleeping anyway."

Sophie worked a finger gently into the corner of the baby's mouth to unlatch him, and then she turned him to the other breast, his tiny arms thrown up as if he'd found himself unmoored and falling from the night's only comfort when she did. "What I want, Karel, is for you to think about him if you have to."

"I have been," Karel said. "I am."

"That's not what I'm saying. What I mean is, I want you to try thinking about him when thinking about me isn't enough."

Two hours before the reluctant winter dawn, Karel pulled his trousers on and buttoned his shirt. Child and mother both were sleeping, and before he went to make the coffee and light the stoves, Karel stood over the bassinet where, in a sliver of moonlight, the child lay with his face pinched up and a fist at his mouth as if he were conscious, even in slumber, of his mother's distance from him. There was something familiar and unsettling in the seriousness of the boy's expression, and Karel couldn't help himself. He reached down and flattened a hand on the boy's chest, felt the faint, fluttering rise and fall of his breathing, and then, before he turned to the awaiting labor of a day not yet fully made, he traced a finger over the little furrows creased into the tender skin of the boy's fine neck.

After an hour of chores in the barn and about the house, before even the suggestion of dawn backlit the eastern treeline, Karel unlatched the stable door and found the lantern in the dark. The air was close and stagnant, the scents of urine and hay and animal exhalations soured overnight by the onset of decay up in the loft. Karel breathed deeply through his nose, growing himself used to the smell while he led the filly out of the stall and cross-tied her, stroking her long black neck and speaking softly to her about where they were going and who she'd soon see until he had gotten her saddled and coaxed the bit into her mouth.

Outside, after he walked her from the stable and down the drive and out to the cattlegate, she nibbled at the yellow tufts of hay left uncut along the fenceline while he worked the latch. Clouds had come chasing the previous day's stray overnight, and their undersides blushed as the topmost arc of the sun came beaming like some proud suitor over the distant trees. From the water oaks and pines along the northern fork of the creek, a mockingbird called out the first of the day's admonishments. With the gate latched behind them, Karel stood beside the horse and put a foot in the stirrup as he took hold of the pommel and swung himself astride the animal, who sidestepped, tossing her head in protest while he sat her and gave her the slack of the reins and waited her out.

And then they walked, the two of them, out toward the stand of oaks that rose up out of the grazing land and stood old and gray and strung heavy with moss over the soft sod once worn to bare earth beneath the hooves of racing horses. He nudged the filly with his heel and turned her loose with his knees, and while Karel cantered her out toward the trees and then around their wide perimeter, he watched her breath come in steamy jets from her nostrils and thought how long it had been since he'd been on horseback and what a damned fool he'd been for keeping himself from it. And still, he couldn't discount his own hesitation any easier than he could avoid the acreage in which it had taken root, growing as it had alongside cotton and cattle and mesquite trees and farm boys reared on absence and fear. He lived on it, was riding toward it. He had seen it in the labored, moonlit frown of his sleeping son's face, and now, when he brought the filly up short and sat her there beneath the overhang of the trees, the past comes to meet the present, the connection between the two no less certain than the tethers strung taut through time between a man's father and son.

It comes. The hard, mineral scent rising from the soft, flooded land. The raw wind and the stinging rain. The swinging lantern throwing its transient light onto the standing water. The ankle-deep mud and the heavy steps away from a suffering horse, and then there he is on his back, Karel's father, his shoulders driven into the mud, his eyes squinting against the rain, his mouth bubbling at the corner with a dark upwelling of blood and tobacco. Karel sees himself kneeling beside him and feels the cold, puddled water wick into the cloth of his trousers. He sets the lantern burning by his old man's shoulder, and when he puts a hand on his father's chest, the man groans and his eyes come wide and Karel feels the damage done there. The ribs caved inward, crushed and sunken. "Jesus, Pop. The horse come down on you?"

The lantern throws the man's shadow long against the ripples of rainfall in the pooled water, and Vaclav's lips move in a pale whisper, his arms twitching at his sides. "You boys promised me a bale of cotton before my birthday," he says, "and here it is almost daylight and you're just now out of bed." Sliding his boot heels in the mud, he gasps and bends his knees as if readying himself to stand.

The cold works into Karel as if born up as liquid from his soaked trousers and into his skin, washing up in little waves until he's shivering in earnest and shaking his head. "It's wintertime, Pop. Cotton ain't even planted yet. Hold still. I'm going to get you out of here." But before he can stand, his father's hand is on him, gripping the same arm that, just days before, the Janek woman had held. He can't remember the last time his father has touched him any more clearly than he can fathom, now, how he'll get the old man to the house. The breathing comes labored and gurgling, little spent strings of tobacco floating in the blood that films the man's teeth and bubbles along the seam of his lips. He needs his brothers. He can't get it done without them, and he knows the old man is going to die here on his back in the mud.

He coughs, spraying Karel's face, moaning and cinching down harder on his son's arm, and the boy tastes the sour metallic mist of his father's blood on his own lips. He wipes his mouth with the sleeve of his coat, and the wind shifts such that a wet nest of moss falls from the oaks onto his head and blinds him with his own soiled hat. He jerks the thing off and blinks his eyes and pries his father's hand from his arm. "I'm going to get you to the house," he says. "I'm going to rig the other horse and pull you out of here."

Vaclav glares into the lanternlight, his eyes washed yellow with rage around their hard gray centers. "The hell you are. Ain't none of you setting foot in the house until you've picked me a goddamn bale of cotton. Now get your brothers and get your scrawny asses into the fields."

In the heartwood of Karel's history, at the onset of his remembering and way back in the days when his father was first teaching him to sit a horse, when his brothers would bet him a day of their corn shucking on a game of spoon, the end of which they'd foreseen with a careful orchestration of cards, when bobwhite cocks still came out brazen and pale-bellied from their coverts to steal some seed beneath the sunlight, and when a boy's sleepless thoughts told him, as they ever do, to play at being a man without ever once telling him how—there had come a Sunday when Karel sat pressed between his brothers in the pews of St. Jude's while Father Carew's homily had found the priest leaning over the lectern, his eyes afire despite the tears welling up in them . . . *So often, when we pray for the dead, we fall prey to the belief that they must so long for their earthly lives, for those they've left behind, for us, when what is certain is that they long, in the company of the Lord, for nothing at all. So don't pray for them because they might now be suffering. Pray for them because they have been released from the temporal world, because they have been lifted from the binds of time as we have yet to be. Pray because for them there is no past or future, and, inasmuch as this is so, our prayers can ease the pains they suffered while they walked the earth as sinners among us.*

Now, astride the black filly, Karel reins her out to the creekside pines, and together they weave themselves through the trees as the sun breaks free of the horizon and squirrels come alive in the branches overhead. When they reach the bank, Karel sits watching the shadows of the trees on the water, waiting until the horse folds her ears softly to the sides of her fine head and begins working the bit gently in her mouth, and then he takes her into the water and guides her toward good footing and leans forward in the saddle as she comes up the other side onto the soft silt of the slough, where he bids her to stop so that he can look back as the evidence that they've come through the water widens behind them before it subsides and heals itself and slides downstream.

He's not sure he can bring himself to do it, even now, even with Sophie's words so clear in his memory, and so he comes down from the horse and walks her out of the slough and up into the unplowed field where he can smoke a cigarette and run his eyes along the outstretched fencewires until their shimmering melts into the distance.

Some hundred miles to the west, there's a boy slumped in his seat with a gun in his pants, his scarred cheek pressed against the window glass as the Sunset Limited gathers speed on the outskirts of San Antonio, its locomotive trailing smoke out over the length of the cars rolling behind it toward California. Behind him, a dead brother but not the thorn of his memory. That he'll hold with him as surely as, back in Dalton, at St. Jude's parish, Father Carew holds the Eucharist before the aging, penitent few who've come for early Mass.

In her room, with her daughters curled up beside her in the quilt and giggling softly, Sophie Skala holds her hungry, sleeping boy to her breast. She shakes her head at the thought of her husband, at the memory, only two hours old, of his awkward, half-dressed frame leaning over the bassinet so carefully, so quietly, to touch his son while she pretended to sleep.

Outside, beneath a sky flung wide over Lavaca County and hung sparsely with sun-blanched clouds that promise, instead of rain, only shade, the youngest of the Skala brothers smokes the last of his cigarette while the black horse turns her head toward the gentle sound of creekwater behind her. In time, Karel will ride her three-quarters of an hour to the north, stopping to open and close his neighbors' gates along the way, and when they arrive, they'll find Graciela emerging from the chicken coop with an apron full of eggs, her husband on the back porch cleaning his gun, awaiting news, raising his head at the arrival of his brother. But for now Karel stands of a bright winter morning in an unbroken field not far from his house, seeing his boy's face, so much like his father's, as he grinds his spent cigarette into the earth. He gathers the horse's lead and puts a foot in the stirrup, wondering just how in the hell a man is supposed to go about asking the dead to forgive him for ever finding comfort at another woman's breast. Or for going on living at all when she could not. Or for doing his father's delirious bidding and leaving him to die in the mud alone. Or for leaving their children so long at odds with one another in the world.

And then he wonders if he's just done it, if it could be that simple.

The horse sidesteps, and, when Karel corrects her, she offers a coy little halfhearted buck. Her body shudders beneath his weight, sensing, before he gives her a heel, that they are about to run.

A New, Warm Offering

FEBRUARY 1895

COME EVENING, she appeared with Edna Janek on the back porch, and Vaclav Skala opened the door to find a girl who looked, despite her slumped shoulders and tired eyes, like she mightn't be old enough to do what she'd come to do. Edna made the introductions, and Skala took the girl's hand, which was rough-skinned and cold and so fragile in his own that he felt, just holding it, as if he might do it some harm. He glanced at her compact frame, looking her over, wary as a bidder at auction. The girl's slight bosom only just swelled the front of her dress, which was black and home stitched, the uneven hem a testament to the haste of its seamstress, and, estranged by grief from reason and amenities, he nodded to the hallway, toward the sound of the crying baby in the back bedroom, thinking the girl had sewn the dress out of respect for the dead.

She had, but not for *his* dead, and while he returned to his cup of coffee at the kitchen table, this girl who would one day bear twins listened to the hollow sound of her own footsteps echoing beneath the floorboards, hearing again the empty, earthen sound of her son's little box coming to rest on the hard bottom of its grave.

Edna led her past the front bedroom, where long, shapeless shadows fell over a bed frame orphaned of its mattress, and in the back room they found the boys in the bedclothes they'd stayed in all day, the younger two on their bellies in their shared bed, watching while Stan stood leaning over the bassinet, his hands gripping the rail while he whispered some consolation to the crying infant.

When the women entered the room, the boys looked up with the startled, expectant faces of those awakened from troubling dreams to the blinking, muddled hope that the known world would now be returned to them.

Stan loosed his hold on the bassinet and took a step backward. "I was just counting to him. I can count to fifty."

"You're a bright boy," Edna said. "This is Miss Hildi. She's going to feed the baby."

Stan turned toward the window where the day's last light fell against the panes. "My mama's in heaven now," he said.

"Yes," the girl said. "I know. My little boy is there, too."

Stan considered this, his hands gathering and releasing the soft cotton of his nightclothes. "Then maybe . . ." he said, turning to watch as Edna helped his brothers off the bed. When the woman led the boys from the room to give the wet nurse her privacy, Stan looked back as if awaiting the spoken answer to his unspoken question.

"Yes," the girl said, her voice soft, her smile a weary one. "Maybe so."

Alone with the child, Hildi gathered him in her arms and sat in the lone chair in the corner with her dress unbuttoned to the waist. The infant was hungry but unaccustomed to this new, warm offering, and the girl winced when he found the nipple only to turn it loose, wailing, his legs working beneath his swaddling, his little muscles seizing with the frustration of his effort. She whispered to him, adjusting his scant weight on her lap and cradling his head more firmly in her hand, brushing the nipple against his lips until he opened his mouth and she felt the sharp stab of him taking hold.

It would take time, but this would become, at last, on some evening later in the week, an undertaking softened by ease and familiarity, by skin, by the soft, wet sounds of satisfaction. For now, the girl leaned back into the chair as he floundered, as he started and stopped, took and surrendered and screamed, until at last he found a way to work from her what was meant for another.

When his rhythmic suckling began to yield in earnest, a cold eddy swelled beneath her collarbone, building in pressure until she found that she was holding her breath. Outside, the dark came on, and she closed her eyes as the child's hand came up, his tiny fingers curling and relaxing against the side of her breast. And then her milk let down, the cool weight of it falling within her and warmed all at once as if by the friction of its own motion or by the newfound proximity to the heat of her heart. It felt so loud that she imagined she heard it, imagined the hot surge of it falling through the flume of her body, and for a time, before she opened her eyes and moved the child to the other breast, she pretended that the comfort she felt was her own.

ACKNOWLEDGMENTS

I am indebted, first and always, to the teachers: Lee K. Abbott, Stephanie Grant, Jim Robison, and Melanie Rae Thon.

For their steadfast friendship and encouragement, I thank Steve Almond, Michael Bell, Johnny Goudie, Michael Lohre, Andy Mullinax, Bryan Narendorf, Daniel Rich, Chuck Rudolphy, Craig Schilling, Ron Wight, and Marvin Williams.

I'm beholden to Brenda Lincke-Fisseler and the other fine folks at the Friench Simpson Memorial Library in Hallettsville, whose holdings and help were essential to my understanding of Lavaca County history and culture.

My greatest debt is owed to my readers — Matthew Batt, Marya Labarthe, and Steve Sansom — whose insights were so often keener than my own.

I have the deepest fondness and appreciation for my intrepid agent, Irene Skolnick, and for Adrienne Brodeur, my insightful and impassioned editor.

I thank my parents and siblings, who have dealt with so much, and sometimes so little, so that I could do what I do. To Marya, for graces innumerable and nameless. And to my darling boy, Dalton Zane, after whom I've named the geography into which I've let wander these ghosts of my imagination.